**A Gestalt Institute
of Cleveland
publication**

Becoming
A Stepfamily

Becoming
A Stepfamily

Patterns of Development
in Remarried Families

Patricia L. Papernow

Jossey-Bass Publishers · San Francisco

A Gestalt Institute of Cleveland publication

Substantial discounts on bulk quantities of Jossey-Bass books are available to corporations, professional associations, and other organizations. For details and discount information, contact the special sales department at Jossey-Bass Inc., Publishers. (415) 433-1740; Fax (415) 433-0499.

For sales outside the United States, contact Maxwell Macmillan International Publishing Group, 866 Third Avenue, New York, New York 10022.

Manufactured in the United States of America

 The paper used in this book is acid-free and meets the State of California requirements for recycled paper (50 percent recycled waste, including 10 percent postconsumer waste), which are the strictest guidelines for recycled paper currently in use in the United States.

Library of Congress Cataloging-in-Publication Data

Papernow, Patricia L., date.
    Becoming a stepfamily: patterns of development in remarried families/Patricia L. Papernow.—1st ed.
        p. cm.—(The Jossey-Bass social and behavioral science series)
    Includes bibliographical references and index.
    ISBN 1-55542-551-8 (acid-free paper)
    1. Stepfamilies. 2. Stepfamilies—Psychological aspects.
I. Title. II. Series.
HQ759.92.P35 1993
306.874—dc20   93-21716
                                                                      CIP

FIRST EDITION
HB Printing   10 9 8 7 6 5 4 3 2 1   *Code 9354*

The Jossey–Bass
Social and Behavioral Science Series

CONTENTS

List of Figures   xiii
Acknowledgments   xv

PART I
BECOMING A STEPFAMILY:
ISSUES AND CONCEPTS   1

Chapter 1   *Introduction*   3
              The Need for a Developmental Map   7
              The Stepfamily Cycle   9
              Overview of *Becoming a Stepfamily*   19

Chapter 2   *Stepfamily Structure: Bonds Without Blood*   21
              Conceptual Tools   21
              What Is Different About Stepfamily
                Structure   41
              Becoming a Stepfamily:
                Developmental Challenges and
                Dilemmas   50
              Conclusion   62

PART II
THE STEPFAMILY CYCLE: NORMAL STAGES
OF STEPFAMILY DEVELOPMENT   65

Chapter 3 *The Early Stages: Getting Started Without*
            Getting Stuck   70
              Stage 1. Fantasy: The Invisible
                Burden   71
              Stage 2. Immersion: Sinking Versus
                Swimming   84

ix

Stage 3. Awareness: Mapping the
                Territory   118
            Conclusion   150

Chapter 4   *The Middle Stages: Restructuring the*
             Family   152
            Stage 4. Mobilization: Exposing the
                Gaps   156
            Stage 5. Action: Going into Business
                Together   171
            Conclusion   195

Chapter 5   *The Later Stages: Solidifying the Stepfamily*   197
            Stage 6. Contact: Intimacy and
                Authenticity in Step Relationships   198
            Stage 7. Resolution: Holding On
                and Letting Go   212
            Conclusion   230

**PART III
MOVING THROUGH
THE STEPFAMILY CYCLE:
PATTERNS AND PROBLEMS**   233

Chapter 6   *Patterns of Development: Four Paths to*
             Resolution   235
            What Makes the Difference?   238
            Four Stepfamily Types   248
            Four Case Histories   267
            Conclusion   301

Chapter 7   *Problems in Stepfamily Development:*
             Intervention   304
            Basic Principles of Working with
                Stepfamilies   305
            Early Stages: Helping Stepfamilies
                to Get Started   311
            Middle Stages: Facilitating the
                Restructuring Process   337
            Later Stages: Helping Families to
                Hold on and to Let Go   355

Special Issues: New Babies,
Stepfamilies Formed by Death,
and "Older" Stepchildren 357
Conclusion 370

PART IV
EPILOGUE: WHAT STEPFAMILIES CAN
TEACH US 373

Appendix A: Stepfamily Cycle Summary 381
Appendix B: Self-Help Guide for Stepfamilies 388
Appendix C: Summary of Clinical Intervention
Strategies 397
Appendix D: Family Profiles 400

Bibliography 411
Index 419

LIST OF FIGURES

2.1.   The Gestalt Experience Cycle   23
2.2.   An Ideal Picture of the Gestalt
        Interactive Cycle   27
2.3.   Simple Stepfamily: A Parent-Child
        Minifamily and a Single Stepparent (the
        Salvi Family)   34
2.4.   Complex Stepfamily: Two Parent-Child
        Minifamilies with Two Different
        Interactive Styles (the Black/Jones
        Family)   37
2.5 a–f. From First-time Family to Stepfamily:
        Structural Changes   48
2.6.   "Action Family": Stepcouple as Insiders,
        Stepchildren as Outsiders (the Allen/
        Betts Family)   58
II.1.   Relationship of the Gestalt Experience
        Cycle to the Stepfamily Cycle   68

To Michelle and Bill

ACKNOWLEDGMENTS

A project of this scope does not come to fruition without the help and support of many people. This has been particularly true for me as a single working parent. The effort of writing this book has stretched over eight years through several major life transitions and two moves. I have been blessed with very good friends and several great editors, as well as colleagues, teachers, mentors, and family who helped bring this book to fruition. I want to say thank you:

To Pam and Phyllis, my stepdaughters, without whom this book would not have been conceived. I feel especially blessed that they have remained my stepdaughters despite many changes in all our lives, and have given me the gift of a rich "intimate outsider" role in their lives. I also want to acknowledge their father, who despite our differences engaged fully with me in creating a stepfamily.

To all of the stepfamily members whose voices we hear in this book, your willingness and generosity in sharing your stories with me made this work possible.

To my GIC Press editors, without whom this book would still be in pieces in my computer. Ed Nevis got me started, helped me see more clearly what I was trying to say, and made sure it got written without ever being intrusive or critical. His deceptively simple but elegant feedback helped solidify crucial sections of this book. Gordon Wheeler understood better than I what was needed in order to bring this book to a conclusion. He inspired me, encouraged me, and stayed with me until it was done.

To all of the people at Gardner Press including Gardner Spungin, who believed in this book early on, and Margo Morse whose heroic attention to detail helped bring this manuscript to maturity. Special thanks to Suzi Tucker who edited like a soulmate. And finally thank you to Rebecca McGovern of Jossey-Bass whose intelligent and responsive midwifery brought this book to publication.

To my good friend Beverly, who gives me the gift of knowing me deeply and telling me what she knows, who has loved me, held me, confronted me, giggled with me, stepparented with me, and who gives me hope.

To Bill, who is my love and who is living this with me with grace and good humor.

To Sonia Nevis who has taught me more than I can say about holding on and letting go and about what is involved in living well in relationships. To Jerry Sashin who taught me to ask.

To all of the people in my life who cared about me while I was doing this, asked how it was going, talked with me about writing and about stepfamilies, some of whom read and edited parts of the book. Thank you to Corky, Pam, Joan, Michael, Donald, Hope, Arnie, Sheila, Steven, Andy, and Charlotte. Special thanks to my cousins Paul and Ev, whose home was a sanctuary for me and in whose hammock the ideas for Chapter Six were conceived.

To the national network of colleagues whose work has enriched mine, who cheered me on, assured me this would be a good book, asked me endlessly (and seemingly patiently) "Is it done yet?" gave me feedback, sent articles, provided citations, and chewed over ideas with me: Kay Pasley, Emily and John Visher, Marilyn Coleman and Larry Ganong, Connie Ahrons, and James Bray. To the Stepfamily Association of America, which has received my work so warmly and given me lasting friendships all over the country, especially Joan Howard, Mala Burt, Susan Borkin, Judy Mize, Sharon Hanna, and Teresa Adams.

My heartfelt thanks to the people at Bromley Engineering who kept my ancient Morrow computer functioning through to the end, who laughed like everyone else ("You have a *what!*") but who, unlike the others, fixed it.

Almost last, but certainly not least, and maybe more appropriately first, to my parents Leon and Felicia Papernow, who read all my work, whom I can still call when I do something good, and whom I can count on to *kvell* with spirit and intelligence.

And finally I want to thank my daughter, Michelle, who shared her Mommy with the computer, and whom I love very much.

Newtonville, Massachusetts   Patricia L. Papernow
February 1993

THE AUTHOR

Patricia L. Papernow is a psychologist in private practice in Newton and Cambridge, Massachusetts. She received her B.A. degree (1969) magna cum laude from Harvard University, her Ed.D. degree (1980) in counseling psychology from Boston University, and her advanced Gestalt training from the Gestalt Institute of Cleveland

Papernow's work focuses on describing normal developmental dynamics in stepfamilies, identifying factors that delay or block developmental progress, and designing preventive and clinical intervention for people in remarried families. She has long had a special commitment to bringing together a strong theoretical framework, existing research, and clinical observation, and to reaching both professional and lay audiences. Papernow is widely published in both the professional and popular literature and has authored numerous articles as well as several book chapters on stepfamily dynamics. She teaches seminars and workshops for stepfamilies and for the professionals involved with them throughout the United States. Because of her ability to communicate complex information clearly and vividly, Papernow is frequently asked to comment on step issues in the national print and television media. In 1978 she received the Practitioner Teacher award from Boston University in recognition of her outstanding ability as a clinician-educator.

From 1973 to 1977 Papernow was director of Community Training Resources, a preventive mental health education program cited as one of the best in the country by the Joint Information Service of the American Psychiatric Association and the National Association for Mental Health. From 1981 to 1987 she directed the Charles River Gestalt Center.

PART I

BECOMING A STEPFAMILY:

Issues and Concepts

Chapter 1

INTRODUCTION

"It was a wonderful weekend," says Tom Tolman, the biological parent of 8-year-old Ricky, "until Jenny messed it up as usual." "It was an awful weekend," says Jenny Tolman, Tom's second wife, "right from the start." Tom's story:

Well, we got up nice and early on Saturday, and we got a really good start. We drove up to New Hampshire and picked up Ricky right on time. It was so good to see him. Then we all went together and watched this neat parade. Ricky was beside himself having a good time. And I felt wonderful, there with my whole family—Ricky and me and Jenny. Then we went out to McDonald's for lunch. Then I had this great idea for us all to end the day by driving to our favorite spot on the beach and watching the sunset together.

All of a sudden Jenny turns completely sour. Out of the blue, mind you. We ended up having a fight in front of Ricky. The day was ruined. We drove back to the cottage absolutely silent. We haven't been able to talk about it since. I'm so bummed out. My one weekend with Ricky and she messes it up. I can't believe she'd do this to me.

Jenny's experience of the same day went like this:

It was an *awful* weekend right from the start. First of all, after working all week, and I really had a bad week, Tom gets us up at the crack of dawn on Saturday. Then we raced up to New Hampshire and picked up Ricky. Ricky chattered a mile a minute to Tom, the entire way back to the cottage. I felt I was invisible. I *was* invisible. Nobody talked to me. Tom didn't even look at me. Ricky didn't have the slightest interest in me. This is the time I need to reconnect with Tom, especially after such a hard week. And I felt like I lost him to this 8-year-old. An 8-year-old who didn't know I even existed.

Then we went to this dumb military parade. So there I was, standing in the rain, watching Tom and Ricky watch this parade. I was tired and my feet hurt, and I just wanted to go home. Then we went to McDonald's. Ricky's favorite. I *hate* McDonald's. At last I thought we were going to go home where I could at least be comfortable. And then Tom asks me, in front of Ricky, if I want to drive a half an hour to the beach to watch the sunset. Not only that, it's the spot on the beach where I most like to be alone with Tom, our special spot. It was the last straw. I lost it. I know I did. And then Tom got so critical and withdrawn. And that was the real last straw.

Although much of the tension, confusion, and inability to resolve differences we see in the Tolmans may appear in any troubled biological family, the particular breach in understanding presented by this couple is a normal occurrence in early stepfamily life. Furthermore, in new stepfamilies these painful knots often happen with relentless regularity and with an intensity that is disturbing and frightening to a new couple, as well as to helping professionals involved with them.

In the last two decades we have begun to shift our attention from the high rate of divorce and its effects on families (Ahrons, 1980a; Bohannan, 1971; Wallerstein & Kelly, 1980; Weiss, 1975) to what happens when divorced parents remarry, as 80 percent of men and 75 percent of women do (Furstenberg & Spanier, 1984). Until recently we have perhaps considered divorced parents who remarried as "normal" again, and as no longer requiring our attention. Perhaps the stigma that remains associated with divorce, much less "stepparent" and "stepchild," blinded us to the fact that whether one or both adults bring children from a previous relationship, remarriage creates a very different kind of family: a stepfamily. The result is a family with a very special set of developmental tasks and challenges. A rapidly expanding academic, clinical, and popular literature is exploring this fact (Ganong & Coleman, 1984, 1986, 1986a; Stepfamily Association of America and National Council on Family Relations, 1988; Pasley, 1991).

Current statistics tell us that 20 to 30 percent of children will spend some time in a stepfamily before they are young adults (Glick, 1979). Ten million children under 18 now live in a stepfamily (Cherlin & McCarthy, 1985). Demographers predict that by the year 2000, stepfamilies will outnumber all other family forms (including nuclear and single families) (Glick, 1984; Glick & Lin, 1986). Stepfamily living offers opportunities for healing past hurts, and for richness and diversity in relationships not possible in biological families. It also requires traversing a geography quite different from biological family living, with a terrain full of rocky, confusing passages and many casualties. The divorce rate in stepfamilies is a staggering 57 percent. Remarrying couples often think of themselves as returning to the mainstream when they start their new family. In fact, as Gregory Burns, a single stepparent, will tell us in Chapter Four, the experience is more like being deposited in the middle of the rapids.

Not surprisingly, members of stepfamilies appear for help in the offices of school counselors, medical personnel, employee assistance programs, clergy, and many others in the helping professions. Whether because of shame or lack of information, few identify themselves as members of stepfamilies. Jenny Tolman had originally sought help from her physician when she found herself grinding her teeth again, a childhood habit that had mysteriously returned since her marriage to Tom. (The Tolman family will be described in detail later on, as Case Two in Chapter Six.) And like Jenny and Tom, few are aware of the degree to which stepfamily dynamics contribute to their pain:

Beth Roberts and George Danielson, a remarried couple in their thirties, come into therapy complaining that they are fighting constantly. Both work. She has two daughters from a previous marriage who live with them. He says he has no time alone with her. She says he is insensitive to the needs of her children. He says she is overinvolved with her children and her ex-husband. She says she feels torn and exhausted from the pressure of trying to please everyone.

Molly Ricci, age 10, is referred to counseling because she is failing in school. In the family interview, her adoptive mother begins talking about how unresponsive this young girl has been despite her efforts to provide the parenting missed from an alcoholic mother. The father sits uncomfortably between his daughter and his wife, and the child looks sullenly at the floor.

Hope Franklin, a single parent, expresses concern to her daughter's nursery school teacher that her children are not getting along with the man she is seeing. Is her dating detrimental to the children, and how should she handle the children's responses?

A minister helping Joanne Gray and Jeff Rudnick to plan their baby son's christening begins discussing what she thought would be a simple matter of who would will stand where. The couple begins a tense, highly charged struggle over the place in the ceremony of the man's son from his previous marriage.

Trisha Greenfield, age 37, consults her family physician about the risks of childbearing as she approaches 40. She seems barely able to hold back her tears. She has been married for a year to a man with two college-age children. Further questioning reveals that he is reluctant to have more children and that she finds herself suddenly wanting children of her own. They have just begun to talk about this as a couple, and her biological clock is running out.

Fred O'Brien is referred to an employee assistance program because his work is suffering. While asking for a family history, the counselor discovers that he has been divorced, is the noncustodial father of two daughters whom he rarely sees, and is now married to a woman with two young children. Fred reports that his wife is concerned that he doesn't seem involved with her children. He wonders if this is a sign of his "inability to love" and is worried that he might fail at yet another marriage.

Timothy Levi, a 20-year-old college student, has been in therapy for a year around issues of identity and self-esteem. He casually mentions that his father has announced his engagement to a woman with two young children. The counselor doesn't pick up on this theme. Timothy misses his next appointment.

These cases may involve clinical, spiritual, medical, and educational issues unrelated to stepfamily dynamics. However, understanding the developmental dilemmas and tasks created by membership in a remarried family will be crucial to fully understanding each person's distress and will be central in any helpful response.

It is worth repeating that none of the people described above attributed their struggles to involvement in the normal developmental process of becoming a stepfamily. In fact, what is most striking in my own work with members of stepfamilies is that they do not see themselves as members of a special kind of family facing unique challenges. Rather, they regard themselves, and are often viewed by helping professionals, as members of poorly functioning biological families.

As long as normal stepfamily dynamics remain unfamiliar, none of the people described above will be adequately assisted with a central dilemma of their lives: the complicated process of making safe, reliable, nourishing relationships in a stepfamily.

The Need for a Developmental Map

The first time my 18-month-old little daughter threw a temper tantrum, I remember the rising sense of panic, replaced fairly quickly with, "Oh, my goodness, this must be her first temper tantrum!" This capacity to be interested rather than panicked was augmented by our family physician, who asked us at our daughter's next checkup, "Has she thrown her first temper tantrum?" as if it were a predictable developmental event. Proudly we answered, "Yes!" My remaining anxiety was replaced the next time with, "Well, didn't she throw a good one this time!" and the tension in our household receded as my husband and I set almost cheerfully about the task of working together to help her (and ourselves) through her tantrums.

Our capacity to place these disturbing events within a normal developmental context provided us great comfort. Most important, it freed us to attend to the work of dealing with our daughter constructively. Likewise, were my daughter still throwing tantrums at age 9, our developmental framework would have signaled trouble requiring a different kind of attention, and an astute pediatrician would have referred us for outside help.

Stepfamilies and helping professionals involved with them need such a developmental map. Early stepfamily living is full of surprising and sometimes painful experiences. Though all family life involves some hard and confusing times, these experiences in stepfamilies tend to be extraordinarily divisive at a time when all the members of the family are feeling especially vulnerable and needy, and when the couple is still the weakest unit in the family. And they present themselves just at the time when the couple most expects an intimate, romantic honeymoon period.

Most important, members of remarried couples experience the same children fundamentally differently: When Tom and Jenny are with Ricky, Tom feels "like my life is finally whole again." Jenny feels isolated and exhausted. Each feels panicked and abandoned by the other's experience. Like Ricky, children in new families are involved in their own struggles with multiple losses and confusing loyalty conflicts. Often their parents and stepparents have few clues about how to support their children or themselves through this major transition.

Placed within a developmental context these events can be seen as the normal, though not particularly pleasurable, effects of early stepfamily realities. Like dealing with a 2-year-old's tantrums, stepfamilies that expect these difficulties know that with some work, each stage will pass. However, Tom, Jenny, and Ricky, as with so many stepfamilies, are adrift with little notion of what they can realistically expect of each other. The power of a developmental model is that it offers workable ideas about what is normal and predictable as opposed to what signals a crisis. It provides a realistic notion of where to start. It offers a guide for where to spend energy that will help move the family forward. It offers reassurance that a difficult stage will not last forever. And it helps to prevent spending energy wastefully and even destructively to make the impossible happen.

With the knowledge that Ricky's loyalty conflict is inevitable, Tom and Jenny could turn their attention to helping him articulate his struggle to include his stepmother in a way that doesn't compete with his relationship to his mother. They could provide some guidelines ("You must be civil to your stepmother, but you don't have to love her.") that protect both Jenny and Ricky. Without this knowledge, both Jenny and Ricky remain burdened with the impossible expectation to love each other as mother and son. Ricky's loyalty conflict intensifies so that he is forced to reject his stepmother all the more fiercely. Jenny is caught in a cycle of trying to win Ricky over and withdrawing, feeling rejected and ever more inadequate—and Tom becomes more hurt, disappointed, and frightened with each negative cycle.

Armed with a developmental framework, Tom could tell Jenny how hard it is for him that this new family doesn't blend easily, turning to her for comfort rather than blaming her for the family's difficulty in joining. Jenny could voice her jealousy without frightening Tom or blaming him.

A developmental model might have helped Tom and Jenny use this time to complete the primary tasks of early stepfamily life: to build individual and shared understanding of each person's very different experience of this new family, and to create some separate space and time for each of the "minifamilies" (the adult couple, the biological parent and child, and the stepparent and stepchild) within the new family to be alone together.

The Stepfamily Cycle

Background

Starting with Fast and Cain's ground-breaking article in 1966, attention to stepfamily issues has increased slowly over

the last two decades, with a veritable explosion in the literature during the past ten years (Pasley, 1991). Although much
of this information is just becoming available to stepfamily
members, many of the themes, strains, myths, and difficult
tasks of stepfamily living have been identified. Increasing
numbers of newspaper and popular magazine articles ad-
monish remarried families against expectations of instant
parenthood and immediate family bliss. For this warning to
be useful, however, stepfamilies and helping professionals
involved with them need a sense of what is supposed to *happen* over time to create this non-instant form of family
bonding.

Sager et al. (1983), McGoldrick and Carter (1980), and
Ransom, Schlesinger, and Derdeyn (1979), each building on
the others' work, have made an exciting beginning to the task
of describing stepfamily development. Others have defined
developmental tasks for stepfamilies (Goetting, 1982; Keshet, 1980; Visher & Visher, 1979; Waldron & Whittington,
1979).

Drawing on family systems theory, work thus far primarily describes life cycle tasks as viewed by the helping professional. The Stepfamily Cycle presents a developmental
model built from the viewpoint of stepfamily members. We
know intuitively that many developmental tasks for stepfamilies are fundamentally different from those in biological families. But what are they? We know something has to happen
over time for stepfamilies to "make it," but what? And when?
And in what order? There is some agreement that stepfamilies "make it or break it" within four years (Visher & Visher,
1978, 1979; Mills, 1984). We know that divorces happen
more quickly in remarriages, with 50 percent occurring
within five years as opposed to the national norm of a little
over seven years (Furstenberg & Spanier, 1984). What makes
the difference in moving on or getting stuck? Is it possible
to describe a healthy stepfamily? And finally, in what ways
can a developmental model guide interventions that might
better support the millions of people living in step relationships?

The Stepfamily Cycle is based on data that answer these questions primarily through the eyes of stepfamily members. It is hoped that their vivid stories not only will provide support, comfort, and a sense of community to those living in stepfamilies, but will also give helping professionals a clearer map of the territory through which stepfamilies must travel.

This book began as a research project that aimed to describe the experience over time of becoming a stepparent. The original research was an in-depth interview study of nine stepparents from which the developmental model described here first emerged. The original model focused on the stepparents' developmental process.

It has always been clear to me and to other clinicians writing about stepfamilies that stepparent role development is dependent on changes in the entire remarried family structure (Kleinman, Rosenberg, & Whiteside, 1979; Visher & Visher, 1979; Waldron & Whittington, 1979, among others). Over the past years, my goal has been to evolve a developmental model that describes both individual and systemic change throughout the entire stepfamily. The result is the Stepfamily Cycle.

The data include direct transcript comments from over 50 family groups. To protect confidentiality, all names (both first and last) have been changed and identifying data has been removed or altered. In a few cases several families have been combined.

About half of the families are couples and families from my clinical practice. The other half are nonclinical individual adults, couples, and families I have interviewed over the years. Of the 30 children's voices we hear, approximately 10 were clients, primarily well-functioning late adolescents and young adults. Another 9 or 10 were latency and teenaged children whom I interviewed. The balance were young adults I interviewed or who had been members of a Teen Panel I chair each year for our local Stepfamily Association. The latter children usually meet with me between one and three times, first without adults present and then as part of the formal panel.

The over one hundred people quoted here do not constitute a random representative sample of the stepfamily population—the group is white and mostly middle class. I did attempt in my interviews to choose people who would give me a mix of stepfather and stepmother, and simple (only one adult brings children) and complex (both adults bring children) stepfamilies, as well as a range in ages of children. Brief interviews lasted 15 minutes to half an hour. More extensive interviews lasted from one to three hours—most took about two-and-a-half hours. Some subjects (individuals, couples, and families) were interviewed more than once over the 10-year span I have been working on this data. Again, this is not a carefully crafted longitudinal research design. It is a qualitative look at the experience of becoming a stepfamily as seen by the people who speak in these pages.

It may be useful to note that I personally find the division of "clinical" and "nonclinical" uninformative in identifying the level of pathology that might be present. In a number of cases, subjects in the clinical population were actually a great deal healthier than those from the nonclinical population. This seemed to be particularly true for some of the young adults. Perhaps in these cases the willingness to go for help is actually a better indication of healthy functioning than lack of contact with mental health professionals.

Developmental Stages

The Stepfamily Cycle describes, through the eyes of family members, what must happen so that the strangers and intimates who come together to create a stepfamily can succeed in their task. It draws on Gestalt and family systems theory to illuminate the process by which boundaries (individual, intergenerational, couple, interfamilial) move from biological to "step." It provides a developmental map that delineates the stages involved in forming nourishing, reliable relationships among steppeople, and establishing a workable stepparenting role. It describes the impact of stepfamily history and structure on individual role development, as well as the role of individuals in the family in furthering developmental movement.

The Stepfamily Cycle describes seven stages of individual and family system development—the three *Early Stages*: Fantasy, Immersion, and Awareness; the two *Middle Stages*: Mobilization and Action; and the two *Later Stages*: Contact and Resolution.

In the three Early Stages, the family remains primarily divided along biological lines, with most nourishment, agreement on rules and rituals, and easy connection happening within the biological subsystem(s). The **Fantasy Stage** sees the adults in the family yearning to heal the pain created by divorce or death. Biological parents hope for a new spouse who will be not only a better partner, but a better parent than the previous spouse. Stepparents hope to provide what had been missing (and be appreciated for it). Both partners may imagine that because the adults in the new family adore each other, stepparents and stepchildren will also. Stepparents may have fantasies about marrying a nurturing parent, and biological parents may imagine that adding a new adult will at last ease the load of single-parenting. Children, in contrast, often continue to have a powerful and enduring investment in seeing their parents back together again, or at the very least, reclaiming an exclusive relationship with their single parent.

In the **Immersion Stage**, the reality of stepfamily structure begins to make itself felt, particularly for the stepparent who occupies an outsider position to the intensely connected biological parent and child (and often an ex-spouse as well). Stepparents find themselves assaulted by unexpectedly strong and negative feelings—jealousy, resentment, confusion, and inadequacy—as they are subtly but consistently excluded by the powerful, already established biological parent-child (and ex-spouse) relationships. The biological parent may be somewhat less uncomfortable in this stage, as he or she has a source of nourishment and support in his or her children. In this phase the biological parent may interpret the stepparent's difficulty joining the new family as evidence of lack of commitment to the new family, a frightening thought, as it signals another failure or loss. For adult family members, the experience of the Immersion Stage is marked by the uneasy feeling that something's amiss, but there is great difficulty in sorting out just *what* it is. For stepparents, the conclusion in this stage often is, "It must be me."

The **Awareness Stage** sees stepfamily members making more sense out of the confusion. For stepparents this means beginning to put names on painful feelings, as well as experiencing them more fully. Greater clarity about the power of the biological parent-child (and ex-spouse) bond enables stepparents to see patterns to their experience and to feel less self-deprecating ("I'm jealous not because I'm neurotic, but because I'm an outsider!"). Greater self-acceptance allows stepparents to form more definitive statements about their needs from their spouses and stepchildren, laying the foundation for the more active engagement of the Mobilization Stage. Relinquishing fantasies of an instant family and increasing clarity about the impossibility of shifting to an insider position quickly also frees the stepparent to accomplish a crucial developmental task: getting to know the strangers she or he has joined.

Just as stepparents become clearer about their outsider position in the Awareness Stage, biological parents become more aware of the pressures of their insider position and their role as the one person in the family who is involved in each subsystem: couple, parent-child, and ex-spouse. Biological parents may also be engaged in resolving a previous loss: increasing awareness of exactly what was gained and lost, and what was learned. Just as stepparents need to free themselves of fantasies in order to engage fully in the slow task of getting to know their spouses and stepchildren, biological parents must relinquish enough of their hope of easy caring between their new spouse and their children to participate actively in facilitating this process. However, because their role exposes them to less rejection and exclusion than the stepparent experiences, biological parents may move more slowly on this until the Middle Stages.

The developmental tasks of the Early Stages include bearing the confusion and disappointment of early stepfamily living without giving up; beginning to identify and articulate the very different experience stepfamily structure creates for each individual in the new family; and relinquishing fantasies enough to engage actively in the step-by-step process of building a family out of strangers.

In the two Middle Stages, the stepfamily begins the tasks of loosening old boundaries and restructuring itself to strengthen step subunits.

The **Mobilization Stage** finds the family, particularly the couple, much more openly airing differences between step and biological family members' needs. Often this is a chaotic and intensely embattled period, as stepparents begin speaking up with more energy and strength about their needs for inclusion and for change. Although stepparents often express relief at being able to state their feelings more openly, the biological parent's insider position now becomes much more painful. The latter is now torn between a spouse's need for new rules and more intimate couple time, and the children's needs for stability and access to their parent. A stepparent's more vocal desire to create distance from an ex-spouse may conflict with the biological parent's need to maintain a civil relationship. The fights in this stage may appear trivial—What is the appropriate thing to do with dirty laundry? Which is better, white bread or wheat bread? What is the appropriate bedtime for an 11-year-old? However, these arguments are struggles over whether the biological subsystem will be able to meet its needs for some stability and continuity after a series of losses and changes, or whether the steppeople in the family will be able to generate enough change to make themselves comfortable. Thus a family arguing wildly about bedtime may actually be struggling about whether a teenager and her father will continue to have special time together in the evening, as they had throughout a very painful postdivorce period, or the stepmother will have that time alone with her husband.

The developmental task of the **Action Stage** is to negotiate some new agreements about how the family will function. The moves of this stage actually change the family structure, drawing new boundaries around the step relationships in the family: the stepcouple, stepparent-child, stepsiblings, and the stepfamily itself. The Action Stage sees the end of the uphill portion of the Stepfamily Cycle, as families now have enough understanding in place so that every family activity is no longer a potential power struggle between insiders and outsiders.

In the two Later Stages, contact finally becomes regular and reliable within step subsystems, ushering in a period of structural solidification. The family begins to be able to function without constant attention to step issues.

The **Contact Stage** gives the family its honeymoon at last. The moves of the Action Stage have given the stepfamily new areas of agreement within which they can function easily. The triangulated relationships of earlier stages give way to one-to-one pairs. Children have been pushed out of the marital relationship and biological parents out of the stepchild-stepparent relationship. Intimacy and authenticity now become possible in step relationships. The marital relationship becomes more of a sanctuary and source of nourishment and support, even on step issues. Stepparents and children begin to forge real relationships. It is only now, *after* the major structural changes of the Middle Stages, that a clearly defined stepparent role emerges.

The **Resolution Stage** finds the family with solid and reliable step relationships. Norms have been established, a history has begun to build, and step relationships no longer require constant attention and yeoman work to function well. Although some children may be more inside the family than others, there is clarity about and acceptance of this fact. The mature stepparent role now brings satisfaction and nourishment as the stepparent is solidly established as an "intimate outsider." He or she is intimate enough to be a confidante, and outside enough to provide support and mentoring in areas too threatening to share with biological parents: sex, career choices, drugs, relationships, remaining distress about the divorce. The Resolution Stage also sees the family facing the remnants of its fantasies—it is a time of grieving once more the reality of nonbiological and noncustodial parenting. Step issues continue to arise: disagreements about who will handle college costs, decisions about childbearing, shifting custody arrangements, weddings. At stressful times (for instance, the reentry into the family of a child who had been living in another household), the family may reexperience the entire Stepfamily Cycle, with divergent fantasies about how it will all work out, a stretch of confusion and lack of articulation, periods of panicked conflict, hard work to forge some new agreements, and the relief and intimacy fostered by having succeeded once more. However, even large differences no longer threaten the couple or stepparent-stepchild relationship.

In biological families each developmental phase has its own kind of starting and finishing points marked by the biological clock, as well as by the child's changing behavior. As the infant becomes a 2-year-old, and the stubborn 2-year-old matures into an articulate and fanciful 3-year-old, biological parents come to each beginning and completion with some sadness and regret, as well as relief and excitement at the inevitable move toward maturity. It is hoped that the Stepfamily Cycle will begin to provide just such marking points for stepfamily members.

Just as in biological development, stages of stepfamily development do not happen neatly and precisely—a family may move ahead in one area but remain at a much earlier stage of development in another. And just as children do not suddenly and forever stop having tantrums, stepfamilies and their members slip back and forth between stages, moving to earlier stages of development in times of crisis or when new challenges present themselves. Nonetheless, I believe the Stepfamily Cycle provides a larger framework within which stepfamily members and the helping professionals involved with them can make sense out of the challenges of remarried family life.

Family Differences in Cycle Completion:
How Long Will It Take?

Expecting a 2-year-old to throw one tantrum and be finished with that stage of development is very different from preparing to live with a 2-year-old for a year or two. Psychological research corroborates that knowing what to expect lowers stress.

Preliminary data about the amount of time this process takes indicates that faster families complete the entire Stepfamily Cycle in about 4 years. Average-paced families take about 7 years to reach Resolution, and slower families remain in the Early Stages longer than 4 years, a few for as many as 12 years. Some of the last group end in divorce, others remain stuck in the Early Stages, and a small number eventually move on to complete the Stepfamily Cycle. Although this data is far from statistically reliable, the approximate time frames seem to hold up in my experience with both clinical and nonclinical stepfamilies.

Most interesting to me is that the differences among these three groups lie primarily in the amount of time it takes to negotiate the awareness work of the Early Stages. Faster families complete the Early Stages in about a year. Average-paced families take two to three years, and slower paced and stuck families remain in the Early Stages for more than four years. As was previously mentioned, stepfamilies tend to "make it or break it" by the fourth year. It is interesting to note that my experience indicates this is the time by which the fast and average families have completed the "uphill" portion of the Stepfamily Cycle and have moved through the Action Stage (where the couple begins functioning as a team).

Whatever the particular number of years involved, my data clearly indicates that speed and ease of movement through the Stepfamily Cycle are often closely related to the amount and timing of support, particularly in the Early Stages. Support is defined as the presence of someone or something that provides validation for and understanding of intense painful feelings involved in early stepfamily living, and some indication of what to do next. Only in the few faster families (those who complete the Early Stages within about a year and the entire Stepfamily Cycle within four years) has this early support come from within the couple. In those faster couples the biological parent has been able to hear the stepparent's jealousy and confusion right from the start, and the stepparent has been able to sympathize with the intense pull that biological parents experience from their own children. In addition, these families also came to step-family living with fewer deeply held fantasies and more real-istic expectations.

On the other end of the spectrum, the "stuck" families in my initial research (Papernow, 1980) were distinguished by the fact that those stepparents had talked to almost no-body who understood their experience. Those who moved on did so because of an infusion of support to the stepparent, or a crisis that reorganized the family and supported further movement.

In my data the faster families are the minority. How-ever, subsequent literature suggests that stepfamilies may be coming together at a somewhat faster rate than we had thought (Chollak, 1989; Dahl, Cowgill, & Asmundsson, 1987; Pill, 1988, 1990). Perhaps these later studies reflect the fact that our culture is becoming more supportive of stepfamilies, particularly in the form of better information about what to expect in early stepfamily life. As we will see, this can make a world of difference in progress through the Early Stages.

Overview of *Becoming a Stepfamily:*

Becoming a Stepfamily addresses the needs of several groups of readers: remarried family members, helping professionals involved with stepfamilies, and students of family dynamics. Toward this end it draws on highly diverse information, in-corporating a strong theoretical framework, citing relevant research, quoting from extensive interview material, and of-fering guidelines for intervention illustrated by clinical vi-gnettes. This combination of theoretical and practical, aca-demic and richly personal is designed to help all readers more fully appreciate the complex processes involved in becoming a stepfamily.

Chapter Two introduces concepts of healthy individual and family process drawn from Gestalt theory. These phenomenologically based models then provide an underlying theoretical framework for understanding the unique challenges posed by stepfamily structure.

We then move on to the Stepfamily Cycle. In Chapters Three, Four, and Five respectively, the Early, Middle, and Later Stages of development are delineated. In these chapters the predictable, interdependent changes that occur over time in remarried families are richly characterized through stepfamily members' own stories.

Chapter Six outlines factors that influence the pace and ease of stepfamily development. Four patterns of movement through the Stepfamily Cycle are described. A longer case history illustrates each family type giving the reader a feel for these four very different paths to a successful, satisfying stepfamily.

Chapter Seven is devoted to intervention strategies. It begins by stating four primary principles for working with stepfamilies. The Stepfamily Cycle then becomes a basis for assessment and a guide to appropriate educational and clinical intervention.

The appendices were developed to provide a highly focused distillation of important material. Appendix A summarizes the essentials of the Stepfamily Cycle. Appendix B provides a self-help guide for stepfamily members. Appendix C summarizes therapeutic strategies. So that each quote or case can be placed in its family context, each speaker has been given a last name which enables the reader to locate that person's Family Profile in Appendix D.

Chapter **2**

STEPFAMILY STRUCTURE: BONDS WITHOUT BLOOD

Conceptual Tools

A full understanding of the developmental tasks involved in becoming a stepfamily requires an appreciation of the context within which this developmental process must take place. We begin Chapter Two with two theoretical models of healthy functioning: the Gestalt Experience Cycle, and the Gestalt Interactive Cycle. These models help us to set the stage for stepfamily development. They help to illuminate the unique qualities of stepfamily structure and to highlight the dilemmas and opportunities it creates for members of remarried families. Chapters

21

Three, Four and Five together provide a full description of
the Stepfamily Cycle, which draws its language and sequencing from the Gestalt theoretical framework.

The Gestalt Experience Cycle

Stepfamily structure and history make both intrapsychic and
interpersonal functioning very different in stepfamilies and
in biological families. The Gestalt Experience Cycle, a model
of healthy process, offers tools to clarify this distinction. The
Gestalt Experience Cycle describes healthy functioning in
an individual (Zinker, 1977). The Gestalt Interactive Cycle
applies these principles to families (Zinker & S. Nevis, 1981)
and organizations (E. Nevis, 1987). The ability to move regularly to completion through the cycle signals optimum functioning and creates a feeling of well-being and satisfaction.
Interruptions in cycle completion signal problems in functioning and create a sense of incompleteness and dissatisfaction (see Figure 2.1).

The Gestalt Experience Cycle begins with *sensation*,
characterized by the inarticulate feeling that "something new
is happening, but I don't know what it is yet." The healthy
person moves from sensation to *awareness* by paying attention
to those sensations that deserve attention, struggling to name
them accurately, and gathering data from the real world
about what might be happening ("How am I feeling?" "What
actually happened in my world that might have made me
feel this way?" "What is actually happening right now?"). The
last task of this phase is to organize one's awareness so that
a need or want emerges clearly (a good "figure" emerges
from the background) and noncompeting interests recede
into the background.

Common interruptions to a healthy awareness phase
include depression (remaining lost in sensation), hypochon-
dria (responding to all sensations as danger signals), premature value judgments ("I shouldn't be feeling this way"), and
naming sensations habitually and/or inaccurately ("I'm uncomfortable so I must be hungry." "Something's not right

Figure 2.1 The Gestalt Experience Cycle.

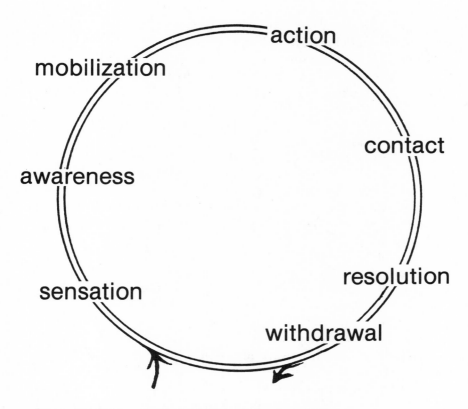

Source: Adapted from the Gestalt Institute of Cleveland, 1978.

here and it must be me."). All of these distort or block information the individual needs in order to function well in the
world. As we will see, the conviction that stepparents and
stepchildren should and will love each other as biological
parents and children do leaves stepfamily members vulnerable to many distortions in awareness. For instance, seeing the
stepparent's very human response to the outsider position
(rejection, jealousy, confusion) as pathological, selfish, cold,
or weak blocks both the stepparent's and his or her partner's
awareness of the outsider's needs for comfort and support.

    "Awareness . . . is supported or limited by the amount
and nature of energy mobilized" (E. Nevis, 1987, p. 24). In
moving to the next stage, *mobilization*, the healthy person
must generate enough physical energy to do something
about his or her awareness. In traditional diagnostic terms,
the obsessive person remains mired in early awareness, with
no clear figure emerging and therefore no energy mobilized
for action. The hysterical person chronically skips from sensation to mobilization, generating intense feelings without
focused awareness of underlying needs or wants. The stepfather who finds himself exploding in anger at a stepchild or
bursting into tears after months (or years) of discomfort,
appears hysterical because he has skipped to mobilization
without sharing his awareness along the way with other family members.

    "Once developed, energy must be used" (E. Nevis,
1987, p. 25). Moving from mobilization to the next stage,
action, requires directing and focusing one's energy: acting
to meet a specific need that emerged as figural, to complete
a task, to make a request, "tying together the aroused energy
with . . . behavioral skills, knowledge or competence . . . in a
way that some appropriate action takes place" (Nevis, 1987,
p. 27). A temper tantrum without a clear request is mobilization without action (and probably energy without sufficient
awareness to direct it). On the other hand, the stepmother
who immediately steps into a disciplinary role has jumped
into action without building enough awareness of this particular child's needs, culture, and history. When awareness is

distorted, inaccurate, or incomplete, the resulting action is much less likely to meet real needs. Thus the stepparent who attributes difficulty in befriending her new stepson to her own inadequacy may redouble her efforts, only to find herself rejected more forcefully—or she may withdraw in hopelessness. The stepmother who responds to rejection by trying to learn something about stepchildren may be more likely to give herself and her new stepson some time to get to know each other, at a distance, while turning to friends or her spouse for support.

Action, based on solid awareness, and supported well physically, makes *contact*—a satisfying connection, either internally with a part of oneself, or with another person or thing. Good contact may also include fully facing what is *not* possible, as in the moment when a biological parent fully understands that his new partner cannot love his child as he himself does.

The last two stages of the cycle ensure good finishing so that the experience can be digested and moved to the background, adding to, rather than distorting, future experience. *Resolution* is the first step in this digestion process: beginning to wind down, savoring what has happened, putting words to the experience, naming what was satisfying and what was missing, and articulating what was learned.

Finally, *withdrawal* is necessary to complete the cycle, marking a clear finishing point and allowing a blank space (a moment of silence, a break between projects, a breath between paragraphs) so that the next new experience can emerge. In stepfamilies, where the sheer number of people and the complexity of their relationships is very high, making time for withdrawal (after a decision is made, at the end of the day, between activities) is especially crucial and challenging.

The Gestalt Interactive Cycle

As we move from a single person to a system of two or more people the process is similar, except that the attention is focused on the complex task of bringing together the interests and energies of a number of individuals, each with his or her own Experience Cycle. Now the task of coming to completion requires building a shared awareness across the diverse experiences of several different people or subunits, bringing together varied energies, creating contact across many different individual and subsystem boundaries. Family therapists Joseph Zinker and Sonia Nevis (1981) have captured this process in the Gestalt Interactive Cycle to describe healthy couple and family interaction. Edwin Nevis (1987) has taken this work a step further, applying the Interactive Cycle to organizational behavior (see Figure 2.2).

The Interactive Cycle begins with the *awareness* phase. As in the individual Experience Cycle, the first task is to attend and put words to one's experience. However, now the awareness must be voiced out loud, preferably in a way that is most likely to get heard. The awareness phase in a family or organization also involves soliciting with curiosity and interest what other people are thinking and feeling about the subject at hand, and staying interested long enough to fully and richly understand the other person's experience.

Although this active sharing and solicitation of awareness are less necessary when functioning alone, they become crucial when functioning jointly with other people. If I am fixing supper alone, I can make an entire meal without ever putting my decision making process into words. When I am cooking with a friend, I have to identify and articulate how hungry I am, what my taste buds long for, what I feel like cooking, and how much effort I'd like to expend. And if I want the pleasure to be shared, I need to ask about my partner's wants, and listen to the answers. The less alike our hungers are, and the less familiar we are with each other, the more effort we will need to expend in the awareness phase to explore our different needs in order to come up with a plan that is mutually satisfying. Here, as we will see, lies the primary challenge for members of stepfamilies who come together in a structure that creates huge gaps in family members' experience of everyday events.

Figure 2.2 An Ideal Picture of the Gestalt Interactive Cycle.

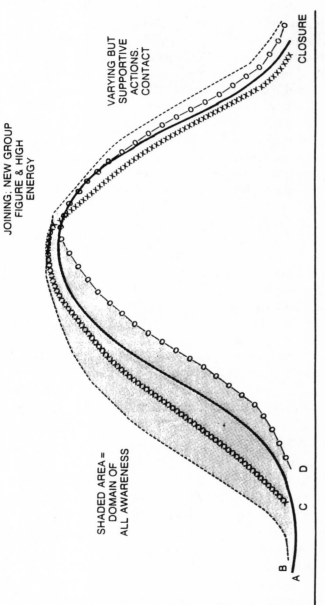

JOINING: NEW GROUP
FIGURE & HIGH
ENERGY

VARYING BUT
SUPPORTIVE
ACTIONS.
CONTACT

SHADED AREA =
DOMAIN OF
ALL AWARENESS

AMPLITUDE OF ENERGY

TIME

CLOSURE

PERSON A = ―――――

PERSON B = ―――――

PERSON C = xxxxxxxxxxxx

PERSON D = ―o―o―o―o

Source: Nevis, 1987, p. 32.

The awareness phase of the Interactive Cycle is interrupted or attenuated when one or more family members do not voice feelings and thoughts, when members demean or discount each other's statements, and when members do not remain curious long enough to understand each other fully. Early stepfamily life brings together a group of people with very uneven levels of awareness about each other's experience. Biological parents and children share a deeper, richer, and longer history than the stepcouple, stepsiblings, or the stepparent and stepchild. Awareness between stepparent and biological parent and between stepparent and stepchild must be built actively and with effort across these different histories and different cultures, and often very different needs. Families that get stuck in awareness can talk endlessly with each other about their feelings. However, they never move on.

Successful systems end the awareness phase with a fairly full sense of their own and each other's perceptions, feelings, needs, and ideas on a given subject. With this shared understanding, the organization or family or group can move to act in a way that feels good to all concerned. And even if there is not full agreement on the course of action taken, differences are understood and accepted.

In the *energy-action* phase the task is to actively influence each other and make a decision. In this phase family members must begin to engage each other with more excitement and intensity. Skills include being willing to jump in and try to influence each other, generating ideas that bring diverse interests together (versus pushing for one idea that meets only one person or subsystem's needs), and checking for fairly equal energy and commitment among members (versus allowing some family members to dominate decision making while others languish on the sidelines).

Several other kinds of problems can emerge in the energy/action part of the cycle. Some family systems jump too quickly into this phase, beginning to actively influence each other before they fully understand one another. Often in

early stepfamily living, one subunit (usually a biological parent and his or her childlren) moves into action (sets the table
a particular way, plans a holiday, focuses the dinner table
conversation) without awareness of the very different needs
and interests of new steppeople. A single stepparent, visiting
stepchildren, or the parent and child unit with a less active,
quieter style will find themselves constantly in foreign territory, unable to join wholeheartedly, and feeling inadequate
and left out. Some families remain mired in energy/action,
engaging each other actively and frequently over differences,
but not moving toward a joint solution (often because they
have skipped the awareness phase).

In the *contact* phase, healthy families eventually find a
way to join around a new "common figure," coming together
in a fresh understanding, a creative synthesis of the varying
needs of family members, or a fully shared notion of what
to do. Good contact is a moment of healthy mutuality: "Yes,
let's do that!" "You're right, we'll just have to let that go."
And again, good contact may involve the couple or family
fully grasping what cannot be. New stepfamilies that spend
enough time and effort in the awareness phase, voicing and
understanding their diverse interests and needs, will honor
some ways of functioning that leave intact some of what is
familiar to each of the subunits of the new family. They will
also invent some new ones.

In the Early Stages, the pull in many stepfamilies, especially those that hold strong fantasies of functioning as a
"blended" biological-like family, is to move too quickly to a
kind of pseudo-contact. The family will appear to be joining
around an idea that in fact only meets the needs of one
subsystem (often the more dominant biological parent-child
unit) without considering the needs of others (the stepparent,
or the less dominant parent-child unit). In this case, those
whose needs were not considered do not join wholeheartedly
and the contact is not lively and full.

As in the Experience Cycle, *resolution* involves finishing
well, turning awareness backward over experience. People in
intimate systems that do this well ask each other what was

successful about a joint effort and what wasn't satisfying. Together they acknowledge what is done, recognize what is undone, and admit what may never be done. "Remember that rainy afternoon when we had that awful picnic in the car?" "My favorite was the evening we spent in that little dive. What was yours?" "What did you love best about what we did together?" "What would you do differently next time?"

Over time good finishing ensures that a family can do some things without effort (plan a successful vacation that meets the needs of most family members, come together at the end of the day, discipline a child) because family members have come to understand each other's needs by checking regularly with one another about what worked and what didn't. People in stepfamilies have much to learn about each other. Stepfamily life, especially in the Early and Middle Stages, involves trying many things together for the first time. Some of these experiments go well, and some create various levels of disaster because participants do not know each other well enough to anticipate each other's needs and feelings. For this reason, stepfamilies need to spend a lot of time in the resolution phase of the Interactive Cycle in order to keep learning enough to do it a little better each time.

When finishing is incomplete, families find themselves trying to solve the same problem over and over again. Couples in stepfamilies are particularly vulnerable to skipping this phase. The press of family business in a complex family system militates against taking time for reflection. Family members may fear reliving difficult experiences. When stepfamilies habitually rush on from event to event, the same bad plan may be repeated again and again. For instance, a "family" vacation with stepchildren may consistently include very little couple time and no special time for the child to be alone with his or her biological parent. The result is an exhausted stepparent and a resentful child in constant competition for a biological parent who feels torn and disappointed.

Finally, *withdrawal* in a family system involves stopping together for a moment to rest, to let events sink in and to mark a clear ending point ("Whooh! I'm glad that's over!" "Hey, we solved something!" "Are we done?" "So that's it, huh?"). Withdrawal makes a clear space in the family for a new event. Families that do this poorly move from one event or subject to another without clear differentiation. The more complex the system's tasks, the more crucial are these small moments of withdrawal in enabling the system to continue without undue stress. Stepfamilies particularly need to make space and time to sit back and take in what has been done, to rest between efforts at getting to know each other and resolving differences.

Stepfamily Process from a Gestalt Perspective

The Experience Cycle, then, describes the ways in which a healthy individual makes sense of his or her experience and finds a satisfying way to act upon it. The Interactive Cycle shows us how a group of different individuals with varying degrees of interest and intensity can build enough shared understanding to bring their energies together in a way that is satisfying to all involved.

Different individuals may have somewhat different patterns of moving through the cycle—getting stuck and moving quickly in very different places. Likewise, different intimate systems may have different paces and rhythms of building awareness, coming together and completing (and interrupting) cycles together. Whatever the pace, Gestalt theory states that individuals who regularly complete cycles feel healthy. Likewise, couples and families who regularly complete cycles together build a sensation of well-being and satisfaction.

Figure 2.2 describes the Interactive Cycle as it would work ideally. The vertical axis represents energy levels, ranging from low to high. The horizontal axis represents time. The entire horizontal axis may represent a few minutes, a few hours, several days, or several years.

In this figure we see four people, A, B, C, and D, who do not all begin at the same place in relationship to this particular family issue or task. Person A becomes interested in the issue first, but remains rather low in energy about it for a while. Perhaps she or he simply has a slower pace or perhaps this person is less interested in the topic at hand. Person B then joins in and becomes quickly energized, followed by C. Person D gets involved, not as intensely as the others but clearly engaged with them. The shaded area on the left side of the cycle represents the breadth of shared understanding (awareness) that needs to be generated by these four people around this issue in order for them to come together. Each person begins at a slightly different point of interest and involvement. Each engages with the issues at a different pace and intensity level. It is the *shared* awareness that evolves from their interaction that allows them to create a fresh, shared understanding, to evolve a collectively generated idea about what to do.

Ed Nevis (1987, p. 31) eloquently describes the work to be done in the awareness phase in order to achieve this fresh creation. Nevis tells us that the work of traversing the shaded area as a family

requires a great deal of sharing among the people involved and a lot of solicitation and interest in what the others are thinking and feeling about the subject at hand. The aim . . . is to achieve the fullest, widest band of awareness possible. *If this phase is rushed or curtailed, there is diminished opportunity to get at the relevant data needed to form a new group figure.* However, done well and unhurried, the interaction results in a joining together around a fresh figure of interest to all [italics added].

This joining together leads to actions that may be somewhat different for each of the four people involved. However, they are now unified by a common understanding. Nevis continues:

There may be varying degrees of intensity in the contacts among the people, and the . . . meaning of the experience may be different for each, but their behavior is synergistic.

As we see in Chapters Three, Four, and Five, and from the cases in Chapter Six, completion of this work is absolutely crucial to satisfying stepfamily functioning.

A stepfamily consists of at least one, and often two, parent-child "minifamilies" (Keshet, 1980), each of which has evolved its own particular rhythm of cycle completion as well as its own pattern of getting stuck. A more in-depth exploration of this phenomenon is offered in the next section on stepfamily structure.

Figure 2.3 illustrates what we call a "simple" stepfamily. A biological parent, Maria, with two children, marries Joe Salvi, who has no children of his own.

Already this "simple" family has a rather complex task to tackle in order to function as a unified group. Maria and her two children have been a single-parent family for a number of years. They share a history and a moderately high energy style. Joe has "joined" the family, but Maria and her two children are continuing to function as a unit with Joe as an outsider. Joe may appear to be joining in, but his lower energy level indicates that he is not wholeheartedly with them. Maria and her children have not stopped to ask him what he needs, and he has not insisted that they slow down so he can tell them. The critical awareness work (represented by the width of the shaded area on the left side of the figure) remains undone. As a result, this new family cannot come together on this issue. Resolution work is also not done, so that each family event ends with no new understanding being built that might enable this group to function more as a whole.

This picture illustrates what often happens when stepfamilies bring strong fantasies of being able to operate like a first-time family. Maria and Joe's stepfamily is functioning "as if" they are working as a unit, but because the work of understanding the territory that divides them is not complete, they do not have enough information to make truly joint decisions in the energy/action phase. This means that even such simple decisions as what to have for breakfast and more complex decisions such as what television show to watch may be determined by Maria and her children, without awareness that Joe may have quite different tastes.

Figure 2.3 Simple Stepfamily: A Parent-Child Minifamily and a Single Stepparent (the Salvi Family).

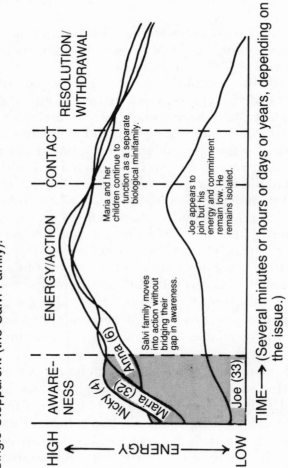

HIGH ◄——————— ENERGY ———————► LOW

AWARE-NESS | ENERGY/ACTION | CONTACT | RESOLUTION/WITHDRAWAL

Nicky (4)
Maria (32)
Anna (6)
Joe (33)

Salvi family moves into action without bridging their gap in awareness.

Maria and her children continue to function as a separate biological minifamily.

Joe appears to join but his energy and commitment remain low. He remains isolated.

TIME ——► (Several minutes or hours or days or years, depending on the issue.)

Note: Shaded area represents awareness gap that must be crossed for this family to function as a whole.

In Figure 2.4 we meet the Black/Jones family. Rather than a biological parent-child unit and a lone stepparent, we now have a "double" or "complex" stepfamily in which both adults bring children. Don Jones and his two children have a slow, rather quiet style, with a relatively long awareness phase. They rarely raise their voices or move quickly into action. However, Lu Anne Black and her daughters have a much more energetic and active style, mobilizing quickly, forcefully attempting to influence each other and anyone else who happens to enter the fray.

The shaded area in Figure 2.4 represents the considerable gap in awareness that must be closed before members of this new stepfamily can begin to function as a whole. In this figure, although there is some coming together of interests and energies within each minifamily, the awareness work necessary to bring the two biological parent-child units together has not been done, and there is no joining of energies between the two subsystems. Furthermore, the resolution work also remains undone, so that there is no learning taking place from each experience of bifurcated family living. Thus, as the figure graphically illustrates, this family begins its life not as a blended family, but as two separate minifamilies.

In Figure 2.4, the higher energy and quicker closure of Lu Anne and her children's family style is likely to dominate in the early life of this stepfamily, determining the pitch and pace at which decisions are made (in this case, quickly, leaving Don and his children bewildered and silent), how space is used (Lu Anne and her children are used to a high level of noise and mess throughout the house, in contrast to the tidy, ordered household familiar to Don and his children), how holidays will be celebrated (Christmas stockings opened at a huge Christmas Day gathering, not quietly at a small family gathering on Christmas Eve, as was the custom in the Jones single-parent family).

Figure 2.4 may also describe a double stepfamily in which one parent-child unit, in this case the Blacks, has the more dominant position for other reasons besides its different interactive style. This might be a family where Lu Anne's children reside in the home full-time, whereas Don's children visit. Or the new stepfamily may be living in Lu Anne's house, giving Lu Anne and her daughters the clearer sense of knowing where the silverware goes, and "how things are done around here," and leaving Don and his family feeling like guests trying to figure out the rules. In each of these cases, the Blacks control the territory. Some members of the Jones parent-child unit (Don and his son Bobby) may appear to be going along. However, because they are operating on completely foreign territory and their own needs have not been included in the plan, they may be physically present but without much energy and commitment, much to Lu Anne's disappointment. Meanwhile, Trisha, Don's daughter, remains very much the outsider of the family.

If we reverse the living situation and imagine that Lu Anne and her daughters have moved into Don and his children's residence, we can imagine the acute feelings of "having been invaded" that the Blacks' louder, quicker style would engender for the Jones family. We can also imagine the "bull in a china shop" discomfort that might be felt by the Blacks as their dirty boots make all too obvious footprints on Don's clean white rug.

As these figures begin to illustrate, stepfamily living, particularly in the Early Stages, requires considerable work in the awareness phase. In Figure 2.3, it will require that Maria stop and ask Joe about what he needs and wants and that Joe speak up and voice his preference in breakfast cereals. In Figure 2.4, it will require that Lu Anne and her daughters slow down and become more curious about Don and his family's thoughts, feelings, and ideas. On the other hand, Don will need to "speed up" and express his feelings with enough intensity and conviction so that Lu Anne can hear him. If the two subunits of this family can traverse the awareness gap between them, they have a great deal to teach each other. Lu Anne and her daughters know how to mobilize but have trouble slowing down and listening. They have very little sense of order and not much of an idea about how to make things peaceful. Don knows how to keep things steady,

Figure 2.4 Complex Stepfamily: Two Parent-Child Minifamilies with Two Different Interactive Styles (the Black/Jones Family).

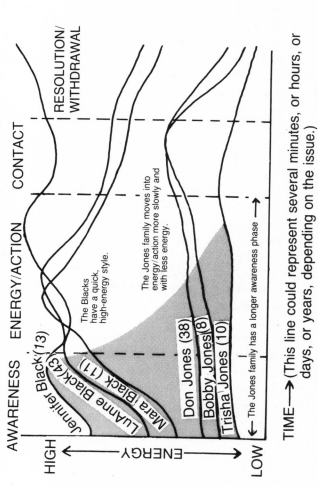

AWARENESS ENERGY ENERGY/ACTION CONTACT RESOLUTION/ WITHDRAWAL

HIGH

LOW

Jennifer Black (13)

LuAnne Black (11)

Mara Black (11)

Don Jones (38)

Bobby Jones (8)

Trisha Jones (10)

The Blacks have a quick, high-energy style.

The Jones family moves into energy/action more slowly and with less energy.

← The Jones family has a longer awareness phase →

TIME → (This line could represent several minutes, or hours, or days, or years, depending on the issue.)

Note: Shaded area represents awareness work to be done for this stepfamily to function as a whole.

but he and his children have trouble rocking the boat even when it is necessary. Perhaps for this reason, Don's daughter Trisha's response to the family's stress is withdrawal, and the family is particularly missing information about what she is feeling and thinking.

As we will see, coming together as a new family will require not only work in understanding each other in the awareness phase, but some very creative efforts in the energy/action phase to generate solutions to address the diverse needs that must coexist in this new stepfamily. In addition, this new stepfamily will travel through its early life together with much less anxiety if family members can savor and heighten even small connections in the contact phase and begin to ask each other, after family events, what worked and what did not (a fuller resolution phase).

Sometimes it is a child's apparent misbehavior that brings the family's attention to these tasks. In Chapter Six, Case Four describes intervention with a family like this. In Figure 2.4 the obvious candidates for this role are Lu Anne's daughter Jennifer, whose highly mobilized response to family stress may tend toward acting out, and Don's daughter Trisha, whose apparent lack of mobilized energy may indicate depression.

The awareness work of articulating and building understanding of differences is one of the major developmental challenges of early stepfamily living. In Chapters Three, Four, and Five, the Stepfamily Cycle will illustrate the course of this developmental challenge over time. In Chapter Six, we will follow four families as they take very different paths through the completion of these tasks. In Chapter Seven, we will see how the Gestalt Experience Cycle and the Gestalt Interactive Cycle guide the therapist in diagnosing the point of stepfamily dysfunction, teaching the individual or the system about its particular strengths and stuck places, and facilitating the development of missing awarenesses or behaviors necessary for more reliable cycle completion.

We are now ready to draw a clearer picture of how stepfamily structure differs from biological family structure.

To do this we need to delineate more fully the dilemmas and challenges involved in completing awareness tasks and traversing the "shaded area" in a beginning stepfamily. Another Gestalt concept, that of "middle ground," provides a useful tool for this task.

The Importance of Middle Ground

Crucial to our understanding of Figures 2.3 and 2.4, and therefore to our understanding of the developmental process inherent in becoming a stepfamily, is the Gestalt concept of "middle ground." Middle ground in a couple, family, or organization consists of areas of shared experience, shared values, and easy cooperative functioning created over time:

> The repetition of successful experience in completing cycles develops a sense of well-being in couples or families, a sense of growth and accomplishment. Such repeated success helps to build the stabilizing "middle ground" of easily achieved common figures. Gestalt small systems theory proposes that this stable and ever expanding "middle ground" is the "gluon" which supports the system's continued enduring over time. (S. Nevis & Warner, 1983, p. 41)

For some families, shared religious beliefs or cultural values, where the path to resolution is paved by already established values and practices, offer areas of easy cycle completion within the family and provide stabilizing middle ground. A couple may come together with a shared love for classical music, a penchant for cooking midnight meals, or similar religious upbringing, all of which provide avenues for easy, satisfying contact.

Other middle ground may be formed from a similar approach to the world, or a shared style of cycle completion. For instance, a stepfather and stepdaughter may both be rather thoughtful and cautious, spending a great deal of time in awareness before moving into energy and action. Shared realistic assumptions about the tasks involved in early stepfamily living can, as we will see, provide substantial middle ground in early stepfamily life. Still more middle ground is created over time through successful efforts to work through familiar problems. What begins as uncharted territory for such questions as how we handle meals, holiday rituals, and bedtimes becomes an automatically traveled, well-defined path over time. Each phase of the cycle no longer requires such intense and active effort.

As new differences arise—because one partner voices previously unarticulated needs, or the family moves to a new developmental phase (the birth or departure of a child)—active effort is again required. When new effort is not expended at these transition points, the family may get stuck, continuing to operate without enough shared awareness of new needs and without a fully shared idea of what they are doing. When cycle completion is interrupted or attenuated in this way, satisfaction decreases, and interaction is no longer fresh and nourishing. The formation of a stepfamily requires such effort.

All life with other people inevitably involves living with differences. Although some of these differences soften or are transformed over time, others remain. Two people who love to cook and go to concerts together may also find that she is comfortable with a cluttered kitchen table whereas he needs a more ordered environment. Likewise, a couple with very different interpersonal styles (he is outgoing and loves to party, she is more contemplative and likes one-to-one conversations) may come together in their religious practice. Some of these differences may remain forever irritating. Others may become more tolerable as deeper understanding makes them more acceptable, and even lovable.

Healthy couples need a balance between the stabilizing effect of easy middle ground and the excitement and energy that come from experiencing their differences (Zinker, 1983). Too many similarities (i.e., too much middle ground) create stagnation and boredom. Too many polarizing differences create anxiety and panic. Remarried couples and their families must contend with a balance that is significantly weighted toward the latter. This imbalance creates a variety of dilemmas for stepfamilies.

Stepfamilies often begin their lives together with deep cracks in their foundation, created by thin middle ground in the adult couple relationship and stepparent-child relationships. Fundamental and highly charged differences in understanding must be bridged for the new "executive team" to succeed in the primary task of integrating step and biological subsystems. Beginning with the awareness phase, becoming a stepfamily often requires extra attention in every phase of the Interactive Cycle. Families that meet these challenges find themselves in the midst of an exciting and rich family life, full of fresh understandings, newly created rituals, and the depth and variety that come from the contactful experience of difference.

What Is Different About Stepfamily Structure

First-Time Family Structure

Couples in first marriages often have a honeymoon period that provides a kind of sanctuary within which the couple can experience their commonality. They usually have some time and space before children arrive for cycle completion around shared pleasures, time to appreciate and heighten "the ways we're just alike." They usually have a while to develop a rhythm of cycle completion—time to develop ways of solving problems together, create shared rituals, build common aesthetic sensibilities and define shared values. Although much of this may happen without full awareness, areas of comfortable functioning begin to emerge. More and more can be done without much thought or effort.

By the time the honeymoon wanes and the two come face to face with how very different they really are, there is often enough middle ground established, enough things that come easily, and enough experience of likeness that the inevitable differences can be borne without threatening to crack the foundation. As a result, couples in first-time marriages also have more opportunity to encounter their differences in the context of experiencing their connection. They have time before children arrive to revel in their shared appreciation of spicy food while coming to grips with the fact that one partner leaves the cap off the toothpaste tube, and the other feels discombobulated unless the cap is replaced and the tube put away. Successful resolution of conflicts adds further "thickness" to the couple's middle ground. Gary and Sharon both love the sun, but he relaxes by "visiting every tiny museum he can lay his hands on." For Sharon, his wife, a real vacation is sitting by a pool with a book for hours at a time. They now take great pride in finding vacation spots with enough historical interest to engage Gary, a pool for Sharon (with big cushioned beach chairs, if possible), and enough good restaurants so they can indulge their passion for good food together.

First-time couples such as Gary and Sharon have time to build middle ground before children arrive. They start with the similarities they bring to their marriage, deepen their understanding of their differences, and forge some new ground to accommodate some of those differences. Nonetheless, the birth of a first child often threatens a couple's equilibrium, requiring that both partners struggle to articulate new awarenesses, face new differences, join together in new ways to do things and establish new areas of middle ground. How do "we" handle a crying baby? How do "we" handle diapers, how do "we" divide money-making versus home-making tasks? Couples in past generations had automatic middle ground in the latter arena, but couples in two-career families must expend more conscious effort to invent a shared path through this dilemma. The birth of a child may highlight new areas of easy middle ground in shared rituals as the family comes together in a bris or a christening, or it may expose painful differences. (Shall we circumcise this child? What do you mean, you shouldn't pick up a crying baby?)

Furthermore, the birth of a child blocks some formerly easy paths to satisfying completion. Friday evening meals at a nice restaurant become an ordeal with a crying baby. A few hours of sleep become infinitely more precious than midnight cooking. The fact that cycle completion becomes hard work again, and new effort must be expended in the search for middle ground, is part of the disequilibrium of having children. However, the interruption in easy cycle completion does not crack the foundation as long as the middle ground is "thick" enough to hold the couple together.

First-time families also differ from stepfamilies in that children usually arrive one at a time, giving parents time to get to know each other as parents, identify some shared values, create family rituals little by little, and evolve a co-parenting style. Thus by the time the second child is born, the family has some middle ground that supports parenting tasks and relationships. They have found a local Chinese restaurant for Friday night dinners that provides a time and place for winding down and coming together at the end of the day. They've found neighbors they both like, have developed some understandings about limits and rules with children, have a favorite family breakfast cereal, and always open their Christmas stockings on Christmas morning. She still leaves the cap off the toothpaste (as does their 5-year-old daughter), and he still talks louder and faster than she does.

Single-Parent Family Structure

The dissolution of a marriage, whether by death or divorce, changes the family structure radically, tearing apart much of the family's middle ground, leaving in its place a single-parent family that will carry on some pieces of the former family's ground but must now also carve out much new middle ground for itself. In divorced families, children often enter a "double-single-parent stage" (Sager et al., 1983) in which they actually become part of *two* single-parent families, each engaged in holding on to some bits of the old family's middle ground and finding and creating new middle ground. Dad may continue to take the kids to the old Chinese restaurant on Friday nights, but Mom doesn't come anymore. Evenings in which Mom and Dad had gone out together (or had spent fighting in the last year) now find Mom and the kids cuddled in front of the television set watching a rented movie.

The context for the task of establishing new middle ground is a structure with a very different shape and texture from a two-parent family. Intergenerational boundaries have softened as the single parent turns to his or her children for nourishment and support previously provided by the spouse. Decisions that had been made by adults are now made jointly by children and adults. Activities that would have been opportunities for adult-adult intimacy (going to a movie, going out to a restaurant) are now more often times for adult-child intimacy and fun. The sheer demands of managing a household, a job, and children require that children take on some adult roles.

Discipline loosens as attention and energy are focused on grieving and healing, and recreating a life after a divorce or death, leaving little energy or desire for confrontation and limit-setting. Limit-setting is hard work with two parents, and doubly difficult for single parents. Registering a problem, deciding upon reasonable rules, and sustaining commitment to enforcing them in the face of children's discomfort is difficult enough when one has another adult to turn to for confirmation ("Did he do that?" "What should the guidelines be, anyway?" "*Is* this fair?" "She sounds like I just told her to hang by her toes—am I that cruel?"). If the marriage had been difficult for a long period before the divorce, or if one parent had been terminally ill, the family may have entered a single-parent stage well before the divorce or death actually occurred. When you add that in a single-parent family both parents and children are often in pain and one's children are a major source of support, the difficulty of sustained limit-setting becomes obvious ("How can I be hard on her when she's missing her Daddy so?").

For these reasons, parent-child relationships in a single-parent family are likely to be quite close (Glenwick & Mowrey, 1986; Weiss, 1979; Weltner, 1982). The intensity of the single-parent–child relationship has been described in the literature with a variety of pathological terms: "overcathexis"

(Neubauer, 1960), "pathologically intensified" (Fast & Cain, 1966), "intense overdependence" (Messinger, 1976), loss of the "echelon structure" (Weiss, 1979), loss of "executive functioning" (Weltner, 1982), and more simply, "exceptionally close" (Visher & Visher, 1979). By whatever name, enmeshment, which would be seen as pathological in a biological family, is a normal part of the new middle ground of single-parent–child relationships.

Stepfamily Structure

As we now move from single-parent family to stepfamily, it begins to become apparent that the stepfamily starts out with a history and structure that are radically different in family systems terms. Most people agree that families work best when individuals in the family have fairly firm, though not rigid, personal boundaries; the adult couple is a strong unit with a clear, but permeable, intergenerational boundary; the family has a fairly well-defined permeable boundary with the rest of the world; children have equal access to both parents; and the parental hierarchy is not pulled out of whack by grandparents, aunts, and others.

In family systems language, stepfamilies begin their lives together with a weak couple subsystem, a tightly bounded biological parent-child alliance, and "interference" in family functioning from a variety of people outside the nuclear subsystem (particularly the ex-spouse). In addition, biological parents and children are often comparatively enmeshed. All of this would signal pathology in a biological family (Minuchin, 1974). (In fact, Minuchin presents a case stepfamily as "pathological" without ever acknowledging the normality of the structure for that time in the family's life!) This structure is simply the starting point for a normal stepfamily.

Figures 2.5a through 2.5f illustrate the differences between biological and stepfamily structure. Figure 2.5a shows a couple in a first-time family. The couple has some time alone together. However, as Sager et al. (1983) describe so fully, things may already be complicated by intergenerational alliances with in-laws.

In Figure 2.5b, a child is born, requiring some shifts in middle ground. Some easy areas of functioning are lost; some new ones must be developed, and some previously unknown differences have been exposed. By the time a second child is born in Figure 2.5c, *some* easy ways of functioning as a family have been established. Still, much readjustment is required.

With divorce, children become part of two single-parent families (Figure 2.5d). Single-parent–child relationships, as we have discussed, tend to be more intense.

In Figure 2.5e, a potential stepfamily begins to form as a new adult enters the picture. In this case it is a single adult with no children (or with nonresidential children). The new adult in Figure 2.5e enters as an outsider to an already established parent-child relationship, a very different position from the beginning experienced by the man in Figure 2.5a.

In the right half of Figure 2.5f, we see what happens if both adults bring children, creating a structure that from the start includes two fully developed parent-child teams—again, a very different beginning from that of the couple in Figures 2.5a through 2.5c.

Despite its title ("Simple Stepfamily"), the illustration we see in Figure 2.5e is now extraordinarily complex. By Figure 2.5f it is even more so, particularly given the possibility that both new spouses may also have been married at least once before. The entire stepfamily system also includes in-laws on all sides. Even visually it is obvious that this suprasystem involves many more complex relationships than those in the first-time family of Figure 2.5c.

This structure creates a fundamentally different experience of family than that in first-time families. First, living as a stepfamily requires extending one's picture of "family" across two households. Stepfamilies (and helping professionals involved with them) who attempt to function as if they can ignore the presence and influence of the child's other parent are ignoring a large piece of reality: children are psychological, if not physical, members of two households. Recent research is showing us that children's postdivorce well-being is more dependent on the adults in these two households operating cooperatively in relationship to the children they share, than on the presence or absence of joint custody or amount of time spent in each home (Hobart, 1987; Isaacs, Leon, & Kline, 1987; Johnston, Coysh, Kline, & Nelson, 1988; Johnston, Gonzales, & Campbell, 1987; Wallerstein & Kelly, 1980). Connie Ahrons, among others, has suggested a new term, the "binuclear family" (1979, 1980a), to help create a new framework for thinking about remarried families. Doris Jacobson (1987) offers "linked family system," and Sager et al. (1983) suggest the term "remarried family suprasystem" to include all extended stepfamily members. Thus both the new stepfamilies we see in Figure 2.5f are affected by the psychological or physical presence of adults outside their boundaries with strong attachments to children.

When we look at the experience inside each stepfamily, more differences appear between first-time and second-time "familying" (Ahrons, 1979). In a first-time family, the adults in the new family have equal history with their children. As these images make clear, the adult team in a stepfamily begins with one member as insider and one as outsider to each child in the new family. The result, as we shall see, is that stepparents and biological parents feel fundamentally different about the same child, the biological parent feeling much more attached and engaged, and the stepparent more excluded and ignored.

The new stepfamily is also complicated by in-laws with long relationships with and concomitant loyalties to the previous spouse, which make it difficult to welcome a new adult in their children and grandchildren's lives.

Furthermore, children in stepfamilies experience biological parents and stepparents very differently. For children the stepparent may be not another nourishing adult but an intruder who threatens to disrupt their close single-parent–child relationship, thereby inflicting yet another loss. Stepparents also place children in a loyalty bind: If I care

Figure 2.5 From First-Time Family to Stepfamily: Structural Changes.

2.5a. Couple in a First-Time Family.

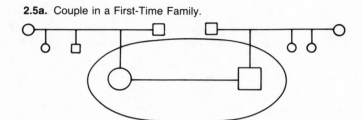

2.5b. Birth of First Child.

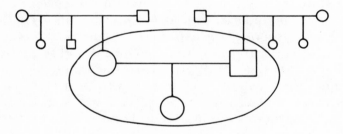

2.5c Birth of Second Child.

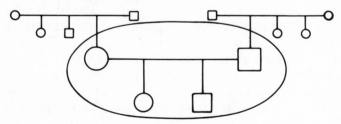

2.5d. Divorce: Two Single-Parent Families.

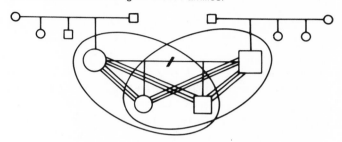

2.5e. "Simple" Stepfamily (only one adult brings children).

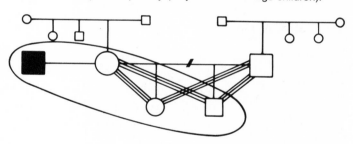

2.5f. Complex Stepfamily (both adults bring children).

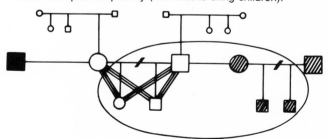

about my mom's new husband, am I betraying my father? Children in first-time families almost always want their original parents to stay together. Loyalty binds, multiple losses, and the remaining, often fervent wish for their biological parents to reunite may combine to make children in stepfamilies much more ambivalent about their parents' remarriage.

Last, but not least, stepfamilies bring together a multiplicity of diverse, well-established cultures. In the final picture, the family at the right brings together two fully established minifamilies, whereas in the stepfamily at the left, an adult (often older than an adult in a first-time marriage, and therefore more set in his or her ways) is joining an existing family. In the next section, we see how these differences create a unique set of dilemmas and challenges for new stepfamilies.

Becoming a Stepfamily: Developmental Challenges and Dilemmas

With these illustrations in mind we can now describe the developmental issues posed by early stepfamily structure.

Stepfamily structure poses a number of dilemmas and challenges to becoming a "whole" satisfying family. We begin by talking about *competition for middle ground*. We then explore more deeply the content of the "shaded areas" we saw in Figures 2.3 and 2.4: the gaps in awareness created by stepfamily structure. As we have noted, these gaps include differences caused by a family structure that chronically places some of its members as *insiders* and some as *outsiders* at every family event. Stepfamily living involves facing great differences in step versus biological parent-child *attachment*. And stepfamilies must find a way to live comfortably with several well-established, diverse *cultures* under one roof. In the following pages we explore the ways in which each of these differences can create a gulf of awareness between stepfamily members in their experience of even the smallest everyday events.

Competition for Middle Ground

As we have seen, the new stepfamily actually consists of several minifamilies. As Figures 2.4 and 2.5f illustrate, when both adults bring children, the family consists of two biological parent-child(ren) subsystems, each with its own separate history and its own shared rhythms, rules, and ways of operating built over years of connection and often intensified in the single-parent stage. As Figures 2.3 and 2.5e show, when the new family consists of a biological parent-child subsystem and a single stepparent, the latter begins life in the new family, not as a member of an established executive team, but as the outsider to a more intimate unit.

Much of the shared understanding in the biological minifamily is no longer in awareness—it can't easily be explained or described or its rules stated, it simply *is* a certain way. It is often not until an unsuspecting new family member violates the territory that a basic assumption about family living suddenly pops into awareness. It may never have occurred to Don Jones that he and his children had a clear agreement about exactly how you put away the silverware ("forks in the fork place, knives in the knife place, teaspoons and soup spoons separated—where they belong") until Lu Anne Black and her children proceeded to do what they always did (throw them all into the drawer—"Why spend precious time separating them?"). The sense of betrayal when these by now unaware bits of middle ground are violated may be surprising to all members of the new stepfamily.

The middle ground in the new stepfamily, then, lies not within the adult couple, but between each biological parent and his or her children, who share memories, rhythms of fighting, playing, and nourishment, not to mention agreements on what the right thing is to do with wet towels, what we do on Sunday mornings, what television shows are "good," and whether junk food should be eaten. As we can see in Figures 2.5e and 2.5f, the solid middle ground of this biological subsystem can extend beyond the biological parent and child to include an ex-spouse, dead or alive, with intimate ties to the children. Unseen in these figures, but very present to the new stepfamily, is what Sager et al. (1983) call the remarried suprasystem: friends, aunts, uncles, and grandparents with ties to the former spouse and the previous family constellation. If the new couple lives in the previous family's community, then church, neighbors, the hairdresser, and even the local hardware store are also part of the familiar ground of one subsystem, but not the other.

In well-functioning families, the couple relationship offers a kind of sanctuary (Minuchin, 1974) to which adults can retreat for comfort, understanding, and problem solving. In the language of Gestalt systems theory, this sanctuary provides a bounded space within which the adults in the family can experience the middle ground between them. It provides a place to heighten shared pleasures and rest on what has been established. It also provides a place to struggle to some resolution in areas of conflict (i.e., to complete new cycles of interaction) without interruption from children or in-laws.

In the new stepfamily, the place to retreat, where the middle ground has sufficiently thickened and the understandings come more easily, is the biological parent-child relationship. Thus, from the start, the biological parent-child subsystem *competes* with the couple subsystem as the sanctuary, the place where nourishment is found, decisions are made, and the family is directed.

The dilemma for the new couple is that in the beginning, the biological subsystem usually wins. Completing interaction within the new couple (and within the stepparent-child relationship) takes much more work and effort. Things that can be done automatically, and with predictable results, within the biological parent-child relationship (deciding what to eat, talking about how to organize the day, playing a familiar game) require much more active effort, producing awkward unreliable results when attempted within new step subsystems. The pull in the new stepfamily is often to continue to complete cycles within the biological parent-child subsystem. Meanwhile interaction within the new couple, and between the stepparent and stepchildren, is continually interrupted.

Thus the dilemma is that the stepcouple, which must function as a strong team in order to bring the pieces of this new family together, begins stepfamily life vulnerable to being interrupted and pulled apart, chronically, forcefully, sometimes subtly and often very obviously, by a competing biological subsystem with greater middle ground.

To effectively guide the process of becoming a stepfamily, the new couple must stay engaged long enough to complete interactive cycles in the face of this often fierce competition. The challenge is to hold on to the still thin middle ground that brought them together, while building a broad enough shared awareness of the often divisive differences stepfamily structure creates. This challenge is made more formidable by the fact that even the awareness work of asking questions and articulating feelings, not to mention the work in the energy and action phase required to create some good enough ways of functioning together, requires that the brand-new couple face fundamental and painful differences that lie at the heart of their new family. These differences lie in needs for intimacy, needs for acceptance, and the need to have some things in life be familiar and easy, especially after a difficult and disturbing loss.

Maria and Joe, the couple in Figure 2.3, illustrate this challenge. Maria has two children, ages 4 and 6, who live with the family. Joe is the noncustodial father of two teenaged daughters, to whom he has had very little access after a bitter divorce. Joe's children do not appear physically in Figure 2.3, nor in Joe and Maria's household, but they remain psychologically part of Joe. A vignette of a dinner table conversation contains all of the dilemmas we discuss in this section:

During a long-awaited romantic dinner, Joe tries to tell Maria that her children rarely speak to him, and that he is having trouble getting enough of her time and attention. He tells her, with more bravado than he actually feels, that he is always in competition with her children and would like more time alone with her. Maria, who has been feeling frustrated and frightened by Joe's apparent inability to join "the family," tells him it is childish to be jealous of her children. She chides him, asking him to join in and be loving to his new children, particularly at the supper table where he is very quiet. He withdraws and the conversation stops. The evening becomes awkward and disappointing for both Maria and Joe.

For Maria and Joe, the task of traversing the gap in awareness between them requires articulating and empathizing across a number of differences created by stepfamily structure: differences between the insider and outsider positions at every family event, differences in the experience of step versus biological parent-child attachment, and myriad differences in family cultures. Just as Jenny and Tom Tolman experienced their Saturdays totally differently, so Maria and Joe experience an evening meal from opposite sides of an experiential gulf. The process of building awareness of each other's very different feelings and perceptions of the same event becomes crucial and challenging. Let us look more closely at these differences, the content of the shaded areas in Figures 2.3 and 2.4.

Insiders and Outsiders

All families have times when some members are more inside and others are more outside. However, in healthy families these positions rotate, with each member being inside sometimes and outside at other times. In a new stepfamily, these positions get stuck. The stuck insiders are usually a biological parent and his or her children. The stuck outsider may be a single stepparent like Jenny Tolman, who has no children of her own, or a stepparent like Joe, whose children reside elsewhere.

In a double, or complex, stepfamily where both couples bring children, the biological parent and child who have moved into the other subsystem's home become the outsiders. They are strangers in someone else's already established territory. As we saw in Figure 2.4, sometimes one biological subsystem, like the Black parent-child unit, simply has a louder, more active style or a faster rhythm of cycle completion, so that subsystem's wants and needs get articulated and acted upon more easily. Thus in Figure 2.4, the Blacks' more dominant style made them the insiders and the quieter sub-system, the Jones parent-child unit, became the outsiders in family events and decision making.

The primary dilemma for the new stepfamily is that the members of all of these adult couples are split experientially. One member of the couple chronically experiences most family events as an insider and the other as an outsider. For insiders, cycle completion comes comparatively easily within the biological subsystem. For Maria, engaging in conversation with her children at the dinner table about their soccer triumphs and the ups and downs of their friendships comes without thinking. She feels included, satisfied, and eager to reconnect with them after a long day of work for her and school for them. Although Maria's children may be purposely ignoring Joe, Maria may be quite unaware of excluding him. She is simply doing what comes naturally with her children.

When Joe attempts to voice his experience of being excluded, Maria has no experiential base from which to understand the subtle ways in which Joe is excluded, and she has no experience from which to draw some understanding of how hard it would be for him to join them. Furthermore, her central position (as the one person in the family who is insider in both the parent-child and the adult couple subsystems, not to mention with her ex-spouse, her ex-in-laws, and ex-friends) leaves her feeling torn when Joe expresses his dissatisfaction.

For Joe, the quick verbal pace, not to mention the content, of the conversation is foreign. Nobody looks at him. Maria's eye contact is with her children. His few attempts to start a conversation, whether with a child or with his wife, are easily overwhelmed by the power of the interaction between Maria and her children. Joe has no place in the family where he can complete cycles easily, leaving him feeling constantly uneasy and unfinished. Maria's inability to empathize with him when he attempts to voice his discomfort only heightens these feelings, and he withdraws in defeat, leaving Maria, who longs for a new family to replace the broken one, feeling abandoned and betrayed.

To bridge this gap in awareness requires work—work to name the feelings, to gather the courage to voice them to each other, and to hang in long enough to build some understanding between the insider and outsider experience of family events. This is the work of the Awareness Stage of the Stepfamily Cycle. When this work is completed, the family has a good enough "map" of the territory they inhabit together to move on to find some satisfying ways to support both the insiders and the outsiders in their new family. When this work is not completed, stepfamily life remains unsatisfying and discouraging.

A second inside-outside split forms between children and adults in a new stepfamily. Children in any healthy family must spend some time as outsiders to the adult couple relationship. However, moving children to the outside in a new stepfamily requires pushing them out of their single-parent–child relationship. Stepchildren may experience their new outsider position as another in a series of unexpected and painful losses. The original parental team in which their sense of self is rooted has been torn apart. Often the family has moved, adding the loss of friends and school and familiar territory. Changed financial circumstances may substantially alter children's life-style. The absence of one parent changes the flavor and shape of comfortable family rituals. We may still play board games on Sunday nights, but Dad isn't there. And Mom doesn't take us out for Chinese food anymore because she can't afford it. Everything—from how we spend the evening to the tone and pace of holidays—is altered in the new single-parent family constellation.

Eventually, this new family develops its own integrity and comfortable ways of functioning. The entrance of a stepparent, not to mention another adult with children, not only disrupts the hard-won, newly familiar single-parent family, but extrudes the child from his or her close relationship with that parent, beginning another cycle of losses. Mornings a child had spent snuggling in bed with Mom are now spent alone as Mom is behind closed doors with her new mate.

New couples in stepfamilies must find enough time alone together to build the sanctuary Minuchin talks about without losing their empathy for and curiosity about children's feelings. Fully facing the fact that the stepfamily is not a unified family but a group of minifamilies can free couples to arrange some clear time for themselves as well as separate private time for each child to be the insider with his or her parent.

It is important to note that in some stepfamilies the new couple can become such a strong insider unit that they force children too quickly into a stuck outside position. These couples may create an adult bond that excludes children from access to their biological parent. We describe these Action Families in Chapter Six. Figure 2.6 illustrates such a family.

This couple has moved quickly from awareness into energy/action with respect to the children. They have come to agreement on a whole host of new rules without enough awareness of what it might be like to ask children to function immediately in entirely new territory. Though stepfamily living requires all members to abandon some familiar middle ground, the process requires an aesthetic that meets both the needs of outsiders for change and those of insiders for stability. The ideal is to make a few changes at a time, leaving something familiar in place for each member of the family. The problem is that the children in Figure 2.6 have been asked to completely discard any familiar middle ground. Furthermore, because the couple unit is so tight, the children do not have adequate support from their biological parent for such a difficult task. If these children, as often happens in a remarriage, have also lost their old neighborhood, and have changed schools as well, they are bereft of any comforting routine or supporting relationships to ease the transition. In these cases the children become stuck outsiders, with no access to easy cycle completion and no comfortable middle ground to ease the transition.

Figure 2.6 "Action Family": Stepcouple as Insiders, Stepchildren as Outsiders (the Allen/Betts Family).

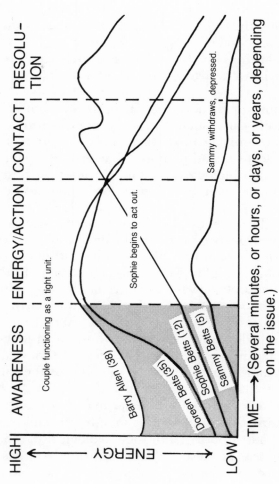

HIGH AWARENESS | ENERGY/ACTION | CONTACT | RESOLUTION

Couple functioning as a tight unit.

Sophie begins to act out.

Sammy withdraws, depressed.

Barry Allen (38)

Doreen Betts (35)

Sophie Betts (12)

Sammy Betts (5)

ENERGY — HIGH ← → LOW

TIME →(Several minutes, or hours, or days, or years, depending on the issue.)

Note: Shaded area represents awareness work necessary for this family to function as a whole.

Doreen and Barry move quickly into action as a team. However, they fail to understand Doreen's children's needs for continuing access to their mother and for a somewhat slower pace of change.

No resolution work with children, so no new understanding of children's needs is created for the next time.

Thus a central challenge in a new stepfamily is to gain as detailed an understanding as possible of how insiders versus outsiders experience each family event. Members of the insider unit, usually a biological parent and child(ren), have to become curious about what is foreign and uncomfortable about their normal everyday interactions. Insiders, particularly the adult biological parent insider, need to take in how differently their new mates experience their children. Stepparent outsiders have to become curious about what foreign but favorite rituals mean to the insider participants. Outsiders also need to learn about how hard it is, particularly for children, to include a stranger in an intimate relationship, especially when whole sets of intimate relationships have been ripped apart by death or divorce. All members of the new family have to struggle to find words for a set of brand-new experiences, in order to be able to talk with each other about them.

Differences in Attachment

The chasm between Joe and Maria Salvi's experience of their family not only lies in their different places in the family structure, but also in the very different quality of each adult's attachment to the children in the family. Like Joe and Maria, and Lu Anne Black and Don Jones, couples in stepfamilies begin their lives with children present. The normal difficulties involved in taking on the challenge of parenting while forming a brand-new relationship are only the beginning. One of the parents in a stepfamily is intimately connected to each child. The other must compete with that child for attention, nourishment, couple time alone, and even the opportunity to start (let alone finish) a conversation.

The result is that like Maria and Joe, and like Jenny and Tom Tolman, whom we met at the beginning of the book, the biological parent and stepparent begin their lives as a couple experiencing the same children fundamentally differently. Biological parents are more likely to feel pulled, engaged, and needed by their children. They feel guiltier when intimate couple time excludes children. Stepparents are more likely to be rejected, ignored, and treated with hostility by the same child. However, they are also more willing and able to tolerate their stepchildren's pain and disappointment without feeling guilty! The biological parent feels nourished by, anxious about, and easily mobilized to do for the same children what the stepparent is more likely to feel jealous of, competitive with, and much more exhausted by.

This difference in the couple's experience of the children lies at the new family's heart. And it must be faced at a time when the couple's middle ground is very thin indeed.

As we have already seen, stepfamily history and structure also dictate that children feel fundamentally different about biological parents and stepparents. Though some children feel very welcoming toward their new stepparents, children in stepfamilies are more likely to engage with, fight openly with, greet warmly, ask questions of, and pull toward their biological parent, while ignoring, competing with, and pushing away from their stepparent. This differential treatment can deepen the chasm within the adult couple, particularly when neither member of the couple can validate or empathize with the other's experience.

Children in stepfamilies also have a parent outside the new family to whom they are more likely to feel attached than they are to either of the adults in the new family. Pauline Boss and her colleagues (1977, 1984) remind us that family membership is both physical and psychological. It is important to remember that whether or not parents are physically present, they remain psychologically present for their children. Parents are inextricably part of a child's physical and emotional identity. Even a parent who has died may remain much more emotionally present for children than for the surviving spouse, who can move on more completely. For the same reasons, divorcing an alcoholic or abusive partner leaves an adult deeply relieved while his or her children may maintain a strong attachment. You can divorce a spouse. You cannot divorce a parent.

Differences in the depth and nature of the attachment felt by various members of the new stepfamily add to the challenge of getting to know each other well enough to form a family that meets enough of its members' needs. The dilemma is that each new awareness of the other's experience can expose a tremendous, often frightening, gulf between the new couple and between the adults and children in the new family.

Couples and families who are cherishing, respectful, and curious about the differences between the step and biological, the adult and child, experiences of their family seem to move most quickly to identify and build the new middle ground that will hold the family together. This is partly because these stepfamilies develop an accurate picture early in their lives together of both the insider and outsider experience so that they have sufficient information to provide supports that will make all family members more comfortable.

Differences in Culture

Remarried families are not only split by differences in attachment and by differences created by their insider versus outsider positions in the family structure. Their primary task is to bring together at least two intact cultures, with potentially different tastes in everything from breakfast cereal to discipline to the way boundaries are handled. A working mother and two teen-aged daughters used to eating melted-cheese sandwiches on the run find themselves married to a father and two children accustomed to formal meals at the table each night. A father and son used to leaving wet towels wherever they fall move in with a woman who is used to finding her towels dry and hung up for her morning shower.

Even a hostile biological parent-child relationship has a familiar rhythm: Perhaps in one family differences simmer for a bit in the awareness phase, suddenly surface in an explosion, and then finish with a loud satisfying (to that subsystem) bang. The other family may be used to long, calm conversations (a long awareness phase), moving eventually to a calmly considered solution. Sudden loud explosions are terrifying to the latter and quiet logical lingering in awareness is frustrating to the former.

Each of these matters may seem trivial, but they are the threads out of which the fabric of our existence is woven. As Virginia Goldner (1982) says so eloquently, when they unravel all at once, they "tear apart all the rituals of private life that make the world feel orderly and natural, and that maintain, invisibly, a stable internal sense of self" (p. 194).

Differences arise in any new couple. However, in a stepfamily at least one adult comes with a team that is fully invested in its already established comfortable middle ground. In addition, team members have already experienced a great deal of unwanted change. The basic rhythms of life offer tremendous comfort in a period of disequilibrium and loss.

When you combine the need for stability created by recent losses with fantasies of a loving, blended family, and add the lack of empathy engendered by the split in the step and biological experiences of the new family, the difficulty in engaging around differences can be intense. As we see in the Middle Stages of the Stepfamily Cycle, the challenge is to stay engaged fruitfully enough to create new middle ground that includes some of what is familiar to outsiders, some of what is comfortable to insiders, and some brand-new inventions for all. The process must proceed quickly enough so that the outsiders in the family do not languish, and slowly enough that the insiders in the family are not subjected to too much disruption. Families that come to this task having completed the work of the Awareness Stage of the Stepfamily Cycle are much more likely to have an accurate map for guiding them in this process.

Conclusion

Stepfamilies must do conscientiously, deliberately, and simultaneously what people in first-time marriages can do over time, with less conscious effort. Individuals in a new stepfamily must struggle to put words to a host of new, often unexpected and disturbing experiences. They must share these awarenesses across great gulfs dividing insider and outsider, step and biological, and child and adult perspectives.

We have said that every couple and family need a large enough area of middle ground to provide peace and stability, and challenging enough differences to provide interest and excitement (Zinker, 1983). Too much middle ground leads to stagnation and boredom. Not enough creates anxiety and chaos. The remarried couple is clearly much more at risk for overwhelming anxiety than for boredom.

A primary developmental challenge then is to identify enough existing middle ground and to forge new middle ground solid enough to hold the new family together. As we will see, to meet this challenge, remarried families, particularly the adult couple, must first come to an accurate enough picture of the territory they inhabit as a stepfamily to attend to the needs of both insider and outsider family members. Stepfamilies holding tightly to the fantasy of an easily "blended family" will be hampered in this task. Paradoxically, those who attempt to make themselves whole by doing everything "as a family" expose themselves at every family event to all of the differences we have described above. This reality makes the term "blended" family one of the cruelest in our lexicon for remarried families.

In contrast, faster families actually provide some separate time and space for each of their minifamilies. These are the "Aware Families" of Chapter Six who intuitively or consciously create little sanctuaries in which each pair in the family can experience its connectedness without competition from outsiders or from more intimately connected insiders. This one-to-one time allows middle ground to be experienced and thickened in each of the stepfamily's separate subsystems, which in itself provides some of the glue necessary to hold the new stepfamily together as it confronts its differences.

The hallmark of a mature stepfamily in the Later Stages, when members have been able to get to know and trust one another, is the emergence of solid middle ground in step relationships. Biological ties remain special and different, but are no longer primary. Satisfying contact among all members is commonplace, a clearly defined stepparent role has formed, and outsider discomfort is a fading memory. While mature stepfamilies have looser boundaries and function less cohesively than first-time families, they often exude a sense of vitality and mastery that comes from knowing their success was achieved, not given.

We now take a closer look at how stepfamilies accomplish this feat.

PART II

THE STEPFAMILY CYCLE:

Normal Stages of Stepfamily Development

H aving set the context, we now turn to the Stepfamily Cycle to delineate the process by which the structure we described earlier becomes a nourishing, workable family—a stepfamily. The Stepfamily Cycle draws much of its language and sequencing from the Gestalt Experience Cycle (see Figure II.1).

The stepfamily, as we have seen, begins its life together biologically organized, with most agreement on rules, shared history, and easy nourishment—most middle ground—lying within biological parent-child relationships. This structure usually remains intact through the Early Stages of the Stepfamily Cycle (Fantasy, Immersion, and Awareness) and begins to shift in the Middle Stages (Mobilization and Action). By the Later Stages (Contact and Resolution), the middle ground in step relationships is finally thick enough to give the family a sense of identity and solidity as a stepfamily.

In Chapter Six we shall see that various families have distinctly different patterns of movement through the developmental challenges of becoming a stepfamily. Even within these patterns, few stepfamilies move neatly through the Stepfamily Cycle. They may move quickly to Action on one issue, while they remain mired in Immersion on another. On any one issue, stepfamily members may slide back and forth, moving to the clarity of the Awareness Stage, slipping back to the confusion of Immersion, and jumping to the polarized conflict of the Mobilization Stage. This is particularly true in the uphill portion of the Stepfamily Cycle (from Fantasy through Mobilization). Even a family that has reached Resolution may find itself reworking the Stepfamily Cycle as new issues expose old fractures (weddings, the birth of a child, custody shifts). However, thicker middle ground in step subsystems usually ensures that these "stress fractures" no longer threaten the family's foundation.

67

Figure II.1 Relationship of the Gestalt Experience Cycle to the Stepfamily Cycle.

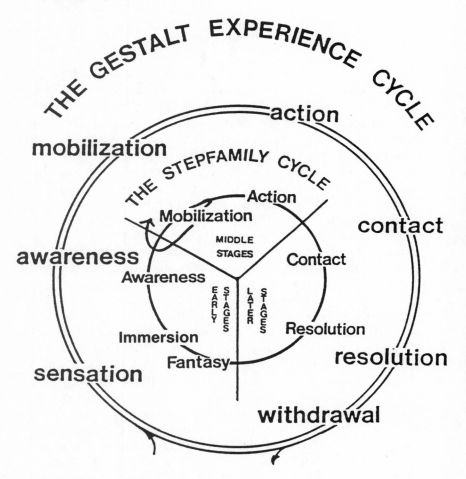

Source: Adapted from Papernow, 1984a.

Underlining the fact that insiders and outsiders, children and adults in early stepfamily life experience the same events very differently, the reader will note that the Fantasy, Immersion, Awareness and Mobilization Stages are described separately from each point of view. It is telling that from the Action Stage on, when the family has become more whole, we can move to describing development in terms of subsystems rather than individuals.

My data indicates that children may move at a very different developmental pace and rhythm through the Stepfamily Cycle than adults. Although children's voices are placed alongside those of the adults at each stage of development, it is crucial to note that children and adults in the same family may actually be at different stages at any one point in their family history.

Furthermore, different children *in the same family* may move at very different paces through the Stepfamily Cycle. One child may move comparatively quickly and easily into a stepparent-stepchild relationship, whereas a sibling in the same family may need to move much more slowly. The children who speak to us in Chapter Three tell us more about why that is.

Though many a stepparent feels that his or her stepchildren's voices are heard only too well in determining the course of family events, there is in fact very little in either the research or the clinical literature that describes the inner experience of children in stepfamilies. Because my own research, clinical practice, and educational efforts have concentrated on adults in stepfamilies, my data on children remains relatively sparse compared to the material on adults' experience of stepfamily living. Nonetheless, the children here speak with conviction and depth, and they have a great deal to tell us. Thus it is hoped that this section offers at least a solid beginning in the understanding of how children experience stepfamily living over time.

Chapter **3**

THE EARLY STAGES: GETTING STARTED WITHOUT GETTING STUCK

T he wish that remarriage will immediately create a new united family, and the gathering awareness that it does not, mark the progression through the three Early Stages: Fantasy, Immersion, and Awareness. For many stepfamilies, the key to getting started with the work of the Early Stages lies in relinquishing enough of the fantasies and "shoulds" they bring to engage in the real work needed.

STAGE ONE
Fantasy: The Invisible Burden

Looking back, most stepfamily members remember bringing a complex set of fantasies, wishes, and unspoken expectations to their new relationships, some conscious, and some barely in awareness. Later experience may prove these fantasies embarrassingly inaccurate. However, their presence in early stepfamily life is almost universal. Stepfamily structure and history uniquely influence the content and intensity of these fantasies. In turn, these myths, wishes, and yearnings exert a powerful influence on the pace and ease of the developmental process.

The courtship period in which adults in stepfamilies can believe wholeheartedly in their wishes is unmercifully short. However, the unspoken sense of "how it should be" often remains as an unseen knot beneath the surface of tangled interactions. All too often, further progress is impossible until family members can be helped to articulate, accept, and grieve over their own, and each other's, fantasies.

In fact, many authors have commented on the wish for "instant family" expressed by some of the stepfamily members who speak in this chapter. All note the danger that this expectation poses to stepfamily development (Jacobson, 1979; Schulman, 1972; Visher & Visher, 1979). However, it is important to remember that the fantasies and hopes described here are often deeply rooted and intimately entwined with stepfamily members' sense of mastery and self-esteem. What may look like an unrealistic whim to a helping professional may feel to a stepparent, stepchild, or a previously divorced or widowed parent like the only shred of hope. Furthermore, most of the speakers in this chapter looked back on this phase with a sense of chagrin and self-deprecation bordering on shame. As we will see, it is often quite painful for stepfamily members to identify and bear the loss of fantasies. Though it may be enticing for the newly informed helping professional to wade in and divest stepfamily members of their wrong-headed expectations, it is essential to approach the task of acknowledging and relinquishing these fantasies with the same gentleness, empathy, and respect we would accord any other loss.

As we see, adults and children often experience this stage very differently. We start with the experience of the adults in a stepfamily, and then move to the children's voices.

Adults' Fantasies

Being Loved and Loving

"I wanted Diana to sit on my lap while I talked to my little boy on the telephone," said Alan Simmons, a noncustodial father devastated by his girlfriend's lack of interest in his son. "I longed for her to listen on the other line while I talked to him and be filled with the same adoring feelings I have."

What emerges most clearly for adults as they recall their thoughts about what their stepfamily experience would hold for them, is the wish that the new family would immediately provide the reliable and nourishing relationships they had been missing. Biological parents recall the drive to have their children loved and well-cared for by a new mate. Stepparents remember the yearning to love and be loved by their new partners and their partners' children. Recent popular media attention to stepfamilies is increasing the numbers who enter stepfamily life with a realistic picture of the obstacles stepfamily structure places in the way of realizing this wish. However, all too many adults still begin stepfamily life with expectations similar to those of Rachel Sax:

We had planned this whole scenario of how I would meet the children and they would gradually get to know me and love me and think I was wonderful. And when Ira would say, "I'm going to marry her," they would jump for joy. I just knew they would love me to pieces. I mean, how could they not!

Many people come to stepfamily living with biological parenting as the model for what is expectable, right and good between stepparents and children. This is especially true in a culture which, as Larry Ganong and Marilyn Coleman's review of the lay media corroborates, continues to see biological families as "intact" and "normal" and stepfamilies as "broken" and embarrassing (Coleman, Ganong, & Gingrich, 1985). The very words "stepparent" and "stepchild" conjure up a host of images and feelings for most people that are neither comfortable nor friendly.

It is not surprising, then, that one of the myths that stepfamily members may find most painful to relinquish is the belief that stepparents and children can love each other from the start (or at least soon!) with the same intensity and depth that biological parents and children experience. The expectation to step in and "love these kids" falls particularly heavily on stepmothers, as our culture creates the additional burden that women can expect to step easily and quickly into mothering. For stepfathers, there is often the expectation that as men they will step quickly and easily into a disciplinary role.

Fixing What Was Broken

Idealistic fantasies about parenting also occur in first-time marriages. However, the history of divorce or death that precedes stepfamily life intensifies these wishes, underpinning them with fantasies of fixing what had been broken, healing a family torn apart, and "making it better this time around." The pain and anxiety about healing the hurt only makes the fantasy of creating a new and loving family more powerful. Tom Tolman:

I left my marriage when my son Ricky was a baby. I never really had a family with him. Then when I married Jenny, I felt I was finally going to get the chance to have a family with Ricky. It just seemed natural that we would all do everything together. Jenny is such a solid person I just knew she'd be great with him. It never occurred to me it would be any different. It was such a disappointment to me that she didn't enjoy him the way I did.

The hurt that wants healing in a remarriage stems not only from the precipitous end of the first family but from disappointments in the experience of parenting the first time around. A remarried mother (Lu Anne Black):

In my first marriage my husband was in sales and he traveled a lot. Even when he was home he didn't see much of the children. Then he started drinking. It hurts so much remembering what my children and I didn't get from their father. I missed having a family during their childhood. When I remarried I really wanted to make the family my children never had. When my second husband and my kids didn't get along, I was devastated.

This mother's poignant wish for the family she lost places an invisible burden not only on her husband, but also on her children, who were at the time in their late teens, developmentally ready to move out, not in. To relinquish the fantasy, however, requires facing a double loss: not only for what can't be in her new family, but also for what she lost in her first family.

For adults, the hurt of a broken or dysfunctional family may extend even further back, to the family of origin. A biological mother, Jane James, looks back with chagrin on her "desperate need" to have her new family work:

My own childhood was hard. My mother was an alcoholic. I don't ever remember being happy. I remember always wishing I could have a family like my friend Becky's. I so much wanted to start my own family. Then my first marriage failed. So the stakes were really high in my second marriage. The wish was really strong to make this loving wonderful family that I'd never had—not as a kid and not in my first marriage.

Being Better Than . . .

The fact that stepfamilies come together as the result of divorce or death breeds another fantasy, the wish that the new adult will not only step into an empty spot, but that he or she will do a *better* job than the previous parent of the same sex: "This man will be the father my ex-husband wasn't." "This woman is so much more reliable and loving than my ex-wife." From the stepparent's side: "I'll be the woman her mother wasn't." "I'll cook and sew for them." "I'm such a much better listener than their father was." "I'll put some order into their lives." And most troublesome is the common expectation: ". . . and the children will be so grateful."

Though the wish to create a loving family and to do better the second time around is normal and even commendable, the intensity of the need for stepparent and stepchild, or stepsiblings, to love each other creates an impossible, though often invisible, burden for all members of the new family. If we return to the Tolmans, whom we met at the beginning of Chapter One, we can now see that a large measure of Tom's sense of disappointment and betrayal, and Jenny's guilt that she "messed up the day," is rooted in their wish that Jenny would adore Ricky as Tom does. Likewise, some of Ricky's apparent indifference toward Jenny is his way of resisting pressure to replace his mother with a stranger—and a stranger who threatens to steal his father away!

Easing the Load

For biological parents, years of single-parenting, with all the strain on resources and energy that it implies, breeds the hope that adding a new adult will ease the burden for both parent and child. "I expected it to be half the burden," said a woman who had been a single parent for five years. "Instead it was twice!" Robert Keefe expresses the fantasy from the stepparent's side:

I expected to come in and make it better. I sensed Elizabeth was overburdened with being a single parent and that I could help. I know I was thinking, "Now we'll have two people to do what one person had to do before. And it's got to be easier." It was so much harder than either of us had ever imagined, and that made me feel totally inadequate.

Abigail Evans, looking back on her early experience with her second husband and his teenaged son, said:

I thought I understood that we wouldn't and couldn't be an "instant family." But you know I was so relieved that Bob was interested in us. I would daydream about how he'd help me with disciplining Jeremy, who was driving me crazy at the time, and how we'd make decisions together. And

I just knew Jeremy would be so glad to have a man around the house, and so thrilled to have a kid his age to live with. I know it's really dumb, but I really didn't count on how hard it would be. I was totally unprepared.

Parents bringing together two sets of children may have a related set of fantasies—the hope that adding new children to the family will ease their own children's loneliness and hurt. "They'll be able to help each other." "They'll love having other kids their own age around." Like Abigail, even adults who can talk reasonably about not expecting to have an "instant family" find themselves unprepared for the hostility, discomfort, or indifference that may emerge among stepsiblings and between stepchildren and stepparents as reality hits in the Immersion Stage.

The Nurturing Mate

All intimate relationships evoke "unfinished business" about the quality of parenting we received, and the level of caretaking and attention we want from our mates. The fact that at least one member of a stepfamily is already a parent, and that the new adult is being called upon to provide parenting, adds an evocative twist to this need to be cared for. As a child, John Smith was the youngest in a highly dysfunctional family:

When I met Lena and her kids I think some little voice said, "Wow! A ready-made family!" I think I so badly wanted a family that would be the ideal family, that would be the loving peaceful place my family wasn't. Lena was so good with her kids. I just knew she'd be good with me, too. I was so surprised by how hard it was.

Lena, when asked to recall her memories of their early relationship, said:

I began feeling that he wanted me to be his mommy. I was already a mommy! I didn't want another child. I wanted a father for my kids. . . . Maybe I wanted a father for both my kids and me!

Lena and John's awareness of these early fantasies emerged only much later in their couples work, as they began to search for the roots of their intense disappointment in each other. For others, the prospect of being involved with a nurturing mate is a more consciously articulated theme right from the start. Barbara Abramson, another stepparent, said she remembered thinking about her new lover:

I thought he was a wonderful father. He talked about his daughter, Emmie, all the time. It just made him more attractive to me. Not only is he an incredible lover and fun to be with, but he's a wonderful father!

The Picture on the Dresser

Just as the biological parent-child relationship is the model for stepparent-child relationships, adults in stepfamilies often enter second marriages with expectations that would be normal for first-time marriages, but create constant heartache as stepfamily structure makes itself felt. The pain and anguish experienced by some of the stepparents whom we will meet in the Immersion Stage may be rooted in a picture of marriage that doesn't include constant interruptions by children, the need to negotiate the most ordinary vacation and recreation arrangements with an ex-spouse, and the constant reminder of a previous unshared intimate history.

By the time we see a stepfamily, many of these fantasies may not be visible, or even conscious, though they remain as controlling forces in family interaction. Joanne Gray, a previously unmarried stepparent, found herself enraged at the inclusion of her husband Jeff's son from a previous marriage in their new daughter's christening. No amount of explaining Jeff's feelings softened her position, until she came to the following awareness:

I've never said this out loud, but I'm a southern girl, I grew up looking at my mother's wedding picture on her dresser and imagining my wedding day. We used to play "Wedding Day" when I was a child, and it was always this picture that I had in mind. But my wedding pictures are so different from that picture on my mother's dresser. They have this strange little boy in them. Jeff's son. And I guess I just wanted at least the christening pictures to be just us.

Whereas some stepparents imagined that their step-children would, as Joanne said, "just disappear," adults who have been ambivalent about having their own children, or who have put off parenting in favor of professional or personal development, may have a different picture—that step-parenting will provide a way to "partially have children"—an ideal way to solve the problem with the best of both worlds. And it is worth noting that mental health professionals carry their own set of fantasies: "We understand this so we won't have the lumps and bumps other people experience!"

"Just Us"

Joanne and her husband, like many couples consisting of a previously single stepparent and a biological parent, had radically different fantasy pictures of "just us." For Joanne "our new family" included "me and my husband and our daughter." Her husband had a different picture: "Me and Joanne and our daughter and my son." This may explain the finding by some researchers (Santrock & Sitterle, 1987) that the birth of a new child may actually have a negative effect on the adult couple's ability to work as a team in parenting the family's stepchild.

Joanne and Jeff's divergent pictures of "us" actually began when they were courting. Jeff, noncustodial father in a nasty divorce suit, had very little access to his son until his remarriage. Jeff:

I had a lousy lawyer when I got divorced, and it was a time when men really didn't stand a chance with their kids. I had visitation rights, but my ex-wife would tell me my son wasn't home, or that he was sick or that he didn't want to see me. Then they moved away and it got really impossible. So I finally gave up. One of the most painful things that ever happened to me was losing contact with him. When I remarried, the possibility of having a family with my son felt real again. So I went back to court and got permission to have him on vacations. I was so thrilled—to have the chance to have a real family with him, to have the family with him I never got to have.

Jeff was fantasizing about having the chance to have a "real family" with his son, but Joanne had a different picture:

I thought it would be just my husband and me. Jeff never saw his son while we were dating. I just assumed he wouldn't be a factor in our marriage.

The picture of a new couple relationship that can proceed without feeling the impact of previous children is even more powerful for older remarrying couples. "I'm 55, my wife is 50. Our kids are grown. I really thought they would just not be a factor," said Dennis Berry whose fantasied "fresh start with no children" was painfully exposed only when his wife's daughter moved back in after having lost her job.

All of these fantasies may in fact carry some truth. Children do come to appreciate having new adults in their lives. A remarried couple with partial custody does have time alone together for a "fresh start." Stepparent and stepchildren can come to care deeply about each other. A new family that works does heal the hurt of previous disappointments. However, stepfamily structure, as we saw in Chapter Two, makes it unlikely that the new family will start this way. We are learning that families with more realistic expectations and assumptions are more satisfied with their stepfamily life (Pill, 1988, 1990) than those who come in expecting a blended "Brady Bunch."

As I often tell my clients, for adults, fantasies in stepfamilies are like alcohol in a recipe. You may burn off the liquid during cooking, but the taste remains. For some members of stepfamilies the remaining flavor sours all further experience. Others have learned to work with the flavor, even using it to advantage.

Of the adults whose voices we have heard thus far, Barbara, Robert, and Abigail are looking back with the sense of resolution that comes from having truly moved forward in their development. However, for Joanne and Jeff further development will not be possible until they can return to their fantasies, articulate them to each other, explore them deeply, and, most important, grieve for their loss.

Children's Fears and Fantasies

Children enter stepfamily life with a set of fantasies that may differ markedly from those of the adults in the family. As a consequence, at no time is the experience of adults and children in stepfamilies more likely to be divergent than in the Fantasy Stage.

Fixing What Was Broken

Although divorce is unsettling for most adults, there is ultimately a sense of relief in having escaped an unsatisfying relationship, a sense of mastery that comes with creating something new and better out of the pain. However, children rarely experience divorce as a gain, almost never feel it is their choice, and with surprising universality, wish it had never happened. Thus, for children, the theme of "fixing what was broken" may mean not creating a new family, but finding a way to put the old one back together again. So, as adults are fantasizing about new and loving relationships, children are often wishing that their parents would reunite. Research is showing us that this wish can persist for years beyond the original divorce, and even beyond both parents' remarriages for some children (Wallerstein & Kelly, 1980). Rusty Peabody, a 30-year-old computer programmer:

I think I fantasized for *years* about how I would get my mother and father back together again. I didn't even really think of it as fantasy. I just daydreamed a lot about how I would arrange it. They would come to my birthday party and see that they loved each other again. Or I would get hurt and then they'd know they had to come together again. I don't think it really sank in until my freshman year in college.

When asked what made the difference, he replied:

I really don't know, I have no idea, because both my parents had remarried by then. It's odd, isn't it!

To help adults understand the intensity of this fantasy, I use the image of a person who has lost a leg. For children, the loss of a parent through divorce or death is like losing a real leg. Even the best artificial limb cannot replace the real one. When stepparents enter the family when children are babies, the "real" parent, like the real leg, often remains the biological one in the child's psyche. It is hardest for adults to understand this when the "real" parent has been abusive. It may help to remember that even a badly broken leg is more real, more "mine," and more "me" than an artificial one. Pressure to love the new artificial leg, as nice as it might be, does not change the reality of "I'd rather have my real one back." In my own experience, it is often the oldest child who feels this wish most strongly. This may be partly because that child carries the longest memory of the "real" family. Or it may be that the family "delegates" the task of carrying the banner of the old family to this child, so that the others can move on with less ambivalence.

Making Things Whole Again

Though the addition of a stepparent is seen, at least at first, as a gain by adults, many children see a new stepparent as yet another loss. Some children do welcome a new stepparent. However, for others the fantasy is not instant love but "Maybe if I'm just mean enough or just indifferent enough this new person will go away." "Making things whole" for these children means restoring the hard-won comfort of their single-parent family. A brother and sister team, now 17- and 11-year-old children of a single parent, said (with the sister acting as spokesperson):

We did everything to get rid of Mom's boyfriends. I guess we thought we could keep her to ourselves. I don't even know if we thought it out loud. But I know we felt it, that it was enough already, with the divorce, and we didn't want any more changes, and that we *could* keep these guys out of our lives if we wanted to. Finally, I guess, she got wise. Or maybe she just fell in love and what we did didn't matter so much.

Losing Again

Most adults, as they enter a new marriage, must confront their fears of another failure. Often by the time they are ready to announce their plans to marry or live together to their children, adults have resolved enough of these fears to believe Samuel Johnson's wry observation that "remarriage is the triumph of hope over experience" (Boswell, 1979, p. 153). Though wedding plans, or the decision to move in together, may signal a resolution for adults, it may spur the beginning of the process for children of articulating and facing their own grief and their sharpened fear of potential loss. Adults with some awareness of this developmental lag can be sensitive and curious about their children's thoughts and feelings at this time. Gabby Davidson (age 9) and Kevin Miller (age 10), stepsister and brother, talked in tandem about their initial reactions to the news that their parents had decided to marry each other. This family is described at length in Chapter Six, Case One. Gabby:

What scares me is if my mom and Chuck get married and then they get divorced again. Maybe it might happen again. Maybe they're just no good at it and that's why they got divorced in the first place!

Kevin:

Yeah, you've moved in and you get to know each other. And then you'd have to move out and have to live in a new neighborhood all over again. You'd spend Christmas together for a few years, and then your family would be separated again! Being torn apart again is scary. That's my biggest nightmare. I have that nightmare a lot. I wake up just when they say, "Now, you're legally divorced."

It is also important to remember that many children enter a new stepfamily still burdened by the fear that they caused their parents' divorce or death. Fears that misbehavior will result in further loss haunt some children. One 6-year-old girl said she imagined living in a castle "with a wall in between. Only I am the only one who can go back and forth between the two sides. But only if I behave myself."

Getting More: Hopeful Fantasies

Not all children's fantasies are negative. Some children begin stepfamily life with positive fantasies very much like the ones adults voice. The wish to heal old hurts, to "have a more fun daddy than the one I have," and to have instant brothers and sisters is expressed by children as well as adults.

Children often talk to me about their wishes for a "real family" and their excitement about having more people in their family. "Now maybe people will come to our house for Passover," said one little girl. "We always have to go to my grandma's. Now we have more people, maybe the holidays will be at our house."

Children, like adults, vary in the particular flavor of the fears and hopes and fantasies they carry into their new stepfamily. Some are primarily looking forward with excitement, others need more time to resolve the past, and still others bring a mixed collection of fearful and hopeful fantasies.

Fantasy: Summary

For most adults in stepfamilies, then, the earliest stage of becoming a stepfamily is suffused with positive fantasies of stepparents loving the children of the person they love, and being loved by them; of being welcomed into a ready-made family; of filling an empty spot for children, spouse, and sometimes the stepparent; of being able to parent without the burdens and obligations of full-fledged biological parenthood. For many looking back, these fantasies have become clouded by disappointment and self-deprecation. Children's fantasies differ markedly from those of adults at this stage, creating a gap in experience that adults may find difficult to bridge. Children's wish for their biological parents to reunite is powerful and enduring, as is the fear of losing or injuring a parent if they come to love the stepparent of the same sex.

It is often too painful for adults in stepfamilies to become aware of and relinquish their fantasies, and so these fantasies remain an invisible burden upon both adults and children. In Chapter Seven we look at how helping professionals can gently, and with great respect and support, help adult members to articulate and bear the loss of their fantasies. We also explore some of the ways that parents can help children with the task of acknowledging and allaying their fears and fantasies, and coming to terms with the loss of their "real" family.

STAGE TWO
Immersion: Sinking Versus Swimming

We thought we would just add the kids to this wonderful relationship we'd developed. Instead we spent the next three years in a sort of Cold War over them.

As the fantasy of a new family that will heal previous losses and hurts is assaulted by the reality of early stepfamily structure, expectations of "blending" meet with countless subtle disappointments and irritations. In this stage, stepfamily members may find themselves immersed in constant and confusing "glitches" and misunderstandings, as insiders experience family events very differently from outsiders, step relationships feel very different from biological reltionships, children's needs and adults' needs clash, and the different cultures and histories of the minifamilies that constitute this new family begin to make themselves felt.

A mother and children used to leaving their dishes in the sink find themselves involved with a man who likes to find his kitchen neat and clean. Children used to doing homework in front of the television set encounter a stepparent who was raised on two hours of public television a day—and only after homework was completed. A father and child used to quiet, low key discussion find they have moved in with a mother and teen-agers accustomed to quick, noisy bursts of conversation. The discomfort caused by these constant clashes of step and biological cultures can be disorienting and irritating. When they are expected they can also prove to be interesting and exciting. For those who do not know they are part of normal development, it is terrifying.

As in the sensation phase of the Gestalt Experience Cycle, family members, particularly those who expected a biological-like family, sense that "Something isn't right here, but I don't know what it is." Families with more realistic expectations (the Aware Families of Chapter Six) spend much less time in this phase, moving fairly quickly into the Awareness Stage. These families are free to spend less energy blaming themselves and each other for their disappointments and more energy trying to learn about each other.

However, when the fantasy of a "blended family" remains the guiding sense of what is supposed to be happening, each deviation from the wish is felt as disappointment in self or others. "Something's wrong here," extends to "And it must be me," particularly for the outsider stepparent in these families. Often the spouse agrees, and the children do as well!

The term "assimilation" previously used to describe this stage (Papernow, 1984a) captures the intention but not the accomplishment of this phase as family members (particularly the adults) strain to fulfill the fantasy of a blended family, even as they are plunged into the realities of early stepfamily structure. Confusion abounds as reality and fantasy, familiarity and strangeness continually clash.

The challenge in this stage is to "keep swimming," to keep trying to put words to experience, to keep holding on to curiosity about what is happening and what will work, rather than sinking into self-doubt and blame. Good information about stepfamilies can make the difference between meeting this challenge and getting stuck in the Immersion Stage trying to make a biological-like family.

As we have said, stepfamily structure in the Early Stages dictates that each person will experience the family differently depending on his or her place in that structure. Because the experience of the Early Stages depends so heavily on one's place in the family structure, Immersion and Awareness are described separately from the stepparent's, biological parent's, and children's points of view. In complex families, where both parents bring children, each adult in the family is both a stepparent and a biological parent. In these cases, adults may experience both sets of feelings, but at different times. When this works well, the adults in the family can use their experience of both roles to empathize with and support each other: "I know just how you feel. I feel the same way sometimes when you and your daughter are real close. It's hard, isn't it? Do you need a hug?" When it works poorly, this mutual experience becomes ammunition for competitive fights: "I don't get angry when I'm jealous of you and your son. What's wrong with you that you're so upset?"

As we have said, in some of these double, or complex, families, one parent-child minifamily may be more dominant. This unit may be louder or quicker or larger. The new stepfamily may be living in what was originally the dominant minifamily's home. Or the children of the more dominant family may be custodial and the others noncustodial. Whatever the reason, the dominant minifamily will be more likely to determine the flow of everyday family events: how space will be used, how family rituals will be celebrated, how meals will (or won't) be organized, what will happen with wet boots, and where the dog will sleep. In these families, members of the dominant unit will experience the family more as insiders and members of the more subordinate unit will experience the family more as outsiders. The adult in the insider unit will feel most like the biological parents described below. For clarity, I have called this person the *insider biological parent.* The adult in the outsider unit will more often feel like the stepparents described below. I have called the latter the *outsider stepparent.*

Immersion: The Outsider Stepparent's Experience

As stepparents join their new families, the positive aspects of their fantasies may evaporate quickly and painfully, leaving a residue of pressure, both internal and external, and ushering in a qualitatively different experience. This can be a painful, lonely, and confusing period for many stepparents as they begin to experience the ramifications of having entered as outsiders into an already established, often intense, parent-child system. For stepparents, the subtitle of this phase could be, "We're glad you're here, but don't come in." As biological subunits continue to operate under their familiar norms, often reacting with knee-jerk quickness to any threat of still more change, stepparents may find themselves mysteriously unable to join or influence the powerful rhythm of cycle completion firmly established in the parent-child relationship.

Becoming an Outsider

Stepparents straining to join this intimate biological parent-child unit often find themselves assaulted by unexpectedly powerful and negative feelings—jealousy, confusion, resentment, inadequacy—as the realities of their place in this system begin to make themselves felt. Christine Erickson, part-time stepmother to two young girls, describes her feelings this way:

When Kate and Pam first came to stay with us it was definitely competition. . . . I had to get used to sharing Roger. I had to get used to sharing him with these two other women. And the fact that they were 8 and 4 at the time was irrelevant to me!

Though jealousy may seem a pathological response to being excluded by an 8-year-old, it is important to recognize that stepparents are constantly confronted with being excluded from an adult couple relationship by children who have a previous and more intimate claim. Lovemaking is interrupted by children used to snuggling with their single-parent fathers in the early morning. An intimate candlelight dinner is brought to an abrupt close by one partner's child's nightmare. Precious time on weekends that would be used for recovery and closeness in a new couple is absorbed with children who are emotionally linked to one member of the couple and not to the other. If those children are visiting, the biological parent is all the more intently absorbed in making the most of the few moments of contact he or she has with them. In this context, jealousy is often a normal response to real events.

Acting on their normal eagerness to be liked, fueled by fantasies of building a new family, stepparents in the Immersion Stage reach out to their stepchildren, only to find them rejecting or indifferent. "For two whole years, Julie would march in the front door for weekend visits, walk right past me and throw her arms around her father," said Trisha Greenfield. Children who had been friendly and welcoming during courtship may suddenly become more indifferent and hostile as the realities of their loyalty bind become more intense, and the loss of the first "real" family becomes more vivid.

Stepparents engrossed in the effort of creating a new couple relationship and building a new family may have no more than an inkling of the bind their overtures create for their stepchildren. Barbara Abramson speaks about the constant rejection, or at best, indifference she experienced in her early relationship with her stepdaughter Emmie:

Emmie really pushes me away. She likes me. But she isn't particularly warm to me. She doesn't greet me. Lots of times I go to hug her, and she doesn't want that. Most of the time she really pushes me away. And if she wakes up in the middle of the night and I go to her room, she won't talk to me. She wants her daddy.

Understanding that children's rejection is their normal and expected attempt to deal with their place in the system helps soften the sting, but it is still hard for most healthy people to be treated with indifference or hostility with regularity by intimates. A spouse who understands that the stepparent's feelings are real and normal can make a huge difference in the stepparent's comfort level. Stepparents who feel supported and heard by their partners are much less likely to sink into self-blame and are more apt to move quickly into the Awareness Stage (Papernow, 1980). Unfortunately, this level of empathy is all too rare in the Early Stages.

Watching Your Lover Love Another

Rejection by stepchildren and difficulty getting enough intimate time with one's new spouse makes it that much harder
for stepparents to watch their partners' often intense attention to their own children. In stepfamilies, the adult couple
relationship is the newer, less established relationship.
Whereas patterns of nourishment have not yet been solidly
established in the adult couple, they are often firmly in place
in the biological parent-child relationship. Stepparents who
had been attracted to their new partners' capacity to nurture
their children now find themselves watching their spouses
provide children with a quality of attention and caring to
which they themselves do not yet have access.

Biological parents have their own children to turn to
for nourishment and validation on rules and values. However, single stepparents who bring no children from a previous marriage, and noncustodial parents whose children reside elsewhere, find themselves feeling especially stranded
during this phase.

Being the Less Expert Parent

Stepparents who have no children of their own struggle with
many of the feelings other first-time parents find familiar:
ambivalence about being grown up, sorting through inherited "scripts" about what it means to parent, finding themselves acting precisely the way they had always promised
themselves they would *never* act toward children, and trying
to develop their own style of parenting.

However, for stepparents, this process of becoming a
parent takes place in front of and in supposed cooperation
with another parent having a more direct claim on the title,
a more intense and often more cooperative relationship with
the child, and an apparently exclusive monopoly on exper-
tise. Gregory Burns, stepparent to Lynn Lippman's two latency-age children, described the problem vividly:

If I had had a kid, it would have been similar in that there would have been this shock in the beginning, just as there was for Lynn in the beginning when she first had the kids. But that's a tension point! The biological parent is used to it and the stepparent is not!

It's kind of like you could choose to enter the Mississippi way up in Minnesota and float all the way down on a raft. Or you could leap in at the middle of the rapids way down in St. Louis and go right up to the falls!

Like in all the small ways down the Mississippi from Minnesota, the biological parent kinda gets used to bouncing off rapids. But if you leap in down in St. Louis, it's a fast ride to New Orleans! And that's really the feeling of it for me!

Confusion for all stepparents is heightened by the fact that the biological family members hold firm perceptions of each other's needs, character, strengths, and weaknesses. Stepparents, as outsiders, often have a very different point of view, but most find themselves acceding to their mate's interpretations of which kid was at fault, and what needed to be done despite the fact that their own initial inclinations may have differed considerably. In fact the biological parent *is* the more expert parent. However, finding the balance between educating the stepparent, and interrupting his or her attempts to get to know the child on his or her own terms is difficult. Robert Keefe, married to Elizabeth and her daughter Becky, said: "Elizabeth would speak for Becky to me. She would say when I suggested something to do, 'Oh, Becky wouldn't like that,' so that inhibited me. I took that at face value because it was easy for me to take it that way."

Because stepparent and stepchild are strangers, their task in the Early Stages is to get to know each other. However, this task must take place in the presence of a "more expert" biological parent and a more compelling biological relationship, which constantly interrupts stepparent-stepchild one-to-one contact. Robert also had a graphic image for the dilemma many stepparents experience as they attempt to build a relationship with their steppchildren:

It's like everybody in the family is carrying around an image of how the step relationship should be. And you're trying to get to know the kid, and all of a sudden somebody sticks themselves in there between us, "Here, look at this"—like these little signs from a protest march stuck in between you and the child.

Stepparents also find themselves constantly interrupting their own perceptions, and replacing them with those of the "majority" biological system. This constant self-interruption is accentuated by the fact that stepparents are parenting in the face of the "expert" parent. Barbara describes the feeling:

It's his kid. I feel scrutinized. It's like he's the boss. Whatever I do with his kid, he evaluates. I don't feel like an equal, I don't feel like a parent, that I can just go in and do what I want to do.

And, of course, Barbara is right—she's *not* Emmie's parent and she is not equal to Jim, particularly at this stage of her relationship with Emmie. Barbara's pain in being pushed away in the middle of the night, as well as her awkwardness getting to know a child who wishes she never had to have a stepmother, is made more intense and more confusing by the fact that it is a surprise. Both Jim and Barbara had expected her to be able to step in easily with Emmie. With more realistic expectations, Barbara might have anticipated that she would not be welcomed by Emmie, and in fact, that Jim should be the person to go to Emmie, until Barbara and Emmie knew each other much better. Instead, both Jim and Barbara are vulnerable to blaming Barbara for "doing it wrong." Furthermore, both are frightened that Barbara's difficulty with Emmie means their family is not working, when in fact they are experiencing a normal developmental event.

Outsider to the Masses

Another reality begins to make itself felt in the Immersion Stage. The new stepparent is not only an outsider to the majority biological system in his or her own nuclear stepfamily but to an extended network of ex-spouse, grandparents, cousins, favorite aunts, old friends, etc. Jane James recalls the first extended family occasion, a wedding after she and her daughter had joined households with Anton Grinnelli and his two sons:

> I couldn't believe how uncomfortable I felt. Here I am, a 30-year-old woman, and I felt like an awkward ugly teenager. Nobody spoke to me except one of Anton's cousins by marriage. Anton's mother kept telling stories about his first wedding. His Aunt Betty, who was seated next to me, treated me like I was invisible, and Anton spent all his time talking to his cousins and didn't even look at me most of the day.

Again, note the quality of the Immersion Stage for the outsider stepparent: "Something's wrong here and I feel ugly." In the Awareness Stage it will be, "Something's wrong here and there's a good reason I feel so lousy." In the Mobilization Stage, it will be, "I feel lousy and I need your support." As this couple maneuvers into and through the Middle Stages, Anton is likely to gain some understanding of the difficulties of Jane's outsider position. As we will see in Chapter Six, a "fast" couple would have gained that understanding in the Awareness Stage. Jane and Anton will have to fight their way across their experiential gap. By the end of the Action Stage this couple may have thrashed out some strategic plans that will get them through these family events—an agreement to exchange looks every time someone mentioned Anton's ex-wife, or perhaps an intimate date to "repay" Jane for "doing time" in the outsider position. By the Later Stages, Jane may still occupy an outsider position at some extended family events. However, she is likely to feel much more supported by her couple relationship with Anton and less panicked and confused by her outsider status.

It is also important to remember here, that what seems rude and unwelcoming to the stepparent, may be experienced by members of Anton's family as their own awkward struggle with a new stepfamily. A woman in Anton's mother's position put it this way:

> I just didn't know what to do with my son's new wife. I kept seeing his first wife, Betsy. I'd known her for 15 years. She was like a daughter to me. It's as if they took away one of my children and replaced her with another and said, "Here's the new one." I can't make the switch so fast. I don't

know how to treat this new woman, and what about my relationship with
Betsy?

In early stepfamily life, stepparents may also feel a minority to the ex-spouse–spouse relationship. When Michelle
Gunnars married Dan, he was minimally involved with his
ex-wife, Susan. Yet the force of Dan and Susan's values and
similar styles of operating with their daughter, Meggan, left
Michelle very much outnumbered for years.

Dan and Susan were part of the liberal movement: "Well, the kid's slow to
learn, leave her alone." Dan and Susan were both C students in high
school, so that's all they've expected of Meggan. In my family, school was
really important. When I learned things in school, my mother went over
it with me, even though she was just learning English herself.

This difference over the importance of schooling would have
emerged as an issue between Dan and Michelle with their
own mutual children. As a stepmother, however, Michelle
arrives as a minority voice in a well-established system. Her
need to act on values that matter to her is constantly
thwarted, not just by her husband, but by an established
pattern that includes her stepdaughter and her husband's
ex-wife.

The presence of an ex-spouse as an "other" parent
who has more history with every member of the biological
minifamily than the stepparent can create many confusing
and disorienting moments for stepparents in the Immersion
Stage.

As Barbara Abramson talks about Katerina's (her husband's ex-wife, and Emmie's biological mother) desire to be
included, as has always been usual, in Emmie's birthday dinner, we can hear her confusion and self-doubt:

I feel so guilty. It's so hard to put words on my feelings. When Katerina
asks to have dinner with us I get so confused. I want two separate families,
and when we get together, it feels like one family. And *I'm* the outsider.
It doesn't just change me when Katerina's present. The family changes.

In the Immersion Stage, Barbara's minority position leaves
her feeling guilty and inadequate. Later as she moves into
Awareness she will feel clearer and less self-deprecating.

Full-Time Stepmothering: The Impossible Mother

Full-time stepmothers are especially at risk for Gregory's image of being dumped in the middle of the rapids, and without a life preserver. Often in these cases, the biological mother has given up custody, or has lost it in a heated custody battle. Such a mother is often seen by both members of the new couple as inadequate and in need of replacement, making the fantasy of "being a better mother" particularly intense for full-time stepmothers and their partners. Barbara describes the pressure that such a fantasy creates for her:

Jim feels so bad about what Emmie didn't get years ago. He feels that Emmie was really deprived because her mother was depressed for a number of years, and Emmie had to take care of her. So I feel guilty, like I'm supposed to be the really good mother!

Children rarely see it this way, though. In fact, it is my experience that for children whose mothers have relinquished custody, issues of loss and loyalty may be even more intense. Many of these children have not only lost a mother, but endured a stiff custody battle that exposed them to vituperative condemnations of one parent by the other, deepening the loyalty bind for the child. Thus, though full-time stepmothers often face particularly high expectations to step fully and immediately into a mothering role and to do it better than the previous mother, they are often faced with children who are particularly unwilling and unable to accept their advances. Without part-time visitation to offer replenishing intimate time with their husbands and a break from feelings of inadequacy and failure, full-time stepmothering can be especially frustrating and demoralizing.

Full-time stepmothers who quit satisfying jobs to take on their new role and who expect, and are expected by their spouses, to step competently and quickly into mothering their stepchildren, are particularly at risk. These women have relinquished a source of mastery and connection for a role that offers, especially in the Early Stages, little opportunity for gratification or intimacy. They are sitting ducks for failure and frustration.

As the nuclear family with Dad at work and Mom at home with the kids becomes less the norm, full-time stepmothers are increasingly likely to be balancing the demands of a career, a new marriage, and needy but unwelcoming stepchildren. Again, the experience of the Immersion Stage for these women is, "I can't do this well enough, what's wrong with me?" In the Awareness Stage, it will shift to "I can't do it all, something has to go." In the Mobilization Stage, these women will often begin to shift some of the responsibility for their stepchildren back to their husbands, or to the children's mother. In the Action Stage the adult team will solve the problem together.

Stranger in a Strange Land

Many stepfamilies begin their lives together in the home or apartment of one of the biological subunits. This often makes financial sense, and may protect resident children from yet another disruption, but it also creates a new set of dilemmas for all concerned. Resident children and their parent agree on everything from which pictures go where to which rooms are "mess rooms" and which ones are "clean rooms." Any move by outsider adults (or their outsider children) to make a change that would make them comfortable, requires taking on an already established biological parent-child alliance and asking them to change. Outsiders often feel surprisingly weak and disenfranchised in this situation, and insiders feel invaded and disoriented by having their space threatened and their routines interrupted.

In a striking metaphor for the difficulties outsider adults may experience in this phase of trying to make space for themselves in an already established system, Robert reported that the only space he could claim as his own after living with Elizabeth and Becky in their apartment for two years was a small unused closet in which he built a small office for himself.

Grown Stepchildren: Into the Nest Again

Contrary to many remarrieds' fantasies, having grown stepchildren sometimes provides little protection against this experience of being an outsider. Dennis Berry had been referred to his company's employee assistance program after
an unusually poor performance review. He had acknowledged that he was depressed, but said, "I don't know why."
Within the first half-hour, he revealed that his wife's grown
daughter had moved into their home after she lost her job.
He had given up his study and his privacy with his wife. He
is furious, but he also feels terribly guilty about not welcoming the daughter, and he is shocked that his wife does not
understand his difficulty.

    This "full nest again" syndrome can pose difficulties
for any couple, but it is handled in a first-time couple by an
adult team with many years of experience together, and a
somewhat equal attachment to the child. It is tackled in a
new stepcouple by two adults who are just getting to know
each other and who have a very different attachment to the
returning child. The adult child's parent is likely to feel more
connected and more interested, and quite dismayed by his
or her new spouse's intolerance for a child in need. The
stepparent is likely to feel more intruded upon, ignored by,
rejected by, and much more irritated by the returning child's
needs. For both, the fantasied "fresh start" in a new marriage
clashes with the reality of this potentially divisive experience.
In the Immersion Stage, stepparents will feel especially disoriented and confused as they find themselves suddenly and
unexpectedly thrust into an outsider position.

Shame: "Something's Wrong Here and It Must Be Me"

In the absence of information about the realities of early
stepfamily living, stepparents in the Immersion Stage are
particularly vulnerable to blaming themselves for their lack
of caring for their stepchildren, their apparent inability to
get heard by either stepchildren or spouse, and their feelings

of disorientation and confusion: "Something's wrong here, and it must be me." Hank Haley, 42, is an adoptive stepfather to three children whose father was killed in the Vietnam War:

I overheard Daryl, who was then 6, saying to the others that he wished I had never married their mother, and that he wished I wasn't his father. And that really hurt. And it fulfilled a suspicion. We'd only been married four or five months and it made me scared—that I had probably failed and that here I was locked into this lifetime situation of being father to these children who didn't want me here.

Feelings of rejection, a normal though difficult developmental event, are experienced here as evidence of failure. Embarrassment and shame make the pain difficult to share, imposing further isolation. Christine Erickson again:

I felt ridiculous being jealous of Pam. I was 20 whatever and she was 6. How can I be jealous of this child who just wants to be with her father?

Because it is so shameful, the pain during this period may be a "deep dark secret" for many stepparents, shared with no one. Rachel Sax, speaking about the first year of her experience living in her husband's apartment with his children, said:

The first nine months were horrible, I don't know how I ever lived through it. But I didn't say anything to anybody. I was the nice silent bride. I was the waitress, and I did supper and cleaned the dishes. When the boys complained that my cooking wasn't like their mother's, I tried and tried to figure out how to do it so they'd like it.

In the Awareness Stage, Rachel would begin to feel more entitled to resent her stepsons' criticism; in the Mobilization Stage, she started telling them about it with vigor and conviction. The Action Stage might find a stepparent in Rachel's position cooking some dishes "sort of like their Mom did it" and others "Rachel's way." In the Immersion Stage, however, Hank describes the effort to win over his stepchildren:

I was into a game of wanting to win their approval. And always doubting that I would. And looking for signs that either I got it or I didn't get it. And mostly seeing signs that I didn't get it.

Even looking back, few stepparents can forgive themselves for how weak and disoriented they felt. Rachel ended her above statement with, "I was pathetic, really."

The difficulty in facing and accepting negative feelings is made greater by the lurking image of wicked stepparent. As Christine put it:

All the negative stuff that was coming up for me personally meant to me that deep down I was the wicked stepmother. And what would come out is that I would try and be so nice. I'd try and counteract it so it wouldn't appear that way. But I still felt terrible.

For men the cruel stepfather image appears to be overlaid by fear of failure as a father to their new stepchildren. The stepparenting role for those who remain for any time in the Immersion Stage places both sexes between Scylla and Charybdis. The fantasied image of the superparent who can form immediate relationships and take over difficult discipline problems and straighten them out looms over them on one side. Waiting on the other side for each inevitable failure is the fear of becoming the wicked stepmother/cruel stepfather, or, equally bad, a disappointment like the previous spouse.

It is important that helping professionals understand that the level of shame and embarrassment many stepparents feel makes sharing these feelings with any but the most supportive person almost impossible. Although one's spouse may seem like the obvious place to go for support, biological parents are all too often unable to serve in this role. They not only often have no common experience from which to empathize, but, as we will see, they are in the grip of their own feelings and needs. This lack of understanding from one's most intimate other only intensifies feelings of shame. Many stepparents must turn outside their new family for support and understanding in this phase—to other stepparents, to organizations such as the Stepfamily Association of America, to books and articles that help make sense out of the pain and lift the shame (see Appendix B and Bibliography).

Straining to Join and Withdrawing

The effort, confusion, and lack of support stepparents experience if they spend very long in the Immersion Stage can be exhausting. The need for withdrawal is powerful. Stepparents in this period seem to vacillate between efforts to assimilate and periods of withdrawal. However, stepmothers and stepfathers are likely to experience their need for withdrawal differently from one another. Gregory Burns again:

I had the habit of coming home and just reading books. I'd cook meals and do other functional kinds of things around the house. But I don't think I was very emotionally present. Lynn would complain about it, but looking back, there just didn't seem to be a way to get in.

Marsha Salzman:

I feel guilty when I go out for an evening with a friend instead of spending it with the family, and my husband feels terribly betrayed when I'm not home to have dinner with him and his kids. So I feel like I'm copping out on the job of making this new family. But the truth is I have such a wonderful time and I come back feeling so much better.

The differing experience of stepfathers and stepmothers is affirmed by Carol Gilligan's work (1982). Gilligan notes that in our culture, men are more likely to draw their sense of self-esteem from separateness, whereas women are more likely to feel their sense of self in relationship to others. Thus, though withdrawal is permissible and even necessary for men in our culture, it poses difficult dilemmas for many women. Likewise, for stepfathers, the difficulty often lies in moving from the outsider position *into* the stepfamily. For stepmothers, the difficulty lies in allowing themselves to turn away from relationships inside their families that cannot yet provide nourishment or mastery.

The particular character style and family history that stepparents bring to their new families may intensify the experience of the Early Stages for stepparents. Stepparents who were outsiders in their families of origin, and stepparents who bring a deep fear of abandonment, may find the feelings evoked by their outsider role almost unbearable. Likewise, stepparents with a deep-seated need for control and order will find themselves particularly unable to abandon the losing battle to impose their will on the single-parent–child unit they have joined.

However, it is crucial to remember that the stepparent role itself is enough to create the appearance of pathology in the healthiest of us. The stepparent's place as outsider in the new stepfamily structure creates feelings of jealousy and resentment in most normal adults. And these are nobody's favorite feelings. In addition, in the Immersion Stage, many stepparents feel confused about the validity of their own perceptions, inadequate in the face of difficulty in achieving intimacy with their new children, and ashamed that they cannot live up to the expectations of their new partner. When these intense feelings are combined with lack of information about the normality of their experience, stepparents are at risk for feeling crazy and ashamed and inadequate. Even without complicating psychodynamic issues, stepparents without outside support may languish here in the Immersion Stage.

Immersion: The Insider Parent's Experience

The insider biological parent in the Immersion Stage occupies a fundamentally different position from the outsider stepparent in the family structure. As stepparents struggle with rejection, confusion, and disenfranchisement inherent in their outsider position, biological parents face a complicated set of feelings and tasks determined by their insider position. However, like stepparents, biological parents find that the Immersion Stage is marked by the sense of being immersed in an unexpectedly confusing and disorienting stress of events, and an inability to make sense yet out of what is happening.

Immersed in Multiple Tasks

Most divorced parents remarry within three years (Vital Health Statistics, 1980). Workers in the field of bereavement (Parkes & Weiss, 1983) and divorce (Weiss, 1975) estimate that it takes three to five years to complete the process of resolving a divorce or death. Taken together, these two pieces of information tell us that remarried parents are often beginning a new family while still immersed in ending an old one. The relationship with the ex-spouse may remain unfinished and raw at the same time that the relationship with a new spouse requires attention. Lessons from a previous unsuccessful marriage may still be being digested as new relationships are being formed. Parents involved in a new adult relationship have children who are coping with grief, hurt, anger, and abandonment and who require attention and support. Stepparents, feeling lost and inadequate, are often unable to speak articulately or convincingly about what they need, and may withdraw at crucial moments when the biological parent had anticipated the presence of a supportive partner. For the remarried parent, simultaneous immersion in parent-child, ex-spouse, and new couple relationships can be unexpectedly overwhelming. Jane James, a newly remarried mother with a young daughter, Ellen:

I'm not sure what I expected, and I'm not sure what's wrong with me, because I thought it would be better. And just when I need my husband's support with my daughter, he's off reading or walking his dog.

Mixed Blessings

By the time a stepparent appears in their lives, most divorced or widowed parents have struggled to create a workable single-parent family in the face of loss. The addition of a new adult (and often, his or her children) poses a complicated

task, that of including a new person in established, comforting rituals. Jane James talks about the unanticipated difficulties involved in welcoming Anton and his sons into her
home:

When my first husband left, my daughter had a lot of trouble sleeping. So
we developed this ritual. I would read her three bedtime stories. Then
she'd fall asleep on the couch while I read or watched television. After she
was asleep I would put her in her own bed. It took months of fussing and
fuming for her to do this peacefully. Anton thinks I'm pampering her.
But his sons are much older. And they visit on weekends, when he doesn't
have to worry about a bedtime. He doesn't know what it's like to be left
alone with a small terrified screaming child, night after night after night.

The worst is the morning. My daughter used to wake up screaming in the
night when she found herself in her own bed. I finally got her to sleep in
her own bed by promising her that when she woke up she could come into
mommy's bed for a big cuddle. That was a *huge* accomplishment, to get
her to stay asleep when I moved her into her own bed. And then that
morning cuddle was such a sweet time for both of us. We would tell stories,
tell each other our dreams and plan the day together. Now when she
comes into our bed in the morning, I can feel Anton get dark and grumpy.
He really doesn't understand, and it puts me in a bind.

In families with stronger fantasies of easily blended
family life, both stepparent and biological parent will continue to feel disappointed and confused by events like this.
The person in Anton's position may remain withdrawn and
hurt, or may take a rigid stance about the inappropriateness
of Jane's limit-setting behavior. The person in Jane's position
may tell her partner to "grow up" or may chastise him for
his unloving behavior toward his new stepdaughter. Confusion and blame will impede the information sharing and understanding necessary to move the family into the Awareness
Stage. These families are more likely to linger in the Immersion Stage, with the biological parent-child unit remaining
the insiders and the stepparent remaining the disenfranchised outsider.

Fast-paced families (the Aware Families in Chapter Six)
are distinguished by the fact that they can name these binds
and can talk about them without blame or panic. These families move more quickly from the Immersion Stage to the

curiosity and shared information of the Awareness Stage. While the morning ritual may not change in the Awareness Stage, Anton will at least gain some understanding of Jane's dilemma, and Jane may come to understand more fully how difficult Anton's outsider position is. Together they may eventually design a way to slowly shift this ritual.

In the Action Families described in Chapter Six we see how the anxiety and confusion of attempting to add new players propel some remarried parents to jump precipitously into the Action Stage, immediately shifting rituals and rules to accommodate their new partners. In these cases the developmental tasks of the Awareness Stage—information sharing and mutual understanding across all of the experiential gaps in the new family—will remain undone, and the children will become the disenfranchised outsiders.

Someone to Turn To

Despite these dilemmas, biological parents, particularly those married to noncustodial or previously single stepparents, often find the Immersion Stage less uncomfortable than do their partners. Although the Early Stages of stepfamily life may not be easy, remarried parents do have a source of nourishment and validation in their relationships with their children. At the beginning of this book we see Tom Tolman standing with his son at the parade. He doesn't feel left out or excluded. He feels powerfully pulled toward and interested in the same child Jenny experiences as an intruder. Because he feels "whole and peaceful," Jenny's discomfort doesn't become obvious to him until late in the day, at which time it is a total surprise.

Furthermore, the insider biological parent is usually part of the majority voice in any glitch over norms and rules. In the Tolman family, the weekend together was designed by Tom and Ricky, who were perfectly satisfied watching a parade and eating fast food; Jenny found the first boring and the second disgusting. Remarried parents are often dismayed and uncomfortable in the Early Stages, but they also feel less crazy and inadequate than do stepparents, and they are less likely to appear for help until the Mobilization Stage, when stepparents begin to make their demands more vividly felt.

I Have a Dream . . .

Unlike stepparents, biological parents are not assaulted by their children's rejection or indifference and therefore they may hold on to their fantasies of a blended family longer. For Tom Tolman, the picture of "Jenny and my son and me" fulfilled a long-held dream of having a family again, after seven years of single-parenting. However, Jenny's experience as an outsider starkly confronts her with the unreality of her fantasy of an instantly nourishing family. The day leaves Tom's dreams much more firmly in place. By the time we meet Jenny and Tom in Chapter One, they are approaching the Mobilization Stage and have begun to openly acknowledge this fundamental difference in their experience of their weekends with Ricky. However, in the Immersion Stage neither had the words to describe their experience, although both sensed that something didn't feel good. Jenny didn't feel entitled enough or clear enough to describe her experience, and Tom feels, looking back, how painful it would have been for him to even acknowledge the validity of Jenny's discomfort:

It was just one weekend a month that I could see Ricky. I so wanted it to go well. Looking back, I think it was so hard to bear that Jenny found it painful. I could hardly stand to see in her face that she wasn't enjoying my son.

Anton Grinnelli, the noncustodial father to two boys, talks about his sense of vigilance in the Early Stages:

A good part of looking for a mate was looking for a woman who could help me out with these kids. Someone who would love my children with me. It wasn't so conscious, but it was a real strong drive. But I'm not sure I realized it.

So it was really important to me that the kids and Jane meshed. I was always watching, "Is this going to work out? Or isn't this going to work out?" I saw them so little, that every moment with them was precious. I watched Jane like a hawk, and every time she looked unhappy with them, my heart sank.

Looking back, Anton can say:

I can't believe the pressure I put Jane and myself under. I wish we'd known then what we know now. It would still have been hard, but we could have been so much more supportive of each other.

Feeling Abandoned

Without accurate information about what to expect, remarried parents may interpret stepparents' very different experience of the children, difficulty becoming part of the new family, and intermittent withdrawal as a lack of desire to be part of the new family. Maria Salvi:

I thought Joe would be such a good father to my kids. I don't know how conscious that was. Except when he'd go and watch television after dinner during what I thought of as family time, I was so disappointed. I just didn't get it. I felt so abandoned and betrayed.

Several years later, this mother can say, "Now I understand how left out he felt. And how much my kids needed that time alone with me. God, do I wish I'd known that then."

Noncustodial Fathers: Old Loyalties, New Ties

Although custody patterns are shifting in some areas, 9 out of 10 children live with their mothers following a divorce (Furstenberg & Spanier, 1984). We know that 80 percent of divorced fathers will remarry within three years (Glick, 1980), and many of them will marry women with children. Thus the male partner in a remarriage is quite likely to be the noncustodial parent of children who may not be physically present in his household, and yet who may remain emotionally present for him.

We have paid some attention in the literature to the loyalty conflicts stepfamilies impose upon children, but we are just beginning to attend to the dilemma of the noncustodial parent, usually a father, who must balance his ties to his own children from a previous marriage at the same time that he is being expected to step into new attachments to his spouse's children. Clingempeel and Brand (1985) note that these fathers must negotiate the allocation of time, money, and affection between two households. Furstenberg and Spanier (1984) found that noncustodial parents who take on new responsibilities in their remarried family may become less able to sustain their commitments to children and ex-spouse from their first marriage. In fact, in their study of divorced and remarried families in central Pennsylvania, Furstenberg and Spanier (1984) found that by the five-year mark 50 percent of children had lost contact with their noncustodial parent, usually a father.

The fact that many noncustodial fathers have lost touch with their own children can be interpreted as lack of interest. The fathers tell a different story, however. Many feel their ex-wives made it too painful and difficult to maintain contact with their children. Alan Simmons:

She would tell me my kid wasn't home when he was. I would drive an hour to pick up Brad for visitation and she would appear at the door and tell me he was sick and couldn't come with me. He would wake up crying in the night when he was with me, and tell me that his mother had told him that the divorce was my fault, that I didn't give them enough money, and that I didn't see him because I didn't love him. He was irritable and withdrawn when he was with me, and would cry so bitterly when we parted. It just got too difficult. And so I gave up. And it haunts me.

Noncustodial stepfathers like Alan who have no contact with their own children may become outsiders in both their first and their second families. That we do not encourage men to talk about their feelings in this culture makes voicing them that much more difficult. And because we are only beginning to acknowledge the importance of their parental role to men's self-esteem, this loss all too often remains invisible to friends and family as well. Fred O'Brien is the father of two daughters, now 23 and 25, who were 14 and 16 when he and their mother divorced. A bitter custody battle resulted in minimal contact with his daughters until they left their mother's home. Fred:

> If I were a woman, everybody and their brother would have felt sorry for me that my kids weren't visiting. Somehow, because I'm a man I think it was not supposed to matter. I had trouble talking about how pained this all made me. And when I did, people would say things like, "Oh, you'll always be their father." Which is true. But it didn't take away the pain of not seeing them become young women, not helping them with their homework, not hearing about their boyfriends, and not watching them learn how to work. I still feel really alone with this.

In the Immersion Stage, the sense of loss and shame may remain a dark, unspoken, and often unconscious undercurrent for these men. Though it may not be articulated, it has a powerful impact on stepfamily functioning, as these men may find themselves inexplicably depressed and they may find it particularly difficult to engage with their residential stepchildren. Now the shame at not being able to provide for their own children is multiplied by the apparent "inability" or "unwillingness" to provide for their stepchildren. We will return to Alan Simmons in Chapter Seven ("Individual Awareness Work with Biological Parents", p. 322).

Straining to Join Versus Denial

Whereas the outsider stepparent may swing between straining to join the new family and withdrawal, the insider biological parent is often caught between trying to make it all work, and ignoring or denying the conflicting needs foisted upon him or her by stepfamily structure. Some remarried parents vacillate between these poles. Others err more on the side of exhausting themselves trying to meet everyone's needs. On the other hand, panic about yet another failure may strengthen the need to deny the fact that this family doesn't blend. Looking back, Tom Tolman acknowledges that he was one of the latter:

When Jenny was jealous, I just thought she was being immature and overreacting. I really had no idea what she felt until she dragged me into couples therapy. It was just too frightening. Because I think I felt that if Jenny didn't love my son, there was no way our new family could work. And I had waited so long as a single parent to have a "real" family.

Retreating Versus Coupling

Trying to accommodate conflicting needs may also push remarried parents into retreating to the more solid middle ground and relative comfort of the biological parent-child relationship. For many parents in the Early Stages, this retreat happens without awareness, much to the chagrin of their stepparent partners. Lynn Lippman:

My husband says that every time we have a fight I go off and spend time with my daughter. I denied this for the longest time. And now I see that it's true.

Families who, like the Davidson/Millers in Chapter Six, operate with the assumption that each of the minifamilies within their stepfamily needs its own time and space, are more likely to purposively arrange special biological parent-child time, and can enjoy the advantages of "taking turns." For families in the Immersion Stage still laboring to be a blended family, the experience is more conflicted. Beth Roberts:

When my husband is late coming home from work, my daughter and I are alone again. It feels delicious and so much easier, but I feel guilty.

For some, the belief that making separate parent-child time is unfamily-like can be immobilizing. Terry Peterson, a biological father in a gay relationship:

When I go to the grocery store, my son asks to come along with me, but only if my lover isn't coming, too. I feel caught. If I say yes, I feel like I'm giving in to my son's idea that he can have me alone. If I say no, then he's furious at me, and I feel like I've sided with my lover against him.

Children in the Immersion Stage

Like adults, children in this stage find themselves immersed in powerful feelings generated by the structure and history of their new families. And, like adults, children are often surprised, mystified, and ashamed of the strength of their feelings. Some children languish for a long time in the Immersion Stage, feeling lost and unable to articulate their experience, and others move through it into the Awareness Stage more quickly.

Sudden Shifts

Adults in stepfamilies are often stunned that positive engaging behavior from children in response to their stepparents and stepsiblings can shift with surprising quickness. This apparently mysterious change in behavior often coincides with a major transition in the new family's status—a stepparent goes from being "Mom's date" to a member of the household, or parents remarry. Although children have a very difficult time articulating their feelings in the Immersion Stage, they are very clear, looking back, about the reasons for their new behavior. Kevin Miller, a 12-year-old in a double family:

In the beginning it's fun. Then you realize that your whole life is going to change. Everything changes. We had just us before, my Dad and me. And now there's all these new people and new rules.

When a new stepparent moves in, familiar routines that had been very comforting are broken because mom has a new boyfriend, or dad has a new wife. Saturday evenings eating pizza and watching videos with Mom disappear because Mom is now out with her new husband—the kids watch television with a babysitter. Furthermore, Mom's new husband doesn't like eating in the living room. Aaron Cohen, a 10-year-old boy:

I always did my homework in front of the television. In my stepfamily they didn't do that. They thought it was wrong. But for me it was so weird sitting in my room all by myself. I couldn't concentrate and I felt so lonely.

Shifts in the family's status may also increase the weight on children of adults' fantasies:

It's like you're supposed to be intimate with all these strangers. Someone you'd played with and sort of had fun with, now you're supposed to live with and love.

Loyalty Binds

Most difficult for children in stepfamilies are the loyalty binds created by the addition of new adults in their lives. In the Awareness Stage, children become very articulate about the pulls and pushes of these binds. In the Immersion Stage, children often feel the pulls intensely but cannot sort out their own feelings. They may have many questions they can't ask yet. Often they find themselves expressing their feelings indirectly in ways that can be confusing and upsetting to adults. Kevin Miller:

I beat kids up in school. I guess it was because I had two mothers, and I didn't know what to do. I didn't know how this would work, and what holidays would be with whom.

Divorced parents can make a difference in whether their children languish in their confusion and worry, or move into a clearer understanding of the complex relationships in their lives. Kevin needed a place to ask his questions. He needed information about what would change and what would stay the same. And he needed some words to describe the ways in which his step and biological relationships would be different from each other. Parents and caretakers can expect children to be struggling with these issues and can take the lead, significantly shortening the amount of time children spend in the Immersion Stage. A number of books are available to help adults and children with this task (Burt & Burt, 1983; Bradley, 1982; Craven, 1982; Evans, 1986; Fassler, Lash & Ives, 1988; Getzoff & McClenahan, 1984; Hyde, 1981; Lewis, 1980; Vigna, 1984). Many of these can be ordered from the Stepfamily Association of America in Lincoln, Nebraska (see Appendix B). For a very thorough review of books for stepchildren see Larry Ganong and Marilyn Coleman's *Bibliotherapy with Stepchildren* (1988a).

Knowledgeable friends and school personnel can help immeasurably. When Nicole's mother, Hope Franklin, began living with her boyfriend Julian, Nicole began telling her mother, "I miss Daddy." Hope feared that her daughter preferred her father over herself. A sensitive nursery school teacher suggested that Nicole's "I miss Daddy" was actually her way of saying "I'm afraid of losing Daddy." Armed with that information Hope took her daughter on her lap and talked to her about her worries. "Are you afraid if you love Julian that you'll lose Daddy?" Nicole nodded silently. "Daddy will always be your Daddy," Hope explained. "And Julian will be something different." "Can he be my special friend?" said Nicole. "Yes," answered her mother. "Are you still worried that if you love Julian, you'll lose Daddy?" The child nodded yes. Hope then offered to have Nicole talk to her Daddy, who was more than willing to reassure Nicole that he would always be her Daddy and that she could have a special, different relationship with Julian.

If children whose divorced parents are so cooperative feel this torn and confused, we can only imagine the feelings of children whose parents compete for their attention and who bad-mouth each other and each other's new partners. This is one of those children, a 9-year-old girl, Ellen James:

On Mother's Day I didn't know what to do. I didn't even know what I should do or could do. If I went with my stepmother, my mother would be furious. If I went with my mother, my stepmother would be upset. I couldn't even think about it. It's the worst situation I ever had in my life.

Not only young children find themselves confused about their loyalties. And not all loyalty pulls involve obvious bad-mouthing of one parent by another. Sally Kelly, a young woman in her mid-20s whose father had just remarried, tries to sort through her feelings as she plans her graduation:

It's all so confusing. It's supposedly my day. But if my father brings his new wife, my mother is going to be a wreck. But if I ask him not to bring his wife, he'll have a fit. I can't sort out what I'm supposed to do here.

Operating on Foreign Territory

Living in a new stepfamily creates shifts not only in relationships and routines, but often in the physical environment as
well. For adults, living in a new environment can be rather
difficult, but for children, whose identities are less formed,
operating on foreign territory can be especially disorienting.
Gabby Davidson talks about what it was like for her when
she moved into her stepbrother's room:

What was hardest was suddenly living with a boy who loves combat. All of
a sudden I'm living in a house with green all over and camouflage things
all over. It was so strange. There were all these guns on the wall. It was
weird.

For many stepchildren, environmental changes often involve
not only new family members and a new household, but a
new school and a new neighborhood as well. Kim Schmidt
was 11 when her parents divorced and 12 when she and her
mother and brother moved in with Ed Brewster:

First we moved out of the house we had with my dad. It had a swing in
the back, and I really liked it. Then we had a house with my mom, and I
remember she used to play the Beatles every morning, and I loved it. I
really grew to love that place. Then we moved in with Ed, and it was
completely different. First of all, he didn't like the Beatles, so we didn't
play them anymore. And I was in a new school where I didn't know
anyone, and in a city. I'd never lived in a city before, and now we had
sidewalks and streetlights. It was all so foreign. And Ed was so foreign. He
had rules about table manners, which we had never had before, and rules
about how you treat adults, which we had never had before. I was completely lost.

Adults, busy trying to establish a working new household,
are often unaware of how hard it is for children to adapt to
a new set of standards and rules. Zoe Becker, at 18, recalls
the first years at her stepmother and father's house:

My stepmother made me eat tomatoes, clean my plate, and do housework.
I never did those things before. I did them. I was good. But I felt *terrible*.

As Zoe goes on, note her feelings that "Something's wrong here, and I can't make sense out of it," typical of the Immersion Stage:

> I don't even have words for it. I was scared there. I used to take a picture of the Rolling Stones with me and look at it under the covers just so I would know that familiar thing from my other house still exists and I'm OK. I'm just getting clearer about it now. I still can't make sense out of it.

It is important to note that Gabby, who moved quickly from Immersion into Awareness, had some help from the other members of her new family. Her mom helped her decide which of her toys she wanted to bring with her for what was a temporary move while their house was being renovated. She helped her put up a picture of herself, "and I put my stuffed animal in the corner." Gabby's stepfather helped his son to take some of the "stuff" off the wall, and to move some of his toys out to make room for Gabby's things. David Jacobson (1988) is discovering that having adequate space can make a difference in how stressful the transition into stepfamily living is. This family's ease in making space for both children is partly due to the parents' sensitivity and partly attributable to the fact that the stepbrother Kevin had two rooms and could clear his "stuff" out of one room but still maintain his primary territory.

Losses

The change in children's behavior relates not just to what had been added to their lives, but also to the fact that stepfamily living imposes a number of losses on them. Danny Wilson, whose mother died when he was 7, had been "delightful" until his stepmother-to-be, Donna, and his dad got more involved with each other. Looking back, Danny is very clear about the reasons for the change in his behavior:

> I remember that until they were getting more serious I liked her. And then when they got more involved he gave more attention to her. I didn't like it. Because she was taking him away. I wouldn't listen to her. I'd only listen to my father. The same thing my dad would tell me, if she told me, I wouldn't do it. I really didn't like her then.

Many children at this time find themselves grappling not only with current losses but with reawakened old ones as well. In this stage these losses are hard to voice and hard to make sense of. However, they remain powerful. Gabby Davidson, 11 at the time of this quote, has had almost no contact with her father since she was born. The entry of her stepfather, Chuck, evoked powerful old feelings:

I lived without a father for a long time. When I found out about Mom and Chuck I had these fits at school. I'd get mad at my friends. I didn't know why. It turned out to be about my Dad, that I was mad at my Dad. Having Chuck made me mad at my Dad.

The timing of remarriage means that children, like their parents, are often still resolving their feelings about their parents' divorce, having lost a family ("Is it my fault?"), and grief over not being able to have both parents at the same time. Even children whose parents' divorce took place many years before may find themselves re-grieving the fantasy of reuniting their parents. I now tell remarrying couples to expect their stepchildren to grieve at their wedding. When these tears (and anger) are expected, both children and adults find them easier to bear. When they arrive unexpectedly, adults may feel betrayed and children may feel confused and surprised by their own responses. Kevin Miller, Gabby's stepbrother, recalls his response when his father told him that he was going to marry Jan:

I started to cry. I was watching TV and my eyes started to tear up. I don't even know why.

Zoe Becker, faced with one more change in something familiar, finds herself inexplicably in tears, and forced to deal with them on foreign territory:

My Dad shaved his beard. And when I saw him, I burst out crying. I didn't know why. And so I said to him I didn't know why and I would talk to him when I did. And I walked out.

My stepmother believes in dealing with feelings and she marched me back downstairs and made me confront him. And I couldn't talk. I just didn't know what to say.

For many stepchildren grief and hostility pass fairly quickly. However, some stepfamilies report that one child, often an oldest, becomes chronically formidable, treating the stepparent with particular bitterness or indifference, or with-drawing quite completely from the new family. This child, especially if she or he has lived the longest in the original family, may have the most to lose in moving on. The problem is compounded for these children when other stepfamily members rigidly adhere to the myth of a biological-like new family. In these cases it is important to remember that a "resistant" child may be attempting to remind everyone of the fallacy of an immediately blended family and the need to grieve the break-up of the original family. Arlene Goldfarb Wentworth's daughter Leah (Chapter Six, Case Four) and Lena Taylor's oldest child Jenny (Chapter Seven, "Helping Children Complete Awareness Tasks", page 327) provide examples of this later on.

Balancing Gains and Losses

Not all the changes are losses. In the Awareness Stage, chil-dren can clearly articulate the balance of gains and losses. Even in the early months, many children can name both sides. Kevin Miller:

We had dinner a lot later when we moved in with my stepmother. She came home from work late, and we had to wait for her. I got so hungry and so tired from school. But on the other hand, we got to ski much more and do lots of other sports that we never did when I lived with just my dad or my mom.

His stepsister Gabby Davidson:

It was hard in the beginning that my mom had someone living here, because it meant my mom wouldn't spend as much time with me. But it was nice that there wasn't a new person every few months. I liked that.

Where Did My Feelings Come From?

In the Immersion Stage, children, like adults (particularly outsider stepparents), are somewhat mystified by the power of the feelings stepfamily living evokes. Some children respond with tears; others find themselves inexplicably angry. Zoe Becker echoes what many children of all ages have said to me:

> I hated my stepmother. I don't know why I hated her because she was a nice person, really. I could even see that she was a nice person, and yet I hated her. And I felt terrible that I hated her. I still feel guilty about it sometimes. I don't know why I hated my stepmother. She was a nice person!

Jessie Nelson, like Zoe, was 15 when her mother remarried, precisely the age bracket in which the literature tells us stepdaughters of stepfathers have a particularly difficult time (Hetherington, 1987; Lutz, 1983). Jessie's stepfather was stunned by the force of her anger at him. And, it turns out, so was Jessie:

> I gave my stepfather such a hard time. And I really don't know why. I yelled and screamed at him, whatever he did. Once when my Mom was away I called her up and told her he beat me. I don't know why I did that.

It is interesting to note that Jessie's mom and stepdad had a particularly close and loving new marriage. Contrary to accepted family systems thinking that the better the marriage, the happier the children will be, researchers are discovering that at least for stepdaughters the opposite is true (Clingempeel, Ievoli, & Brand, 1984), a finding that Jessie's experience supports.

Both Jessie and Zoe were angry at their stepparents. Zoe, too, had a hard time making sense of her response, which was quite the opposite of Jessie's:

> Z.: I clammed up. I couldn't talk. I couldn't say anything about what was happening to me . . . [long pause]. I wish I hadn't clammed up.
> P.: I wonder what you would have said if you hadn't clammed up.

Z.: I don't know. I don't even have words for it now.

Typical of the Immersion Stage for all these children was the combination of being mystified, at a loss to describe where such powerful feelings could emerge from. For many children like Jessie and Zoe we can hear that the mystery is tinged with shame. These children, like the adults we have described above, might have benefitted enormously from some information about what to expect, and from some help "mapping the territory" into which their new stepfamily had thrust them. In fact, all of these children looked enormously relieved when, at the end of the interview, I talked to them about the many other stepchildren who share their feelings.

Immersion: Summary

For adult and child stepfamily members, the experience of the Immersion Stage is much like the sensation phase of the Gestalt Experience Cycle—a strong sense that something's not right, and great difficulty figuring out just what it is.

The fact that stepparent, biological parent, and child may experience the same family event in quite different ways can make the communication necessary to move the family to the Awareness Stage difficult. Fear and this very different experience of family functioning combine so that biological parents may find themselves responding to the stepparent's even tentative expression of negative feelings with disbelief, protectiveness toward children, and sometimes criticism. Conversely, the stepparent's struggle to join, in addition to feelings of inadequacy, make it difficult to hear the pain behind the biological parent's apparent deafness. Parents and stepparents in the throes of their own fantasies and fears about becoming a stepfamily may find themselves surprised and dismayed by their children's reactions. The drive to create a new family that works may make it especially tempting to dismiss their children's discomfort, and difficult to listen carefully enough to understand their underlying concerns.

When all of these forces combine, it is no wonder that many families languish in the Immersion Stage.

It is interesting to note that, as in first marriages, women in second marriages are less satisfied than men. In addition, remarried women are significantly less satisfied than women in first marriages (Glenn & Weaver, 1977; White, 1979). It may be that the orientation for women to relationships as a primary source of satisfaction makes the strain of both the biological insider and the stepparent outsider role particularly meaningful and painful.

The popular literature is full of exhortations for stepcouples to "talk to each other right from the beginning." However, the stepparent's difficulty moving to awareness, in addition to the biological parent's anxiety and immersion in the biological minifamily, can make this an uneasy task.

Realistic information can mean the difference between sinking and swimming through the difficulties of the Immersion Stage. As the case studies in Chapter Six illustrate, families with realistic expectations can work together to make both insiders and outsiders, and both adults and children, as comfortable as possible in the Early Stages. These families experience the chaos and confusion of the Immersion Stage as a challenge rather than as evidence of failure, helping each other to put markers on the territory in which they find themselves, to put names on their feelings, to voice their needs, and to make it safe for both insiders and outsiders.

STAGE THREE
Awareness: Mapping the Territory

The challenge of the Awareness Stage is to begin to map the territory of the new family: gathering data about what each position in the new family feels and looks like, identifying which parts of the terrain feel familiar and which parts do not, seeing patterns to wrong turns and right turns, flagging the boulders and rough spots, finding out how deep the swamps are, measuring the ravines that divide the family, and identifying some shared ground where the family can come together easily.

The challenge in the Immersion Stage was to keep swimming, to bear the confusion and disorientation that early stepfamily structure can create without sinking for too long into blame and shame in the face of each disturbing event. For those stepfamilies that can keep moving (or get moving), "mapping the territory" in the Awareness Stage actually involves a double set of tasks: a set of individual tasks and a set of joint or shared family tasks.

In the Awareness Stage, the *individual task* for each stepfamily member is to map his or her own territory in the family: to begin to put names on the feelings that his or her place in the structure evokes, and to voice what he or she needs from other family members. The *joint task* is to begin to reach across the experiential gaps that stepfamily structure creates, and to start forming a "good enough" (Winnicott, 1958) picture of the territory inhabited by people in the other positions in the structure. To return to Figures 2.3, 2.4 and 2.6 (Chapter Two), the joint task is to fill in the shaded gap in awareness. Insiders and outsiders, biological parents and stepparents, and adults and children must gain a deeper understanding of what each other is feeling and needing. Members of the different cultures that have come together in the new stepfamily need to start forming some understanding of each other's history, rules, rituals, and assumptions about the world. The information generated in the Awareness Stage provides the foundation for truly joint decision making in the Middle Stages. As in every stage of the Stepfamily Cycle, individuals and families may proceed into Awareness on one issue that is less charged, while remaining stalled in Immersion or catapulted prematurely into the Middle Stages on another issue. On any one issue, individuals and/or families may slide back and forth between Immersion and Awareness, or may jump from Immersion to Mobilization and then work their way back to Awareness. Furthermore, different children in the family move at very different paces. One may be fairly clear about his or her experience, and have even developed some understanding of how his or her stepparent feels, whereas another may be lost in Immersion, or may simply choose not to be part of the new family.

Families vary considerably in the speed with which they complete this double set of tasks in the Awareness Stage. Faster families move fairly directly into the Awareness Stage and complete both individual and joint awareness tasks in about a year. Average-paced families spend two to three years completing Awareness Stage tasks. The slowest families may spend more than four years together before they can complete both individual and shared awareness tasks. Some of these families get stuck and never move on. Others move on with an infusion of outside support or when a family crisis loosens the family structure, providing a forum for unheard voices and helping family members to complete the task of making a more realistic picture of their new family.

The Stepparent's Experience of the Awareness Stage

For outsider stepparents, the individual task in the Awareness Stage involves naming the feelings evoked by their outsider position (jealousy, resentment, inadequacy) with less shame and more clarity. At first falteringly, and then with more confidence, stepparents begin to make sense out of the confusion and chaos. Often the pain does not abate, but the source of discomfort and the patterns of interaction that create it become less mysterious. Even when the pain persists, stepparents often experience some relief as their greater self-acceptance lifts the burden on their self-esteem. As their awareness deepens, outsiders move from "Something's wrong here and it must be me!" to "I'm not crazy, I'm just feeling terrible about being an outsider."

By the end of the Awareness Stage, stepparents can name some of their needs for changes that would make them more comfortable in the foreign territory they are curious about; and unthreatened by their deepening awareness, they can move much more quickly from Immersion to Awareness and on into the Middle Stages. Unfortunately, as we have seen, the insider biological parent may be too immersed in his or her own experience of the family and too frightened to be able to offer the validation and empathy that ensure easier, quicker movement through the Early Stages.

I'm Not Crazy, I'm Just an Outsider

Bit by bit, stepparents put words on their feelings and begin to believe their perceptions about what is happening in their new families. Alicia Winston, an outsider stepmother married to David, talks about her stepson, Mark. In the Immersion Stage, Alicia attributed her isolation to her own lack of self-esteem. In the Awareness Stage, she is able to identify real events that leave her feeling confused and alone.

It's not my imagination! Mark really does treat me differently than he treats his father. He makes faces at me behind his father's back. He talks to his dad at the supper table as if I'm not there. And I'm realizing David really doesn't see these things. Because it's not happening to him, it's happening to me!

As they begin to believe their perceptions about what makes them so uncomfortable, the self-deprecation and shame of the Immersion Stage begins to lift. During this period, stepparents are increasingly able to separate their own feelings and perceptions from the shoulds and standards they and others have for them. The following statement is from Hank Haley, adoptive stepfather to his wife's three boys, and father to a joint child, Billie:

I always used to try to deny that my relationship with Billie was different than the rest of them. But it is. It's very different. For whatever reasons. Whether it's a blood reason, or just that he was a baby with me. Whatever it is, as much as I love the others, it's different with him. I have finally allowed that it was OK to have it one way with one and another way with another of my kids.

The fact that Hank had adopted his sons may have impeded his awareness process, leaving the fantasy of a biological-like family in place well beyond the time when his outsider experience began to make itself felt. He remained in Immersion feeling confused and inadequate, and explaining his mismatched feelings with the self-deprecatory belief that "there must be something wrong with me."

The "Biological Force Field"

It is especially a relief for stepparents to put some shape and pattern to the set of elusive but potent biological alliances they have entered. As the areas of clarity widen, stepparents can begin to appreciate the power and impenetrability of what one stepparent called "the biological force field." Ann Lieberman, stepmother in a double family, talks about the way her relationship with her stepsons, Aaron and Josh, changed in the presence of their father:

Aaron and Josh and I would be cooking and actually having a fine time together making pancakes or something. And then their father would come downstairs. And it was as if I would suddenly be left standing all alone with the pancake batter on the other side of a thick glass partition! And that's the way it would be for the rest of breakfast. It used to be mysterious to me. Now I can predict it. But it still hurts and I still don't know what to do about it.

Going It Alone

As is implicit in Ann's quote, though the source of discomfort becomes clearer, many stepparents in the Awareness Stage of the Stepfamily Cycle remain very alone as they attempt to map their understanding of what is happening in their family. Stepparents who come to their new families with a character style that is more introverted and shy, who are particularly prone to blaming themselves when something goes wrong, or who have learned not to ask for help, will be particularly alone through the Awareness Stage.

However, as in the Immersion Stage, the block to engagement with a spouse is not only intrapsychic. It is rooted in the vicissitudes of stepfamily structure. The biological parent's insider position creates a fundamentally different experience from the stepparent's outsider position in early stepfamily life, making it difficult for the biological parent to provide the empathy that would make the negative feelings easier to bear and express. Furthermore, stepparents in this stage may be getting clearer, but they do not yet have the strength of conviction to engage their spouses or step-children in satisfying communication about their experience of the family. The embarrassment of feeling jealous and re-sentful has abated somewhat, but not enough to withstand any resistance. Alicia Winston:

It's like they're saying, "Come on in," but they don't understand what it's like to be the foreigner. They don't understand what it's like to sit and listen to them telling stories about people you've never met, or playing board games you've never played before, or looking only at each other so I feel invisible. They don't understand because it's not their experience!

Keeping the Focus

Stepparents often talk about having dismissed early flickers of awareness about the difficult geography of the stepfamily system they were entering. Rachel Sax, for instance, remem-bered that on her first date with her husband-to-be, Ira, and his two sons, the seating arrangement at the basketball game was:

Me on the end, then Ira close to his younger son, Adam, on his other side, and then Ben, his older son, way out on the opposite end. Ben did not talk. He obviously wanted nothing to do with this whole thing. And that has been, I think, a sort of sculpture of the relationships in this stepfamily ever since. I remember thinking, "What am I doing? I don't need this!"

In the Fantasy and Immersion Stages, the yearning to make a new family leads stepparents to push aside these bits of awareness. When asked "How did that feel?" Rachel responded:

Terrible. And I must have blocked it off. I was just so in love with Ira and I wanted Ira to have what he wanted. So I just ignored things like that. I didn't even talk to him about it at that point.

Alicia again:

I know I had anxiety in my stomach for ages! I think I knew it was about this stepfamily stuff—that things weren't as hunky dory as I thought. But I think I panicked. Panicked that it would all blow up if I acknowledged those feelings.

Even on a single issue, it is not surprising that moving through Immersion to the Awareness Stage is not a linear process for most stepparents. The shift from Immersion to Awareness is a particularly difficult one for stepparents in families where stepparent and biological parent cannot share their experience easily. The picture, their place in it, the power of the expulsive forces, and their needs for support will get clear and then confusion will set in again, often sending stepparents back to the disorientation and confusion of the Immersion Phase. Furthermore, stepparents may have gained full awareness in one area of their family lives, and remain lost in confusion in another. Likewise, a shift in the family—a major visitation change, arrival in the family of a stepchild who had resided with the absent parent—may send the entire family, including the stepparent, back to the Immersion Stage.

Getting to Know You

On the positive side, as the fog clears and things begin to make more sense, the Awareness Stage of the Stepfamily Cycle is a crucial time for stepparents to get to know the people they have married. The fantasy of a blended and immediately loving family, obscures the fact that members of the step and biological subsystems in the stepfamily are strangers to each other. The Awareness Stage of the Stepfamily Cycle is a time for strangers in the family to get to know each other. This is a time for stepparents to learn about the children they have married—their likes and dislikes, their friends, the kinds of games they enjoy, their memories—without trying to influence them. Stepparents need the chance to let themselves be known to their stepchildren, at a slight distance, remaining in their outsider position, without an expectation of a close relationship. David Mills (1984) goes even further, suggesting that stepparents provide a completely accepting presence to their stepchildren until a bond can be formed.

It is important to note that in this phase, though relationships with stepchildren remain strained in the presence of their biological parents, interaction between stepparents and stepchildren may become surprisingly easy when the biological parent is absent. The stepparent-stepchild relationship is then free to map and explore its own middle ground in the absence of the thicker, competing middle ground of the more firmly established biological parent-child relationship. Small threads of middle ground begin to appear as stepparent and stepchildren begin to engage with each other without the competition of the stronger biological middle ground. Although these threads may disappear with startling (and disappointing) quickness when the biological parent reappears (as in Ann Lieberman's experience of making pancakes with her stepsons), they nonetheless provide an initial opportunity for satisfying interaction.

Likewise, when the children are away for visitation, the members of the adult couple may suddenly find themselves more able to turn toward each other for intimacy and nourishment (especially if the subject is not children), as they are freed from competing with the more powerful middle ground of the biological parent-child relationship. The implications are clear: step pairs (the adult couple, stepparents and their stepchildren, stepsiblings) need to begin to spend time alone together without the extra biological member of the triangle, so that each pair can map its own territory and begin to establish its own middle ground in the Early Stages. The belief that the family will become unified only if time is spent as a whole family will, of course, impede this process.

Sounding Board, Not Savior: The Stepparent Role in the Awareness Stage

In marked contrast to the Contact Stage, when asked about what their role is, stepparents in the Awareness Stage cannot yet form a coherent statement. Neither can their stepchildren describe a role for their stepparents. My data indicates that a mature stepparent role does not emerge until *after* the major structural changes of the Middle Stages, at which point both stepparents and stepchildren can quickly and easily describe a clearly formed role.

Accumulating evidence from both researchers and clinicians suggests that in the Early Stages, unless children are very young and/or very open to a new stepparent, stepparents cannot successfully take on a traditional parental role. The work of Hetherington (1987) and Bray, Gershenhorn, and Bennett (1987) corroborates that stepfathers who move into a disciplinary role too quickly have stepchildren with more behavior problems. As one chagrined stepfather put it, "Things went better in the beginning when I began to function as a sounding board for my wife rather than as a savior for her children."

I find David Mills's (1984) model of stepparent as babysitter useful in the Early Stages—the stepparent is in charge when the biological parent is absent. Mills suggests that stepparents begin by enforcing the biological parent's rules, much as a babysitter or a visiting aunt would, adding perhaps only a minor change here and there. Mary Whiteside (1988b) describes the way in which the stepparent's stance in the Early Stages needs to be supportive of the parent, not directive of the child:

This support must be given directly to the parent, and not by taking over the enforcement with the adolescent. This is the difference between, "Do what your mother says," and the statement to the mother, "I agree with your expectation that he come in on time. Keep at it."

James Bray's research on Early Stage stepfamilies (Bray et al., 1987) turned up the apparently discrepant findings that girls who reported that their stepfathers were affectionate had fewer behavior problems. However, stepfathers who reported that they were more affectionate, had stepdaughters who exhibited more behavior problems. Looking again at the data, Bray discovered that, in fact, stepdaughters and their stepfathers had different definitions of positive affectionate behavior (Bray, 1988b). The girls were describing verbal affection, whereas the stepfathers were talking about physical affection.

Stepparents who come to their new families with some information about what to expect are more likely to be able to begin in this somewhat outside, but still available, position. Others will enter the role with more force and less success.

ea... nd child know
flu... nake more in-

Na...

As... ndividual task
of... orm a few de-
fin... now why I get
so... comes "I feel
ter... late at night
fro... nny Tolman:

I wa... *not* in the middle
of th... office, where he
can... 's not!

... me when she comes into a room where I'm sitting," says a stepfather in this phase. "She doesn't have to love me. I'd just like her to be civil with me." "What I want is some clear time alone with my wife," says another stepfather, "*without* one of her kids on her lap."

Laying Down the Load

In their attempts to clarify their place in the family, some stepparents in this stage begin to acknowledge their needs not only for more closeness, but for more distance from one or all of their stepchildren. Women who had given up outside friendships and interests to "make a new family" begin to give themselves permission to hanker for the easier nourishment and sense of mastery that come from satisfying work and friendships outside the marriage. Stepparents who had stepped precipitously into a parenting role become aware of the need to pull back. "I began to realize I was trying too hard," said one stepfather. "I started backing off and taking it easy more."

On this subject, Carolyn Moynihan-Bradt (1983) has done some very interesting work describing the particularly intense overload for full-time stepmothers who also work and who then go on to have a baby of their own. Bob Weiss (1985), in his study of men in divorce and remarriage, describes the other side of the coin, the ways in which these men had expected their new spouses to simply step in and take over the mothering responsibilities in the new stepfamily. The fact that Doris Jacobson (1987) has found the highest rate of behavior problems in father-custody (i.e., full-time stepmother) families may be due to many other reasons—a more conflicted custody battle, poorer predivorce parenting, and more behavior problems before the divorce. However, it is also likely that the invisible burden of fantasy weighs particularly heavily in these families. Consequently, behavior problems may be attributed to the loyalty bind created for children as their stepmothers attempt to act as replacement mothers. In the Immersion Stage, these stepmothers wade in expecting to realize the fantasy of becoming a "better mother" to their stepchildren. In the Awareness Stage, stepparents, particularly full-time stepmothers who had taken over from an ostensibly inadequate noncustodial parent, begin to acknowledge that they are overwhelmed and exhausted and want less of a role.

For stepparents who have until now been unable to get heard, things are now in place for the Mobilization Stage, when stepparents have enough self-support to begin to voice their needs and perceptions more energetically and with more conviction in the face of conflict.

Mapping the Other Side: The Stepparent's Tasks

As we have seen, the outsider's place in stepfamily structure can evoke powerful feelings. Often stepparents are so busy with their own awareness tasks that they are not able to look up long enough to imagine, or ask about, what others in the family might be feeling. For stepparents the joint tasks of "seeing the other side" include gaining some empathy for their adult-insider partner's position in the family—feeling torn, feeling immersed in both forming a new family and finishing an old family, and needing to speak for the needs of people with whom the stepparent does not yet have a direct relationship (children and ex-spouse, particularly).

Most challenging for many stepparents is understanding the feelings behind their stepchildren's difficulty in welcoming them into the new family. Stepparents need to begin to appreciate the loyalty binds their stepchildren experience. They need to understand the depth of children's feelings about losing their first family. They need to become curious about what rituals and bits of history are meaningful to their stepchildren.

Remaining curious and empathic in the face of rejection and indifference is a tall order for a beleaguered stepparent. However, understanding their stepchildren's dilemmas helps stepparents to ease the pain of their outsider position. It also helps them to leave the right amount of distance in the Early Stages and to gauge effective moves in the Middle Stages. Often stepparents cannot glean this information from their stepchildren. If the topic is charged, they sometimes cannot get it from their spouses either. For stepparents who cannot yet communicate with their partners on step issues and who have no access to outside resources, this task may remain uncompleted until the fuller engagement of the Middle Stages, and even later for some. As we see in Chapter Six, stepparents in families that communicate better in the Early Stages have more opportunities to gather this information earlier in their family's development.

This is an area where public education and media attention to stepfamilies can provide invaluable information that is difficult to obtain from other stepfamily members. I particularly find children's books helpful to stepparents, as they provide the children's point of view in simple, very accessible language. These books seem to give stepparents an opportunity to listen to children voicing their feelings and thoughts, without the charged relationship that may cloud communicaton in a difficult stepparent-child relationship. Beth Roberts, a stepmother:

I really had very little idea of what my stepdaughters were thinking and feeling. I just felt their behavior was "bad." It's interesting because I usually think of myself as an empathic person. Then I read the Burts' (1983) book, really so I could decide whether to give it to my stepdaughter or not. And some things sank in that I just never got before. I especially understood how many losses this kid had had. I mean I already knew it in my head, but somehow I never understood what it means when your stepmother asks you to change one more thing.

The "one more thing" always seemed simple enough to me—put your clothes in the hamper, drink milk with meals. . . . But I guess it was one more change for her. I still want to ask some changes of her. Otherwise *I* can't live with her comfortably. But now I understand more what I'm asking of her, that it will be hard for her, and that she *won't* say, "Thanks for helping me make some order in my life."

Contrast the above statement with a stepparent (Angela Ricci) who can clearly state her own needs, but has not yet completed the task of understanding how this will impact her stepdaughter:

When she's in my house, I want her to follow my rules. She can follow her mother's rules in her mother's house. I don't see why it's such a big deal. I want her to learn some manners. I want her to clean up her room. I want her to set the table. Her mother hasn't taught her any of these things, and it's about time she learned.

Because this stepmother had great difficulty imagining her stepdaughter's experience, her list of needed changes was too long for this stage of development. She was headed for a precipitous move into the Action Stage that was bound to meet with failure and frustration. Her stepdaughter could not, and would not, accommodate such a long list of changes. Her husband, although he initially supported her verbally, could not back her up when he felt his daughter's extreme discomfort. We will discuss this case at length in Chapter Seven, (page 349) when we focus on intervention.

Finally, stepparents will function much more effectively in their new families if they can extend their understanding to the territory inhabited by their partner's exspouse. Research is showing us that it is the mother-stepmother relationship that is more intense and most likely to be difficult (Ahrons & Wallisch, 1987). Stepmothers who understand a little bit about what is at stake for what I call "the ex-wife-in-law" ("You married her, too!" I always say) will be able to tolerate a little more apparent "craziness." Some will be able to design moves that head off trouble. Ann Lieberman (whose stepchildren now live with their mother but visit in the summer):

Now that I have my own child I finally understand how my stepchildren's mother must feel about me. What it must be like to share her children with me, a potential rival, who might take them away. It just never occurred to me that her crazy phone calls while they were here must come from that feeling.

So this might sound nuts, but now I call her once or twice when they're here for the summer. I ask her advice. I tell her what they're doing. I definitely do not want to be this woman's friend. But I want to get her off my back. Now I have enough information to do that. And it seems to be working. She's calmed down a lot. And so have I.

Let us turn now to the other adult in the new stepfamily, the insider biological parent.

The Insider Parent in the Awareness Stage

Whereas stepparents must struggle primarily to bring awareness to their outsider position in the family, biological parents experience this stage through the very different eyes of their insider position. As in the Immersion Stage, this position creates a very different experience of the family. For biological parents, or the insider adult in the family, the task is to name the feelings evoked by the insider position. For remarried parents, this often involves finishing unresolved feelings from the previous marriage.

In the Aware Families we meet in Chapter Six, the biological parent moves right along with his or her stepparent partner in completing awareness tasks. However, as we saw in the Immersion Stage, in many stepfamilies, the insider position provides some protection from the strains of early stepfamily living. In these families, the insider adult may not move actively into completing awareness tasks until the stepparent moves into Mobilization and begins making more active demands. Now as the biological parent begins to feel torn, the strains in the insider position become more obvious and the need to make a more accurate picture of the family territory becomes stronger. In these families, the stepparent must function as the family change agent pulling his or her partner into awareness. The joint task of empathizing with the feelings created by the stepparent's outsider position may involve considerable loss for these remarried parents and may not be accomplished until after the more active engagement of the Mobilization Stage.

"I'm the Meat": Mapping the Multiple Pulls

Whether they come to it easily or through the intensified efforts of their stepparent spouses, remarried parents in the Awareness Stage begin to feel the multiple pulls involved in their insider position in the new family. The presence of another adult does relieve the intense loneliness of single-parenting. It also makes life more complicated, placing more demands on small bits of time. Evenings, particularly, can create these multiple pulls. Terry Peterson:

I feel like I'm rushing my kids to bed now. When you're a single parent, you *linger* over these things. Then when you get involved in a relationship, you do the opposite.

"I'm the meat!" said another custodial father, Reginald Cox, in exasperation. "Everyone wants a slice of me!":

We went for a walk in the woods yesterday. Me and my wife and my kids. We used to come back from these walks and she would be a wreck. I never understood it. Now I'm beginning to get it. I could feel my kids wanting to be next to me, and my wife wanting to be next to me, and I only have two sides and there are two kids and my wife, that makes three. I'm just starting to see all the feelings and all the maneuvers that can go on in a simple walk in the woods! My wife has been feeling them for months!

Straining to Make It All Work

In the Immersion Stage, the insider parent often struggles with little awareness to make the pieces of the new family fit. Some deal with the lack of fit by denying it. Others greet each new fissure by straining to close it. In the Awareness Stage, not only the strain but the impossibility of managing this feat begin to dawn on the insider parent. Jane James:

I'm starting to see I have tried to make everyone like each other. And by gosh they don't like each other! My daughter doesn't like her stepfather. They may never like each other. I think I've decided they just have to be civil. They don't have to love each other. What a relief!

As another remarried mother put it, "I finally realized, it's not that I'm inadequate that they don't adore each other. It's that they're strangers!"

Remarried parents like Reginald who are adult children of dysfunctional families have a particularly difficult time letting go of their "fix-it" role. For them, awareness work also involves seeing some of the roots of their urge to "make it all better":

I'm beginning to see that when things go awry between my wife and my kids, I just want to get in there and fix it. It's as if I can't stand it that there's pain and trouble and I just *have* to smooth it over. And then my wife gets furious at me, which used to flabbergast me and make me feel so betrayed. I'm just starting to see that mostly she just needs me to listen to her. But it's so difficult for me. Sometimes I can do it. And sometimes I can't. I know that makes it hard for her. It makes it hard for her to tell me when she's upset because I get so anxious. And when she doesn't tell me, then she really gets weird.

Just as stepparents begin to see patterns to their interaction, insider parents also begin to see patterns. Angela
Ricci:

I come from a family where everything went wrong. All the time. And I
held it together. I cooked for my brothers. I held them when they cried.
I made sure they went to school. I went to the bar to get my dad when he
was drunk. And I'm damned if I can stop now that things are going nuts
in this new family.

Clarifying the Biological System's Needs

Some remarried parents are very articulate from the beginning about the needs of the biological subsystems in the family (parent and children), sometimes to the exclusion of the
needs of the stepsubsystems in the family (the adult couple,
particularly). Other parents find that the press of a new relationship obscures their sense of their needs as parents and
their children's needs. Jane James again:

I've been trying to go along with my husband on all these rules changes
because I really want to make him happy. And I guess I'm afraid he'll
leave if I don't make him comfortable.

But now I'm beginning to see that I'm asking too much of my daughter.
And of myself. And ultimately of him, because it's not going to work this
way. Ellen can adapt to only so much at a time. And she needs time alone
with me. When we have our time alone together, she can let go of me. Not
easily, but without trauma at least. When we don't have our parent-kid
time together, she screams bloody murder when I want to do something
with my husband.

Just as it is the stepparent's task to name his or her
needs for change, it is the biological parent's task to be able to
articulate how much change his or her children can tolerate.
Mapping this territory accurately is a delicate task that usually requires some trial and error. The trick is to find the
right balance between overprotecting children (which leaves
the stepparent and/or outsider stepsiblings as disenfranchised outsiders), and asking too much of them. Couples

proceeding through the Early Stages as a team have access to much more accurate information about the children in their family. Often biological parents can voice their children's needs for stability, and stepparents, who bring a fresh pair of eyes and less history, can more easily see children's strengths, their capacity to adjust, and, particularly, their needs for limits and structure.

Resentment

In our mythology about stepfamilies, the focus is on the wicked stepmother's resentment. And yet, hidden in the story of Hansel and Gretel is a father who allows his wife to talk him into leaving his children in the woods. Hidden somewhere in Snow White is another father who didn't stop the queen from her murderous attempts on her stepdaughter's life.

The literature, both the popular self-help literature and the clinical literature, have now given full voice and much validation to the stepparent's resentment and its roots in stepfamily structure. But biological parents feel resentful as well, of the many pulls their children's presence in their lives exposes them to, and of the difficulty in pursuing a new intimate relationship while also meeting children's needs. Often these feelings evoke great shame and fear—it's one thing to hate your stepchildren, but quite another to want to be rid of your own children. Perhaps this is why the resentment of the fathers in the fairy tales remains hidden behind the wicked stepmother, who expresses it for both of them!

Just as stepparents often need support and permission to express their negative feelings, biological parents often need empathy and validation for their wishes to be free of so many ties, and the reassurance that murderous wishes and murderous actions are quite different. Putting words to the difficulty of the territory in which insider parents are trying to operate can in itself provide relief. Reginald Cox:

I'm trying to do a lot. That sounds so simple, but it is a great relief to say it. It's like the woodcutter in Hansel and Gretel trying to stretch a few

crusts of bread too many ways. No wonder he left his children in the woods.
I don't think I'll do that. But I do get resentful of my kids sometimes and
that has scared me. I think I just need a break from trying so hard.

Something Old and Something New

Another awareness task for remarried parents is to finish
grieving and digesting and learning from their previous marriage. As we have said, the timing of remarriages is such
that the task of forming a new family must often proceed
simultaneously with the task of resolving the previous family.
When remarried parents remain in the Immersion Stage in
this area, unresolved sadness and anger affect their lives but
remain out of their awareness. As they move into the Awareness Stage, they can begin to articulate more clearly what the
losses and gains have been. Again, some move on their own,
and others, such as George Danielson, are pushed into confronting these feelings by a mobilized stepparent:

My wife read the riot act to me a while ago. She said she wasn't going to
try to make up for what my first wife didn't do with the kids. First I was
stunned. I guess I didn't realize I was doing that, asking her to do what
my first wife didn't do. But, of course, I was.

Then I was angry. Really furious at her. But I didn't know which "her" I
was so angry at. And then I was sad. God, was I sad. I cried and cried.
And I guess I was crying for that marriage. I'm still trying to sort it out.
But I think I'm finally facing how hard those years were in my first marriage, how much happened that breaks my heart. And that my second wife
can't fix what my first wife didn't (and did) do. God, that hurts.

Other bits of awareness come around continuing old
patterns with a first spouse. Anton Grinnelli:

I took care of her in the marriage, and I'm still taking care of her. I'd run
over there and fix her plumbing, and talk to her when her boyfriends
disappointed her, and bail her out when she got drunk. That worked OK
before I got remarried. It doesn't work now. But it's taken till now for me
to realize that I'm tired of it.

And still others as the issue of a new baby is confronted.
Walter Brown:

I realized I was resisting having a baby partly because I'm done parenting. But also because it was so hard to lose my daughter. I'm the noncustodial parent. I lost my kid. The thought of another loss like that is just so hard to bear. I hadn't realized how much that fear is part of not wanting another child.

Seeing the Gains

On the positive side, the task of mapping the territory of the new stepfamily can be exciting for biological parents. The stepparent's presence adds new perspective to the enmeshed single-parent–child relationship. Stepparents see patterns that single parents, operating alone with their children, had perhaps felt, but had not been able to articulate. Hope Franklin:

Julian sees where I don't set limits with my daughter. I'd just sort of given up I guess. He hasn't been critical, which is nice. He just says, "She got you on that one, Sweetheart," and it's so helpful to have another pair of eyes to see what's happening here!

As stepparents get to know their stepchildren, they may evoke new behaviors from them that their parents hadn't seen before. Beth Roberts, a remarried mother, describes her second husband's effect on her third-grade daughter and the light it throws on her own relationship with the child:

He plays with her much more actively than I would. I see a part of her I've never seen before. And I see that both her father and I were actually very delicate and careful with her.

Outsider adults also bring new perspectives on ex-spouses, visitation arrangements, and in-laws. And they bring an extra pair of hands. For divorced women, remarriage often also brings a substantial increase in income (Day & Bahr, 1986; Mott & Moore, 1982). Jane James:

I can't believe how much easier it is to operate with a little more money. My husband sends part of his salary to *his* ex-wife, but even the little bit he adds to our household makes such a difference. I'm only now beginning to realize how hard it really was to make ends meet before.

Naming Needs

Like their stepparent mates, as biological parents work their way through each of these issues, their own needs become clearer. Many of the statements above end with a clearer articulation of needs: for a break from trying so hard for stepparents and stepchildren, and for a slower pace of change. Thus, though naming all the pulls can be disturbing, it does begin to generate information that can be used to solve some of the problems. Hope Franklin:

I'm realizing I need to spend separate time with my kid and with Julian. It's just too hard otherwise! And *I* need some time alone!

Just as stepparents with help from their mates move into awareness and clarity about their needs with more ease and grace, remarried parents whose partners have some empathy for all they are trying to juggle find it easier to name their needs and own them fully. "Oops, I forgot. You feel terrified I'm going to leave when I tell you I'm jealous. Is that what's going on?" is much more helpful to a biological parent who is responding defensively than, "Why can't you ever listen to me?"

Mapping the Other Side: The Insider Parent's Tasks

The primary joint awareness tasks for biological parents are to name the feelings and needs of their new spouses and their children. As the pivotal person in the family structure, the biological parent's awareness of all members' needs is particularly crucial in the Early Stages, when members of stepparent-child subsystems often cannot yet articulate their needs to each other.

Biological parents need to understand what it's like for new stepparents to be left out over and over again, what it's like for the stepparent to try to create an intimate relationship in the presence of a parent-child relationship that often feels more like ex-lovers. Insider parents particularly need to grasp the fact that outsider stepparents experience their

spouses' children fundamentally differently—what is nourishing and pulling and engaging for biological parents is rejecting and lonely and irritating for stepparents in early stepfamily life.

The fact that biological parents seem to hold on more
tightly, and for a longer period of time, to the fantasy that the
new family would create a biological-like bonding between
stepparents and stepchildren may particularly impede this
task. For these remarried parents, as the stepparent becomes
a little bit more articulate about his or her difficulties in
joining the new family, this task becomes increasingly laden
with anxiety. Every indication of the stepparent's unhappiness may be proof that this family, too, may end in a loss.

Parents who are prone to thinking in black-and-white,
either/or terms will have to struggle a little harder to map
the complexity of the feelings of others in the family. "Either
you're happy being a stepmother or let's quit" will not help
with awareness tasks!

Biological parents who develop this awareness across
the experiential gap early feel more torn sooner. However,
sticking with the task of gathering information about the
stepparent's experience also provides clues for how to be
more helpful. Biological parents who create clear intimate
time with their new mates, give them extra eye contact when
children are present, and hear their feelings with less judg-
ment and criticism find that their mates relax considerably.

"Seeing the other side" with children means having
some awareness of children's feelings and needs, particularly
where they differ from adults. Especially at the beginning of
stepfamily living, parents and their children may be in very
different places. As we saw, while adults are nursing fantasies
of a wonderfully blended new stepfamily, children may be
wishing for their original parents to get back together. Their
parents need to be able to empathize with this wish, while
acknowledging that it will not happen. Parents in exciting
new relationships may find they have to look especially hard
across this experiential gap to empathize with children's difficulties in coping with the many changes in their lives. Most

crucial for parents is to gain some understanding of the loyalty binds that divorce and stepfamily structure create for children. Adults who have a strong need for support and are frightened of losing their children to their ex-spouse may blindly bad-mouth a child's absent parent without awareness of the impact on the child's sense of self-esteem and safety in the world.

Children in the Awareness Stage

Children also begin mapping their own territory in the family during the Awareness Stage. Just as stepparent and biological parent may move at different paces into this stage, various children in the same family may move very differently from each other, and from the adults in the family. Like the adults, children may also map out some areas of their lives more clearly than others.

Even more than adults, children move most quickly when they have some help with the task of mapping their piece of the territory in their new family. Children need help putting words on the loyalty binds they feel, naming their losses and gains, articulating the dilemmas that their shifting insider and outsider positions in the family create for them, and identifying what will change and what will stay the same in the new stepfamily. Finally, they need help in naming their needs from the new family.

For some children and in some families, and on certain subjects, becoming aware of needs makes it easy to voice them. Children whose parents need their loyalty, or whose families don't listen well, will have to move into Mobilization before they have enough conviction and strength to get heard.

Children with less active support from the adults in the family for these tasks will move much more slowly in completing an accurate map of their place in the new stepfamily. Some of these will remain stuck in the self-doubt and confusion of the Immersion Stage. For many children, the task of "seeing the other side," understanding their parents' and particularly their stepparents' experience, remains undone or is not completed until many years later.

Some of the "children" who speak here are actually young adults. We are finding that young adults have many of the same intense responses to divorce and remarriage as younger children (Crosbie- Burnett, 1987; Kaufman, 1987).

Naming the Losses

For children, divorce and remarriage involve a series of losses. There are gains as well, but naming the losses must often precede an appreciation of the gains. Children who remain in Immersion feel their losses but cannot quite articulate them and are often surprised by their angry or sad responses. As children move into Awareness, their feelings start to make more sense.

For many the first loss in the new remarried family comes when they are bumped from their close relationship with their single parent. Most children can put words to this experience fairly quickly: "I really miss cuddling with my mom in bed in the morning." "I used to go with my mom to the movies. Now she goes with her boyfriend." "Why can't I go on vacation with you?"

A little less accessible is the fact that the remarriage, or the beginning of living with a new adult, re-evokes unfinished grief for children about the divorce or death that broke up their first family. When they remain in Immersion in this area, children feel the loss but do not have words for it. They may pick fights with their schoolmates as Gabby Davidson did, or cry, aparently inexplicably at their wedding, or burst into tears as Zoe Becker did at the apparently unrelated event of her father shaving his beard. As they move into Awareness, children can begin to name these feelings and identify their sources. Cindy Danielson (12):

I guess I cried at the wedding because I really wasn't sure my dad should get married again. I mean, he blew it the first time. How do I know he's gonna do it OK this time? I'm mad at him for blowing it with my mom.

But most of all, I guess I was crying because I do miss having a mom and a dad in the same house, and it was pretty clear at this wedding that that wasn't ever gonna happen again.

For Sally Kelly, a young adult, her father's remarriage evoked several layers of loss in her relationship with him both current and past:

I never had an easy relationship with my father. He was hard to talk to, and he didn't listen well. When he married Dora, though, it became even more difficult to be with him. She was always there. I'm already almost strangers with my father. Now there's this real stranger there, and I'm supposed to be able to talk to him in front of her?

So, I think my dad's remarriage exposed the tenuousness of my relationship with him. And I felt like I lost him again, only more completely this time.

But what is most painful is watching my dad relate to Dora's children. It's like he became human with Dora. And now I have to watch my father, who never really had the time of day for me or my brothers, lavish attention on Dora's children.

As we saw in the Immersion Stage, children also lose a great deal of comfortable middle ground in a divorce, and again at the time of remarriage. Larry Schmidt, a young adult lists the changes that his mother's remarriage created in the special middle ground of his family:

We just don't do the things we used to do as a family. We always had this special Christmas celebration. We don't do it the same way anymore. And we used to go camping together. My stepfather hates bugs so we don't do that anymore. Lots of things we used to do we don't do anymore. It makes me sad.

Like Sally, adults can have surprisingly powerful responses to their parents' remarriage. They feel the loss of familiar routines: "We can't go to the cabin anymore. *She* doesn't want us there." They often experience a jolt in their "gestalt" of the family: "It just doesn't seem right that this strange guy is sitting at my mother's table pretending to be her husband!" And it may be important to note, "waiting until the children leave home" does not lessen the impact of divorce on children. It simply changes it. Sally was in her 20s when her parents divorced:

> It was like I lost my foundation. I didn't need them to be parents like they used to be. But I just sort of needed to know they were there. So I could use them as a kind of foundation to push off from as I'm going out into the world. Having that foundation cracked makes going out into the world much harder.

In a remarriage, children may also lose access to their grandparents on the noncustodial side of the family. Although it is sometimes a relief for the biological parent to be rid of troublesome in-laws, children may have a different attachment to their grandparents. Custody arrangements may also change children's access to their grandparents. By the Awareness Stage, they can talk about it, at least to themselves. Ingrid Cummings, a teenage girl:

> My stepmother's kids get to see my own grandparents more than I do. When I go to my mom's on the weekend, and they go to Grandma's and Grandpa's. That's really hard for me.

Mapping the Loyalty Binds

As they move into the Awareness Stage, children begin to name their feelings about being pulled between two parents, or between parent and stepparent of the same sex, with more clarity and precision. Parents who bad-mouth each other create particularly painful feelings for children. Ellen James, Jane's daughter, put it beautifully:

> It hurts. Because they're talking about *me* when they talk about my dad.

And as they continue to think about these things, we can begin to hear a more pointed statement of what they need from their families. Kevin Miller, then 10:

> They played tug of war with me. At dinner, my dad would talk about what happened in court and then tell me not to tell my mom what he said. I didn't like it. It felt bad. I realized I didn't like it at all. I realized I needed it to stop.

Good feelings toward stepparents also pose loyalty binds for children. If only her hapless stepmother could have heard Emmie Dayton speaking:

When my stepmother does something really nice for me, it's hard for me to thank her because I feel like I'm betraying my mother.

Shifting Relationships

We have talked about how relationships shift for younger children when their parents remarry. The shift for older children and young adults is colored by their own emerging sexuality. Several young women have talked to me about how odd it is that their mothers and fathers are dating at the same time that they are. Zoe Becker finds words for her own awkwardness with her father after he remarried: "I was like a shy teenager on a date with my father."

Mapping Foreign Territory

By the Awareness Stage, the sudden shifts that placed children in foreign territory have been in place for a while. As in any foreign territory, it is comforting to be able to at least recognize the street names. Now children begin to more fully articulate the differences between their own culture and the one they have joined. They still may not like the territory, but the words seem to help them find their way around a little better. Kate Pierce, a teenage girl in a double family:

They hang their stockings on doors. We open them all together. They have special television shows that are different from ours. They're just a really different family from what I'm used to.

Children living in two households also need words for the differences between their two homes:

In my mom's house, I can eat a lot more junk food and she doesn't mind, but I have to do my homework right away when I get home from school. In my dad's house, I can do my homework whenever I want, as long as it gets done. But no junk food. You can't even get a coke over there!

This is a place where adults can be particularly helpful by simply naming the differences between a child's two households, and between the "old" family and the "new" family, *without value judgments*: "We used to eat at Chef Chang's on Friday nights with your dad. Now we make pizza at home." "In your mom's house, you can't swear but you can watch as much television as you want to. In your dad's house, you can swear, as long as it isn't directly at someone, but you only get two hours of television a day."

Insider and Outsider Children

In double stepfamilies, where both parents bring children, some children are often more insiders and others are more outsiders. The insiders may be the custodial children, whereas the outsiders visit. The insiders may be the children of the parent into whose home the outsiders have moved. One biological parent-child group may be noisier and have a quicker, more aggressive rate of decision making, and so be more likely to dominate the household flow. As children move into the Awareness Stage on this issue, they begin to name the particular territory they inhabit in the new family. Jill Andrews, a member of a quiet, low-key family, talks about her experience of her stepfather's high-energy family:

We're a kind of quiet family. My stepfather's family is real noisy. It's very hard. I feel overwhelmed by him, and especially when his kids are here. When his kids come for the holidays, I feel like our family just fades into the woodwork.

It is interesting to note that Jill is in some ways a member of the insider subsystem in the family—she lives there year round, and the others visit. However, the visitors' noisier style dominates the household, making Jill feel very much an outsider. It can be particularly complex when a visiting child feels like an outsider with his or her own parent. Timothy Levi:

I'm the one who visits. I also get up later. So by the time I get up in the morning, my dad and my little stepbrothers have been up and made breakfast. They sort of have this thing going. It's hard. I feel like such an outsider with my own dad.

Children in joint custody situations may shift insider and outsider positions, being the resident insider in one household, and the nonresident outsider in another. And like Jill, children who had been insiders in their own homes may feel suddenly pushed aside when a nonresident stepsibling visits. In the Awareness Stage, children have words for these experiences. They may or may not be able to voice them and get heard by their families, but they are clear inside themselves. Ellen James:

When my stepfather's son comes to visit, it's like everyone drops everything. He's the center of attention. And he doesn't have to wash dishes or feed the dog or anything. That doesn't feel real good to me. But I haven't figured out how to say anything about it to anyone.

Counting It Up: Losses and Gains

Children who are not pressured to feel terrific about their new family can also begin to name the gains. As they move into the Awareness Stage in this area, they are ready to make a statement of the account. Kevin Miller in an interview that took place before his dad married Jan:

Before it was just me and my dad. Now I have to share him with all these new people. But actually, now that he and I are living with his girlfriend, I see more of him. Because before he would go out and I'd have to have a babysitter. Now he can be with his girlfriend without going out and I get to be with him.

Children also count as gains "having more people," gaining a stepparent who lets them eat "real sweets" rather than whole wheat cookies from the health food store, and having a "real family" with whom to celebrate holidays.

Children see gains not only for themselves, but for their parents. Leslie Kohl, a very articulate young adult whose parents have both remarried, sees the ways in which their new marriages have changed them for the better:

My parents were always angry and bitter with each other. I think my mother and father married each other because they were each missing something, and they each had something the other needed. And then they were always disappointed in each other, because they couldn't quite fix it for each other.

With his new wife, my dad is more of an equal. And I think my mom feels like more of an equal with her new husband. It's like both my parents are more whole people now.

Unlike Sally, whose father's remarriage broke the last threads of her contact with him, Leslie also sees gains for herself in her relationship with her father:

He's gotten more human, and I've gotten a more human relationship with him.

Leslie appears at the moment of this interview unambivalent about the changes, but other children remain more mixed. One child put it very simply: "I think it was for the better, and I feel cheated."

When Kevin Miller and his father moved into Gabby and her mother's house, the situation was ripe for insider/outsider tension between the two children. However, the adults in this Aware Family managed to arrange a re-sorting of the bedrooms so that both children experienced the move as a gain. Both children are very articulate about this. Gabby:

I didn't feel bad they moved in 'cuz I got my mom's bedroom furniture and my mom's cozy bedroom, so I was pretty happy.

Kevin (who got Gabby's old room):

Well, I was happy because I got the biggest room!

Naming Needs

As we can see in some of the above quotes, the final step for children in moving into Awareness is to identify what they need from the people around them. Children begin to be able to name their needs in a variety of areas. For instance, transition times, when they are shifting between households, pose special dilemmas for children. A third-grade boy articulates this:

I used to get nasty at my mother. Whoever I'm with more, I take it out on the other person. When I'm with one longer, it's much harder to switch.

I need time to make the change between my houses. I need a while to myself. My mom wants to spend time with me before I go. That's not so good for me. I need time to have the change go final.

Like this little boy, children get clearer about what adults do that helps and what does not help. Danny Wilson, a 12-year-old boy whose mother had died describes what teachers did that helped and didn't help:

One teacher was good at it. She would ask me how I thought and how I felt and if I needed anything. On Mother's Day she would say, "If you want to, you can do something for your father or your grandmother." In my other classroom the teacher said, "Just do it anyway," or "Just do something else," without helping me figure out what to do.

Sally Kelly, as she moved from her graduation to her wedding, got clearer about what she wanted from the adults in her world:

It's my day. I'd like them to behave! And I'd like *them* to work it out. I don't want to decide whether my stepmother comes and my mother goes off the wall or my stepmother stays home and my dad is furious at me. It's not my job to take care of all these people at my wedding.

Again, like Sally, the area about which children express the most feeling is that they want out of their loyalty binds. Even as the need gets clear, it is not always easy to express in this stage. Sally:

It's the greatest feeling in the world when my parents can be civilized to each other. There are times in my life when I want both my parents there together. I don't want to be embarrassed. I want to say, "I wish you could do it for me," but I can't say it yet. I'm afraid they'll yell at me.

Mapping the Other Side: Children's Tasks

Families work better when all members make some effort to understand each other's very different territory. My own experience is that children may come to see their own parents' needs and feelings. However, they often don't have an inkling of the territory that stepparents reside in for a very long time. Stepparents may rarely talk directly to them about what it's like to be an outsider. Their own biological parents may not have the information to convey. Even adult children of remarrying parents remain surprisingly uninterested and uninformed. Jerry Burke, a grown man whose father has remarried, laments his stepmother's "coldness" with no understanding of how overwhelming the presence of six adult stepchildren and their families might be to her. Nor does he seem to have any inkling of his dad's need for an intimate life of his own!

It's so sad. We're used to this big family Christmas. But now since my dad's remarriage, his new wife has ruined it! She doesn't want to have us to their house for Christmas. She is so cold. She's really changed him. My parents used to vacation with us. Now she has him running all over Europe, and she doesn't want any of us along.

Zoe Becker had been out of her stepmother's home for several years when she made this statement:

I'm just starting to see it from my stepmother's perspective. I'm just realizing that when I visited she had to give up time with my dad and had to use extra energy to be with me, and that I was as much a stranger to her as she was to me. I never thought about it that way before.

Awareness: Summary

The Awareness Stage of the Stepfamily Cycle is necessary for the members of the new stepfamily to get to know themselves and each other in this new system before moving on to more actively changing the structure. The task of "mapping the territory" includes both the individual task of mapping the part of the family each member inhabits, and, particularly for the adults, a joint task of gathering data about the family members who reside across the experiential gaps created by stepfamily structure. Successful stepfamilies usually allow themselves to remain biologically organized during this period, with most discipline continuing to be carried out by each biological parent with his or her children, while the strangers in the family get to know each other.

Conclusion

The Early Stages see stepfamily members grappling with the consequences of their unique family structure: (1) gaps in empathy and "common sense" between members; (2) hostility, discomfort, or indifference children often bring to their step relationships; (3) the negative valence of normal feelings engendered by outsider status (jealousy, resentment, inadequacy); (4) the impact stepchildren have on the developing new couple relationship; (5) the challenge of negotiating even the most trivial of everyday family decisions; (6) the inappropriateness of a traditional parent role for the new stepparent; (7) the effect of unshared histories; (8) children's loyalty binds; (9) the lingering influence of an absent ex-spouse and the previous extended family in the new stepfamily's life; (10) the many, often hidden, losses incurred by both children and adults in the formation of a new stepfamily.

The Early Stages end with increasing clarity and diminishing shame about these realities, and with the biologically organized family system still in place. Chapter Six describes four paths stepfamilies take in traversing the challenging territory of early stepfamily structure. Aware Stepfamilies begin with realistic expectations and enter the Middle Stages having a good start on both individual and joint mapping tasks. Immersed Families flounder for longer before completing awareness tasks and often do not complete the joint mapping tasks of understanding each other's experience of stepfamily life until differences are aired more explosively in the Middle Stages. Mobilized and Action Families skip the anxiety of Early Stage tasks, and have to return later to complete them before successful developmental progress is possible.

For some family members awareness work may include exploring family-of-origin and personality factors that bear on the degree of difficulty of forging satisfying step relationships: An outsider position in a previous family situation may make even a temporary experience of this intolerable. Fear of abandonment may make the innumerable differences encountered in early stepfamily life more disturbing. A person with a strong need for control and order is at a distinct disadvantage amidst the multiple surprises of bringing together strangers from two different cultures. Shyness, a tendency to blame oneself, difficulty asking for help, loss of previous children (for remarrying noncustodial parents) will all bear on the degree of difficulty involved in "getting started versus getting stuck." We will touch on these factors in Chapter Six and will address therapeutic intervention in Chapter Seven.

Implied in all of the above, Awareness Stage tasks are critical to moving on. Their completion will primarily determine the stepfamily's developmental pace and pattern. Fast families (Aware Families, primarily) complete the Early Stages in a year or two; average families take from two to three years; slow families require four years and more. Stuck families may not leave Immersion.

Chapter 4

THE MIDDLE STAGES: RESTRUCTURING THE FAMILY

The Early Stages involve deepening awareness for each member of the stepfamily of his or her place in the system and the feelings, perceptions, and needs it engenders. By the beginning of the Middle Stages, individuals in the family are clearer about their own experience. Both outsiders and insiders have words for their feelings. In faster families members have begun talking to each other and have developed some understanding of each other's place in the family structure. In average and slow families this does not happen until the Middle Stages.

At the beginning of the Middle Stages, individuals in the family have moved: They have relinquished some of their fantasies and they are clearer about their perceptions and needs. If they have accomplished the tasks of the Awareness

Stage, they have a fairly decent map of the territory they are inhabiting together. In faster families, large portions of that map are shared. In average or slower paced families, each individual may enter the Middle Stages clutching his or her piece of the map but with little understanding of the experience of other family members.

Whether fast, slow, or medium paced, if they are proceeding well, the family has begun no earthshaking projects yet. Thus the family's structure remains essentially biologically organized: Middle ground remains thickest in biological parent-child relationships. Biological parent-child minifamilies continue to be the primary seat of decision making around children and remain the site of easier cycle completion. If the family is a double family, with two sets of children, rules for each minifamily may remain somewhat unintegrated. Although some threads of new middle ground may have begun to be established in step relationships, they do not yet form a fabric firm enough to hold the new couple together when they differ about step issues. Nor are these threads strong enough to hold the stepparent and stepchild together in the presence of the biological parent.

In contrast, the developmental shifts of the two Middle Stages (Mobilization and Action) are *systemic*, involving moves that actually change the family structure. The task in the Mobilization Stage is to air differences more fully, broadening awareness of experiential gaps without fracturing the family, as step and biological, insider and outsider, members of the family come into more open conflict. The challenge is to confront differences while holding on to whatever middle ground already exists in step relationships.

In the Action Stage, the task is to more clearly and specifically define the middle ground in which the new couple and family will function. Families need to finish some of the fights of the Mobilization Stage so that the couple can begin functioning more as a parenting team. The couple can now become the "architect" of the new family, beginning to form clearer boundaries around its step subsystems: the stepcouple, stepparent-stepchild relationship, and around

the stepfamily as a whole. The family has more clearly identified some existing middle ground in step relationships and
has also sketched out substantial new middle ground.

The faster families seem to move through the Middle
Stages in a year or two. Of the four stepfamily types introduced in Chapter Six, these are usually Aware Families. The
remaining three family types (Immersed, Mobilized, and Action Families) move more slowly or more precipitously
through this period. Aware Families seem to slide seamlessly
into the Middle Stages, with less commotion and a less obvious shift in family functioning, making a less well-defined
Mobilization Stage. Members of faster families are more
likely to begin the process of actively influencing each other
with a deeper understanding of what is at stake for one another. Having begun talking and listening to each other in
the Early Stages, some items of disagreement have already
been resolved. These couples may start with more middle
ground. However, their ability to work out their differences
with empathy and curiosity rather than blame and self-doubt
enables existing middle ground to become clearer earlier and
stay more fully intact while they deal with areas of disagreement. For these reasons, they experience less polarized conflict in this stage.

Average-paced families require just a little longer, two
or three years, to complete the Middle Stages. They are more
apt to fight their way into the Middle stages, often when
the stepparent begins to mobilize with increasing force and
sustained effort. They spend a longer time in Mobilization
and their understanding of each other's needs and feelings
is harder won. Joint awareness tasks, and some of the individual tasks of mapping the family territory *result* from engaging
more fully over differences, rather than *precede* it. Interest-
ingly, slower paced families move very similarly through the
Middle Stages. The primary difference between an average
and slower pace through the Stepfamily Cycle lies in the pace
through the Early Stages.

In the slowest moving and stuck families, the voice for
change (usually the outsider stepparent's) cannot gain

enough strength, or enough responsiveness from the biological subsystem, to move the family from biological to stepfamily structure. Stuck families often do not reach Mobilization, or, when they do, they cannot sustain the stress and they break apart or retreat to the Early Stages. Occasionally a family crisis will catapult a slow or stuck family into the Middle Stages, as external forces call the established biological subsystem's middle ground into question and pull in enough outside support to enable the family to begin reorganizing itself. (This is often because the outsider stepparent or an unheard child has received sufficient support to get heard.) It is worth noting that once even the slowest paced family has moved into the Middle Stages, completion of the Stepfamily Cycle moves at about the pace of average families, taking two to three years to complete.

Erring on the other side, a few families move too quickly into the Mobilization Stage, dealing with the anxiety and confusion of the Immersion Stage by engaging immediately in a struggle over differences. Some of these families involve two "hair-trigger" adults who mobilize quickly in the face of anxiety. Some involve a very active and aggressive stepparent who moves forcefully and quickly for change, up against an equally powerful biological parent who voices the biological subsystem's need for stability. Still others are members of complex or double families in which the presence of two fairly equally matched and fully formed teams of people immediately exposes hotly contested differences. As we see in Chapter Six, successful Mobilized Families fight their way back to the Awareness Stage, completing the mapping task and then moving into Action. These are lively active families with a lot of energy and vitality. In my experience, unsuccessful Mobilized Families break apart fairly early or spend their lives together alternating between chronic conflict and withdrawal.

Occasionally a couple moves precipitously into the Action Stage, dealing with the anxiety and chaos of the Immersion Stage by forming a tight couple system. As we see in Chapter Six these Action Families eject children from the biological parent-child relationship too completely and quickly, destroying single-parent–child middle ground in favor of a host of new rules and family norms. Although the biological structure of the Early Stages is uncomfortable for stepparents, successful stepfamilies allow previously established middle ground to stand for a while.

Successful work in the Middle Stages rests on the awareness work of the Early Stages. The more complete and more accurate the family members' map of their territory, the more easily and successfully they can complete the primary task of the Middle Stages: identifying and carving out enough shared step middle ground to operate as a stepfamily, rather than as a collection of minifamilies. Aided by a good map of family members' needs and feelings, the challenge is to move quickly enough so that the outsider stepparent or the less dominant parent-child unit is not left languishing, but slowly enough so that children can maintain some sense of security and stability.

The Early Stages through Mobilization constitute the "uphill" part of the Stepfamily Cycle. Families who make it to the Action Stage will find that the balance of work is much more "downhill" from that point on. In my experience, families that break up after they have completed the Middle Stages rarely break up over step issues.

STAGE FOUR
Mobilization: Exposing the Gaps

I stayed on the shore a while, I tested the water. I walked up and down to see if it got any better north or south. And finally decided it didn't! So I jumped in! [Gregory Burns, stepfather to Jason and Judy.]

Gregory's image of finally plunging into the Mississippi is an apt metaphor for many stepparents for the Mobilization Stage. Outsider stepparents who had not been able to voice their minority position strongly enough to be heard yet begin to wade into the family with more focus and confidence, voicing their needs and perceptions with more sustained force and energy. With each move, it is as if outsiders in the family decide to move further into the family and rock the boat, rather than moving further out and abandoning the family ship.

Insider biological parents, too, describe a Mobilization Stage in which they begin to more actively voice their needs for relief from the insider position the stepfamily structure places them in. And stepchildren who have not until this time been able to voice their needs begin to speak up with more force and conviction.

Barbara Abramson describes the quality of the shift that takes place as family members begin to be more able to mobilize around their unmet needs. She is describing the change in her stance as stepparent to her husband Jim's daughter:

I started realizing that I'm different than Jim is, and I'm going to be a different parent than he is. I spent years trying to be just like him and be sweet and kind and always gentle with his daughter. But I'm not always that way. I think I made a decision that what I was seeing was right. And that I had to move on it even though Jim didn't see things the same way.

It's really sort of a mind-set, that instead of trying to get in with them and not cause trouble and not be a problem, what I've done in the last year is to say, "I will be a problem."

As family members begin to voice unheard needs and perceptions with more force, experiential gaps in the family, between insiders and outsiders, step and biological family members, and adults and children are exposed more starkly. Faster families who have already mapped these differences in the calmer, more curious, atmosphere of the Awareness Stage are less panicked and surprised by their presence, and less likely to erupt into polarized conflict. Families that have not yet made a jointly shared picture of their family structure find this stage much more frightening and challenging.

Many of the issues that families fight over in this stage may appear trivial: whether jackets can be left in the living room or should be hung up in the coat closet, whether children should drink soda or milk with meals, when and how the table should be set for dinner, whether and when the television will be turned off for the night. However, each issue represents a struggle over who will be the insiders and who will be the outsiders in the new family. The stepparent is fighting to gain entrance, to feel at home, and to shape the family so that it includes his or her needs and tastes. The biological parent and children are fighting to retain some of their familiar and comfortable routines. Children particularly are fighting against becoming the new outsiders.

Taking a Stand: Stepparents in the Mobilization Stage

Stepparent as Change Agent

During the Mobilization Stage, in their efforts to get heard, stepparents who until now have been rather quiet outsiders in the family begin to function as family change agents. As we have said, establishing a workable stepfamily requires loosening intense biological parent-child ties and creating new middle ground in step relationships. Middle ground is particularly needed in the adult couple so that it can become a place of nourishment for both adults and can begin to operate as the seat of decision making in the new family. However, it is often the stepparent who is most interested in this task. In double families, it is the adult in the outside position who is most likely to push for change.

A few stepparents find their more clearly articulated needs greeted with relief and eagerness by their partners, who welcome a clue as to how to make their new spouses more comfortable. In most cases, however, the biological parent receives the news with panic ("This must mean this relationship, too, will end."). Unfortunately, the biological parent's difficulty in understanding and bearing the reality of the stepparent's outsider position all too often combines with the stepparent's newly found urgency and lack of empathy for the dilemmas of the biological parent's insider position to polarize the couple on step issues. Predictably, the stepparent is on the side of more discipline, more boundaries around the couple, and clearer limits with the ex-spouse, whereas the biological parent defends the need to spare the child more loss and change, to remain available to the children, and to keep a modicum of peace with the ex-spouse. For the insider biological parent-child unit, creating new middle ground requires relinquishing old, comfortable ground. After the losses and changes involved in divorce or death, this is particularly hard and uncomfortable work. What for the biological pair is yet another loss is for the stepparent a matter of emotional survival. What is familiar and comforting for the biological parent and child is isolating and disorienting for the stepparent.

We have said that the presence of strongly held fantasies of a biological-like family creates major obstacles to the task of restructuring the family. On the biological side of the experiential gap, the stepparent's more vocal description of the ways in which the family is *not* working now more powerfully confronts many insider biological parents with their as yet unrelinquished fantasies. Beth Roberts, an insider mother, describes her experience:

I just kept dismissing my husband's complaints. I thought he was being childish to be jealous of my daughter. I guess I thought we would become this wonderful instant family. Really, it sounds stupid now, but that's what I'd dreamed about all those years single-parenting. He kept withdrawing and going off with his friends, and I'd feel betrayed and abandoned. I really thought he could love Melissa the way I loved her, if he would just try. He kept wanting us to go away without my daughter, and I kept trying to arrange these wonderful family camping trips like the ones I had when I was a kid and had always wanted with my first husband.

Finally, he read something about stepfamilies in some magazine, and he brought it to me. "See," he says. "I'm normal." We had a huge fight. But this time he didn't back off. And he also said there was no way he would stay in our family unless I took some vacation time alone with him. It's not that we hadn't talked about this before, but this time he really stood his ground.

I was devastated. I cried and cried. It was the first time that he got through to me that we weren't going to be the family I dreamed about, that he'd never feel about Melissa the way I do. Since then I've learned an awful lot I wished I'd known when I started. And actually, our family works better now that I'm not trying to make it into something it's not. But I still feel sad sometimes.

Two years later, this family completed the Middle Stages, and proceeded into the Later Stages of its development. Like most average-paced families, they had spent two or three years in the Early Stages before the stepfather felt solid enough about his needs to stand his ground. Implied in this quote, as well, is the crucial importance of good information in facilitating movement through the Stepfamily Cycle.

It is the outsider stepparent's need for an insider position, then, that often drives the family toward completion of the developmental tasks of the Middle Stages, pulling the biological parent to spend more intimate couple time, lobbying for changes that will firm up existing middle ground and establish new shared experiences and goals in the family.

Moving In: "I Belong Here"

Many stepparents who began to function in this period as family change agents can clearly mark a time when they experienced a qualitative change in their expressiveness with their stepchildren, as well as their spouses. Now that stepparents and stepchildren know each other better, stepparents can begin to deal more directly and forcefully with their stepchildren. One woman remembers the night she threw a pan of lasagna at her stepchildren when they compared her cooking with their mother's one too many times. Barbara Abramson described the change in her relationship with her stepdaughter Emmie this way:

The other day I tried to comfort Emmie, and she pushed me away. Instead of withdrawing and feeling hurt, I told her that it was hard for me that she doesn't like me to kiss her or hug her. I asked her how come she doesn't like that. I wanted to find a way we could do that. She said she doesn't like me to kiss her. But it's OK with her for me to hug her. So we hugged each other. Things are really changing between us, a little bit at a time.

The Mobilization Stage also sees stepparents moving to take more insider positions with their spouses in relationship to their ex-spouses. The solidity and differentiation gained by stepparents as they more clearly map their piece of the family territory during the Early Stages enables them to hang in longer when they are not heard. The following quote illustrates Barbara moving from Immersion through Awareness to a clearly stated need, and then sustained Mobilization in a series of encounters with her husband Jim:

It's really been a series of struggles, especially struggles to make a boundary between the two families.

When Katerina (Jim's ex-wife) comes to town to see Emmie, she borrows Jim's car. It took a while for me to get in touch with how I didn't like that. That made the boundary fuzzy for me. I started feeling unsafe. And I remember when I got in touch with how much I didn't want her to use that car, how threatened I felt. And I didn't think it was a good thing for Emmie either—too confusing.

And so I talked to Jim about it, and we had this big fight about it. I sort of expected him to agree with me easily, but he didn't! He really didn't see what the big issue was. For him, it was just a practical thing. She was borrowing his car. It was a good fight. I talked about how it was a way to hang on. Why didn't she get her own car fixed? Why didn't she borrow from the people she stayed with?

I tried and tried to convince him it was not a good thing. Finally, I realized that it didn't matter. What mattered was I didn't want it! It took a couple of months of saying, "I don't want her to borrow your car, it makes me feel unsafe," over and over again until he told her she couldn't borrow his car.

As always in looking at stepfamily events, it is important to keep in mind that the biological parent's feelings about this struggle would be just as strongly felt, very different, and equally convincing. Were Jim telling us his experience, he might say something like, "I don't know why Barbara is making such a fuss. Katerina sees Emmie so little. Katerina never quite gets it together, and I feel so badly for Emmie. Besides, it used to be Katerina's car. So why shouldn't she borrow it, especially when it gives them some time to do something together?"

Stepparents also begin to mobilize around issues within the adult couple. The amount of adult private couple time is a frequent focus, as the stepparent pulls with more conviction for a more intimate couple relationship, while the biological parent tries to protect his or her children from further abandonment. The bedroom door is a frequent focus of painful conflict within the couple. The close parent-child relationships of single parenthood, the mutual need for comfort, and the lack of another adult make early morning and late night cuddling and talking in bed a natural and soothing activity for single parents and their children. However, what is comforting and affirming for biological parents and their children feels invasive and disorienting to a new adult who finds even his or her most intimate time with a new spouse interrupted by children.

Issues between the two families form another focus. Stepparents now become more actively engaged in areas that in the Early Stages they (appropriately) left to the biological parent to work out with his or her ex-spouse: visitation arrangements, use of shared property, time and duration of phone calls between ex-spouses.

In some cases, a crisis where the stepparent's more outside position is needed as a resource in the family, provides a less conflicted entry point for stepparents. Harvey Roseman describes finding a way to step in when his stepdaughter Cory had major surgery on her mouth. Cory's parents were immobilized precisely *because* they were much closer to her. Harvey's somewhat less involved relationship with his stepdaughter enabled him to provide something that her parents were incapable of offering at that moment:

When I walked into Cory's hospital room, she was lying there looking absolutely awful. Her whole face was black and blue. She was a mess. Cory's dad and Jannine were standing there on either side of her bed. And they just looked stricken. Nobody was saying a word.

For a moment I had my usual feeling that I really didn't belong there. Literally, Cory had her parents on either side of her bed and there was no place for me. And then something shifted in me, and I decided I *would* go in, not only that I belonged there, but that I was the only one with enough cool to cheer poor Cory up! So I walked in, and I started joking with Cory about how awful she looked, and it was like the tension broke, and there I was, the one who had made a difference! It was a real turning point for me in the family.

Moving Out: "I Quit"

Though many stepparents mobilize to move more firmly into their families, some mobilize themselves to *move out* of stepparent roles that have thrust them too precipitously into parenting. Ann Lieberman, a full-time stepmother:

I realized I was doing *too* much. I was working. I had a new baby. I had almost full-time responsibility for Mickey's sons. I finally decided that if he wanted them here, *he'd* have to do more of the work; more of the disciplining; more of the rides to hockey practice at the crack of dawn; more of the talks about homework.

And I actually think it was better for all of us when I finally put my foot down. It was like we were doing something unnatural out of this wish to be a "regular" family. And I think the boys really needed their dad back.

Stepparents who move into families where a parent has died are particularly vulnerable to stepping blindly into a bereaved family with the expectation that they will replace the absent parent. Cathy Olson was just beginning to relinquish the full-time mother role she had inherited 14 years earlier when she married Nick, whose wife had died of cancer, leaving him with a 2-year-old. The 2-year-old, Betty, is now 17, and had just been kicked out of school. Cathy:

I've tried to parent this kid for 14 years. I've poured my heart into her. And what do I get? She treats me terribly. It's like we've been trying to do something unreal all these years. It's time for me to stop and let Nick take more of the load.

And you know, I so wish I could call this kid's dead mother up. I'd like to call her up and say, "Come get this kid. She's yours. She's got *your* blood. And she's driving me nuts."

After several frustrating years of straining to make a relationship with him, Rachel Sax's stepson Ben demolished her car and took no responsibility for it. She waited for a

week for him to call and work it out with her, and then she
finally exploded:

> Finally I called him up. I was yelling at him so loudly that I could hear his
> mother on the other end of the phone say, "*Who is* that?" And Ben said,
> "It's Rachel." And for once in her life, she shut up. She didn't say another
> word.

> And I just told him he was irresponsible, and I had had it with him and
> that this was it. I said that he was an adult now and that any other time he
> wanted to make plans with us, come down for his father's birthday, or be
> part of holidays, then he could call me. Because I'm not going to chase
> after him anymore.

> It was the best thing I ever did. And it was the first time I ever laid into
> him. Of course, Ira wasn't there.

Feeling Torn: The Insider Adult's Experience of the Mobilization Stage

For most couples, this period is a noisy, frightening, chaotic
time as the stepparent's greater expressiveness exposes painful differences between the biological and step experience
of the family. The locus of discomfort now shifts from the
outsider stepparent to the couple. The biological parent's
inside position, which had afforded some protection from
the stresses of the Early Stages, now becomes much more
conflicted and painful, as stepparents' more vigorous demands for change place biological parents between their children's needs for stability and the stepparent's needs for
change; between the need to maintain a stable cooperative
relationship with an ex-spouse and the stepparent's needs
for more distance from the previous marriage. Reginald Cox,
biological parent to three teenagers, describes the pain of
being caught in the middle:

> So my wife and my daughter have a fight. My daughter is sulking upstairs,
> crying that nobody loves her. My wife is crying in the bedroom. If I
> comfort my wife, my daughter will accuse me of abandoning her. If I talk
> to my daughter, I'll catch hell from Gina for "giving in" to my daughter.
> What do I do?

Ben Wilson, remarried to Donna and biological father to Danny, who was 8 when he and Donna began engaging more actively over stepparenting issues, echoes the same theme:

> I *always* feel split these days. I'm always aware of what Donna is going to think, and how Danny is going to feel. He loves potato chips and Donna doesn't believe in them for kids. When I give Danny potato chips, he's so pleased and she is *so* pissed. When I say no to Danny, who has always eaten potato chips, I feel awful. I'm always in the middle, always aware of both of them. I feel like I just can't win.

"And it feels so much better" is, in contrast, the oft-repeated statement for stepparents as they describe the many small ways they begin to make themselves feel more like insiders, making their needs and feelings known to their spouses and stepchildren, and making more demands of them.

However, for biological parents, the greater intensity of stepparents' demands can be frightening. The emergence of intense conflict after an apparently peaceful Early Stages may feel like failure to the insider parent. Reginald Cox describes his feelings when his wife Gina became more vocal about her needs in the family:

> It just felt like we'd gotten nowhere. Here we were three years down the road, and we were fighting like crazy. It just felt like we should give up. I was so disappointed in Gina. I had felt like she was on my side, and then I feel like no matter what I do, I did something wrong.

Some understanding of the fact that despite the chaos and anxiety, he and Gina had actually progressed far enough to air their differences openly was very comforting to this biological parent. The Mobilized Family in Chapter Six demonstrates that when couples understand that struggling over these differences is crucial to building a satisfying stepfamily life, they maneuver through the Mobilization Stage with a little bit more equanimity.

"I Don't Want to Be the Meat": Getting Out of the Middle

Just as stepparents take a clearer position in this stage, further into (or further out of) the family, biological parents may also begin voicing their needs for a shift in their family position. Now that stepchildren and stepparents know each other better, it is time for biological parents to move out of the middle. Some are asked firmly to move out of the middle by their stepparent spouses. For others, particularly women who have been the go-betweens in stepfather families, the new clarity in the Awareness Stage is that they are tired of being the only one in the family with all the pieces of the map. They now confront their families with a resignation notice. Joan Davis, a remarried mother:

They each only have one set of feelings they know about—their own. I have *three*—mine and my daughter's and my husband's. And I'm ready to say, "It's time for you all to begin understanding each other. I'm tired of being the bridge! Go talk to each other. I'm getting out of the middle!"

Going Nose to Nose

Several of the quotes in this section highlight another important fact: stepparents in the Mobilization Stage often begin taking on their stepchildren when the biological parent is absent. Even when biological parents are eager to step out of the middle role, it is difficult to watch another adult fighting intensely with one's child without intervening. When they are present, biological parents often step in to mediate. This is appropriate in the Early Stages, when children and stepparents are still relative strangers. However, it becomes not only less necessary in the Middle Stages, but obstructive to stepparent and stepchild developing their own relationship.

Though biological parents may continue to experience themselves as being helpful or as protecting the child from further harm, stepparents now feel diminished and interrupted by their spouse's efforts. Michelle Gunnars talks about trying to confront her stepdaughter when Dan (Michelle's husband and Meggan's father) intervenes. She and Meggan have known each other for several years by this time:

When Meggan gets angry at me, she swears at me. I don't mind her swearing, but it's not OK with me that she uses that kind of language to my face. I tried to tell her that, and Dan immediately jumped on me and said, "Well, you're the one who's irritable." And then Dan would act as a kind of observer and treat us like two peers.

I wanted it to be a parent-child thing. She was talking as if she's bigger than me. And I feel I am older than she is, and I am in the parent role. And from my family tradition, you don't talk to your parent in that way. Dan never said anything like, "You're the child and we're adults." He would never do anything that would show she was in a one-down position in terms of power. That feels humiliating to me to have him tell me she and I are peers fighting and that he is between us.

Michelle, a member of one of the slower-paced families, is traveling alone through the Awareness Stage on this issue. She is getting clearer about her needs, but neither her husband nor her stepdaughter understands her position. In contrast, support from the biological parent spouse seems to enable stepparents to move into this more expressive stance with a greater sense of ease and competence. Bill Hobbes, a member of one of the faster families, speaks of the impact upon him of the support he received from his wife Paula when he was angry at her daughter Patsy:

Paula has been really wonderful in facilitating that. She saw when I was angry, and in a sense she really gave me permission. She'd say, "Hey, it's OK you're angry. Patsy needs to see you angry. That's important, too." So I really do feel successful in that I'm very straight with my anger with Patsy, and she's really receptive and really straight back with me.

Slow Down, We're Moving Too Fast

Many of the cases thus far have described a stepfamily system in which the stepparent has been the more silent partner through the Early Stages. Although the disenfranchisement generated by the stepparent's outside position in early stepfamily structure makes this balance of power most likely, the opposite also occurs. Some stepparents handle the extremely uncomfortable feelings of jealousy and resentment by moving too quickly into Mobilization, demanding change on many fronts. Their spouses may deal with the anxiety of being put in the middle by making the new couple relationship primary at the expense of the biological parent-child relationship, asking children to adapt to an entirely new set of rules, and demanding that ex-spouses sever any but the most necessary communication.

In many of the cases I see, this is a first and late marriage by the stepparent, who has functioned very autonomously, built a successful career, and operated in an arena where, with enough discipline and effort, she or he could control the outcome. When such a stepparent marries a somewhat passive biological parent, the result will be a family in which the couple becomes a closed system very quickly, making children the new outsiders at a time when they can least afford it. In these family systems, the biological parent is the confused, more silent partner. When stepparents mobilize too quickly, they often find themselves frustrated and exhausted. Because they cannot wholeheartedly support so much change, biological parents will appear to concur but then will often undermine apparent agreements. Children in such families feel invisible, confused, and discarded, and, in fact, stepfamilies with this arrangement frequently present with a depressed or acting out-child.

For these families to succeed, the biological parent and the stepchildren must begin more fully to articulate the needs of the biological subsystem for some stability, for some protection of already established middle ground, and for quality time together.

In these families, the Mobilization Stage may see a biological parent advocating more strongly for fewer rule changes and more time alone with his or her children, or fighting more forcefully for longer visitation of a noncustodial child. Children may also become more vigorously recalcitrant as they attempt to slow down the process of change.

Finding a Voice: Children in the Mobilization Stage

Perhaps the most charged area children begin to move on in their own Mobilization Stage is the loyalty binds they have found themselves in. The pulls between their parents, or between a parent and a stepparent, were often felt (but wordlessly) in the Immersion Stage. In the Awareness Stage, children can more clearly articulate the patterns of the pulls and even state their needs out loud. However, they often cannot make themselves heard. Children who move into the Mobilization Stage on this issue gain enough strength and conviction to make the adults in their lives pay attention. Leslie Kohl (26):

My dad used to tell me one thing, and my mom would tell me another. And I didn't know what to make of it. One of them would ask me to tell the other one something. And then *I* would get to hear how angry it made the other one. I thought, this stinks. It's horrible. After the 50 millionth time I said, "That's your problem. Talk to each other about it," and they didn't do it again.

Kevin Miller, then age 10:

The worst thing has been when my parents argue. They'd fight and hang up. And then my dad would call back and my mom would say, "Answer it." Finally, I sat my parents down and told them, "I'm not your messenger! You tell each other yourselves or it's not gonna be said."

Pamela Danielson, a 15-year-old girl, tells a similar story:

My parents would send messages to each other through me. "Tell your dad . . ." "Tell your mom . . ." It seems like they didn't know how to use the phone! Finally, I said to them, "You're not beyond talking. That's a bit immature. Grow up!"

Children also mobilize around other issues. Some more clearly state their needs for time alone with their biological parent. Others finally voice a need to shift a visitation schedule. Just as some stepparents in this stage get clearer about the need to move out of a stepparent-stepchild relationship, some children more firmly voice their need not to be part of a new family. Timothy Levi is a college-age young man whose

father had remarried a woman with two young children.
Timothy's father, who is now a recovering alcoholic, was eager for Timothy to be part of the new family. Like many
stepfamilies with college-age or late adolescent children,
Timothy's normal developmental need to move out of the
family and off on his own contrasted with his father's need
to pull him into the new family. In the Immersion Stage,
Timothy had felt guilty and confused:

My dad wants me to go home for the High Holidays. I don't know what I
want to do. I feel so guilty if I don't go, and so awful if I go. I can't sort
it out.

As he moves into the Awareness Stage, Timothy is clearer
about his place in the new family. He is also clearer about
the difference between his needs and his father's:

My dad's new house isn't "home" for me. It's home to him. It's *his* second
chance. And I think he wants to give me the family I never had with him.
But that's gone. His new family isn't my family. I don't feel good there.
I'm the outsider there. I don't like watching my dad give her children what
I didn't have from him.

But mainly, I want my own life now. And my life isn't there with him. I
can't imagine saying all this to him though. I think it would break his heart.

By the end of the next year, Timothy has moved into the
Mobilization Stage on this issue:

I told my dad I'm not going "home" this summer. Home is here with my
friends. I'm never going to live at home again. And certainly I'm not going
to live there with him. It's right for him, maybe, but it's not right for me.
It makes me sad. And seeing him so upset is hard, real hard. But it's his
loss that he was drinking when I was a kid. My loss, too, but I can't make
it up to him. It's not my job to fix that.

Mobilization: Summary

For most families, the challenges of the Mobilization Stage
are substantial: the couple system must often bear intense
struggle over differences without either fracturing or slipping permanently back into the unspoken disequilibrium of

the Early Stages. The stepparent's task is to identify a few changes that matter and sustain the effort to get heard while maintaining respect and empathy for the biological subsystem's needs for some stability. The biological parent's task is to voice the needs of children and ex-spouses while supporting and empathizing with the stepparent's needs for change. Children more vociferously voice their needs to ease their loyalty binds. Though most families do not maneuver smoothly through these challenges, those who can stick it out and begin hearing each other widen the band of shared awareness, and complete the accurate map that is so crucial for successful moves in the Action Stage.

STAGE FIVE
Action: Going Into Business Together

In the Action Stage of the Stepfamily Cycle the family can begin to make larger moves to reorganize its structure. The primary task of the Action Stage is to use the clearer and wider understanding created in the Awareness and Mobilization Stages to make some truly joint decisions about how the family will operate. The family is now ready to actively thicken the middle ground in step subsystems in a variety of ways, drawing new, firmer step boundaries and creating new step norms and rituals. As in other stages, the family may be ready to take Action steps on one issue, while remaining in an earlier stage with each other on other issues where the territory has proven more difficult. Couples that have trouble bearing the anxiety of the Early Stages may move precipitously to the Action Stage without doing the work of getting to know each other.

Drawing New Lines

Successful moves in this phase are based on a good enough understanding of the needs of all involved and have the shared investment of both spouses. They actually change the family's structure, lessening the dominance and exclusiveness of the biological parent-child relationship, and strengthening step relationships in the family.

In the Action Stage stepfamily members change the internal geometry of the family by creating new boundaries around step relationships. In large and small steps the family begins to shift insider and outsider positions in the family. Biological parent and child continue to need time alone together. However, it is time for the stepparent to move more actively to the inside of step subsystems, pushing out the biological family members who do not belong in each family subsystem.

As the outsider adult's need for intimate couple time is heard and understood, stepcouples who have not already made separate space for themselves begin to work together to create time alone without children. Stepparents and stepchildren who have begun to grapple more directly with each other in the Mobilization Stage can now more actively push the biological parent out of their interaction. Stepsiblings begin to relate to each other as a unit, separate from their parents. As we have said, faster families do some of this right from the beginning. Other stepfamilies arrive at the need for separate space for each minifamily with more effort, through the open airing of family members' needs in the Mobilization Stage.

The new family is now ready to define itself more separately from the old family, and clearer boundaries are established with ex-spouses. Occasionally stepparent and the absent parent of the same sex also begin to make a more direct one-to-one relationship, rather than working through the biological parent.

Thickening the Middle Ground in Step Relationships

The work of the Awareness Stage, often combined with the greater engagement of the Mobilization Stage, has widened members' understanding of each person's very different experience of the family. This often hard-won, deepened awareness in itself adds much "glue" to step relationships. As stepparent and biological parent, insider and outsider, come to accept and understand each other's fundamentally different experience, they can more often hold hands across the "chasm" created by their family structure. Trisha Greenfield, after several years of marriage to Walter:

> We still feel very differently when his daughter comes to visit. But now at least we understand each other. He can say, "I know you feel left out. I know it's hard for you." I can say, "I know you feel torn." It's funny. I'd still rather have the time alone with him, but we don't become enemies over it anymore.

Equally important, this wider awareness gives family members enough information to begin to invent some new rules and norms that respect both the insider system's need for stability and the outsiders' need for change. The primary work of the Action Stage lies in this effort to delineate the stepfamily's unique middle ground. The family must preserve some of each biological subsystem's familiar territory and also create some new norms that combine bits and pieces from each culture. In addition, families begin to invent some brand-new norms and rituals that are special to this family.

The successful stepfamily ends the Action Stage with much firmer middle ground in step relationships. The family has now clearly identified some areas where they can operate automatically, where an agreed-on path has been hacked out and can be walked upon without too many unpleasant surprises. By the end of the Action Stage, the middle ground in the stepcouple, and in some (but not all) stepparent-stepchild relationships, is at last thick enough to compete with the biological parent-child unit.

The presence of some reliable middle ground in step relationships in itself provides stability and hope, particularly in the couple relationship, which in turn makes it easier to face remaining differences with less panic. The Action Stage of the Stepfamily Cycle marks the end of the uphill portion

of the developmental struggle to forge a workable new family
out of the minifamilies that come together in a new remarried family.

The Action Stage, as do all the stages of the Stepfamily
Cycle, happens in a series of moves. Families may be able to
cooperate early to create new understandings in some areas,
though in others, where the gap between their needs is wider
or the territory is rockier, they come to agreement only after
considerable struggle. Still other regions of disagreement
may receive no attention or remain sources of bitter conflict
(or objects of silent despair) until much later. Different stepchildren in the same family may clarify their positions in the
new family at very different paces, some moving quickly to
insider relationships with their stepparents and/or stepsiblings, and others remaining very much outside the new family until well after the rest of the family is in the Resolution
Stage. Boundaries around some step subsystems may become
firmly established, whereas others remain fuzzy or don't coalesce until much later.

Something Old and Something New

Existing middle ground in the new family may offer some
areas of easily agreed-on functioning early in the new family,
well before the major earth-moving efforts of the Action
Stage. Already existing shared middle ground may include
shared realistic assumptions about the new family's structure
("For now, we are a collection of minifamilies that each need
time and space."), shared religious practices ("We go to St.
Botolph's Church." "We do not celebrate Christmas."),
shared energy levels ("We are a low-key family." "We love to
entertain."), and shared values ("We are both left-leaning
liberals.").

Again, shared realistic expectations can offer substantial shared middle ground in a new couple, easing the family
though the first years. For instance, some families begin their
lives together with both members of the adult couple agree-
ing on the need for intimate time without children. Thus

agreements about the need for vacations without kids, breakfasts alone, and intimate dates come fairly easily. When these families also agree that children and their biological parents need time alone together, couple needs and biological subsystem needs can be balanced, often with some effort, given limited time and energy, but without undue conflict.

These shared realistic expectations help the family to experience its existing middle ground even while facing areas of difference. When separate minifamilies each have their own time and space, biological subsystems have some territory in which they can operate on familiar ground without worrying about whether the strangers in the family are comfortable. Members of step subsystems can experience their shared middle ground without competing with the thicker preexisting middle ground of biological subsystems. This continued experience of existing middle ground significantly lowers the panic and anxiety that are often generated when experiential gaps are exposed.

Because our culture has not yet normalized the stepfamily structure (Cherlin, 1981), most stepfamilies feel they are inventing the wheel as they toil, often somewhat blindly, at the task of moving from a biological minifamily with a stepparent appendage or two separate biological parent-child minifamilies to a workable stepfamily. The following section describes some of the specific action steps that thicken middle ground in step relationships.

A Step at a Time Saves Nine

The work of the Action Stage of the Stepfamily Cycle is built on earlier stages. Some couples deal with the anxiety and confusion of early stepfamily structure by jumping precipitously into the Action Stage, immediately operating as a firm adult parenting team. Although this may appear to speed the process of becoming a workable stepfamily, it often backfires. Because the work of the Awareness Stage is not complete, it is as if the adults have set off on a major trip with children, without an accurate map of the territory in which they are traveling, asking children to treat complete strangers as trusted guides. In Chapter Six we meet such an "Action Family," the Wentworths. Many of these couples immediately create a tight adult relationship that excludes children so completely that they do not have adequate access to their biological parent. Though complete exclusion of children gives adults much-needed intimate time, it does so at the expense of the children just when they need support from their parent to weather major shifts in their world.

We have often assumed, extrapolating from what we know about biological family systems, that the better the adult stepcouple relationship, the happier and better adjusted the stepchildren will be. This assumption, which has been carried through the step literature for some years, may be what Ganong and Coleman (1987) identify as a "whoozle effect," a made-up "fact" that people assume is true simply because others have said it. Actually, some researchers have found that close couple relationships make for more conflicted stepparent-stepchild relationships and poorer stepchild adjustment. It may be that these closer stepcouples have moved precipitously into the Action Stage. Children can be very articulate about the cost of this precipitous move to the Middle Stages. Sarah Fishman, age 16:

It just didn't feel right. My mom and stepfather were saying to us, "We are a unit." But we had just met! I'd ask one about something, and then they'd go off and come back and talk as if they agreed. It felt untruthful and weird. And it made me feel really lonely. Like I didn't exist there. Who was I there anyway? I didn't recognize my family!

Sarah is very clear about how she wishes her mom and stepfather had made the shift to new rules more openly and more gradually:

I wish they'd sat down with us and my mom said her rules and my stepfather said his and we talked it out. But this was too fast and too weird. My brother and I went along for a while and then we just stopped. We couldn't take it.

Sarah goes on to describe the abrupt shift in her stepmother's behavior when the adult couple married:

My stepmom was my friend. The *day* they got married she tried to become my mom. She started with the discipline. As if because they were married, my relationship with her could change overnight! Before, if something bothered her, we talked about it. Overnight she started saying, "Do it because I say so." It was too soon! Maybe if it were more gradual, it would have been easier for me. I couldn't do it. We started really fighting. We'd never fought before.

Larry Schmidt, who was 16 when his stepfather entered the family, describes the sabotage he and his younger sister waged:

My stepfather came into our family feeling we hadn't been disciplined and he would be the one to do it. He wanted lots of changes fast. It was too fast for us. Boy, did we make it hard for him. Not doing what they tell you to do is one way to get to your stepparent. And when he told us to put our napkins on our lap we'd do it, but we'd say, "Sails down!"

Action Steps at the Couple Boundary

Making a Sanctuary

Biological couples usually begin their marriages without children, and, therefore, have time alone together before children arrive on the scene and pose a whole new set of complex relationships and couples tasks. Stepcouples are in the unique position of having to exclude at least one partner's children in order to create a private couple relationship. As we have seen, a few stepcouples may move too completely in this direction, forming a rigid boundary that does not allow enough access for children. My own experience is that this is rare. Some stepcouples never come to this understanding that the adult couple needs its own territory. Hank Haley, a member of a stepfamily that remained in the Early Stages after 13 years, talks about the difficulties this created for him:

I never had a life with one other adult, with just Helen and me. After the honeymoon was over, we always had her kids. We've hardly ever been away together since the honeymoon without having the kids along. Vacations, the kids come along. We don't go on vacation just the two of us. I could count the times on one hand, it seems, in 13 years. So we never had that. So I sometimes wonder about our marriage relationship. How has it suffered since we haven't had the time to be alone with the two of us? At least we would have had the 10-11 months prior to Billie (their biological child) being born. We never had that.

This couple never made it to the Action Stage. They had no information about normal stepfamily functioning, and in fact didn't consider themselves a stepfamily. Both adults expected the family to operate as an immediately blended family. Evidence that it was not working was taken as proof of Hank's inadequacy. The adult couple relationship could not become a separate intimate system in the constant presence of children, much less children deeply attached to one adult and not to the other. This couple divorced within a couple of years of my interview with Hank.

All couples must work harder after children are born to make time for their intimate relationship. Stepcouples must begin this effort in the presence of one, and often two, sets of biological parent-child relationships that powerfully and unevenly pull at least one of the adults in the family away from the marital relationship. As we have seen, it is the outsider stepparent who has felt most adrift and bereft and has the most to gain from a closer couple relationship. In the Mobilization Stage, he or she often becomes the primary advocate to carve out separate space for the adult couple: pushing to put doors on bedrooms, advocating for times when children are not to interrupt the couple, asking children to knock before entering the adult bedroom, and urging their spouses to take vacations as a couple without children. In the Action Stage, the couple begins to act as a team to accomplish some of these moves. In making them, successful couples respect both the needs of the outsider stepparent and children.

As a single parent, Lynn had been living in a small apartment, and had been using an open alcove off the living room as her bedroom so that each child could continue to have a separate bedroom. Though this arrangement felt comfortable and supportive to her and her children, it was disturbing to her new partner, Gregory, who felt her children could interrupt them "morning, noon, and night!" In the Early Stages, Gregory had suffered silently, remaining somewhat withdrawn from the family. Lynn had felt abandoned and betrayed by his apparent lack of interest in her children. The Mobilization Stage for this couple began when Gregory, a budding family therapist, read enough about "triangles" to buttress his contention that, "There are some weird boundaries around here and I don't like them anymore!" Lynn and Gregory tangled bitterly, as Lynn fought against disturbing the hard-won stability of her single-parent family by putting her latency-age children together in one bedroom, and Gregory equally vociferously defended his desire for a private adult bedroom. In the Action Stage, the couple finally agreed to move into one of the two private bedrooms and they made some new rules about when children were and were not welcome in the adult bedroom. They also agreed to look for a larger apartment that would give each child a bedroom.

As families move more fully into the Action Stage of the Stepfamily Cycle, the voice for change is less often the stepparent advocating alone, and more often the insider biological parent and outsider stepparent functioning together as a team. When stepchildren intrude on the adult relationship, biological parents increasingly move to protect the couple's boundary, as in this brief vignette told by Rachel Sax:

Ira's son and his girlfriend were taking pictures and Ira was hugging me. And his other son said, "Let me get in between the two of you and Dad can hug us both." And Ira said, "No, I'm hugging Rachel."

Arranging adult time alone is particularly difficult in stepfamilies, due to the presence of children from the beginning of the marriage and the intensity of children's needs for support during a painful transition. Visitation arrangements may further complicate the problem: one spouse's children may regularly arrive for the weekend just as the other's leave. Noncustodial parents may have time with their children only during weekends and vacation periods, placing needs for couple time in direct conflict with needs for time with children.

In the Early Stages, these needs may remain unexpressed, or only weakly voiced, and the new family limps along, often meeting the needs of one subsystem over another, usually the biological unit at the expense of the new couple—although, as we have said, occasionally the new couple forms a rigid boundary too early and leaves the needs of the biological parent–child system unmet. In the Mobilization Stage, unvoiced needs begin to be expressed, but fear of another failure, lack of empathy, ongoing wishes that stepparent and biological parent would have the same needs, the strength of the feelings on both sides, and lack of a road map for navigating this territory may prematurely end these conversations in despair or polarized conflict.

In the Action Stage, the challenge is for the couple to gain enough awareness of all the needs in the family to become a more creative team in balancing the need for enough couple time, with the need for biological parents and their children to have time together. Again, some solutions come easily, and others emerge only after bitter warfare. Couples may assign one time of day in a household with teenagers as "adult time"—no teenagers in the living room, no loud music, and no interruptions barring a life-threatening emergency. The couple may take a walk together on weekends when children are visiting, have an intimate date on Thursday night before a child arrives, take "minivacations" by "running away" for the day together when children are at school. They may arrange regular breakfast or lunch dates.

Becoming a Parenting Team

Couples in stepfamilies need to become a team in two very different ways: They need to build an *intimate relationship*, so that the couple is a sanctuary for nourishment and support, and they also need to become a *decision-making team* for the new family. The former involves making intimate time together. The latter is more task-oriented and involves making parenting decisions together.

In the Action Stage of the Stepfamily Cycle, parenting decisions that would have appropriately been made in earlier stages by the biological parent alone, or in consultation with the ex-spouse, now begin to be made by the new couple together. Stepparents and their stepchildren are no longer strangers, and biological parents increasingly confer with stepparents about rules, visitation arrangements, and financial matters involving children and ex-spouses. Stepparents can now begin to move more directly into the disciplinary role with their stepchildren, and their requests of their stepchildren around eating habits, bedtimes, and chores are increasingly supported by their spouses. Rachel Sax:

> I had my stepson Adam clean my cellar out two weeks ago. A filthy dirty rotten job. If I had told him to do that three years ago, Ira [her husband] would have gone bananas. Now he says, "Do what Rachel tells you."

Some joint decisions come easily. Others are more hard fought and require support from outside the family for a successful solution. Liz Pierce and Andrew Raskin's family moved at an average pace through the Stepfamily Cycle struggling through a highly conflicted Mobilization Stage with the help of family therapy. As they entered their third year of marriage, Liz was beginning to mobilize around her concerns in the new family.

Liz and her then 8-year-old daughter, Kate, married Andrew and his boys who were then 12 and 10. Liz and her daughter have moved into Andrew's home. They are the "subordinate" minifamily in this new family, by virtue of their smaller number, their quieter style, and the fact that they were the physical newcomers in their new home. The couple came into therapy after a disturbingly fierce fight over television. Andrew and his two children treated television "like wallpaper." It was on all the time, and his children did their homework in front of the television. Liz, on the other hand, had rarely allowed Kate to watch television. In the Early Stages, the television came on as soon as Andrew's children walked into the house. Liz's pleas to turn the television off, particularly in front of Kate, fell on deaf ears. In the Early Stages, Liz complained to Andrew occasionally, but the conversations ended when Liz withdrew and Andrew threw up his hands. Andrew's children experienced the dilemma this way. Joe:

> Here's this stranger moving into our house, and the first thing she wants to do is tell us not to watch television. She's got this little kid who won't leave us alone, and she wants us not to watch television in front of her. I don't know why my dad lets her do this.

In the Early Stages, Liz, the outsider, had felt unheard and discounted. She and her husband had both expected her to move into a full-time stepmothering role, and she felt confused and inadequate that not only her stepchildren, but her husband did not respond to her. Her stepchildren, the insider children in the new family, felt invaded and put upon. Her husband, the insider parent, found Liz's increasing unhappiness frightening and confusing. He began to dread coming home and started working late several nights a week. Andrew's absence pulled Liz even more firmly into a full-time stepmother position, a move her stepchildren resisted quite successfully.

In the Middle Stages, Liz had begun what Andrew experienced as a "civil war." She began to speak up with more force and conviction for a workable solution. With help, in the form of better information about the kind of family territory they were traveling in, and assistance in hearing each other's very different needs and feelings, this family moved into the Action Stage on the television issue. They worked out an agreement that met the needs of all family members. They moved the television into the den. Liz's daughter, Kate, was now not allowed in the den unless she had finished her homework. She is still allowed only an hour a day of television. Two nights a week (the nights to be negotiated with each new television season) there is no television on at all in the house. This truly shared decision maintained some of the separate values of its original biological minifamilies, while carving out a new area of agreed-upon functioning.

Again, couples may move too quickly to become a parenting team, establishing a host of new rules that require children to function in entirely new territory. Some change is required early on for the stepparent (or the less dominant minifamily) to become comfortable in the new family. However, changes need to be made a few at a time, so that children are not summarily stripped of their comfortable middle ground. Furthermore, as we have said, in the Early Stages when stepparents and stepchildren remain strangers to each other, it is appropriate for discipline to be carried out through the biological parent.

At the other extreme, in some families the biological parent continues to carry full responsibility for discipline and decision making for his or her children, never shifting decision making to the couple. When the couple has a strong intimate relationship, families can sometimes function comfortably enough this way without making the transition in the parenting team. They may consult only about major decisions that affect the new couple (money, a major shift in custody arrangements). In these families, a full stepparent role may never completely emerge and stepparents and stepchildren remain somewhat distant from each other. These families can function quite comfortably as long as the structure meets the needs of all involved.

Action Steps at the Stepparent-Stepchild Boundary

In the Action Stage, just as establishing an adult couple relationship requires easing stepchildren out, creating workable stepparent-stepchild relationships involves pushing the biological parent out. In the Early Stages, when stepparent and biological parent are still comparative strangers, the stepparent needs to remain at a bit more of a distance. The stepparent enforces the biological parent's rules and standards, leaving much of the children's old middle ground in place. As stepparent and stepchild get to know each other, it becomes time for them to develop a direct relationship. Gregory Burns put it succinctly:

I think one of the most difficult things for me as a stepparent is getting to know the kids on *their* terms, not Lynn's terms. It's really important for me to have my own relationship with the kids that doesn't have anything to do with Lynn, but really has to do with our relationship!

The twin tasks at this boundary in the Action Stage involve the stepparent and stepchildren pushing toward each other with more firmness, and the biological parent letting go of responsibility and control. Beth Roberts, a biological mother:

It was hard for me to let George take over with my daughter. He'd do things I thought she wouldn't like, and I just felt so protective after the hell I put her through with the divorce. In the beginning I think it was right of me to step in between them.

But I think there came a point when I knew it was time for me to let go, and let them work it out themselves. That was tough for me, especially when they fought. I so wanted it to work between them that it was hard for me to keep my mouth shut. But Melissa helped me out. One day when she and George were fighting and I started to step in, she said, "Stay out, Mom. This is between George and me."

As Melissa's move illustrates, just as biological parents begin to participate more equally in protecting the adult couple boundary, stepchildren often begin, as Melissa did, to become allies with their stepparents in establishing a stepparent-child boundary. Likewise, stepparents are more able to give their partners a firm nudge when they forget and butt in, and biological parents are more able, as Beth was, to let go. Barbara Abramson described this exchange between her, her husband Jim, and his daughter Emmie:

I said to Emmie, "You have to clean up your mess in the kitchen before you go to bed." She was in the middle of watching a TV special the half hour before she was supposed to go to bed. I asked her if she had cleaned up her mess. She said, "No." And I said, "Well, then, you can't watch TV. You've got to clean up the kitchen."

And then Jim stepped in and got pissed at me and said that I hadn't been fair, because I wasn't clear with her about when that would happen. And

I just told him to stay out of it. Yes, that was true, I could have done it better, but I didn't want him to criticize me in the middle of something. It was good. He backed off! And Emmie and I worked it out.

In turn, as stepparents experience their couple relationships strengthening and begin to receive more reliable support from their spouses in their moves toward their stepchildren, their comfort in relating to their stepchildren increases. Christine Erickson's response to the question, "What made it more possible for you to begin to be yourself with your stepdaughters?":

Having a sense of myself in my relationship with Roger. I've gained a tremendous amount of security in our relationship. Just the solidness I feel with him leaves me freer to be with the kids.

It is important to note that not all stepparents and stepchildren are interested in moving toward each other. One child in the family may need to remain outside the family. Sometimes these children get interested in a relationship with their stepparents later, when their loyalty binds ease. Sometimes this never happens. As we saw in the story of Timothy Levi (in the Mobilization Stage), adolescents and older children may get caught between the family's need for their participation in becoming a stepfamily and the child's need to separate. Mary Whiteside (1988b), in a fascinating piece of work, describes the interaction between the child's developmental stage and the family's stage in the Stepfamily Cycle.

In families with younger children, stepparents can sometimes begin shifting to a more direct role late in the Early Stages. On the other end of the spectrum, in families with older children, or where one or more children remain unwilling to form a new relationship with a stepparent, a more outsider stance may continue to be appropriate through the Middle and Later Stages. Research is indicating that 9- to 12-year old stepdaughters in stepfather families may particularly continue to need this kind of distance (Hetherington, Arnett, & Hollier, 1986; Hetherington, 1987). Stepparents in relationships with children who do not

need or want a new adult in their lives can continue to actively
support the biological parent as described in Chapter Three
(Stage Three, "The Stepparent's Experience of the Awareness Stage") without moving directly into a disciplinary relationship with their stepchildren.

Action Steps at the Stepfamily Boundary

Creating a Stepfamily Culture

Mary Whiteside (1988a) uses Wolin and Bennett's description of three levels of family ritual to talk about the challenge
of creating a stepfamily culture. She differentiates among
daily routines of living (eating, sleeping, etc.), family traditions (such as holiday rituals), and rites of passage (weddings
and graduations).

In the Action Stage, the stepfamily begins to work out
some middle ground in each of these areas of family living,
and to find some ways to accept and live with differences
they cannot, or choose not to, resolve. Many of the fights in
the Mobilization Stage concern events on the first level—how
are we going to live together? Stepfamilies are confronted
with differences of opinion regarding everything in their
daily lives from the proper disposal of winter jackets, to the
merits of sugar versus non-sugar cereal, to the amount of
television watched. In the Early Stages, these differences may
be tolerated, or succumbed to with the dominant subsystem
determining the outcomes most of the time, while the family
grows to understand its differences. The Mobilization Stage
sees an upsurge in family members' attempts to influence
each other for change, and the Action Stage sees some resolution of these differences in which both insider and outsider
voices get heard.

A previously single stepmother used to making sandwiches out of whole wheat bread, lettuce, tomato, and "real
meat from a real being" marries a family that prefers a slice
of white bread, a slice of bologna ("fake meat" she calls it),

and another slice of white bread. She comes from a tradition where children drink milk with all their meals and a household in which there was no sugar except in an occasional dessert. She has married a family that drinks Coke and Kool-Aid all day long and with meals.

In the Early Stages, she makes white bread sandwiches and serves them with Coke, cringing internally. In the Mobilization Stage, she begins to insist that her stepdaughters have lettuce in their sandwiches and drink milk with their meals. Her husband objects that there is no way that his 10- and 15-year-old daughters can ever be convinced to eat whole wheat bread and lettuce. She and her husband have what appear to be ridiculous squabbles over the merits of white versus whole wheat bread and his refusal to back her up on this issue. In the Action Stage, the couple agrees that the girls will be taught how to make their own white bread sandwiches, but that the whole family will drink milk with meals. Coke is now allowed only for dessert and "special meals out."

In this struggle, the outsider stepparent began in the Immersion Stage by appropriately, albeit uncomfortably, supporting the majority culture. As her awareness of feeling like a "stranger in a strange land" sharpened, she began to speak up, finally taking a firmer stand in the Mobilization Stage about what she needed in order to feel like the family's daily patterns reflected her needs. As the couple engaged more vigorously over this issue, her husband, the children's biological parent (and also a white bread eater), has come to understand his wife's need for change, while advocating his children's needs for familiar routine. The stepmother has come to understand what it might mean to a 15-year-old to suddenly be asked to change her eating habits. In the Action Stage of this dilemma, the couple has incorporated the stepmother's needs for change as well as the girls' needs for some familiar routine. The girls complained about the new milk rule, but their father, who had now forged a clear agreement with his wife, supported her fully.

This family moved at a pace that aesthetically fit the whole family's needs. It might be worth noting that a more passive, less expressive stepmother and less empathic biological parent might have become mired in Immersion on this issue. A more highly mobilized and impatient stepmother and a less effective, more passive biological parent might have moved more quickly into Action together, with much less satisfying results for all concerned.

Holiday rituals provide an especially intense arena in which struggles over family values take place. In Liz Pierce's family stockings were hung on the fireplace and opened as part of the family Christmas celebration on Christmas morning. In her husband Andrew's family, stockings were hung on the children's doors. They were to be opened by children before the actual family Christmas ritual as parents had a quiet cup of coffee together.

Both Liz's and Andrew's children were very attached to their particular ritual. On the first Christmas, Andrew's children had visited their mother. Andrew, who was usually the dominant insider parent, suddenly became the outsider parent as Liz and her daughter Kate proceeded to celebrate Christmas as they always did. Andrew suffered silently through the day, feeling bereft not only of his traditions, but of his children as well. The next Christmas, Kate spent at her father's, and Liz and Andrew's positions were reversed. The third Christmas, the family spent together. Liz:

> It was awful, absolutely horrible. I don't know what we were thinking. It was our first "family" Christmas with the whole family and we were so looking forward to it. It was a disaster. Kate went up to her room crying in the middle of opening presents, and Andrew and I fought all Christmas Eve and half of Christmas Day.

By the next Christmas, the family was solidly in the Action Stage. They had attended a number of Stepfamily Association meetings, had done some successful work in family therapy and had resolved a number of issues (including the television debacle described earlier). With some solid middle ground under their belts, and greater faith that, "If we hang in there the path will emerge," Liz and Andrew talked at length about what they each needed over the holidays. They talked with their children, separately and as a whole family. After much intense discussion it was decided that the family would celebrate Christmas together several days after the actual holiday (Andrew's children would be at their mother's again on Christmas Day). "We felt we needed to have a family ritual," said Liz, "even if it meant waiting a few days."

The sticking point was the stockings. Kate wanted hers on the fireplace "because that's Christmas!" and Andrew's children wanted theirs on their doors "because we've always done it that way." Andrew's son Joe suggested that each family simply "do their own thing." The adults resisted, feeling that would divide the family too much. Finally Alex, Andrew's younger son, came up with a compromise, "Let's suppose Santa sees double!" he said. It was decided that the family would do both. The children would each have two stockings, one on the bedroom door, and one on the fireplace. The bedroom door stockings were to be opened while parents had their coffee. The fireplace stockings were to be opened with the gifts. In addition, the family added stockings for each of the adults, to be filled by all three children, and to be opened as part of the family gifts. Again, this family successfully managed to respectfully incorporate some old middle ground from each preexisting family, and with Alex's stroke of creative genius the "Santa sees double" stocking tradition became a precious part of their family fabric.

All of this planning and negotiating can feel very unfamily-like to people expecting to celebrate special occasions as they did in their first-time families. However, it is important to remember that traditions in first-time families build a year at a time. Threads are added to the fabric slowly and new pieces are woven over years of experience together. Furthermore, negotiations begin with just two adults present. Children become part of their parents' combined heritage. And they start being inducted before they have any fully formed preferences! The stepfamily brings together two strongly bonded subgroups (or a biological minifamily and a stepparent outsider) with already established traditions. Familiar rituals that worked in the past create disasters in the

new family, as Liz and Andrew discovered all too painfully.
Successful stepfamily rituals require active attention and
well-thought-out plans for integrating and respecting differences. Like the American Automobile Association (AAA),
which provides maps for travelers, local Stepfamily Associations are often extraordinarily helpful models for this kind of
strategic planning, providing pictures of the multiple paths
stepfamilies find through seemingly impossible territory.

Not all new stepfamily rituals require the effort described above. Though Christmas posed a major dilemma
for Chris Campbell and Karen Morrison, Thanksgiving was
an "unclaimed holiday." Neither family had done much with
it. "We lucked into an easy one," says Karen, stepmother to
Chris's two children and mother to their two mutual
children.

We had a very hard time at Christmas. I'm Jewish and Chris's family
celebrates Christmas and loves it. We had a lot of hard talks about that,
about what it meant to each of us, what it meant to the kids. I finally
decided I could live with it as a "pagan ritual," and we could have a tree,
even, as long as I didn't have to decorate it.

Thanksgiving was another matter, though. Both of our mothers hated to
cook. Both Chris and I love to cook. So we sat down with the kids and
figured out all our favorite foods. We found out that we *all* hated cranberry
sauce and sweet potatoes, so we decided we didn't have to have either one!

We also decided we would have a fabulous dessert, and we looked through
all our cookbooks and chose the richest, gooiest chocolate cake we could
find. Really it was gross and wonderful. And we all made it together. That
chocolate cake has now become our family chocolate cake. We make it for
all our birthday parties, and, of course, we make it every Thanksgiving.
And a few weeks ago, Chris's oldest son called me from college and asked
me for the recipe.

The above story takes this family into the Resolution
Stage with a tradition begun in the Action Stage. It is a tradition that emerged from shared middle ground Chris and
Karen brought to their marriage. It is as if they found a
"clearing," an unoccupied space in which they could build
upon their existing middle ground without having to contend with the thicker, competing, already-established middle
ground of the biological subsystems.

Drawing a "Boundary with a Hole in It"

One of the most complex set of Action steps for the stepfamily involves separating the new family from the previous one without depriving children of a relationship with their other biological parent.

The stepfamily's task is to create distance between exspouses on the adults' interpersonal issues, while developing what Mary Whiteside (1988b) calls "a repertoire of courteous and respectful patterns of co-parenting exchanges" that help children to move freely between two families. The trick is to create a "boundary with a hole in it," one that leaves open channels of communication between ex-spouses about children, but establishing distance between ex-spouses on other issues, so that the stepparent is clearly the insider in the new marriage.

In the Early Stages, the new stepcouple may yearn for the apparent safety of establishing the new stepparent and defining the new family by asking children to renounce the absent parent. Research is showing us that this fantasy can be disastrous for children (Wallerstein, 1984), who do best in a divorce if they have access to both of their parents. Connie Ahrons (1979, 1980a, 1980b) suggests that we use the term "binuclear family" to remind ourselves that children remain part of two families that must find ways to function cooperatively. She notes that although we have created norms for civil functioning in the potentially conflicted arena of in-law relationships, we remain without such norms in binuclear family relationships. Recent research highlights the importance of conflict-free, cooperative co-parenting in children's postdivorce well-being. The section on "Children" in Chapter Six (see p. 246) details some of the research which underlines the necessity of meeting this challenge well.

A number of moves draw the necessary "boundary with a hole in it." Late-night and extended friendly phone calls between ex-spouses can be replaced with a regular call-in time during the day. Discussion between ex-spouses can be focused on children, away from the intimate details of daily living, issues from the previous marriage, personal ups and downs. The goal is to establish the stepparent as the intimate insider in the marriage while maintaining open communication about children between the adults in both families.

Equally important to smooth stepfamily functioning is that the adults in the stepfamily must draw this "boundary with a hole in it" for children. Many new family rules and rituals coalesce in the Action Stage of the Stepfamily Cycle, some of which make the new family different from the old family. As Action moves are completed, the task is to articulate the new family's values, while protecting the children's relationship with their other household. This requires neutral statements such as, "In this family, you can swear but you can't watch more than two hours of television. In your mom's house, you can watch as much television as you like, but you aren't allowed to swear." "In your dad's house, you can have a Christmas tree. In your mom's house, we don't have a Christmas tree, we have Chanukkah." Children can feel supported and secure living in two different households as long as the adults in their lives do not expose them to conflict over the differences. Children's comfort may be increased if they can be supported in talking about the differences: which ones are hard for them, which ones are fun, which ones are most irritating. Adults need to listen without trying to influence children to feel differently. "That sounds like it makes you mad" is preferable to "But don't you understand that television is bad for you?"

In the Action Stage, children's and adults' needs may differ. Adults may be engaged wholeheartedly in moving forward into their new family at the same time that children need help talking about their dead or absent parent, hearing what that person was like and keeping the memory alive. Adults often believe they can speed children's movement into their new family by convincing them that it is really better than the last one. When a child says she misses her father, her mother may be tempted to say, "But your stepfather loves you," or "But your stepfather is so good to you. He's so much nicer to you than your father was." Though this mother is trying to help her daughter let go, she in fact is tightening the child's loyalty bind by implicitly asking the child to replace her father with her stepfather. Children need parents to say, "I know. What do you miss most about him?" When the message is clear that children are not being asked to abandon their missing biological parents, they can join more freely in Action Stage moves.

The task becomes more complex when the absent parent was an alcoholic or was abusive or neglectful. Children need permission to love, and to long for, their "real" parents, even while they need help understanding that parent's limitations. "Your mom was sick. She didn't know how to love you, even though she loved you very much" will support children in their new families much more securely than, "Your mother left you. I don't know why you want to keep thinking about her." "I know it hurts. Tell me about it" will help children move into their new families with more freedom and less ambivalence than "You should be so grateful that your stepmother is taking such good care of you."

"Failures"

The Action Stage involves the family in actively making moves that will give the family more common ground, and strengthen the step relationships in the family. If the work of understanding each other's very different needs and perceptions is done well, many of the decisions the adult couple comes to will work reasonably well. However, even with the best of intentions, carefully crafted agreements may prove unworkable. Though this may be disappointing, it is often because a piece of information was missing. The fact that the family has taken a wrong turn simply requires looking again at the map more carefully. The challenge is to become curious about what happened and what awareness was missing, rather than to experience the disappointment as a "failure" or a betrayal. Often a little bit of juggling can turn an apparently failed agreement into something that works very well.

The Pierce/Raskin television agreement offers an example. It worked well for a few months and then began to fall apart. Andrew's children started watching on "off" nights and, of course, Kate joined them, much to Liz's displeasure. Liz had several temper tantrums about this, to no effect. Finally one night when Andrew was away working, a conversation with her stepson revealed that the television season had shifted. A favorite program was no longer available and another one appeared on one of the "off" nights. The "To be negotiated seasonally" clause was added to the television agreement at this point.

At this time, the family also established a regular family conference to which children and adults could bring their concerns. Included in this conference was a "black box" in which requests and problems were collected. The black box almost failed when it became the repository for negative and angry comments about the family's life together. Before the family abandoned what had become "Pandora's box" as Andrew began to call it, it was suggested that each family member put something appreciative into the box before each conference. Though Andrew's children had to be pushed at first, this move transformed "The Box," as it came to be called, from a divisive frightening item into everyone's favorite part of the family conference. It began to hold statements like (from Joe) "I loved the strawberries Liz put in my lunch," and (from Liz) "Alex smiled at me this morning and it made me cry." These simple statements had a powerful impact on the family's feelings about each other, providing some badly needed glue for the family. "The Box" took a more permanent form (it had been an old black shoebox) when Alex made a beautiful wooden one for the family in his shop class and presented it on Liz and Andrew's fourth anniversary.

Action: Summary

The remarried family ends the Action Stage of the Stepfamily Cycle with a sense of accomplishment and mastery that has been missing in earlier stages. Fuller understanding of the very different needs and experiences of insiders and outsiders, adults and children, and step and biological members of the family enables the couple to make moves in which they can both invest. This shared investment gives the moves in this phase a quality of firmness and clarity. The moves of the Action Stage change the internal geometry of the family, carve out new boundaries around step relationships, and establish clearer common ground in the new family.

The family is now living in the midst of much recently completed construction. The impenetrable wall around the biological parent-child unit now has become more permeable. New bedroom walls have been built for the adult couple. Stepparent and stepchild have separate "room" to be alone together in the new house. The new family lives in a home that may have some features of the old family's house, but looks quite distinct. Big front and back doors give children easy access in and out. It is clear to an outsider that the stepparent, or the step subsystem, now lives in this home, not as guests, but as family members. By the end of the Action Stage, many details remain to be worked out—how the molding meets the wall, what the door handles will look like, where the bookcases will go, and exactly how each room will be decorated. However, much of the major construction work is completed. The uphill portion of the Stepfamily Cycle is done.

Conclusion

Stepfamilies enter the Middle Stages biologically organized and leave with many new step boundaries in place. Differences are now more openly aired and joint decision making more regularly reflects the range of insider and outsider needs.

Mobilization Stage conflicts often pit the stepparent (interested in more discipline with children, more private time for the stepcouple, and clearer limits with the ex-spouse) against the biological parent (who hopes to spare children too many new adjustments, maintain previous levels of accessibility to them, and establish a working relationship with the ex-spouse). Children who reach the Mobilization Stage gain stronger voices in areas of concern to them: resolving loyalty binds, spending time alone with biological parents, and continuing familiar family routines.

During the Action Stage, the stepcouple can more effectively serve as "architect" to redefine the new stepfamily system; stepsubsystem boundaries begin to firm up, the stepparent begins to play a more direct role in the family, and the pressure on the biological parent to be all things to all people begins to subside.

As in all stages of the Stepfamily Cycle, Middle Stage processes are not all-or-none. A family may be in Action in one domain and lingering in Immersion in another. One family member may plunge into Mobilization (often the outsider stepparent) while the other remains in Fantasy. The adult couple may have launched into the Action Stage while children remain in Immersion.

Nonetheless, as we will see in Chapter Six, different families have different styles of traversing these two stages. Aware Families experience a comparatively more quiet Mobilization Stage (many of the differences have already been explored in the more low-key, curious style of the Awareness Stage). For Immersed Families, movement into the Mobilization Stage is an accomplishment. Mobilized and Action Families begin their lives together in the Middle Stages and must travel back to complete awareness tasks before they can progress further.

Fast families take one to two years to complete the Middle Stages; average and slow families, about two to three years. Some stuck familes do not reach Mobilization; others remain mired in chronic conflict for many years. Still others cannot abandon precipitous Action, often resulting in problematic children.

Chapter 5

THE LATER STAGES: SOLIDIFYING THE STEPFAMILY

The Middle Stages are a period of hard labor in stepfamilies involving major changes in family structure and establishment of much new middle ground. In the Later Stages, most of the hard construction work has been completed. Family members now shift more easily between insider and outsider positions. Stepparents begin to feel at home and now have a well-defined, satisfying role. Biological parents no longer feel constantly torn between children and spouse. Children feel clear about their place in the family and begin to feel that the family is solid and reliable.

Members of step relationships can now work together to inhabit the new spaces they have carved out in the family.

Only at this point does a fully formed stepparent role emerge, *after* the major reorganizing work of the Middle Stages, and *after* boundaries around step subsystems have become firm enough to allow completed satisfying interaction within step relationships.

Biological parent-child relationships remain special and different in a stepfamily. But now the middle ground in step relationships is thick enough to compete successfully. Intimate, authentic interactions within step relationships continue to thicken their middle ground. New step issues continue to arise (childbearing, custody shifts, college costs, etc.) that may divide the family along the old biological lines. However, they can now be tackled within the context of solid, reliable family relationships. The family has become whole.

STAGE SIX
Contact: Intimacy and Authenticity in Step Relationships

con'tact, n. (L. *contactus*, fr. *contingere*, *-tactum*, to touch on all sides.) 1. A touching or meeting of bodies. 2. A coming or being in touch physically or mentally . . . —v.t. and i. To get into communication with . . . (*Webster*, 1971, p. 179)

As the Action Stage ends, the adult couple has defined space for itself separate from children. The biological parent has been eased out of the stepparent-stepchild relationship. Now one-to-one communication, which had been constantly interrupted by a biological "extra" in early stepfamily life, becomes possible within step relationships. In systems language, the major structural changes of the Middle Stages have shifted stepfamily structure from triadic to dyadic relationships. It is as if this new construction has given each step subsystem its own room, within which step pairs can explore their relationship without competition from the stronger middle ground of biological relationships. The subtitle for this phase of the Stepfamily Cycle might be, "Now that we're alone together, who are we, anyway?"

In gestalt language, members of step relationships can now more regularly move through the entire Gestalt Interactive Cycle together. Communication within step relationships is more often reliably satisfying, and more often has a sense of intimacy and ease and nourishment. By the end of the Contact Stage of the Stepfamily Cycle, stepparents have achieved a well-defined recognizable role for themselves, sanctioned by all family members.

The Stepcouple Becomes an Intimate Sanctuary

In the Contact Stage of the Stepfamily Cycle, the remarried couple relationship at last becomes an intimate sanctuary. Difficulties that were sources of confusion and shame in the Immersion Stage of the Stepfamily Cycle, remained painful and unarticulated in Awareness, and were struggled over in the Mobilization and Action Stages, can, in the Contact Stage, be brought to the couple relationship. Now spouses can reliably provide support and comfort to each other on step issues and they can turn to each other for help in problem solving. George Danielson, a biological father in a double family, speaks:

It used to be that when it would be time for my daughter Cindy to return to her mother at the end of the summer, my wife, Beth, and I would be on different planets. I just couldn't talk to her about it. I felt so depressed, so sad to lose my daughter all over again, and it would be as if Beth was just eager to have her go. We'd just end up fighting.

Now I can go to Beth and tell her I'm really down. And now she can tell me she's had it up to her ears and it doesn't freak me out so much. And I think now Beth misses Cindy, too. And I think I understand more how different Beth and I feel about Cindy, even though she loves her. Now it's as if we can comfort each other. I don't know what's changed. We just seem to understand each other so much better.

The members of this stepcouple still experience Cindy's leaving fundamentally differently. However, now there is a deeper understanding and acceptance of the differences.

When they appear, rather than evoking despair and betrayal and shame, they evoke empathy and caring and comfort.

Intimacy in Stepparent-Stepchild Relationships

This fuller, more intimate communication extends to step-parent-stepchild relationships as well. From in-depth interviews with stepparents (Papernow, 1980), quotes describing stepparent-stepchild conversations that had been contained in a few sentences in the Early Stages became several pages of richly detailed exchanges in the Contact Stage. Stepparents and stepchildren can now explore fully, with more ease, and without an intervening biological parent to remind everyone of how it "was" or "should be," what names they would like to call each other, what it was like when they first met, how they have each experienced the other and the family, what they want and do not want from each other.

Many stepparents can identify a turning-point one-to-one conversation that clearly marked a new era of greater authenticity and clarity in their relationships with their stepchildren. Gene Davis describes such a moment with his stepdaughter Wendy:

> Wendy and I had this conversation, and it felt like some kind of turning point in terms of our relationship. I was saying to her that sometimes it was hard for me to know how to refer to her when I was talking to other people. I wanted to say "my daughter" but it just sort of caught before it came out. I told her there were times when I felt very much like she was my daughter. And she could talk about it some, too, and we talked about what to say that describes our relationship.

Gregory Burns, an expressive, physically large stepfather, describes a simple, and touching exchange with his tiny-for-her-age, and much quieter stepdaughter, Judy:

> We talked about how I'm three times as big as she is. We played with it and figured it out on a calculator. And she said it scares the hell out of her when I'm angry. In a kind of triple way: 200 pounds of anger storming through the hallway! So I told her I would try to put more words on my feelings.

Becoming an "Intimate Outsider"

It is especially interesting that, as the stepparent moves into a more intimate role in the family, the outsider position that had been so painful in earlier phases now gives him or her a unique place in the family, as an intimate who is close enough to children to share very personal things, but yet with more distance than a biological parent could summon. A stepparent, it seems, can be the ideal person for children to talk with about sex, drugs, their feelings about the divorce, and a host of other things too "hot" for biological parents. It was Barbara Abramson's emerging role as an intimate outsider that made the following exchange with her stepdaughter Emmie possible:

One night when Emmie and I were alone together, she started to sob and sob and talk to me about the divorce. "I hate this. I hate them living apart. I like you, but why can't they get back together? And my mommy and daddy fought, and they got divorced, and you and daddy fight, and you're going to get divorced, too. If my daddy ever tries to get married again, I'm gonna stand up in the ceremony and say, 'This man shouldn't be married.'

"And I don't see my mommy very often. So when we're together, I can't complain like Jenny and Julie [her friends] do about their divorce." I told her, "You're a little girl, and it's your mommy who's supposed to take care of you. You can tell her how you're feeling." Emmie finds the words "supposed to" comforting.

And she said, "But I want to make my mommy happy 'cause if I don't, she won't want to see me." That broke my heart. Because I know there's a certain amount of truth in that.

And then I remembered that children of divorce need information. So I told her again why her parents got divorced. She kept switching the subject, but I kept coming back. I said, "They were different in what they wanted," and I told her how they were different.

And it worked. She started to get calmer. And she could relate to how kids have differences. Then I read her a story, and she said, "Can I sleep with you in the big bed tonight?" Jim [Emmie's dad] was away. And I said, "Of course." And I took her with me into the big bed. And she said, "I love you." And I said, "I love you, too."

Barbara thought a moment, and then she said:

> You know, there's something incredible between a stepparent and a child
> about that sadness. Who else can she tell? It's a function that I have, that
> no one else can do. Who else can help the child tell her parents about all
> this?

Step Intimacy in the Presence of the Biological "Other"

The above exchange took place between Barbara and Emmie
when Jim was away. Like Barbara, many stepparents report
that their initial intimate contacts with their stepchildren happen when the biological parent is away (and there is no competing middle ground). However, in the Contact Stage of the
Stepfamily Cycle, intimacy and authenticity in the stepparent-stepchild relationship can be sustained in the *presence* of
the biological parent. And the adult couple relationship can
function in the presence of the stepchild. The following
quote from Gregory captures this quality. This interchange
took place in the context of this family's first long vacation
together, a camping trip across the United States with Gregory Burns, his wife, Lynn Lippman, and her two children,
Jason and Judy. Notice that unlike earlier quotes, this quote
has a beginning, a middle, and an end. This quote is also
much longer than earlier ones due to the fact that in the
Contact Stage, the family is much more likely to stay engaged
until members are finished and satisfied.

> The whole thing had a quality of crescendo and denouement, like a tragic
> opera for a while that got resolved. It was the first time that we had ever
> done a trip for any length of time together, the four of us. On the train,
> the kids were a lot of fun to be with. And then Jason started this fundamen-
> tal kind of "no" position to everything.

> "Let's go see the Air Force base." "No." "Let's walk across the street." "No."
> I'd ask him what he wanted to do, and help him figure out how he could
> do it. But there was always this kind of no, no, no, no. And he kept talking
> about Jack, his dad. I think it was his way of saying, "I don't want to be
> on this trip. I want to be back in Boston with my father. Being on this trip
> really scares me."

By the time we got to a campground near Denver, I was filled up with no's. And Jason said no one more time, and I just grabbed him.

I started saying all sorts of delightfully irrational things, like if he didn't do what we had planned, I was going to dunk his head in the pond until he did. If he was going to act like such a wet head, I was going to make sure he had a wet head he'd never forget.

And he was terrified. He was so scared. And that was what stopped me, I could see the terror in his face. And I realized that I was nearly verging on being out of control with my anger. And I stopped.

And then Lynn started defending the kids' right to say no. And I just lit into her. I had just had it! And I knew the struggle was about the fact that I had planned the entire trip. But I also heard that the kids were having a hard time, and I was willing to change. But what was still coming through was the complaining, not that I was listening to them. And a lot of stuff about, "I want to be back with Daddy."

So Lynn and I went to the car we'd rented, and rolled up the window and I really had it out with her in the car, that I had just had it with not hearing much back from the kids and with hearing about Jack. And I don't even mind hearing about him, but there was sort of a coalition going on with Lynn and the kids. They would turn to her with the goodies, and she was reinforcing them in some way that it was OK to give that stuff to her, and Jack could be talked about in the background, but Gregory wouldn't be acknowledged.

At the pitch of it, I was literally ready to pack my bags and fly back to Boston—that if it didn't change within three days, I would be back on the plane.

After the pitch passed, I said to Lynn, "I need to be silent." That's a real change for me. I used to go silent and not say anything. So it would take on ominous tones for Lynn. Now I tell her, "I'm going to be silent so I can figure out what I need to do from here," so she knows what's happening.

I got silent. And five minutes after I got silent, I was in tears. Because getting silent got me in touch with just the profound amount of hurt that was down behind my rage. The rage was important to keep me motivated and active. But it was also the fuel. And down inside the fuel were the moving parts, and the moving parts were the sadness. You know, just about feeling rejected. That I was always struggling to get my place in this group, but that there was very little acceptance.

I was really crying for a while. And then Lynn asked me if I were willing to share that with the kids. And I think that I needed some help from her to do that. That was really nice. It was a beautiful piece of support from her.

And I got out of the car and I went to the kids and told them that I really needed to talk to them. I can feel the tears right now. It's amazing. And we went over to the side of the stream and sat down and talked for another hour. And I just told them everything that was going on inside of me, about how hurt I felt, and how hard it was to make a relationship with them, and how hearing about Jack gets to be infuriating and frustrating when I got very little feedback from them.

And it really changed our relationship, my being that vulnerable with them. And I was in tears most of the time we were talking. And Jason burst into tears, and Judy burst into tears. We really needed to cry to relieve all the tension that had been floating around.

Jason spilled out a lot of confused feelings he had about me and saying he wanted to be close to me and didn't know whether that was right, and feeling torn between me and Jack. It was an incredibly touching conversation.

So we talked some more and cried some more. And we laughed and then we spent another hour playing in the pond. The pond was like a baptism after the mess we'd been through. And we went over and started walking up and down the stream and playing with each other. And the stream was very healing, the moving water.

This story speaks eloquently of the depth of contact that had become possible in Gregory's family. In the Immersion Stage of the Stepfamily Cycle, Gregory would have withdrawn from the family, leaving Lynn feeling betrayed and all members of the family alone and confused. In the Awareness Stage, Gregory might have named the patterns of exclusion and biological primacy but not sustained himself with enough force to be heard, and Lynn would have been unable or unwilling to hang in with him. Had this episode happened in the Mobilization Stage of the Stepfamily Cycle, Gregory and Jason (and Gregory and Lynn) might have fought openly, but without resolution or understanding. (And, if the communication had stopped there, Gregory would easily have fit the description of a cruel stepfather.) In the Action Stage, the family, particularly Gregory and Lynn, might have come to some decisions about what to do but without the intimate exchange that followed.

The above exchange happened after Gregory and Lynn had much of the Action Stage of the Stepfamily Cycle behind them. They had established enough middle ground (enough clearly marked agreed upon paths for normal functioning), had developed enough faith in each other, and had deepened their understanding of each other's very different positions in the family to help bring the anger and hurt in their family to completion. Gregory was able to push Lynn out of his angry contact with his stepchildren. Together the adult couple retreated from the kids to fight, with Gregory helping Lynn to accept his silence, and Lynn moving to help Gregory share his sadness with her kids. Lynn was then able to stand aside as Gregory and her kids shared their hurt and confusion with each other, leaving them space to come to a sense of completion and resolution. Note the length of this quote, the intimate, authentic, and completed contact in all of the step relationships in the family.

The Emergence of a Stepparent Role

The specific stepparent roles that emerge in the Contact Stage are as varied as the people who inhabit them. Often the very differences that had been so threatening to the family in the Early Stages now serve as the foundation for the roles stepparents occupy, as the stepparent's clearer definition of self joins forces with the biological unit's willingness to acknowledge what is lacking and what is needed in their particular set of family skills, rituals, relational styles, and history. A very expressive woman who entered a highly structured task-oriented family describes her role as "the one who talks to them about feelings. . . . I am the emotional bringer-outer."

A meticulous, well-dressed stepmother whose mother's precious lace tablecloths were a source of derision to the hang-loose liberal family she entered has become "the one who helps them put some order in their lives." After the Action Stage created more support for her parental style, she solidified a role for herself, teaching her stepdaughter the pleasure of having a clean room and taking care of her clothing.

In a double family, Andrew Raskin and his sons had been "the ones who do it right" (sit-down dinners at the table every night, music lessons for all of the children, vacations at music or art camp). With the exception of strict rules about television Liz Pierce and her daughter, Kate, had been "the ones who do it easy" (dinner on the run, standing up, if at all; vacations on the beach). Andrew's minifamily was the more dominant of the two: He and his children had a louder, more aggressive style, there were more of them, and Liz and Kate had moved into Andrew's home. After six years of marriage, from the safety and intimacy of the Contact Stage, this couple looks back over the struggle and describes the unique roles they now inhabit in their family:

L.: Really it was awful. And in a fight over "right" versus "easy," you can imagine who won most of the time! They did!

A.: Are you kidding? You guys could win by sandbagging any old time. [Both laugh.]

L.: But what's wonderful is I feel like we've really learned from each other. I feel like Andrew has really shown Kate something about discipline, and staying with something. Can you believe, my daughter is taking cello lessons? The cello was Andrew's instrument, and he helps her a lot with her playing. Oh, they fight a lot, but I stay out of it now. It's between them. He's really become the one who's teaching her to push herself.

A.: And Liz has really showed us how to hang loose. She's become the one who's helped my kids to be a little easier on themselves, to do an average job every now and then. My son Joe took a year off to work on a boat before going to college. I think . . . I *know* . . . Liz was really influential in helping him decide to do that. He was burnt out. And that was a case where *I* stayed out.

L.: Yeah, you stayed out after you and I had a huge fight and I *kicked* you out. You kept offering your opinions and then he'd clam up!

A.: Oh God, the fights. And we still fight. But I don't get scared any more. I know we'll find a way.

It is important to note that not all workable stepparent-stepchild relationships, even in the same family, are equally close. One child may fully engage with a stepparent, and another may remain more diffident. By the Contact Stage, there is acceptance throughout the family that some kids are more "in" than others, some are more involved in the new family's life than others. The "outside" children may have less need for another adult in their lives, or may be caught in a more intense loyalty bind that requires that some distance be kept from the stepparent.

Qualities of a Workable Stepparent Role

Although the content of the role stepparents inhabit varies, there are some qualities that I believe successful stepparent roles have in common (adapted from Papernow, 1988):

1. **The workable stepparent role does not usurp or compete with the parental role of the same-sex parent.** Children need acknowledgment of their special relationship to their absent parent, whether that person is dead or alive, loving or abusive. Pressure to abandon, to demean, or to ignore the existence of a parent places the child in an intense loyalty bind that will inhibit his or her ability to form a relationship with the new stepparent.

2. **The role requires the sanction and active support of the biological parent spouse.** Developing a workable stepparent role is not the individual task of the stepparent, but a task for the entire family. Viable stepparenting is not simply an extra activity that takes place in an unused corner of the family.

3. **The very differences that were so threatening in earlier stages seem to become the foundation for the stepparent's special role in the family.** The stepparent's role is an expression of the individual style and strengths that the stepparent brings to the new family, and it often complements the style and functions available within the already existing biological unit.

4. **The role must observe an intergenerational boundary.** The "friend" role suggested by Draughn (1975) and Waldron and Whittington (1979) may be useful for earlier stages, but it is not usually sufficient for the later stages and healthy stepfamily restructuring. "Teacher" and "role model" seem to be roles ideally suited to provide a conduit for the stepparent to express his or her special qualities, while maintaining an intergenerational boundary and remaining noncompetitive with the absent biological parent.

5. **The role must be "mutually suitable."** This is a term borrowed from Margaret Crosbie-Burnett (1984), who found that it was not the quality of nurturance or discipline, but the "mutual suitability" of the stepfather-stepchild dyad that predicted marital happiness in a stepfamily. I use Crosbie-Burnett's term to mean that the amount of closeness and distance, the content of the role, the amount of discipline and nurturance given by the stepparent, must be "mutually suitable" for stepparent and stepchild, as well as for both of the adults in the family.

6. **The mature stepparent role often places the stepparent in an "intimate outsider" position with stepchildren**. In even the most intimate stepparent-stepchild relationship, the ongoing presence of another same-sex biological parent (dead or alive) leaves stepparents in a somewhat more distant position with their stepchildren than biological parents usually hold.

In the later developmental stages, as the stepparent role takes shape, this step-removed, yet intimate position enables stepparents to become a very special kind of resource to their stepchildren. Stepparents in the Later Stages often have more emotional distance than biological parents, making them much less likely to overreact on sensitive subjects like sex, "the divorce," career choices, drug use, and struggles to separate from parents. Stepparents in the Later Stages know their stepchildren well, and are often involved enough with them to be a safe adult for sharing very personal things. Thus the stepparent becomes the perfect adult to turn to for support and advice on potentially highly charged subjects. This intimate outsider part of the stepparent role begins to form in the Contact Stage and emerges fully in the Resolution Stage of the Stepfamily Cycle. It is one of the most gratifying rewards of forging a stepparent role.

What Stepfamilies Are Like in the Contact Stage

Family process in the Contact Stage of the Stepfamily Cycle *looks* different. In the Early Stages of the Stepfamily Cycle, differences between the outsiders and insiders in the family, and the step and biological experience of the family, are felt but often not discussed openly or fully. In the Immersion Stage, they are felt, but often not named or understood. In the Awareness Stage of the Stepfamily Cycle, individual family members may become clearer, but often do not have enough grounding to express themselves fully or to sustain the interaction if there is conflict or disagreement. In the Mobilization Stage, differences move out into the open. Often, however, the couple is engaging each other with more energy and commitment, but without understanding or empathy. In the Action Stage of the Stepfamily Cycle, the band of awareness between the couple on the step versus biological, and insider versus outsider, perspective of the family has been widened enough so that the couple can find some solutions that meet the complex sets of needs family members bring to stepfamily life. It is as if the couple can now travel back to awareness, but this time together. This shared awareness in itself adds "glue" to the family. Members of step pairs are increasingly able to come to agreement about how they will work together in the new family. However, some differences remain. As understanding deepens, remaining differences become less charged and anxiety-provoking.

In the Contact Stage of the Stepfamily Cycle, members of step relationships begin to interact with more ease and grace. They stay engaged longer when a difference emerges. There are many reasons for this: some things have been decided, some new middle ground established, finally enabling the family to function without effort in some areas in a way that is satisfying to most family members. As anxiety recedes and hope rises, each new experience of difference is less threatening to the marriage or to the family. Equally important, the firmer boundaries established in the Action Stage protect members of step relationships from interruption, so that conversations are more likely to have a beginning, a middle, and an end rather than coming to an abrupt halt when a third person barges in.

To further understand how stepfamily interaction has changed in the Contact Stage, we return to the model of healthy process introduced in Chapter Two, the Gestalt Interactive Cycle. In the earlier stages when step issues emerged, the thicker biological ground prevailed. Conversation about differences in step relationships often collapsed in confusion or blame. In the Middle Stages, they engaged with more force and vigor. In the Action Stage, interactive cycles in step relationships begin to be completed more often, but there is the sense of hard work and effort.

In the Contact Stage, the whole process requires less effort. When step issues emerge, step pairs move more easily into the awareness phase of the Interactive Cycle, sharing their very different perspectives with less blame and more empathy, and more curiosity, deepening their understanding of each other. This fuller awareness phase of the Interactive Cycle gives members of step relationships enough data about each other's needs and feelings to generate ideas more easily that might bring together their diverse interests (a lively *energy/action* phase of the Interactive Cycle). A fully shared notion of what to do (*contact*) emerges more often, with more ease. Good experiences actually begin to add up enough so that they can be felt palpably. Family members can more often applaud each other's efforts, and failed ideas can more often be treated as learning experiences (good *resolution*). Families in the Contact Stage of the Stepfamily Cycle also seem to do the *withdrawal* stage of the Interactive Cycle with more frequency and fullness, perhaps because it is easier to stop and rest after a satisfying meal than it is after an unsatisfying meal.

The Stepparent Role: Why Now?

It is no coincidence that the ability to more regularly come to resolution within step relationships corresponds with the emergence of a viable stepparent role in the Contact Stage of the Stepfamily Cycle. The stepparent role remains undefined in our culture (Cherlin's [1981] "incomplete institutionalization"). Unlike the role of grandparent, parent, aunt, or uncle, there are few already-established paths within our culture that the family can take to create a workable stepparent-stepchild relationship. A path has to be invented. And, to use Crosbie-Burnett's term again, it has to be "mutually suitable" to the particular family in which it must function.

Continuing to use the language of the Gestalt Interactive Cycle, to invent a set of roles that really works for two or more people requires completed interactive cycles: a full *awareness* phase (deep understanding of what matters to each member of the system), a lively *energy/action* phase (engaging with each other to work out differences and generate solutions that meet as many needs as possible), *contact* (experiencing the connection of really coming together), and *resolution* (learning over and over from experience).

In the Early Stages of stepfamily living, this kind of completed engagement is thwarted. The stronger middle ground of biological relationship takes over step interactions, determining the content and tone, and often drawing attention to the biological parent-child pair, away from step relationships. Further movement in step relationships is halted by the resulting narrow awareness of each other's experience. Efforts to widen awareness may in themselves create panic and anxiety, particularly in a family firmly attached to fantasies of functioning like a biological family. In the Action Stage of the Stepfamily Cycle, the family, often led by an outsider stepparent with a yearning to move into an insider position, begins to draw firmer boundaries around step subsystems. Now step relationships begin to be protected from intrusion and competition from the stronger middle ground in biological subsystems. This protection enables the members of step relationships to experience and explore their existing middle ground. And because they can now complete interactive cycles, they can over time create new middle ground. It is through thickening this existing and new middle ground that the stepparent role emerges.

Contact: Summary

The stepfamily leaves the Contact Stage with the insider/outsider relationships in the family markedly shifted. The stepparent has become a firm insider in the adult couple relationship, and has begun to forge a more intimate, authentic relationship with at least some of his or her stepchildren. The biological parent is relieved of the most painful aspects of the insider position and can now step aside into the outsider position more often as stepparent and stepchild(ren) begin to engage more fully with each other. The family at last has its honeymoon. The fact that honeymoons have to be earned in stepfamilies makes this period all the more precious.

STAGE SEVEN
Resolution: Holding On and Letting Go

In the Resolution Stage of the Stepfamily Cycle, the newly won satisfaction and ease of the Contact Stage become a matter of course. Step relationships begin to feel solid and reliable, no longer requiring the constant attention of the Early and Middle Stages. Paths to cycle completion that were hacked out with great effort in the Middle Stages are now well-traveled highways. Norms have been established, a history has begun to be created. Biological parent-child relationships remain special and different, but the family has a comfortable middle ground, which gains thickness in family interactions.

In response to the question, "So what is resolved now in your stepfamily, and what still feels unsettled?" stepfamily members in earlier stages of the Stepfamily Cycle will answer immediately, "Nothing," or they will name one or two issues on which they have come to agreement. Stepfamilies in the Resolution Stage reply with conviction that a great deal has been resolved, and can go on to describe the many ways in which their family life now feels normal, reliable, and predictable. Bill Hobbes:

I can feel that we've moved. Not easily, because it's been a pain in the ass. But I feel clear that our family works. That is resolved. It's been proved over the years that we could do it, and we're doing it. We're happy for the most part. There's a lot of love. You can feel that the family is working.

Issues that were nagging sources of discomfort in the Early Stages and the subjects of intense discussion in the Middle Stages now require little attention. The family now knows how "we" celebrate holidays, handle meals, and deal with discipline. And the "we" is now the stepfamily, not the biological subunit. The new stepfamily's emerging middle ground that was carved out in the Action Stage and had just begun to feel comfortable in the Contact Stage is now a matter of course. New step issues, such as managing college costs, custody shifts, and new babies, may split the family along old biological lines occasionally. However, these recurring gaps open in the context of a reliable committed family life, and no longer threaten to rock the family's foundation. Not surprisingly, when divorce occurs in the Resolution Stage of the Stepfamily Cycle, it is rarely over step issues, and stepparents and their stepchildren often maintain their relationships with each other.

The literature on stepfamily living is full of admonitions to "hang in there and things will work out." However, the literature provides little detail about just *how* things will work out, and few pictures of what a "worked out" stepfamily looks like! Stepfamilies in the Resolution Stage provide an answer to this important question in remarriage research: How does the mature stepfamily system function, and what does the mature stepparent role look like and feel like?

Stepparenting in the Resolution Stage

The Intimate Outsider Role

Bill Hobbes describes the sense of durability he has come to feel in his relationship with his stepdaughter, Patsy:

Deep down I know that Patsy and I have a very special connection. That can't be threatened by anything. And I know that it is a lifetime connection. And there is a real bottom line of security where I know I've already made a big difference to her, and I know she's made a big difference to me. And I anticipate that will keep growing. And *that* in the long run is going to be what counts.

Gene Davis's stepdaughter, Wendy, is now 10.

I think that in the last year or two my stepdaughter's understanding of the relationship has matured, solidified. She makes more references to "my parents," meaning her mother and me. She's more comfortable when somebody who doesn't know us very well slips and refers to me as her father. It just sort of rolls off her now.

She very clearly knows that she has a father, and a mother, and that each of them happens to be married to another new person. There's been a gradual process for her in sorting who are all these people in her life, including her step grandparents, stepcousins, this, that, and the other—the network of people she has is enormous. She has come to terms with things.

Though not all stepparent-stepchild relationships are equal, for many, the intimate outsider role that had begun to take shape in the Contact Stage becomes fully realized and stepparents finally get to reap the rewards of their efforts. "I'm like a very special adult friend to my stepdaughter," says

Cecelia Johnston of her relationship with her stepdaughter, Mary:

Mary calls me her "motherly friend." Sometimes I think of myself as her mentor. I'm the one [pointing to her chest] who helped her think about going to college. I'm the one who helped her decide she could be an architect.

She confides deeply in me, and it is such an honor and a pleasure to be so intimately involved in guiding her life, and yet to be seen as someone with enough distance that she can trust me not to take what she says personally. It is worth *all* the struggle to have this relationship with her.

Though the particular content of the intimate outsider role will vary, depending on the needs of the stepparent and child in the relationship, the quality Cecelia describes of standing in an intimate, and yet somewhat outside, adult mentoring, or confidante role is the special opportunity stepfamily life provides to many (though not all) stepparents and their stepchildren. Like the parent of a 2-year-old who knows that 3-year-olds are a lot of fun, stepfamily members mired in the early phases of the Stepfamily Cycle could be fortified by the knowledge that this lies ahead for them.

Stepchildren, too, feel the special benefits of having extra adults in this intimate outsider role. Marty Levinson is a teenager who has been in a split-custody family (a week in each household) for many years. Both his parents are remarried, and he is openly appreciative of the extra resources his stepparents have brought to his life. Listening to him, one gets the sense that his experience with his stepmother makes him more hopeful about his much newer relationship with his stepfather:

My mom is a psychologist and my dad is a professor. My stepmother is a businessperson. She's really different from my mom and dad. I can go to her for things they just don't have a clue about. And my stepdad is an artist. I don't know him as well because that's a newer marriage. But I can see there might be lots to learn from him, too.

Achieving "Mutual Suitability": Not All Relationships Are Equal

The Johnston family, described extensively in Case Three, Chapter Six, illustrates another quality of the mature stepfamily system: full acceptance of the fact that not all stepparent-stepchild relationships are equal. When Cecelia and Richard married eight years ago, they brought together his two teen-agers from his previous marriage, Mary and Jon, and Cecelia's 3-year-old son, Corin. Corin's father lived far away and expressed little interest in him, and Corin seemed eager and available for a relationship with his stepfather. Corin and Richard became close within the first couple of years.

Cecelia's intimate outsider relationship with Richard's daughter, Mary, developed more slowly over the eight years the family has been together. Jon, who was close to his mother throughout the divorce, remains very distant from the new family, particularly from Cecelia. Even after eight years, when Cecelia answers a telephone call from Jon, he asks immediately for his father. The difference in the Resolution Stage is that Cecelia no longer feels hurt and outraged by this. She simply says hello to Jon, and hands the phone to her husband.

In the Resolution Stage, Cecelia has fully relinquished some of her fantasies. She experiences her family as an insider now and that transforms her experience not only of her stepson's need for distance from her, but her stepdaughter's ongoing closer attachment to her father:

I feel so good about us that I have more empathy for the kids. Now I don't get threatened when Mary runs in the door and screams, "*Daddy!*" and throws her arms around him without even saying hello to me. Before I was nobody and he was everything. Now I know I have a role with my stepchildren.

Of her stepson's distance, she now says, "If I hold my nut out long enough he'll come and nibble."

The Couple as a Solid Team:
Resolution in the Adult Couple Relationship

One of the most salient features of the Resolution Stage of the Stepfamily Cycle is the experience of safety, solidity, and nourishment in the adult couple relationship. The chasm of understanding created by the step versus biological experience of the family has now been substantially crossed. Members of the couple may still experience events in the family very differently. However, biological parent and stepparent have now developed a much deeper understanding of each other's perceptions and feelings. Step issues still occasionally divide the couple experientially, but acceptance of these differences has replaced the silent disconnection and anxious blaming of the Early Stages. And cooperative problem solving has largely replaced the panicked polarization of the Middle Stages. Much middle ground has now been established, so that the couple not only has many areas of easy, automatic functioning on step issues, but can turn to each other for support and comfort and intimacy, even in areas where they experience the family differently. The couple relationship is now the "sanctuary" Minuchin (1974) describes.

Charlie and Jessica Turner are members of a double family with a total of three children between them. Charlie's son, Wes, remains somewhat outside the family.

It used to be that when my son Wes would push Jessica away, she would get really upset, and I would feel so disappointed that they couldn't get it together. And I have to admit I was critical of her for not hanging in there and making it work. I couldn't understand why she couldn't just "be the grown-up" and make it work. I wanted this nice family, you know, and it wasn't working out that way. She finally got me to understand what it was like for her, and that was very important.

But it's also been very nice for me that she can give him his space now. Because now I don't feel so torn. Wes doesn't seem ready to get close to Jessica. I think he knows his mother would freak out, and he just can't do it. Jessica understands that now, and understands that Wes and I have a relationship that, for now, and maybe forever, excludes her. It's painful sometimes, and I feel lonely for Jessica to be with me and Wes sometimes. But I understand that that's how it is.

But for a while there I thought I was going to lose my relationship with
either my son or my wife! Now I feel I can have both. Wes and I do things
alone together. He rarely comes to stay here with us. He and I may go on
a trip together. We talk on the phone regularly, and I visit him at college
sometimes when I'm in New York on a business trip. It's worked out well.

It's not the picture of "family" I had when I married Jessica. But it's how
our family really is, and I can accept that now. It actually works real well.

As this quote illustrates, as stepparents become insiders in
the adult couple relationship and in some of their stepparent-
child relationships, biological parents are freed at last from
most of the painful components of their insider role. Also
implicit in this quote is the final resolution of Charlie's fantasies about his new family.

Ongoing Realities

Few families feel, even in the Resolution Stage, that all step
issues or differences have been resolved. Christine Erickson,
a stepmother, married to Roger for seven years, talks about
what another stepparent calls the ongoing "biological pulls"
in her family:

I imagine Roger and I will continue to have disagreements about discipline.
I still have times when I will watch him get sucked in by his girls, and I
get pissed as hell. I say, "Are you going to get suckered into *that*?" I can't
believe how he gives in sometimes when they goo-goo eye at him for
something!

Even in the Resolution Stage of the Stepfamily Cycle, biological ties remain more intense than step ties. In most cases,
this, too, remains very much in the background, a normal
part of everyday living. Occasionally issues of inclusion and
exclusion reappear, temporarily fracturing the couple and
dividing the family again along biological lines. However,
these divisions rarely threaten the couple's sense of well-being for long periods of time. Another stepparent, Gregory
Burns bemoans the fact that the biological alliance between
his wife, Lynn, and her children reappears at stressful times
in the family:

My individual relationships with the kids are getting real good, and different than they have ever been. That all feels pretty solid now.

But there is still some sequence of events that happens between Lynn and myself when she's anxious. She does something to block me away from the kids; or doesn't include me in decision making. It's still kind of an assumption on the biological parent's part that has to be worked on over and over again, that somehow they make the final decisions on the kids and don't have to check it out with the stepparent.

So we go over it and over it and over it, how I don't want that to happen. I sort of feel like I'm with an alcoholic who goes out and drinks again and then says they won't ever do it again, they're sorry.

The difference in the Resolution Stage is this statement reaffirming his faith in his relationship with Lynn:

And the thing that makes it work, obviously, is that Lynn and I are willing to work on it. And we usually do.

Not only do old issues remain, but new ones emerge as the family continues to evolve on other developmental tracks. Conflict over financial arrangements between the two families, which may have been dormant for years, may resurface as a child enters college. Children, as they reach adolescence, may opt to shift from one parent's residential custody to the other. Sometimes the latter is accomplished peacefully. However, a child in a loyalty bind may get into trouble as a means of forcing the parent to whom he or she feels bound into the position of having to kick the child out.

Babies?

Childbearing may become a particularly poignant issue at this stage for couples who have not yet resolved it. For single stepparents who do not yet have children of the current marriage, the wish for a child that had been expressed as "a possibility" in earlier stages may become an intense desire in the Resolution Stage. In these couples, the biological parent and the single stepparent are in different "generations" with regard to childbearing, even if they are the same age. A single stepparent who has delayed childbearing for career development, or a difficult first marriage, or previous lack of interest in parenting may find himself or herself crying during diaper advertisements. At the same time, his or her partner may be looking forward to celebrating being done with the work of childbearing. Lynn Lippmann, a remarried mother and Gregory's wife:

I love my children. I've loved being a parent. But it's hard work, and I really don't want to do it again. I started having kids when I was 20 years old. I've never had a life for myself. I want this part of my life for me, for my needs, for intimate time with my new partner, for my career. And for maybe reading a novel, beginning to end without being interrupted so many times I can't remember the storyline.

Gregory, a previously married but childless stepparent:

I never wanted kids before. Maybe I just wasn't grown up enough. I don't know. And I was busy with other things—going to school, then working, then changing careers. I just never thought about it much. And now, it's incredible.

Maybe it's partly seeing what my relationships with my stepchildren can be. They are wonderful. And yet there's a certain something that just can't be there. A certain intensity, a certain holding on. Because I'm always having to move over and make room for another parent.

I want my own. I want a child I can fall in love with, without making space for another father outside our family. And a child I can be furious with without worrying about rupturing the relationship. I can see that Lynn has something with her kids that I can't ever have as a stepparent. I want it for myself.

However, even on issues as painful as differences over childbearing, couples in the Resolution Stage can experience each other as supportive and caring, and can place their differences in the larger context of a reliable, committed relationship. Rachel Sax, who desperately wanted a child, is married to Ira, who firmly does not want more children:

What has been resolved is that Ira and I are committed to each other. And that the kids are not going to break us up, and this thing about having another kid is not going to break us up. We are going to work on this marriage, which sometimes we both wondered about in the beginning. That we are committed to each other as a couple is resolved.

Stepcouples in the Resolution Stage of the Stepfamily Cycle not only have a sense of their relationship as reliable and nourishing, but they often feel that the hard work of the Early and Middle Stages has given them a special vitality and aliveness they might otherwise not have developed. Richard and Cecelia Johnston:

R.: Our relationship is the stronger for it. We were forced to confront a lot of issues real early or kill each other!

C.: And it's not like either of us were good at it! Neither of us fought in our first marriages. It is a gift from my stepchildren that I had to learn to fight.

Letting Go

Normalizing the "Boundary with a Hole in It"

By this stage, stepfamilies have found many ways to normalize the challenges of living in a family that has a "boundary with a hole in it." Differences between the two families are now normal parts of everyday life. Transition times, when children are shifting families, may remain somewhat stressful, but the patterns are predictable and routines for coming and going have been established:

Now we *always* go to McDonald's on the way home from picking up my daughter at the airport. I suppose it's like stopping on neutral ground before going home.

A family with shared custody, a week in each family, allows no visitors for the first few hours after the children arrive on Sundays. Some have earlier or later bedtimes. Where the stress remains, it is more predictable. Bill Hobbes marks the changes over time in how he and his wife, Paula, have handled transition times in their family:

Well, I'll tell you. At first we used to get drawn into it every single time! We'd feel frustrated and impotent and start bonking each other over the head. You could always tell this particular trip was going down by the real level of stupidity!

Now we get into a fight for about an hour. And then we get through it. We still tend to fight. But I think we understand it better. We can catch it and support each other.

Even dealings with difficult ex-spouses can be normalized. Karen Morrison, stepparent to Chris's two teenagers:

Chris's kids used to live most of the year with their mother in Wyoming. We would make plans for Christmas, buy presents, rearrange the house so there would be room for his kids and mine, buy tickets to a special show. And then two days before Chris's kids were supposed to come, she'd call up and tell us she'd decided not to send them. That used to drive me absolutely crazy. It would ruin the holidays, and I'd be a basket case for weeks.

Now we just make two sets of plans. One if they come and another for if they don't. Or vice versa—she'll say she's not going to send them, and then a day before Christmas, we have two extra kids on our doorstep. So now we also make plans in case she suddenly decides she'd like to get rid of them for a couple of weeks. It actually works. I don't get so bent out of shape anymore. It's just a normal part of how we operate around here! We call it the "none if by land and two if by sea" plan. And the kids know it, too! We actually took bets last time!

In the Immersion Stage, Karen remembers feeling, "What's wrong with me that I can't handle this?" In the Awareness Stage, she remembers "being silently angry for weeks. I knew how I was feeling but I couldn't get Chris interested." In the Action Stage, after much discussion, they decided on the "none if . . . two if . . . " plan. In the Contact Stage, "I began to relax a little, and we actually comforted each other instead of fighting and withdrawing when she pulled her usual switch." In the Resolution Stage, Karen accepts the reality, plans for it, and jokes about it. Most important, "none if by land and two if by sea" has become background, now, not foreground. It is the backdrop of her experience, not a major event that grabs her attention and requires her energy. Christine Erickson tries to capture the feeling she now has of facing the reality squarely and with equanimity:

It feels much more like acceptance than resignation. It's a much more powerful position about not being able to change it.

And, last but not least, as is clear in some of the above quotes, many stepfamilies in the Resolution Stage seem to have developed an abundant sense of humor about the foibles and dilemmas of remarried family life. Rachel Sax:

I have this fantasy that if I were pregnant, I would really like to call up my husband's ex-wife and say, "Now look. Really, I've fed your kids, and clothed them. I've tutored them. I take your son on a vacation with me every year, just the two of us. Now I'm having a kid, and I want to know how often you're going to see him. I mean it's only fair!

Grieving What Cannot Be

The Resolution Stage is also a time of grieving, of facing what cannot be. The deepening sense of security in the stepfamily also exposes it for what it is not and cannot be. It is as if the family returns now to grapple on a different level with their fantasies and yearnings for their family. Although stepfamilies enter the Resolution Stage of the Stepfamily Cycle with a distinctive family identity clearly differentiated from the original biological family, they must continue to deal with the ongoing influence of an ex-spouse, and sometimes another entire family with a claim to the insider role with their children. This remains true whether the absent parent is dead or alive. Children continue to have to deal with the reality of divided households. Many a smoothly functioning stepfamily is rocked by a teenager's apparently sudden powerful interest in an absent or dead biological parent, as chidren, too, return to resolve their losses and solidify their identities. Family events such as weddings and graduations that would be occasions for coming together in a first-time family may reexpose painful realities in a stepfamily as both adults and children deal with the awkwardness of double sets of "parents" (who sits at the head table, given that mom still falls apart in dad's presence, especially when he's with his new wife), family pictures (will the stepmother be included in the bride's family wedding picture?), and children and grandparents whose loyalties are divided between the old and new families.

Stepparents in this stage find themselves grieving the reality of nonbiological parenting. As the original first-time family recedes into the background and the stepparent-child relationship deepens, many stepparents find themselves more sharply aware, as well, of what cannot be—that their stepchildren are really not *their* children. Bill Hobbes talks about the juxtapostition of his panic and his sense of security in his relationship with his stepdaughter, Patsy:

At times I get very scared. I still panic. But now I always get that there's a security underneath. I know we have a really loving, important, forever connection. But there is a real primitive level where I want to panic. Like there's something that can be taken away from me.

Gene Davis, talking about the ongoing awkwardness of his stepdaughter Wendy's names—her own, and what she called her stepfather—as he grapples with his wish for a child of his own in the face of several years of infertility in his new marriage:

There's her name. Which at her age is important to her. She's always writing her name all over everything, which is common for kids that age. But it's Wendy Goodman, not Wendy Davis. So I'm always confronted with her last name, different from mine.

And there are times when it hurts me, too, to be out in the store, and there are references to "Mom, Mom," and then "Gene." At this point in my life, I feel the need for somebody to call me Dad. And it hasn't happened. And it's not going to happen with her.

For the biological parent, grief centers around the reality of interrupted parenting. This is particularly painful for noncustodial parents of teenagers, often fathers, whose children begin visiting less as peer relationships based in the mother's community, become primary. "I feel as if the father part of me has been castrated," said one noncustodial father.

Because our culture does not yet offer men much support or affirmation as parents, noncustodial fathers may be at risk for depression at this time.

As in earlier stages, biological parent and stepparent may not initially understand each other's grief. The stepparent's awareness of the painful reality of nonbiological parenthood may initially be met with protestations, "But you and my son are so close!" as the biological parent struggles with the last wisps of his or her fantasy of biological-like relationships between stepparents and their stepchildren. Spouses of noncustodial parents may find their partners' grief puzzling, as this stepmother married to a noncustodial father said, "Doesn't this grieving for his kid *ever* end?" A stepmother may be stunned when her stepdaughter of 10 years announces that she would like to have "only my real parents" on her wedding announcement. The withdrawal, fights, and tears of the Early Stages may reappear as adults air their realizations with their spouses and stepchildren, and stepparents rework territory both had thought was clearly mapped. However, the stuck isolation of the Early Stages doesn't last as long, and the level of panic and polarization subsides more quickly. Again, the sense of family is now solid: "And I know there's nothing I'm going to do to make it go away," says Rachel Sax. Now in step relationships, there is much middle ground to retreat to when the going gets rough. And, often, family members now have bridges in place over which they have walked many times to come to understand each other's very different experience of the family.

Living with a Ruptured Membrane

One area where biological parents, stepparents, and children may now share grief is the reality of living with a "boundary with a hole in it." All families must learn to let go of their children at some point. And children must learn to leave home. Stepfamily life, when custody is shared, requires letting go repeatedly. Bill Hobbes:

It's almost like rupturing a membrane! Over and over again. It's hard to get grounded in being a family physically when periodically one of the people in the family leaves and goes to another family.

Melissa Roberts, whose parents now reside in two different states, talks about facing again the reality that she always has to leave one to be with the other:

All this leaving and saying good-bye. To have to say good-bye to one parent to be with the other. To always have to miss one parent when you're with the other. Even though I love being in each of their houses, and I like my stepfather and really love my stepmother. Sometimes I just want to cry about it all over again.

Comings and goings bring another rub into awareness occasionally. By the Resolution Stage, the differences between the two families inhabited by some or all of the children in the stepfamily have become a matter of course. However, for adults, the ongoing influence of another biological parent's very different parenting style and values may resurface, to be grieved over many times. Beth Roberts, Melissa's mother:

I divorced him, and yet it's like "the divorce that won't go away." It just hits me so hard sometimes, that I have to live with him the rest of my life, because of our daughter. I would never do anything to rupture my daughter's relationship with her father. And yet there are times when it just breaks my heart that I have to send her to him.

But what's wonderful now is that I can cry in my husband's arms. I think it used to scare him, or irritate him. Or maybe he had feelings, too, and didn't know what to do with them. But now we just comfort each other. And sometimes we can even joke about it!

As usual, Bill Hobbes has a graphic image for the experience of living with his wife's ex-husband:

It's like having a beautiful body, and feeling good about your body, and really liking the boundaries and the structure, but also having this appendage, this tumor, that has a different value structure, or maybe a different aesthetic structure. It's like, "Oh, God, what is this?" And it's there and it's like my body, but how do I relate to this thing because it distorts something for me. And you can't just cut it out. It's there.

The Pleasures of Binuclear Familying

A double household also has its joys and pleasures. Children in the Resolution Stage are often very articulate about the special riches they feel that binuclear "familying" (Ahrons, 1979) brings to their lives. Despite the juggling of time and energy that living in two households requires for teenagers, they talk about how nice it is to have two different cultures to draw from. Ingrid Cummings, a 17-year-old, lives with her remarried father and his wife and children during the week, and her single-parent mother on the weekends:

My houses are so different, and I really love it. My mom is a health food nut. Tofu and whole wheat and vegetables. And my mom is really into talking about feelings and we always have these real deep long talks. My dad's into Twinkies and Coke. And he's not much for talking. What I love about my mom's house is you always can talk about whatever's going on with you and she's right there.

On the other hand, she's always *right there*. When I want to space out and just *be* without talking, I love being at my dad's house. He really lets me be. And he lets me eat whatever I want!

What Stepfamilies Look Like in the Resolution Stage

Cynthia Pill (1990), in a study of normal stepfamily functioning, provides some fascinating data with which to end this chapter. Pill found that stepfamilies score much lower on scales of "cohesion" and much higher on scales of "adaptability" than the national norm. Family practitioners have seen more average scores as "healthier" and would rate the stepfamily scores as somewhat pathological. However, Pill found that stepfamilies with "low cohesion" (i.e., families that don't do everything together, have kids who come in and out of the household, include people outside the immediate family in their holiday celebrations, vacation not as a nuclear stepfamily, but with children's friends) are more satisfied than those who try to operate more "cohesively."

Likewise, the scale Pill used actually labels the high stepfamily score on adaptability "chaotic." Nonetheless, these stepfamilies were *just as satisfied* as first-time families that scored more toward the median on adaptability. Most important, those stepfamilies that scored higher on adaptability were more satisfied with their family life than those with lower scores.

Pill's data helps us to picture the healthy stepfamily in the Resolution Stage. The Resolution Stage of the Stepfamily Cycle finds remarried families functioning smoothly but looking a little different from first-time families. There is much coming and going as children move between two homes, sometimes bringing friends along. Not all children are equally close to the family, some having decided to remain outsiders to the new family. Family membership may shift as adolescents switch homes or choose to visit their noncustodial parents less often. Ex-spouses (and their current spouses' ex-spouses) may influence needs and schedules, sometimes predictably, sometimes precipitously.

Resolution: Summary

Despite the fact that the mature stepfamily functions less cohesively and more "chaotically" than first-time families, members experience their step relationships as firm and reliable and nourishing. The stepparent role is now well defined and solid, as stepparents become mentoring intimate outsiders to at least some of their stepchildren. Other stepparent-stepchild relationships have reached a mutually suitable distance. The adult stepcouple has become a sanctuary, a place to turn for empathy and support and cooperative problem solving, even on most step issues. New step issues arise, but within the context of a solid family that cannot be broken. The biological parent-child relationships remain "more special" even in a mature stepfamily. However, the middle ground in step relationships is now thick enough to compete, and insider and outsider roles in the family now shift regularly. The stepfamily itself has a sense of character and a clear identity. Pill's subjects had many images of their stepfamily that capture both the sense of wholeness and the greater looseness of stepfamily living: the "family is like the center of a daisy. While the outside edge of each petal first draws away and then arches back and rejoins the center, the center itself is the focal point which holds everything together" (Pill, 1988, p. 116).

Stepfamilies in the Resolution Stage also find themselves more keenly aware of the realities of nonbiological and noncustodial parenting as well as the grief involved in living with a "boundary with a hole in it." They may return to struggle at this stage, with the necessity of relinquishing the images of family, and parenthood, and childrearing that might have been central to their identity.

The challenges and pleasures of the Resolution Stage seem to be threefold: (1) it is a time to hold on to and cherish what is resolved and reliable about stepfamily living; (2) it offers a kind of reprise, a time to recognize again and let go at a deeper level some of the grief engendered by normal stepfamily living even after restructuring; and (3) finally, the Resolution Stage is a time for reworking and moving forward together on unresolved issues.

As the family begins the Later Stages, step relationships have made a critical shift from triadic (with the biological parent or child intervening between step members) to dyadic (with all members more consistently dealing with concerns one-to-one with each other). By the end of the Contact Stage, a widely accepted mature stepparent role has emerged. This "intimate outsider" role, which begins to take shape in the Contact Stage, is fully formed by the Resolution Stage, becoming one of the unique rewards of stepfamily life.

By the Resolution Stage the hard work previously required for everyday decisions has given way to routine that no longer requires attention. Biological relationships remain special and different. While not all step relationships are created equal (some children may need to remain at a distance) most have achieved the thick middle ground that yields a sense of permanence and reliability. Although crises occur, the family system resolves difficulties more quickly and with less threat to ongoing stability.

The family's more well-defined picture of itself makes attendant losses more sharply drawn, perhaps because they are now clearly unavoidable. These include facing the reality of unfamily-like divided households, the continuing involvement of a child with an ex-spouse, the permanent presence of the ghost of a deceased parent, relinquishing last hopes for biological-like ties with stepchildren, and for some non-custodial parents, final acknowledgment that everyday parenting of biological children is impossible.

The fundamental changes in stepfamily structure which occurred by the end of the Middle Stages enable most families to move through the Later Stages in one to two years. In total, then, fast families move through the entire Stepfamily Cycle in about four years. Average families complete Resolution in about seven years. An infusion of support or a crisis that reorganizes the family can sometimes enable slow or stuck families to move on to completion after many years in the Early or Middle Stages.

Conclusion

Becoming a stepfamily is not an event but a process that requires moving slowly, and in small ways, to engage with strangers and familiars, in making a new family. The Stepfamily Cycle describes the territory families must traverse to find a path through a sequence of developmental stages that involve every member of the new family in forming a new family structure that can provide safety and nourishment for all. Gregory Burns captures the courage and spirit stepfamily living evokes:

It takes guts! You've got to be willing to look at this situation and finesse, kick, love, and scream your way into it. And then persist in staying there until you all get used to it! It means laughing, having a sense of irreverence, and not being afraid to get into trouble.

PART III

MOVING THROUGH THE STEPFAMILY CYCLE:

Patterns and Problems

Chapter 6

PATTERNS OF DEVELOPMENT: FOUR PATHS TO RESOLUTION

F or clarity's sake, the seven stages of the Stepfamily Cycle have been described as a set of sequential, distinguishable steps from Fantasy to Immersion to Awareness, to Mobilization and Action, to Contact and Resolution. However, if we think of the Stepfamily Cycle as a map that describes the terrain of stepfamily living, families vary greatly in how they move through the territory.

As we saw in Part Two, the differences between "fast," "average," and "slow" or "stuck" movement through the Stepfamily Cycle lie almost entirely in the amount of time families spend in the Early Stages. In Part Three, we will see even more specifically that the differences between these families lie in how they travel through or around the crucial individual and shared tasks of the Awareness Stage: naming the feelings and needs of one's own place in the stepfamily structure, *and* being able to describe with some accuracy and empathy the experience of family members in other places in the structure. Without the information generated in completing these tasks, stepfamilies do not have a clear enough map to "go into business" together in the Action Stage. It is as if some families find their way through the difficult stretches of the Early Stages directly and quickly. Others get lost in an unfortunate turn or misleading shortcut and cannot progress further. Still others may not take the most direct route, but nonetheless manage to labor through swamps and over boulders to eventually find a path to creating a nourishing workable stepfamily. Some families move immediately to completing Awareness tasks, proceeding fairly smoothly, if not always easily, to completing the Stepfamily Cycle. Others linger much longer in Immersion while still others skip precipitously to Mobilization or Action. Some families get stuck in these "wrong turns," but others work their way backward (or forward) eventually to complete the Stepfamily Cycle.

Chapter Six describes four different paths stepfamilies may take through the geography described by the Stepfamily Cycle. The four family types are named for the phase of the Stepfamily Cycle where their family compass takes them in their earliest years and describe the family's dominant style of dealing with differences: the *Aware Family*, the *Immersed Family*, the *Mobilized Family*, and the *Action Family*. We begin by introducing them briefly.

Aware Families come to stepfamily life with realistic expectations. They spend little time in Fantasy or Immersion, moving fairly directly and quickly to the tasks of the Awarenesss Stage. The mutual understanding gained here allows them to move into the Action Stage fairly smoothly, without a highly conflicted Mobilization Stage. These are the "fast families" that complete the entire Stepfamily Cycle in about four years.

Immersed Families are slowed by more entrenched fantasies of biological-like family functioning. These families move beyond the blissful Fantasy Stage into the discomfort of Immersion, but continue to function as if the stepparent (or the less dominant parent-child unit) could be assimilated into the more dominant biological parent-child unit. Movement from the Immersion Stage is usually led by the outsider stepparent, who finally finds a voice and engages the family in a highly conflicted Mobilization Stage before the family can travel back to complete Awareness tasks together. Successful Immersed Families complete the Stepfamily Cycle in about seven years. "Slow" Immersed Families may take much longer, and "stuck" Immersed Families may never move beyond the Early Stages.

Mobilized Families may also begin their lives with more unrealistic expectations than the Aware Family. However, unlike the Immersed Family, both step and biological, insider and outsider, voices are heard right from the start. These are the families that go "from courtship to middle marriage," struggling openly and immediately over a raft of issues. These families appear to begin their lives in the Mobilization Stage. Successful Mobilized Families gather enough information from each other enough to complete the work of the Awareness Stage. They can then travel on to complete the work of the Action Stage, and into the Later Stages, completing the Stepfamily Cycle in about seven years. Unsuccessful Mobilized families may blow apart very quickly, or live their lives in chronic conflict.

Action Families, like Immersed Families, begin their lives together with little conflict. However, unlike the Immersed Family, the dominant unit is the adult stepcouple who quickly come to agreement on a whole spectrum of new step rules and regulations. Often the dominant voice is an articulate, strong stepparent. These families appear to be "going into business together" with clear new rules and a solid adult couple. Yet the movement to Action is precipitous. The work of the Awareness Stage remains undone, and the new rules cannot hold. Trouble in these families is often signaled by an acting-out or depressed child. These families either extrude children early, or must go back to the Early Stages in order to reach Resolution.

What Makes the Differences?

Progressing beyond the Awareness Stage requires naming, talking about, and empathizing with powerful feelings most people think of as negative, as well as facing facts most people find disappointing. A number of factors influence the ability of stepfamily members to accomplish this feat, creating varying paths through, or around, the Early Stages. We begin this chapter by naming some of these influences.

Information: Reality Versus Fantasy

Like treating a 2-year-old's temper tantrums as predictable developmental behavior, people who bring good information and realistic expectations to the potentially disturbing events of early stepfamily life can treat them as normal parts of everyday living. Like good childbirth preparation, expecting these challenges and having some notion of how to meet them successfully doesn't change the reality of the labor, but it does prevent the panic, shame, and tension that significantly impede the birth process.

Good information also gives stepfamilies a kind of jump start on both the individual and joint awareness tasks of identifying the geography they inhabit together. It provides a kind of road map for what this stepfamily structure might feel like, so that stepfamily members don't have to create one from scratch. Each family must still work out for itself what bits of middle ground need to stay in place, what can be shifted, what new inventions will work for this particular family, and what pace is fast enough for outsiders and slow enough for insiders. However, as we will see in Case One, stepfamilies with more realistic information about the territory they are traveling in have to struggle less to find the path of least resistance.

Cases Two and Four show us how unrealistic expectations can retard the developmental process. The outsider's jealousy and resentment then signal inadequacy. The insider's inability to meet all needs signals failure. Children's needs are met less well or are met at the expense of the adult couple. Families straining to realize the fantasy of an immediately blended family may attempt to change everything at once; or they may try to assimilate new members as if nothing had to change. In these cases differences in attachment and culture are more likely to be treated with panic and criticism rather than respect and interest. All family members are less comfortable and more anxious, which makes it harder to express feelings and more difficult to listen well to each other.

When unrealistic expectations are simply a result of poor information, an infusion of education about stepfamily living can make a tremendous difference in developmental pace. Case Four provides a good example of the power of good coaching in helping a family to reformulate and set to work on its developmental tasks. The role of organizations like the Stepfamily Association of America cannot be underestimated here.

Previous History: Loss and Shame

I often tell my patients that stepfamily living is very bumpy. Getting bumped hurts. But when you get bumped in a place that was already bruised, the pain can be almost unbearable. When even good information does not seem to make a dent in a stuck belief system, the problem may lie in the amount of pain that information generates.

A remarried parent whose own family of origin was painful and dysfunctional may cling particularly tenaciously to the fantasy of an easily blended new family, and may be especially frightened by the missed connections of early stepfamily living. Information that these misconnections are normal will not be comforting to this person. On the other side of the gap, a stepfather who was an outsider in his family of origin will find his position in a new stepfamily especially evocative and painful. The news that this position is normal may elicit rage, not relief. In these cases the problem is not just one of education; it involves the need to face old as well as new "necessary losses" (Viorst, 1986).

Mental health professionals have begun to tell us that some of us are more vulnerable to shame than others in the face of feelings we aren't "supposed" to have (Morrison, 1983, 1986, 1989). Shame makes the normal painful feelings of stepfamily living even more excruciating and more difficult to acknowledge and voice. "I feel left out all the time. I think I need some time alone with my husband," becomes "I'm jealous and left out. I'm so ashamed to be so childish and selfish. I'll try to do better."

Related to shame is the need for "mirroring," the need to have one's parents' full, empathic attention enough of the time. Heinz Kohut (1977), who introduced the term, believes this is a need that begins in childhood, but extends into adult relationships. Children who experience "good enough" (Winnicott, 1958) mirroring feel seen and heard, feel that their thoughts and feelings matter, and develop a solid sense of self (Miller, 1981). Dysfunctional families cannot provide enough of this kind of empathic attention (Black, 1981).

As we have seen, stepfamily structure creates experiential gaps that make empathic mirroring hard to come by, particularly in the early years. A jealous stepparent is less likely to hear, "Gee, that makes sense. I'd feel the same," from his or her partner, and more likely to hear, "Aren't you overreacting?" A nervous and torn biological parent is less likely to hear his or her spouse respond with, "Gosh, I see you're trying to balance so many needs here," and more likely to hear, "Where are you when I need you?" As we will see, only members of Aware Families reliably empathize with each other from the beginning, a factor that powerfully lowers anxiety and speeds progress through Awareness tasks. However, in most cases, lack of even minimal mirroring may well be one of the most painful "bumps" of early stepfamily living. A person who comes to stepfamily life with a solid sense of self will find this lack of empathy painful and disorienting. Those who come to stepfamily life with a deficit in this area will find the pain much more unbearable and even annihilating.

Some kinds of religious or cultural training also create a greater propensity for experiencing normal "negative" feelings as shameful, creating an especially strong sense of how one "should" feel and act. Whether the roots lie in religious training or elsewhere, people with strong "shoulds" are more likely to repress, attempt to ignore, or criticize themselves (and others) for feelings that don't fit the picture of how things should be. These deeply rooted values about how one "should" feel in everyday life and what a family "should be" can make the territory of early stepfamily living particularly difficult to map out with self-acceptance and interest. All of these factors contribute to experiencing early stepfamily living not as a series of somewhat stressful normal transitions, but as one shameful, confusing interaction after another.

Loss, shame, shoulds, and lack of mirroring can make the path to awareness very painful. Some stepfamily members respond by redoubling their attempts to be "good enough," while others increase their efforts to get others to change ("If only she wasn't jealous, we'd be fine"). All of these efforts are, of course, doomed to failure and are likely to keep a family mired in Immersion or tangled in constant conflict (Mobilization). Continuing "failures," in turn, deepen everyone's sense of inadequacy. In these cases, psychotherapy may be needed to assist with identifying and mourning some of the old losses before the awareness tasks can be completed. Therapy that attributes the feelings generated by stepfamily structure entirely to internal vulnerabilities would be misguided and destructive.

Early losses, shame, deficits in mirroring and "shoulds" brought from previous family history not only make it hard to bear and express one's own feelings, but they also make it harder to hear the negative feelings of others. For a shame-sensitive biological parent, "I feel left out" becomes not a piece of information about a struggling stepparent, but a statement about the biological parent's inadequacy. "I miss Mommy" becomes not a child's longing to have two parents in the same household, but a criticism of the child's father.

Support: Isolation Versus Validation

Closely related to the above, the quality and quantity of support available to stepfamily members make a difference in their developmental pace and rhythm. Support functions most crucially to move stepfamily members from Immersion to Awareness. Papernow (1980) found that speed of movement through the Stepfamily Cycle for stepparents was intimately related to the timing of support. Here, "support" means empathy, others who understand, help naming the feelings and figuring out where they come from, help moving from shame to self-acceptance. For people who do not have complicating psychodynamic issues, groups like the Stepfamily Association of America, a friend in the same position, a good friend who will listen, and even good books (see Larry Ganong and Marilyn Coleman's new book, *Bibliotherapy with Stepchildren*, 1988a), provide support. As we have said, when family-of-origin issues are significantly slowing progress, psychotherapy provides needed support that facilitates the developmental process. However, as Case Four illustrates, psychotherapy without good information about stepfamily functioning may not be enough to help families progress through the Stepfamily Cycle.

In the faster-paced families like the Davidson/Millers (Case One in this chapter), much early support comes from inside the family. Spouses in these families are distinguished by the fact that they are more likely to empathize across the insider-outsider, step-biological and adult-child gaps in their family right from the beginning. They provide each other with the "mirroring" we talked about in the previous section. However, the divisive nature of early stepfamily structure, particularly when combined with lack of good information about what to expect, makes it more likely that stepcouples will have a hard time hearing and understanding each other in their early life together. In some families, like the John-stons (Case Three), each member of the couple can support himself or herself well enough to fight his or her way into understanding and supporting each other. In many stepfam-ilies like the Tolmans (Case Two), the need for support is first experienced by the outsider stepparent, who must turn outside the family for validation and help in sorting things out. With help from outside the family, the stepparent may then become the family change agent, pulling the others into the process of completing developmental tasks. In other families, like the Wentworths (Case Four), children's diffi-culties bring in outside support that helps the family to com-plete developmental tasks.

Support is also needed in the Middle Stages to help generate ideas for solving problems. Here again, Stepfamily Association of America meetings, informal contacts with other stepfamilies, and books and other media help provide a pool of information about how stepfamilies manage myriad cultural differences, celebrate holidays, devise workable cus-tody plans, handle money, and maneuver through gradua-tions and weddings and other multiple-family events.

Thickness of Middle Ground

We have already talked a great deal about the nature of middle ground in stepfamilies. Remarriages, according to some researchers, are more likely to include people of differ-ent cultures and religions than first marriages (Dean & Gurak, 1978). Nonetheless, stepfamilies that come together with more shared middle ground already in place have some areas of agreed-upon functioning that provide what Sonia Nevis calls "gluon" (Sonia Nevis, 1980; Nevis & Warner, 1983) that can hold the family together while they tackle pieces of difficult territory. The new stepfamily's already ex-isting middle ground may lie in shared religious practices, similar ideas about childrearing, similar feelings about mess and order, common political or cultural values, or favorite activities enjoyed by all members of the new family. In Case

One, a similar style of relating, similar feelings about "mess," and shared values about childrearing provided a solid area of middle ground for the Davidson/Millers. In this family, realistic expectations about stepfamily living also provided considerable middle ground, and some agreed-upon paths through the family geography.

Stepfamilies that come together with existing middle ground not only have less work to do, but they have more places of easy, satisfying contact to retreat to, and therefore more opportunities to lower anxiety and take a breath. These little rests make the work easier. New stepfamilies need to provide these respites by carving out time in step and biological minifamilies, where existing middle ground can be explored without competition.

The Family's Mix of Personality Styles

Different positions in the stepfamily structure require different skills and abilities for developmental progress. A quiet, shy stepparent may do well at sitting on the sidelines of the biological parent-child unit for a while. However, a shy stepparent who has trouble voicing his or her own perceptions and needs will remain unintegrated for a longer time than a family with a more outgoing person in the outsider role. I have had several families in treatment where the most disengaged stepparent-stepchild pair were both very shy, quiet, easily shamed people. Both members of the dyad found it excruciatingly difficult to speak their feelings out loud, ask for feedback, or engage each other in conversation, making the gaps in awareness much more difficult for these pairs to traverse. Often another child in the family, who was more aggressive and outgoing, had formed a strong relationship with the same stepparent.

Conversely, a biological parent in the insider role who is used to being the center of things may find it more difficult to step back and allow stepparent and stepchild to get to know each other without interrupting. A stepparent who needs a great deal of control and order to feel comfortable will find the experience of living in foreign territory and in an often (as we have seen) less disciplined, single-parent family, particularly trying and may be tempted to step in much too quickly to restore order. Likewise, a similarly constituted biological parent will have trouble stepping aside when the time comes and allowing stepparent and stepchild to create their own, very different relationship.

Good Awareness and Problem-Solving Skills

The skill level of the couple and family can make a great difference in how quickly they move through the Stepfamily Cycle. Like the proverbial three blind men each feeling a different part of an elephant, stepfamily members have to talk to each other in order to create an accurate picture. As we said in Chapter Two, stepfamilies have to do a lot on purpose, all at once, and out loud that gets done slowly over time and less consciously in first-time families. This makes good awareness skills much more crucial to good stepfamily functioning. In concrete language, couples and families with the capacity to name their feelings accurately, and to share them without blaming each other, are much more likely to turn up all relevant information about how each member of the family might be feeling. Even without good information, stepfamilies whose members get curious and ask questions about each other's needs in the face of problems will create an accurate picture of what is needed to move on together. The assumption that there is "one right way" is less supportive of awareness tasks than the assumption that there are multiple realities.

Stepfamilies whose members have learned to be generous and creative about inventing solutions that incorporate a variety of needs are much more likely to find a path everyone wants to travel. Stepfamilies whose members are in the habit of asking each other "How did it go?" and "What worked here and what should we change next time?" are much more likely to learn more for the next time.

Children

In Case One we meet the Davidson/Millers, a family blessed
with two stepsiblings who liked each other and who were
basically accessible to new relationships. Life was easier for
this family than in a family where children are more hostile,
more resistant, or more troubled.

Children's responses to stepfamily life are mediated
by a number of different factors. First, and most obvious,
children of different ages have different developmental
needs and tasks that may or may not coincide with the developmental needs of the family (Whiteside, 1988b). Some of
the adolescents we met in Part Two spoke of their difficulty
in balancing their parents' strong desire to have them become
part of the new family just when the child needed to be
leaving home. As we shall see in the Johnston Family (Case
Three), younger children are often more ready to accept
a stepparent. Children of different ages also have varying
cognitive capacities to name and understand their experience
of stepfamily living (Bernstein, 1988).

Research is clearly establishing that one of the most
critical factors in children's postdivorce adjustment is the
level of conflict they experience between their parents. Kline
and her coworkers (Kline, Tschann, Johnston, & Wallerstein,
1986) found that the level of conflict outweighed type of
custody (joint or sole) in children's adjustment. Current research continues to support and expand this finding (Hobart,
1987; Isaacs, Leon, & Kline, 1987; Johnston, Gonzales, &
Campbell, 1987; Johnston, Coysh, Kline, & Nelson, 1988;
Kline, Johnston, & Tschann, 1991; Shaw & Emery, 1987;
and Tschann, Johnston, Kline, & Wallerstein, 1989).

Closely related to this finding, the more intense a child's
loyalty bind, the more difficult it is for a child to bond to a
new family. As we have said, the oldest child in a divorced
family often maintains more loyalty to the previous family
than his or her younger siblings, and more need to remind
all present that this new family is not the "real" family. These

oldest children are also more likely to have become the confidante of one or the other of the original parents, entangling them in tighter loyalty binds than younger siblings.

Research is establishing that a child's sex is a major factor in this relationship. Clinicians have sometimes assumed that when mothers remarry, it is their sons who will have the most difficulty with the entrance of a stepfather. The assumption is rooted in the thought that the underlying sexuality between boys and their mothers makes boys more likely to be competitive with their stepfathers. However, researchers, measuring actual behavior changes through videotapes and the reports of family members and teachers, are finding just the opposite. Single-parent mothers and their sons have the most conflicted relationships (Hetherington, Cox & Cox, 1982). But behavior problems in boys recede over time with the entrance of a stepfather (Hetherington, 1987). The opposite is true for girls, who do well in single-parent families but become more troubled when their parents remarry. Stepdaughters between the ages of 9 and 12 exhibit more problematic family and social relations and more behavior problems than do boys (Clingempeel, Brand, & Ievoli, 1984), and stepfather-stepdaughter relationships in this age group remain particularly conflicted or disengaged, even after two years (Hetherington, 1987).

Some of the very dynamics that led clinicians to their initial, incorrect assumption may account for some of these results. Boys may gain safety with the addition of a stepfather, as the adult male may lower anxiety-laden sexuality between boys and their mothers. A new adult male may be a much needed male role model and buddy for a boy, but he may be an anxiety-laden sexual object for a girl.

Girls' behavior, however, is more troublesome in stepmother families as well (Clingempeel, Ievoli, & Brand, 1984; Brand & Clingempeel, 1987). Clearly the presence or absence of anxiety about sexuality does not explain enough of the results for girls. It is my belief that in both stepmother and stepfather families, the addition of a stepparent is more of a *loss* for daughters. We know that single-parent mothers are extraordinarily lonely (Hetherington, 1987; Wallerstein, 1986) and that single-parent mother-daughter relationships are less conflicted than mother-son relationships. Mavis Hetherington's work also tells us that mothers in all kinds of families are more expressive toward their daughters than toward their sons (1987). Single mothers may turn much more fully to their daughters, and then drastically away from them when a man enters the picture. Likewise, single-parent fathers may form closer, more affectionate relationships with their daughters than with their sons. Sons may have a more "buddy-buddy" relationship with their fathers that is less affected by remarriage. Again, when a father turns to an adult woman for affection and companionship, daughters may feel a greater loss. This conclusion is supported by the finding that the happier and closer the marital relationship, the more conflicted and hostile are stepdaughter-stepparent relationships (Brand & Clingempeel, 1987; Hetherington, 1987).

Finally, a number of demographic factors affect children's adjustment. A study of stepmother families found conflict is lowest in simple stepfamilies (where only the remarrying father brought children), with smaller numbers of children, and where the annual income was reasonably high (Santrock & Sitterle, 1987). These results are supported by White and Booth (1985), who found that the divorce rates were highest in double, or complex stepfamilies where both adults brought children, and by David Jacobson (1988), who found that stepfamilies do better when they have more physical space. None of these demographic factors are surprising. Clearly there is more awareness work to do when the number of people increases, and the resources decrease.

Four Stepfamily Types

With some understanding of the forces that may affect the particular patterns of stepfamily movement through the Stepfamily Cycle, we now proceed to a more detailed description of each of these four patterns. Each will be illustrated with an actual case history. It is important to note that these are not "pure" types. Many families may have some characteristics of more than one of these patterns. However, in my experience both colleagues and clients find these four different paths recognizable and helpful in making sense out of the apparent chaos of stepfamily dynamics.

The Aware Family

Aware Families constitute most of the fast families, who move through the entire Stepfamily Cycle in about four years. Members of Aware Families are more likely to bring realistic expectations, few complicating psychodynamic issues, and good communication skills to their lives together. This combination seems to enable Aware Families to carve a path that leads fairly directly into the Awareness Stage, protecting them from languishing in the swampy confusion and reproach of the Immersion Stage and at the same time preventing them from moving precipitously into Mobilization or Action. Aware Families spend a year, sometimes two, in the Early Stages. As the name implies, they spend little of this time in Fantasy or Immersion. Their attention and energy are concentrated on awareness tasks: naming their own experience of the new family, getting to know each other, and learning about the needs of both insiders and outsiders in the family. They are able to use information from their daily lives together to relinquish their remaining fantasies of an easily blended family.

Aware Families bring some skills and attitudes that support them in Awareness Stage tasks. Early stepfamily living proceeds more smoothly when each member is able to say out loud what she or he is experiencing and when family members are interested in each other's reports. Members of Aware Families are more likely to be generous in making the effort to name their feelings and say them out loud without blaming each other. They often involve a highly empathic biological parent, able to understand and undefensively hear outsiders' feelings (feeling left out, operating on unfamiliar territory, needing reliable intimate time, needing a few things to be familiar). When a stepparent says, "I'm jealous," a biological parent in an Aware Family is more likely to say, "Tell me some more," than "You're the grownup." When a biological parent says, "I feel torn," a stepparent in an Aware Family is more likely to say, "What can we do for you?" than "What's wrong with you?"

As is especially clear in the Davidson/Miller case, being in touch with family members' needs guides members of Aware Families to make separate time and space for each of the minifamilies that make up their family. This means that as they do the work of mapping their territory, Aware Families, either intuitively or consciously, provide experiences of the easy middle ground we spoke of earlier. In Aware Families we see biological parents who can compartmentalize—who can give quality attention to their new partners, while still giving separate, reliable one-to-one time with their own children. We see stepparents with a good aesthetic sense of getting to know their stepchildren slowly.

Aware Families move into Middle Stage tasks having helped each other to complete both individual and joint awareness tasks: each family member has a good sense of his or her piece of the family territory and a good enough sense of what other parts of the terrain feel like. They spend a year or two here. Their solid base of understanding enables them to spend less of this time in the Mobilization Stage struggling to get through to each other, and more of their time in the Action Stage "going into business together," working out how to meet the varied needs their new family presents. As in most other stepfamilies, after the tasks of the Early and Middle Stages are accomplished, the Later Stages take a year or two to complete. As with most other stepfamilies, new issues in the Later Stages may take the family back to the beginning of the Stepfamily Cycle.

We can begin to grasp the differences between these four paths through the Stepfamily Cycle in more detail by looking at how the adult couple in each would handle a common occurrence in very early stepfamily life. We will use a mythical family comprised of Andrea, her daughter Amy, and Harry. For the sake of clarity we will make them a "simple" stepfamily (a biological parent with a child marries a previously childless stepparent):

Amy, 8, and her mother, Andrea, are playing cards, an after-dinner ritual remaining from their single-parent family days. Andrea's second husband, Harry, comes into the room, and asks them if they would like to go out for ice cream. Amy is absorbed in the game and barely looks up. Andrea quickly says, "Nope," and goes back to the game.

In our mythical Aware Family the conversation might go something like this:

H.: You know, I felt really left out tonight when you and Amy were playing cards.
   [In an Immersed Family Harry might have withdrawn wordlessly. Here he gets up his nerve and says something to Andrea.]
A.: You did? Gosh, I didn't even notice! What happened?
   [Andrea gets interested and asks for more information. In an Immersed or Mobilized Family she might have accused him of not trying hard enough.]
H.: Well, I came in and asked you both if you wanted to go for ice cream with me. Amy didn't even look at me, and you looked up and said, "Nope," and went back to playing cards.
   [Harry tells her exactly what happened. In a Mobilized or Action Family, he might have launched into accusing her of not being welcoming enough. Here he is simply descriptive so that Andrea can recognize the place where the problem occurred.]
A.: That was hard for you?
   [Andrea responds with an empathic question that invites more information.]
H.: I felt invisible.
   [Harry accepts the invitation and finds a word for his feelings.]
A.: You did? I wouldn't have felt invisible if that had happened to me.

[From her biological parent perspective, Andrea doesn't get it.]

H.: Yeah, but you already know you have a place with Amy. It's different for me, remember?
[Harry hangs in and reminds her that his outsider place in the family is different.]

A.: How do you mean?
[In an Immersed or Mobilized Family, Andrea might have pushed her point of view again—"Why can't you understand that we want you here?" Instead she stays curious and invites Harry to tell her some more about his piece of the territory.]

H.: [Explains some more]

A.: Oh, yeah. I keep forgetting.
[Again, Andrea takes in Harry's different point of view rather than arguing with him to be more like her.]

H.: Why do you keep forgetting? I feel like I've explained this a million times.
[Harry is frustrated, but manages to stay curious about Andrea.]

A.: [Silent for a moment] You have. It's true. Maybe it's just painful to remember that you don't feel the same way about Amy that I do. And partly I just plain forget.
[Andrea is able to acknowledge that she forgets. And she takes enough time to tune into herself and offer Harry some information about what makes it so hard for her.]

H.: Well, in fact, you guys play cards like that almost every night and I feel really left out.

A.: It feels so normal to me to play cards like that with Amy. I don't even think about it. I suppose, now that I think of it, you are left out. Why don't you just join us?
[Andrea offers some more information about her insider position and acknowledge's Harry's outsider position. But she still doesn't quite grasp the difficulty for Harry.]

H.: Well, first of all, I hate to play cards. And second of all, it just seems so intimate between you two.
[In an Immersed Family, Harry might have blamed himself for not being aggressive enough. Here he is willing to say some more about the dilemma for him.]

A.: Like we speak a special language?

H.: Yeah, that's a good way to put it, like you speak some foreign language I don't talk. And it's actually getting really painful for me. It's lonely at night. And then when Amy doesn't even acknowledge me, that's really hard.

[Andrea helps Harry put words on his experience. This seems to enable Harry to talk more freely and fully about his piece of the family territory.]

A.: Why don't you suggest we do something else?

H.: I did! [Getting a little exasperated] That's why I asked if you wanted to go for ice cream. I decided that for once I wouldn't sit around like an outsider and read the paper, and look what happened. You and Amy just chugged along like an express train and left me in the dust.

[Andrea didn't get it. But now Harry is firmly grounded, and he is able to vigorously voice his own internal dialogue so that Andrea has a clearer picture of his experience.]

A.: Ouch. That's a little hard to hear. But you're right. And you're right that Amy didn't even answer your question. That must hurt. I mean she doesn't mean it to hurt you, but it must hurt.

[Andrea takes in Harry's outsider position, and is able to acknowledge that it hurts. A more defensive Andrea might have lashed back. Andrea goes on to fully validate Harry's experience. Again, it is as if Andrea's understanding and validation make more space for Harry to show himself to her. He now finishes the individual Awareness task on this issue, telling her specifically what he needs from her.]

H.: You bet it does. [Silence] And, Andrea, I need some more time alone with you in the evening, and some time with the three of us doing some things that don't so completely exclude me.

A.: Yeah, I see your problem. You feel really left out. And you can't join, or don't want to because it's too tight between Amy and me when we're playing cards. Now, do *you* get *my* problem?

[Andrea again voices her understanding of Harry's piece of the map, completing her end of the joint Awareness task. In an Action Family, she might immediately give over to Harry's needs for change. Here, she ensures that he understands the biological piece of the family geography before they decide what to do.]

H.: I think so. But say it again.
[Now it is Harry who calls on his willingness to learn Andrea's territory.]

A.: Amy and I have played cards like that for three years. It was the thing that kept me sane in the evenings at first. Now it's become this really special thing between us. I really don't want to give it up completely. And I think it's important for Amy to have some things stay the same, that she can rely on. There have been an awful lot of changes in her little life in the past few years.

H.: [Silent for a few moments] I don't think I understood that before. Tell me some more about that. When Amy is rude to me, I just completely forget that there might be a reason for it, because it hurts so much.
[Now Harry makes space for Andrea to fill in the missing pieces for him.]

A.: Your turn to forget! [They both laugh. Andrea now talks some about all the changes Amy has been through.]

H.: OK. I get it better. [More silence] So now what the heck do we do with our evenings? [More silence] Maybe the solution is we can do some of each. Some card playing time for you two, and some time for you and me?

A.: Maybe Mommy-Amy nights and some Andrea-Harry nights?

H.: Or divide up the evening—Mommy-Amy time and some time for just you and me?
[With solid understanding of both the insider and outsider territory in their new stepfamily, Andrea and Harry can move on to invent a solution that meets the needs of both the biological and the step subsystems in their family.]

A.: And it sounds like we need to find something the three of us can do besides playing cards.

H.: [With a silly grin] How about going out for ice cream?

As this somewhat idealized conversation ends, Andrea and Harry have helped each other to complete both individual and joint awareness tasks on this issue. Each has voiced his or her own dilemma, and each has gained an understanding of the experience in the other domain of the family structure. The hallmark of an Aware Family is that they have traversed some fairly slippery ground together, each stopping in the hard places to help each other articulate his or her point of view. The dilemma can then be posed not as "Whose needs will win out?" (Andrea's or Harry's or Amy's), but as "How can we meet all the needs here?" Andrea and Harry now move naturally into devising a plan that leaves some of the biological middle ground reliably in place, while creating some clear space for the new adult couple, and carving out some new middle ground in which the whole family can function comfortably.

The Immersed Family

Now let us imagine the response to the same event had Andrea and Harry been members of an Immersed Family. In the Immersed Family, Harry, as the outsider stepparent, might have remained silent for many many months, perhaps spending his evenings alone with the newspaper or watching television. Andrea would have felt abandoned and lonely. The occasional couple conversations about the family's evenings might have gone something like this:

> [Harry has retreated to the television room again having been rejected in his ice cream offer. After putting Amy to bed, a tired Andrea accosts him.]
>
> A.: Why do you spend all your evenings alone? Why won't you join in? This is a family, after all, and you don't even seem interested!
> [She is lonely and misses Harry's presence with her but has no awareness of what happened to him earlier in the evening. Her question is more an accusation than an attempt to learn about what the family is like for Harry.]
> H.: I don't know. I guess I'll try harder. I was just reading. You guys were playing cards.
> [Harry collapses under Andrea's criticism and withdraws in self-reproach. His attempt at describing what happened inside of him is not vivid enough to get through to Andrea. The conversation stops. Both Harry and Andrea feel uneasy and unfinished, but neither can

maintain the conversation long enough to bridge the gap in their experience of the evening.]

   This Andrea and Harry are stuck in Immersion. Harry feels the impact of his outsider position, but blames himself. Andrea senses his absence but joins him in blaming him. Neither of them has enough words for his or her own piece of the family terrain to give the other a geography lesson. Neither expresses enough curiosity about the other's territory to facilitate this process.

   Immersed Families, then, take a very different path through the Early and Middle Stages. Often the path to the Awareness Stage is impeded by the conviction that the new family can function like a first-time family. The realities of stepfamily living move them from blissful Fantasy to the discomfort of Immersion. But, like the Immersed Harry and Andrea in the vignette above, family members often feel the impact of their unique stepfamily structure but blame themselves or each other for things not going right. This makes it difficult to accurately name the natural feelings created by the structure (jealousy, feeling torn, missing an absent parent, etc.). Thus movement from the self-reproach and confusion of the Immersion Stage to the clarity of the Awareness Stage is strewn with obstacles. As the name implies, these families remain stalled longer in the Immersion Stage and must expend more time and energy to complete Awareness Stage tasks.

   Like this mythical Harry and Andrea, Immersed Families begin their lives together usually operating in the old middle ground of the more dominant biological subsystem. The family may look "as if" they are operating as a unit (hence the title "Assimilation Stage" for this phase in Papernow, 1984a). However, outsiders' needs are not articulated, and therefore usually are not met. The couple may have very little time alone together, as the biological parent-child unit dominates family interaction. In double families where both adults bring children, outsider stepsiblings (those who visit, or those who moved into the dominant subsystem's home) may feel unheard and unseen and especially displaced.

In Immersed Families, the communication and mutual understanding necessary to bridge the gaps created by stepfamily structure become fraught with difficulty as events that evoke empathy and curiosity in an Aware Family create confusion, reproach, and betrayal. Thus access to information about family members' needs is often blocked, preventing real movement into the Action Stage. Because awareness tasks are incomplete, apparent solutions to stepfamily dilemmas may leave out an entire subset of needs and feelings (usually the outsiders' voices are not heard) and so agreements often fail, creating further demoralization. Outsiders' feelings of jealousy and discomfort and their needs for extra support and reliable intimate time remain particularly misunderstood or discounted. The insider adult's grief over not being able to have a biological-like family may remain unexpressed and his or her feelings of guilt and ambivalence may remain unheard, as are children's very mixed feelings about their new family.

Immersed Families often need outside support to move from the Immersion Stage to the Awareness Stage. In healthy families "support" may mean information that helps to validate and voice the unheard awarenesses in the family. Support may also mean helping family members to listen across the gap between the step and biological experience of the family. Support that has made a difference to these families includes attendance at a local Stepfamily Association of America group, new information coming into the family through books and (increasingly) other media, a well-informed therapist, or even a highly empathic friend who helps the disenfranchised member of the family to articulate his or her feelings and helps the couple to sustain efforts at hearing and getting heard.

Immersed Families are sometimes slowed by some of the psychodynamic issues listed at the beginning of Chapter Six, which further complicate communication about step issues. A stepparent whose needs were never heard in his or her family of origin may become discouraged much more quickly than the Harry of our idealized Aware couple. A biological mother whose own father abandoned her may, like our Immersed Andrea, experience her new partner's absence from her new family so intensely that it is difficult to become interested in her own role in pushing him out. As we shall see in Chapter Seven, a therapist who can weave back and forth between dilemmas created by stepfamily structure, and those that are intensified by previous family history, may help the Immersed couple or family to keep moving through the Stepfamily Cycle.

With outside support, at least one member of an Immersed Family can often move into Awareness and finally into sustained Mobilization. In Immersed Families, this is often the disenfranchised outsider stepparent who then drags the other adult with him or her. As we have said, Aware couples travel into the Middle Stages having helped each other to complete both the individual and the mutual understanding tasks of the Awareness Stage. In contrast, the stepparent in an Immersed couple often struggles painfully, and alone, from the confusion and self-blame of Immersion to the greater clarity of Awareness. It is in these couples that the move from Awareness to Mobilization often involves a "last straw" event that gives the outsider stepparent enough strength and conviction to effectively rock the boat. In these Immersed Families, the deceiving quiet of the Immersion Stage then erupts in highly polarized conflict in the Mobilization Stage as the family outsider battles (often with more desperation than grace or empathy) to get heard by the insiders. Let us imagine, then, that our Immersed Harry has just had a conversation with a close friend, a stepmother, who encourages him to push Andrea more forcefully for more time alone together. Harry returns home armed for battle:

H.: Don't you ever have time to spend alone with me?
A.: Amy needs this time. Why don't you just join us? Amy's your daughter, too, now, you know!
   [Harry has become more vigorous, but he is so accusing

that Andrea responds defensively. She does offer a little information about Amy's needs, but sandwiches that in with her wish that Harry treat her like a biological daughter.]

H.: But she ignores me!

A.: You're just too sensitive. You're the grown-up, you know. I can't believe you'd let an 8-year-old hurt your feelings like that.

H.: It's about time you started treating me more like a husband and less like an appendage!

A.: Well, I wish you'd start acting like one!

Our Immersed Andrea and Harry have now lurched into Mobilization without having completed much of the Awareness section of the Stepfamily Cycle. Because the Immersed Andrea and Harry are more likely to sink in despair or hurl stones at each other than to help each other across slippery spots in their family life, their journey is a rough one. Like many Immersed couples, this Harry and Andrea may slip back into the Immersion Stage and catapult into Mobilization several times before they can traverse the uncompleted sections of the Awareness Stage. Successful Immersed Families do finally replace the pseudo-agreement of the Immersion Stage with the truly joint decision making of the Action Stage. Couples in these families will often make this trip from Immersion to Mobilization, back to Awareness, and then forward into Action, one painful issue at a time.

Successful Immersed Families take about seven years to complete the entire developmental process including two or three years in the Early Stages, much of it in Immersion, and two to three years in the Middle Stages, much of it in Mobilization. Then, with the hard work accomplished, they spend one or two years in the Later Stages, for a total of about seven years to complete the entire developmental process. As with all stepfamilies, new issues in the Later Stages may return them to the beginning of the Stepfamily Cycle. They may then progress a little more like an Aware Family as fantasies recede, the family solidifies, and their ability to maneuver through step differences increases.

Immersed Families may become slow (more than three or four years in the Early Stages) or "stuck" families when one or both adult partners bring with them particularly strong longings for a biological-like family that they cannot relinquish. They may simply lack access to any accurate information that would help them to function with more realistic expectations. Some are also hampered by previous family histories that make communication about step issues more charged and complex. This combination of lack of information, strongly rooted fantasies, and complicating intrapersonal issues significantly slows progress on awareness tasks, making the territory much more treacherous.

Slow immersed families may move on, with a sudden heavy influx of outside support, or may suddenly get moving due to a family crisis that unfreezes the family system. "Stuck" immersed families never leave the Early Stages.

The Mobilized Family

Mobilized Families begin their lives together openly airing the differences created by their step structure. Unlike Immersed Families, each of the adult family members is somewhat aware of his or her needs and feelings. Both insider and outsider voices can be heard clearly right from the start. However, unrealistic expectations and/or a highly mobilized family style make the empathy and shared understanding across the differences in cultures, attachments, step and biological, insider and outsider positions in the family hard to come by. Thus, unlike the curious empathic exploration of Aware Families, or the swampy confusion of an early Immersed Family, these families are catapulted immediately into highly charged and polarized conflict over their differences. If we were to transform Andrea and Harry into a Mobilized couple, we would hear a very different interaction. Harry would be more likely to confront Andrea immediately and forcefully, perhaps with her daughter's "rude" behavior and Andrea's lack of support for him. She would reply with equal strength. In distilled form, several months of conversation might go like this:

H.: You guys hardly even said hello to me again this evening. Amy didn't even look up and you give the garbage man more attention than you gave me when I walked through the living room tonight!

A.: What's wrong with you that you can't let us play cards together? This has always been a special time for Amy and me. Can't you let us have our time together?

[The opening volley has been fired. The Mobilized Andrea and Harry are both direct and straightforward. Each is actively trying to give the other a geography lesson.]

H.: Yeah, but it's not OK that Amy treats me that way. That's no way to treat a new father.

A.: You're not her father. She has a father. Your expectations are way out of line.

H.: But at least I have the right to be treated with some amount of civility. And besides, when do I get time alone with you? I feel like I'm always sharing you with Amy. Evenings are a time I'd like to be alone with you, without Amy there claiming all your attention.

[Andrea is able to confront Harry's fantasy of being treated "like a father." He hears her and forms a more realistic request. Note that though this couple is very lively and confrontive, they are, so far, not particularly mean, or blaming.]

A.: Are you dense? I've told you a million times that this is special time for Amy and me. It really helps her feel safe and secure. We need some things to stay the same around here. There's been an awful lot of change in her life.

[Although this last statement was prefaced with an attack, Andrea offers some more solid information for Harry about the biological piece of the territory.]

H.: Yeah, and some things have got to change. Amy has got to begin treating me with more respect, and you have got to make some time alone for me without Amy. I didn't get married to spend my evenings alone reading the paper.

[Harry hangs in, tenaciously voicing his outsider position and his needs for change.]

A.: So why don't you just join us?

H.: Because, first of all, I hate playing cards. And second of all, I feel like a third wheel. It's like you guys have some kind of secret code I can't break.

[Now Harry offers some good information about his experience of the family. Again, this Mobilized couple is informative and is not particularly blaming or nasty, despite their highly engaged style.]

A.: You're really putting me in the middle here. What do you think I am, Superwoman? How the heck am I supposed to meet Amy's needs for some kind of stability and yours for time alone with me? What do you want me to do, clone myself? I'm going crazy in this family!

[Although her tone is becoming more accusing than curious and thoughtful, Andrea begins to tell Harry about the dilemmas of her insider position.]

In this particular Mobilized Family, many of the *individual* awareness tasks are completed. The Harry of this Mobilized Family knows he feels left out. He knows he wants more time alone with his wife. Andrea knows she feels caught in the middle. She knows Amy needs some stability and consistent time with her mom.

What is missing is *shared understanding* across the differences in the insider-outsider, step-biological, and adult-child experiences of the family. Neither Harry nor Andrea has expressed any interest in ("Say some more about that") or empathy for ("Gee, that must hurt!") the other's experience. And neither has articulated the needs of the *whole* system. ("So how do we find a way to give Amy and Andrea special time, Harry and Andrea some time alone, and find some activities we could all do together?") Each is competing to meet his or her needs.

Living through the Early Stages in an Immersed Family is much like living with lots of lumps under the rug—family members attempt to walk as if the rug were smooth, but they keep tripping, and feeling embarrassed by or critical of each other for their awkwardness. In a Mobilized Family, the lumps are visible and openly acknowledged very early in the relationship.

When Mobilized Families are simple stepfamilies like Andrea and Harry's where only one adult brings children, they often include a strong, highly articulate outsider stepparent who may have somewhat unrealistic needs for immediate change, and an equally strong (sometimes equally unrealistic) insider biological parent who voices the needs of the biological subsystem for stability. Complex or double stepfamilies, where both adults bring children, are more vulnerable to beginning their lives as Mobilized Families. In these double families, each set of values and each daily ritual is supported by an entire team. If both units are evenly matched (in numbers, or in claim to "home territory," or in quickness or loudness), the likelihood of an immediate clash is much higher than in a single stepfamily where the biological parent-child unit's middle ground is more likely to dominate at first, leaving the stepparent as the disenfranchised foreigner and silent outsider.

Some mobilized couples like the Johnstons (in Case Three, upcoming) bring enough middle ground, enough areas of shared belief, and enough ability to fight constructively that they maintain a real sense of unity even as they fight. In fact, as we listen to the Johnstons, we get the sense that their willingness to fight provided some of the "gluon" (S. Nevis, 1980; Nevis & Warner, 1983) for their marriage, serving as evidence of their commitment to making their new stepfamily work. Stepcouples with less middle ground but a highly mobilized style of dealing with differences (rather than the quieter, more curious style of an Aware Family) will be in more danger of splitting up.

Although the process is much noisier and requires more effort than in an Aware Family, members of successful Mobilized Families, through their struggles, gain some understanding of one another. "We had to beat it into each other, but now we really understand each other," said one vivacious woman. The family can then move on to the Action Stage together. When all the information is available and articulated in Mobilized Families, they may, like the Johnstons in Case Three, be able to continue moving through the cycle without outside intervention.

Successful Mobilized Families complete the Stepfamily Cycle at an average pace, taking five to seven years to reach the Resolution Stage. They begin their lives together in the Mobilization Stage, and then must move back to the Awareness Stage (often with some slips back into Immersion) before progressing forward.

Slower paced Mobilized Families may have more individual awareness work to do before their lively engagement can provide enough geography lessons. Crucial realistic information about normal stepfamily functioning may be missing, or underlying fantasies may slow progress. A more vicious fighting style may create scars rather than building understanding. In some Mobilized couples, hair-trigger responses to differences may be rooted in deeper psychodynamic issues that will need attention before the family can make developmental progress. These families may need outside support to help them slow down and move back to complete awareness tasks. Unsuccessful Mobilized Families may blow apart rather quickly or they may live in chronic conflict.

The Action Family

If we now transform them into an Action Family, our Andrea and Harry would quickly agree that evenings should be adult or family time. The conversation, distilled from a few months of interaction, might go something like this:

H.: These evening card games have got to stop. I want us to spend time together as a family. I want time alone with you. And I want Amy to start treating me like her father. I expect a hug from her when I come into the room, and I expect you to spend your time with me in the evening, not with Amy.

A.: Gee, I'm sorry. You're right, we're really not functioning like a real family here.

The card games would be stopped. Family activities would be substituted, or Amy would be expected to retire to her room to leave space for the adults. In some cases, she might be told to call Harry "Daddy." In extreme cases, she might be expected to unite with Harry and Andrea against her own father. Amy's objections to this might be treated as "bad" or ungrateful behavior as would her requests for special time with her mother. Amy's response might vary from pained acquiescence, to depression, to "inexplicable" bursts of temper and school problems.

Like the Allen/Betts family in Figure 2.6 (Chapter Two), the adults in an Action Family immediately "go into business together" with each other, coming to agreement on new step rules and rituals. Action Families may consist of an articulate and forceful stepparent and an acquiescent biological parent, as with Andrea and Harry above; or both adults may be in (misinformed) agreement. The unheard voices in the Action Family are the original insiders, particularly the children, who are expected to function in entirely new territory. The eagerness for a fresh start as a new couple and a new family may cloud, or completely block, biological parents' awareness of, or ability to voice, their children's needs to hold on to some familiar middle ground. When a parent has died, or an ex-spouse was abusive, or the absent parent has abandoned the family, the pull to treat the new stepfamily as if the missing parent never existed is particularly strong. As we will see in Case Four, the problem is that though adults can leave their ex-spouses behind, children cannot. A child's biological parent remains forever part of his or her being, both emotionally and physically.

Often in these families, the adult couple becomes a closed insider unit at the expense of biological parent-child relationships. Children in Action Families often lose not only familiar routines, but adequate access to one-to-one time with their parents. In stepfamilies this happens at a time when

children's need for support and for familiar routines is intensified. As we have seen, early stepfamily life for children
often means large changes in not only their internal family
territory but often in the external geography of school and
neighborhood and friends.

Change agents in Action Families are often children,
who, if they can object effectively enough, may be able to
force the adults to slow down and face the reality that forming a stepfamily is a step-by-step process. Sometimes one or
both adults will appear in either a school or clinic setting,
spurred by the need to get help for a troubled child. Figure
2.6 in Chapter Two provides two opposite examples of such
children in Sophie Betts (who has begun to act out) and her
brother Sammy (who has become withdrawn and depressed).
Case Four will illustrate how easy it is to miss the presence
of a stepfamily structure in an Action Family. Stepparents are
referred to as the child's "mom" or "dad" and no attention is
paid to step dynamics, with sometimes near-disastrous results.

For Action Families, the path to successful completion
of·the Stepfamily Cycle requires going back to the Awareness
Stage, to complete both individual and joint awareness tasks.
Sometimes an influx of realistic information and some good
coaching are enough to help an Action Family find a workable developmental pace. It's as if some of these families
simply took a wrong turn, and, now that they have a good
map, they can proceed with relative ease. As step realities are
exposed, some grief work may be necessary. Again, psychodynamic issues may complicate the process—a biological parent with many previous losses may find the loss of the fantasy
of a first-time-like family very painful. Biological parents who
fear abandonment by their new partners may have more
difficulty asking their new mates to remain in the uncomfortable position of an outsider for a while. Stepparents with
intense needs for control will have more difficulty functioning by the biological subsystem's norms until they form a
strong enough relationship with their stepchildren. Adults
who feel very deprived will have difficulty in balancing their

own needs for an intimate new relationship with children's needs for intimate time with their parent. Children in step-families tend to leave home earlier (White & Booth, 1985). This may be particularly true in Action Families. Alternatively, children may shift custody, leaving the adults to themselves.

Perhaps because I work primarily with adults, I see few Action Families. Work in progress by Larry Ganong and Marilyn Coleman in the state of Missouri is showing that many stepfamilies, particularly simple stepfamilies in which only one adult brings children, function "as if" they were a nuclear family. We can imagine that some of those families are Immersed Families (the family is functioning as if the stepparent could simply assimilate into the biological unit) but that many others are Action Families (the family is functioning as if the children could immediately adapt to a new parental authority). Because women still get custody in the majority of cases, most full-time stepfamilies are stepfather families. Differences in perceived power between women and men, and a tired single mom's eagerness to have her new husband take over, may intensify the precipitous pull into the Action Stage.

Four Case Histories

Having described these four paths through the Step-family Cycle, we will now illustrate each with an actual case history.

Case One: The Davidson/Millers, An Aware Family

The Davidson/Millers are a nonclinical "double" family (each adult brought a child) that beautifully illustrate the path that Aware Families take through the Stepfamily Cycle. Unlike the first double family we met in Figure 2.4 (the Black/Joneses) this family has taken the time to complete awareness tasks.

When they met, Jan Davidson, 36, had been a single parent to Gabby, then 8, since her birth. Chuck Miller, 40, the father of a 9-year-old boy, Kevin, was newly separated and just beginning a hotly contested custody battle.

Now, a little over two years later, Jan and Chuck have married and are living together in what was Jan's house. Gabby lives with them full-time, and Kevin divides his time between his dad's house and his mother's house. Information for this case study was gathered in a series of interviews: a long one with Jan a year and a half into the relationship, a two-hour interview with the children a few months later, and a shorter conversation with Chuck at about the same time.

Jan Davidson and Chuck Miller came into stepfamily living with very realistic expectations. Both expected they would initially operate as a collection of very different biological and step units, each needing separate space and time, and each requiring a different pace and level of involvement. This family also demonstrates the ways in which Aware Families support both insiders and outsiders in the new family, maintaining respect for the established middle ground of the biological parent-child relationship, while working actively to create separate spaces in which the middle ground in new step relationships can "thicken."

In this family, each adult inhabits both step and biological roles in the family, a situation that can breed either competition ("But I don't do that with *your* child, why should you with mine?") or mutual understanding. In this case, both adults illustrate the empathy and respectfulness that is typical of Aware Families. Like the Aware Andrea and Harry, the combination of realistic expectations and good communication skills makes Jan and Chuck likely to treat difficult spots in early stepfamily living with curiosity and an "attitude of learning" (Paul & Paul, 1983, 1987) rather than blame and self-reproach.

Jan and Chuck might have completed Awareness Stage tasks just as well with more troubled children. However, Kevin and Gabby, the two stepsiblings in this family, also brought some qualities that may have contributed to an easier start. Both Gabby and Kevin were accessible, emotionally healthy, and likable children. They were on the young side although Gabby at 8 was just under the age when research is telling us that stepdaughter-stepfather relationships begin to become much more difficult.

Jan and Chuck's relationship began when they met at a party given by a mutual friend. Their initial courtship is already part of the shared history of the new family. Gabby and Kevin tell "The Story" together with obvious relish. Kevin begins:

> The mother of my best friend, Bobby, invited Jan to this birthday party dance. And that's how it started.

Gabby continues:

> There was another woman there that Chuck met. He was more interested in her. But she wasn't free. So he called up my mom. Then he sent her a dozen red roses at work with a nice card. And then they went out to a dance together!

About three months into the adult relationship, Chuck began to get involved with Jan's daughter Gabby "in a fairly low-key kind of way."

Because Chuck was engaged in a highly contested divorce, Jan did not meet Chuck's son until six months later. Thus, the family began with Jan and her daughter Gabby as the insider unit and Chuck as the outsider not only to the parent-child unit, but in Jan's home. Many stepfamilies flounder because they cannot or will not appreciate the very different feelings and needs of insiders and outsiders. Jan, however, was very attuned to Chuck's position as outsider in her household:

> Once Chuck started to stay at my house, I wanted to know "Where do you need space? What can I do so you'll feel more like this is your home?"

When Chuck didn't immediately respond, Jan continued to be interested in helping to identify his needs as an outsider:

He didn't have real high demands. I had to offer several times before he would take me up on my requests. Finally, I went out and bought him a metal drawer thing just like the one he had at his house. Just so he could feel more at home and could put his clothes away.

Likewise, Chuck was a sensitive outsider, beginning to build a relationship with Gabby, but continuing to be respectful of her relationship with her mother. Chuck:

It wasn't conscious or cognitive. But it was clear to me that Jan and Gabby had a real close relationship. So I just sort of hung out in the same space with them. If Gabby needed something from Jan, I'd just drop into the background and not get in the way.

Jan:

There were times when one of us would ask her to wait if she interrupted. But if she needed something right away, he could back off.

We can see that Jan and Chuck began their lives together actively (if not always consciously) reaching to understand each other's needs and feelings.

Most important, Jan and Chuck did not attempt to operate immediately as a blended family: "We're not a whole family," said Jan. "It will be interesting to see what shape we have over time." These realistic expectations about the step structure of their new family spawned some purposeful and some intuitive moves to give each of the subunits in their new family its own time and space:

Most of it's intuitive, but some of it is conscious. We each deliberately have time with our own child. We did that by design. We have time for the two of us by design. And we make time for the four of us by design.

Jan and Chuck supported each other's biological relationships not only by giving separate time and space, but by respecting each other's special parenting relationships. Neither adult attempted to immediately take over parenting the other's child. Jan:

I would never tell Chuck's son, Kevin, how to eat his cereal. Chuck does that. He'll say, "Please be careful, there's a tablecloth on the table." That's between Chuck and Kevin. I would never say that to Kevin, not yet. We're each harder on our own child and have a wider tolerance with the other's child.

Many new stepcouples respect children's needs for continuity and special time with their own parent at the expense of the adult couple. It is important to note that although Chuck and Jan supported their existing parent-child relationships by not operating as a unified parental unit yet, they at the same time protected their adult alliance. They agreed not to undermine each other in front of their children when inevitable cultural differences cropped up. Chuck:

We disagreed often in my first marriage, and in front of Kevin. I want us to be supportive of each other. If we disagree, I want us to handle it away from the children. So I don't undermine her and she doesn't undermine me.

Equally important, Chuck and Jan provided protected time for their couple relationship from the very beginning of their new family:

We always did things alone as a couple. Somehow fairly naturally, we would always do things by ourselves. We would go out at night, and go away for the weekend.

Jan attributes Chuck's openness to Gabby and his willingness to include Gabby as a threesome to Chuck's interest in children. However, even the most child-loving stepparent becomes less generous when she or he must always compete with a child for her parent's attention. Chuck's willingness to move aside for Jan's daughter can also be attributed to the fact that his needs for intimacy and for some measure of comfort as an outsider were being met.

Chuck and Jan were also attentive to the need for the two stepparent-child units to get to know each other. Chuck and Gabby, of course, had a head start. As Chuck's custody battle began to become resolved, it was time to introduce his son into the new family, which now had a nine-month history. Again, Chuck and Jan understood that Jan and her new stepson needed an opportunity to get to know each other slowly, and separate from Chuck. A combination of sensitive planning and fortuitous timing gave them that opportunity. Jan:

> Chuck and I had this plan. Once the divorce was final and he didn't have to worry about compromising his chances for custody, his son, Kevin, and I would get to know each other in a low-key sort of way. It turned out Chuck had to leave for a business trip on a weekend when he had Kevin. And I ended up taking care of Kevin.

Although the opportunity for time alone with her new stepson without Chuck was fortuitous, Jan intuitively understood that it was not time yet for her and the boy to be "thrust in each other's laps." She suggested that Kevin bring a friend along with him.

> It was brilliant. Kevin's friend was real friendly and interactive, which left Kevin free to sit back and watch. The first night it was Gabby, and Kevin, and his friend. The second night the friend left and Gabby went to visit a friend of hers. So that night it was just Kevin and me. It was perfect. We played poker, which he's really good at, and he cleaned me out.

The business trip was a lucky break that gave Jan and her new stepson precious space and time to get to know each other without having to compete with the more powerful father-son relationship. However, Jan understood the opportunity, and she used it well. She provided Kevin with the protection of a familiar friend for the first night. (A less realistic pair of adults might have felt that was "unfamily-like.") And intuitively or consciously, she operated on Kevin's ground the first night they spent alone together, playing poker with him and allowing him to clean her out. Even with this fairly comfortable beginning, both Chuck and Jan remained very aware that Jan's relationship with Kevin was in a very different place from Chuck's with Gabby. Jan:

> Chuck is closer to stepping in as a parent with Gabby. He's known her longer. I'm just at the stage of *watching* him with his son. I'm not ready to say anything yet. My daughter and Chuck have known each other for 10 months, and fairly intensely for most of that time. His son and I are only three months old! That's really different.

I will say to Gabby, "Please don't put two pounds of jelly on your toast." But I wouldn't say that to Kevin. Chuck, of course, is a little closer to doing that with Gabby.

Jan and Chuck understand and actively plan time for one-on-one relationships, which is important in all of the complex relationships in a new stepfamily. Jan:

Someone will say, "I need time alone with you," or "I think Gabby needs time alone with you."

Another unplanned but equally well-used event provided an opportunity for the fourth step subunit, the children, to pull together. Jan:

Now the kids have created their own separateness from us. They go off for long conversations. But that was not planned.

It happened at first by accident. Once Gabby knew Chuck and Kevin were moving in, we said to her, "You know all this stuff that Kevin doesn't know yet. And we asked her not to tell him, but to let his dad tell him. And she was able to keep her mouth shut for a while.

Then one day the three of them were in the basement. Chuck was making bird feeders with Gabby and Kevin. And Gabby slipped and said something like, "Well, when you—" (meaning to go on to say something about, "Well, when you move in, we'll . . . "), and then she stopped.

The children pick up the story from here. Kevin:

So we went up to Gabby's room and she told me the whole story. I sort of knew it already. But nobody had told me anything so I didn't ask. Gabby told me the whole thing.

Jan continues:

Then the two of them came downstairs and said, "We just had a big talk and we're not telling you what we talked about."

So that really put them together as a unit. Now they seem to have figured out that the two of them together are stronger. They formed a unit to wheel and deal with us. So they deal as a unit with us, about staying up late, buying gum, getting more dessert.

Some new couples might have been threatened by the power the children had seized, but Chuck and Jan have been able to appreciate the importance of the two children turning to each other.

Talking with the adults, it was obvious that not all of this bonding between the two children happened by accident. Jan and Chuck were not only able to appreciate and support the children's intuitive moves to form a unit, but they also made some active moves of their own to help Kevin and Gabby come together. During the winter, the foursome went away for a ski week together. Chuck and his son are avid skiers. Neither Jan nor Gabby had ever skied. In another new stepfamily, this difference could have split the unit right down the middle along biological lines. In this family, Chuck helped his son give pointers to Gabby. And, in fact, he told Kevin that he would pay for his lift tickets if he would help Gabby learn to ski.

This was a particularly good move for a variety of reasons. Gabby was the insider child, having been "in" on the new family for nine months before Kevin even knew about it, and being the resident child into whose home her new stepbrother would move. Kevin was vulnerable to being "stuck" as the family outsider not only by his historical position in the family, but by the difference in his and Gabby's personalities. Gabby is by far the more active and outgoing of the pair. Jan:

Gabby talks a mile a minute, has her feelings right out there, and will climb in Chuck's or my lap in a moment. Kevin is much quieter, more discriminating about what he'll say. He doesn't like hugs. Both children are strong-willed, but she is closer to the surface. She is a year younger, but she has an easier time with school work.

However, the ski trip placed Chuck and Kevin as the more expert insiders. Skiing is a place where Kevin feels especially good about himself. Chuck's simple strategy enabled his son to move toward Gabby in an area where he is a comfortable and expert insider. Thus Chuck intuitively offered Kevin an opportunity to shift the balance of power between the two children. And again, Chuck didn't expect his son to *want* to teach Gabby "because she's your new sister." He paid him.

Jan and Chuck not only encouraged and supported the children, but they also set some clear limits on behavior they felt was destructive to the new family. Gabby remembers what happened when she teased Kevin about what she called her "backyard ways"—her secret routes through the neighborhood that were familiar to her, but not to Kevin. Gabby:

I got in trouble. My mom heard me say, "You can't go on my backyard route." And she sent me to my room. I think that taught me a lesson. You have to make the other person feel at home.

When Jan and Gabby lived at Chuck and Kevin's house while Jan's house was being renovated, the process was reversed. Kevin:

When Gabby came to live in our house, my dad made me take a lot of my stuff off the walls of my bedroom. He made me move a lot of my stuff out so that Gabby would feel comfortable in our house.

This balance of support for the relationship without expecting these new stepsiblings to love each other, combined with firm and realistic limit-setting, has left the children free to get to know each other without pressure. The adults report that recently the children emerged from one of their long talks to announce as a unit: "We've been talking and we want you to know that we are *not* friends. We want this to be really clear." Chuck responded by asking the children, "Well, what are you?" "We don't know," said the children, "but we're *not* friends." A family with less realistic expectations might have greeted this announcement with protestations, "But you're brother and sister, you're in the same family," and so on. Chuck and Jan responded with acceptance and curiosity, leaving the children free to continue to define their own relationship. They were not only unthreatened by what some stepcouples might perceive as a statement that is disruptive to family unity, but they clearly understood that the children were operating very much as a unit, struggling together to define their relationship, and announcing their results as a very unified team.

The combination of some fortuitous opportunities for the children to "gang up" and the adults' active but unpressured support of the children has paid off. In my interview with the children, their bonding was obvious. They bragged about booby traps they'd set together for the adults. They consulted as a team in the hall when I asked a question they were unsure about answering.

As the time when Chuck and Kevin would make their official move into Jan and Gabby's home came closer, the adults continued actively trying to take care of both insider and outsider needs. They understood that Kevin was particularly vulnerable to feeling powerless and on foreign territory. They also understood that Gabby was about to have to give up eight years of being the only child in her household. Jan and Chuck understood that Kevin needed to feel he had some control and a place in Gabby and Jan's home. Gabby needed help dealing with feeling invaded and displaced. Chuck and Jan masterfully balanced Kevin's outsider needs and Gabby's insider needs. First, they made sure that Kevin could choose his own room in Jan's house. They told him they would totally repaint it. "We told him, 'We're all going to do it together,' " thereby sending a clear message to him of being welcomed, having a place, and having some say.

However, Gabby with her usual quick, active style, "got all the rooms sorted out." Jan:

She decided in her head who would have each room. But we knew that Kevin would need to have some power and choice, or he'd really feel like an outsider.

Chuck stepped in brilliantly. Jan:

Chuck took Gabby aside and he advised her on how to manage this problem. He told her not to tell Kevin which one she wanted. Just let him choose. But he said to her, "If I were you, I would give him information so he chooses the room you don't want."

What was especially delightful to Jan was that Chuck as an outsider was able to bring an approach to the dilemma with Gabby that was brand-new to Jan:

There's Chuck giving Gabby all these manipulative skills. I wouldn't have done that. I might have told her directly just to back off. Chuck said, "If you want what you want, here's how to get it."

We can see in this interaction the very beginning threads of the "intimate outsider" stepparent role, as Chuck is close enough to the situation to understand Gabby's dilemma, and, because he is the outsider, far enough away to bring something new (and needed) to Gabby.

In addition to their realistic expectations and empathic interest in each other and their children, Chuck and Jan also brought with them some solid, already existing middle ground that made functioning as a new family easier. Jan:

Overall, we're fairly alike. The specifics are different. The general overall tone is similar. There are things we do differently, but they're not real big. And Chuck doesn't do things where I have to choke down my response.

For instance:

Our neatness styles are similar. I'm somewhat neater. He teases me affectionately. We're equally *clean*. But I sort things out and put them back in their place where he wouldn't. And he's willing to do that in my house.

The arena of parenting styles offers another good example. Jan and Chuck share enough middle ground to provide some areas of easy functioning. Equally important, where they differ, both are able to be respectful and interested. In the language of the Stepfamily Cycle, both can stick appropriately with awareness tasks: noticing the differences, naming them, describing them to each other, without moving precipitously into trying to change each other. Jan:

As a parent, Chuck would sooner and more clearly say, "Stop it. That's not OK." I tend to hang on longer. I give warnings: "You're pushing my limits!" I say, "Watch out!" whereas Chuck would say, "Stop."

So he thinks I'm not being clear enough to be helpful to Gabby until I lose it. He thinks I need to say "No" sooner. I, on the other hand, think he's too fast and sudden with his "No!" and that the behavior doesn't need that yet.

We're not that far apart. And he doesn't intervene. He's saying it to me in a way of, "I think it would be less painful for you. Why don't you try telling her to knock it off sooner?" *He doesn't intervene and take over, or pressure me about changing* [italics added]. So I feel more that he's trying to take care of me. Not that I'm doing a lousy job.

Again, Jan and Chuck are sticking with Awareness Stage tasks, beginning to describe the differences in their parenting styles to themselves and each other, but not moving precipitously to change each other (Mobilization) or to join their parenting styles (Action).

Jan and Chuck have a partly conscious, partly intuitive aesthetic about timing: They have supported the new step relationships in the family while respecting that the biological parent-child relationships must remain in place. They do not expect this to be the case forever and have moved slowly to come together. They have intuitively been able to stick with the tasks of the Early Stages: getting to know each other, making sense out of their experience, identifying existing middle ground, becoming aware of differences without trying to fix them all.

We don't do all of these things on purpose. But we talk about it. So then we know what to do the next time.

This family at the time of our interviews was poised at the threshold of the Middle Stages. As is typical of Aware Families, they have spent most of the Early Stages in Awareness. As they move into the Middle Stages, the solid shared base of understanding will enable them to move fairly directly into the Action Stage, beginning to make some shared rules, to establish some clearly defined "step" middle ground. Stepfamily living in an Aware Family is not without struggle and hard work. However, as the Davidson/Millers illustrate, these families expend much less effort trying to be what they cannot. As a result, we see Jan and Chuck wasting very little energy struggling against the tasks posed by their new family structure. They are free to devote their attention and energy to things that can make a difference and that move them along the developmental path to becoming a nourishing stepfamily.

Case Two: The Tolmans, An Immersed Family

After a year and a half the Davidson/Millers were poised comfortably on the threshold of the Action Stage. The Tolmans, whom we first met in Chapter One, have had a more difficult path. The Tolmans, like the Davidson/Millers, are a middle-class, dual-career couple. Tom Tolman, 31, had been divorced for six years when he married Jenny, who was 38. Jenny had been married, but had no children from her first marriage. Tom has a son, Ricky, by his first marriage, who was 8 when Tom remarried and who continues to live primarily with his mother. I began working with the Tolmans after they had been married about two years. They had a baby together four years later and now have been married for six years. Ricky is now 14 and Bobby, their new son, is almost 3.

The Tolmans are a successful Immersed Family. They spent two or three years in the Early Stages (much of it struggling in and out of Immersion), and another two or three in the Middle Stages (much of it in highly conflicted Mobilization). After six years of marriage and much hard work, many Action pieces have been put into place. The family now has some areas of step middle ground where they function with the ease and reliability of a Later Stage family. Some areas remain "under construction"; a few other areas still have the swampy treacherous feel of the Immersion Stage.

Like Jan and Chuck, Tom and Jenny brought a substantial amount of shared middle ground to their marriage. They share deeply felt religious and moral values and have much commonality about the kind of life-style they want.

Tom Tolman, like Jan Davidson, had spent most of his parenting relationship as a single parent, as his marriage broke up when his son Ricky was 6 months old. However, unlike Jan, Tom brought deeply rooted wishes for creating the family he never had with Ricky, and giving Ricky the mother he didn't have in Tom's first wife. Furthermore, unlike Jan and Chuck, who came together in the last two years, Tom and Jenny started their new family at a time when little good information was available about what to expect of stepfamily life. Ricky was a somewhat troubled child, having lived with an alcoholic mother most of his life. In addition, though their Catholicism gave Tom and Jenny some precious shared middle ground, it may also have given them a strong sense of what a family should look like and of a "right" way of doing things that combined to block their awareness of the actualities of their new stepfamily. Finally, both Tom and Jenny brought some previous family history that tangled their communication over step issues at critical junctures. All of these components have made communication between Tom and Jenny on step issues painful and complex. Nonetheless, they have been determined to make their family work, and after six years, a lot of hard work, and some outside help, they are close to completing the Stepfamily Cycle.

My contact with the Tolmans began when Jenny appeared for individual therapy after two years of marriage, feeling anxious and depressed. She had been referred by her family physician after being mysteriously plagued by the return of a childhood habit, grinding her teeth. For several years, Jenny had been trying to be the mother Ricky didn't have and Tom very much wanted her to be. She was clearly in the Immersion Stage: "Something's wrong here and it must be me." She felt terrible about herself as a stepmother, that she just didn't measure up.

Jenny and I worked together for several months, helping her to assess her expectations of herself, looking at what she felt she should be offering Ricky, and what she actually could offer him. As she got clearer about her feelings and her needs, it became obvious that she had a number of things she needed to negotiate with her husband. She had moved into the Awareness Stage and was heading fast toward Mobilization, though with very little understanding yet of Tom's experience of the family.

As we began couples work, it became clear that Tom and Jenny each brought some complicating previous family history to the new family. Tom had coped with the difficulties in his early family life by making his world very ordered. He learned at a young age to make decisions by himself ("Who was there to talk to?") and dealt with a series of abusive peer relationships as best he could by "pulling my feelers in so I wouldn't get so hurt." Jenny, as the oldest child in an alcoholic family, learned early to squelch her own needs. Like Tom, she deals with anxiety by creating order. Unlike Tom, her strategy for maintaining control is to keep her antennae out and to adjust quickly when the environment is threatening.

Tom and Jenny's respective roles in their stepfamily exacerbated this difference. Tom, as biological parent, would digest information and come to a conclusion, usually silently. His self-contained style didn't lend itself to asking Jenny questions about her needs, and the fact that his antennae were habitually pulled in meant he did not pick up nonverbal clues about her feelings. He would then go into motion with a plan that seemed perfectly reasonable to him, but which, to his disappointment and surprise, would leave Jenny feeling terrible.

Jenny's accommodating style did not at first lend itself to questioning Tom's decisions. Furthermore, the fact that *her* antennae were out, not in, meant she had little access to her own experience of the family. So she tried to acquiesce. The fact that she felt vaguely uneasy made her feel inadequate. As Jenny became a little clearer about her own needs, she began feeling less inadequate and more dissatisfied. She began speaking up more often, but, as is often true for angry stepparents, without much grace! She would whirl into motion attacking Tom for his insensitivity. Tom and Jenny would then become each other's nightmare. Tom would deal with Jenny's "spraying anxiety like a cat in heat" by trying to make order, which meant trying to get Jenny to see his already firmly formed point of view. Jenny would respond to feeling unseen and unheard by becoming more anxious. As her rising anxiety became more intolerable for him, Tom would pull in further and begin to make decisions about Ricky even more on his own, leaving Jenny feeling all the more outside.

The course of resolving these tangles in an Immersed Family is well illustrated by the Tolmans' struggle with the structure of their weekends with Ricky. Ricky, then 10, lived with his mother in New Hampshire. Tom and Jenny lived north of Boston. They would spend every other weekend in New Hampshire with Ricky at Tom's cottage near Ricky's mother's house. The weekends usually began early Saturday morning. The couple would drive up to New Hampshire, pick Ricky up at his mother's house, and then drive to their cottage. During this time, Ricky would chatter excitedly with his dad, while Jenny often sat silently. As in the vignette that opens Chapter One, the family spent most of these weekends together as a threesome, "being a family."

Jenny, who worked a more than full-time, high-stress management job, began to voice, somewhat tentatively at first, how hard the weekends were for her. She wanted time to rest from the week and more time to be alone with Tom. She found the time with Ricky exhausting and wanted less time with him. This was very painful for Tom, who very much wanted the family he had never had with Ricky. "It's four days out of 30," he kept saying to Jenny. "Why can't you just give me those four days to be with my son?" Although Jenny was clear enough to voice her needs, at least sporadically, she didn't yet have the strength to sustain herself in the face of Tom's disappointment and criticism. Jenny had moved into the Awareness Stage, but in this family there could be little understanding between insiders and outsiders until Jenny reached the Mobilization Stage and could sustain herself when Tom didn't get it.

The Tolman vignette at the beginning of Chapter One is from a session that took place in the middle of our first year of work togther. By this time, Jenny had taken a much stronger position. She had become very clear about what she felt and what she didn't like, as had Tom. The couple had moved fully into the Mobilization Stage and they were actively fighting over their differences. Although each was articulate about his or her experience, it was as if they were in two different worlds, each competing to be right. Because there was no interest or empathy across the experiential gap created by their stepfamily structure, they were stuck in Mobilization. Their fights at this point were often painful and frustrating, and because the work of understanding each other did not usually get done, they rarely reached any resolution. The couple would then slip back into confusion and betrayal (Immersion) or return to a silent, separate, pained Awareness Stage until Jenny rocked the boat again, catapulting them once more into Mobilization.

Weaving between step issues and the family-of-origin issues that intensified them, the work of the next few months focused on helping Tom and Jenny to slow down enough to understand each other. Finally, in one session we listed on a very large piece of newsprint all of the needs the family was trying to meet in a little more than a 30-hour weekend. Tom very much wanted time together as a whole family; Ricky needed one-to-one time with his dad; Jenny needed time alone with Tom; Jenny also desperately needed time by herself; Ricky wanted time alone with Jenny; and the whole family needed to rest and relax enough to return home and gear up for another intense week of work and school.

Both Tom and Jenny walked out of that session stunned by how complex the problem of how to structure their weekends with Ricky really was. Although the complexity was overwhelming, becoming realistic about the immensity of their task removed some of the stigma and blame from their feelings about these weekends and cleared the way for the first time for some real problem solving.

Furthermore, it was as if by laying out all of their diverse needs on paper in front of them together, we had finally loosened the tightfisted hold Tom and Jenny each had on their own piece of the family map. For the first time, they could both see the whole territory. Now there was some chance that they could begin to function as a team and find a path they could travel together.

With this more shared understanding, Tom and Jenny were able to come up with a plan that might work. The new plan went something like this: Tom and Jenny would have an intimate date on either Thursday or Friday night. Often this meant buying a pizza and watching their favorite television program in bed together. This met the need for some intimate couple time and some time to wind down from the week, ensuring that Jenny could go into the weekend with less anxiety, feeling more of an insider. On Saturday morning, rather than immediately picking up Ricky, Tom and Jenny would drive first to their cottage where Jenny would be dropped off. Tom would then go alone to pick up Ricky. This meant a longer drive for Tom, but it gave Jenny some time by herself. Equally important, it gave Ricky time alone with his father without Jenny feeling like a third wheel.

When Tom and Ricky returned, the three would spend some time together. At several points during the time as a threesome, Tom was to look straight at Jenny and/or to put his arm around her. If he forgot, she was to go up to him and put her arm around him and remind him. This gave Tom and Jenny something concrete they could do to help Jenny feel less like an outsider.

At some point in the evening, or the next morning, Tom and Jenny were to take a walk together, just the two of them. We also invented several things Jenny could do alone with Ricky that would give them time together without pressure—go to the store together, play a game, etc. The plan eased tensions considerably.

However, Jenny still found the weekends exhausting. After several months, she timidly asked to stay home alone while Tom went ahead to New Hampshire. A whole new round of intimate negotiations began as Tom struggled again with his needs to preserve as much as possible of his wish for family and Jenny struggled to voice her very different needs without either withdrawing or attacking.

The conflict between Tom and Jenny's pictures of their family was played out again when Jenny became pregnant. Jenny and Tom fought bitterly over how to use the one free bedroom in their two-bedroom home. This had been a combination junk room and Ricky's space when he visited them. Jenny wanted to put away all of Ricky's things to make a "real baby's room." Tom was hurt and outraged that Jenny would deprive Ricky of a stable place in their home. Jenny felt that Ricky's occasional visits didn't warrant "using up a whole room."

Though this crisis again exposed a great gap in their understanding of each other, they moved through the Step-family Cycle much more quickly. This time there was no long silent Immersion Stage. They immediately engaged each other head on. They needed help and support to go back to the Awareness Stage, slow down, and get *interested* in each other's feelings.

Both Tom and Jenny also required some help in identifying the fantasies underpinning this fight. The conflict was actually over two opposing and very different fantasies. Jenny had spent many childless years, preceded by many years parenting her brothers and sisters. For her the picture of having her own baby had become very particular and intense. It included a "baby's room." This "baby's room" did not include an 11-year-old's paraphernalia. Tom, too, had looked forward to the new baby but with a very different fantasy of his son having a sibling and the two children sharing a room.

Both Tom and Jenny felt betrayed by the other's inability to understand their feelings. Empathy across the experiential gap was again hard to come by, but helping them each to feel the loss they faced seemed to loosen the tangle. Jenny particularly explored her longing, deeply rooted after so many years, in great loving detail, and mourned the loss. As the fantasies receded, the couple decided they needed more space and began making plans to buy a larger house.

Three years after I had first seen them, and five years into their marriage, Tom and Jenny came in for a "checkup" having just maneuvered beautifully through a school vacation that Ricky had spent entirely with them and their new baby son. They had clearly moved very firmly through the Action Stage and were heading into the Later Stages. Both glowed about how well the vacation had gone (the last few had been disasters). "What made the difference?" I asked. Jenny replied quickly:

I got enough time alone, so I was rested. And I got enough time with Tom so I felt fine when Ricky was around. I got real clear about my needs, and I didn't get vague about them. I just stood my ground.

She turned to Tom and said, "I *really* appreciate that you could let me go. It made all the difference." I asked Tom what enabled him to "let Jenny go." He said poignantly:

I finally let go that I would have the family I didn't have. I knew what it had felt like to have it. Then I wanted it back. I figured being a whole family is the way it's supposed to be. I just figured that it's the right way until proven wrong.

I just couldn't hear Jenny until I let that go. I guess I finally saw it wasn't working. And I decided to take a real risk and to try it the other way.

It was stunning to me that this statement came fully five years after Tom and Jenny had married. It underlined for me once more how firmly rooted the wish for a "real" family can be and how silently and powerfully it had remained an unseen knot below the surface impeding the process of forging a workable stepfamily life. Equally important, Tom reminded me again of how risky it feels to relinquish these wishes.

We leave the Tolmans poised at the brink of the Later Stages, where life will become easier for them. While some Middle Stages work remains, the Tolmans are becoming a stepfamily.

Case Three: The Johnstons, A Mobilized Family

The Johnstons, a "double" or "complex" stepfamily, demonstrate the lively, energetic, highly engaged style of a successful Mobilized Family. Cecelia and Richard married when Cecelia's son, Corin, was 3. Richard's daughter, Mary, was 15½ and Jon was 13½. Corin lived with the family almost full-time from the start of the marriage. Mary and Jon visited on weekends, moving into the new family occasionally when their mother was in a crisis.

When I interviewed them for the first time, Cecelia and Richard had been married for a little over seven years and had moved fully into the Resolution Stage. Cecelia's son, Corin, then 10, lived with them full-time. Richard's children, Mary, 23, and Jon, 21, had become occasional visitors. The Johnstons are a nonclinical family. Data for this case was gathered in a long interview with Cecelia, Richard, and Corin, and several subsequent shorter interviews with Cecelia. Unfortunately, Richard's children were not available.

It is important to note that the Johnston children, whom we first met in Chapter Five, illustrate the ways in which three children in the same stepfamiy can have very different rates of adaptation. Each of the three has formed a very different but "mutually suitable" (Crosbie-Burnett, 1984) relationship with his or her stepparent. The relationship between Richard and Cecelia's son, Corin, came most easily and formed a solid piece of middle ground for the family within the first year or two. Richard:

Corin accepted me right away. He was young. His father had opted out, so he was really wanting parenting from me. I had missed out on some parenting because I was unhappy in my marriage in the early years of my kids. With Corin I got the chance to be more of a poppa.

Corin soon began to actively participate in making his family whole. Cecelia:

When I married Richard I took his name, but Corin kept his dad's name. So we had two different last names. We used to call him "Corin Cub" as a term of affection. So he made this last name "Bear" for all of us. He called Jon "Big Brother Bear." He would draw pictures for Richard of the Bear family. It was his way of making a whole family out of us.

With Richard's children it was a different story. Jon and Mary were accustomed to a loose chaotic household. Cecelia is a person who likes to provide clear limits, and prefers a certain amount of order to her family life. In the first year that they were married, Richard's son, Jon, chose to live with them. Cecelia now became a full-time stepmother to a child with whom she had never expected to live. In an Immersed Family, she might have tried to adapt silently to Richard and Jon's very different life-style. However, Cecelia, like many stepparents in Mobilized Families, is a powerful, articulate person. She knew what she wanted, and, like many a Mobilized stepparent, she had some strong, unrealistic fantasies about her potential role with her stepchildren. She stepped in quickly to make some changes. Cecelia:

At first there was this honeymoon. Then I started setting down rules, and I became the "bad bitch stepmom." When Jon came to live with us, I really moved in on him. I had only one child. I wanted more kids. I wanted to make up for the kids I didn't have and also for the mothering I thought they weren't getting. I thought that they were very entangled with their mother and that she really didn't set enough limits with them. *Now* I know that's normal when you're a single parent. But I didn't know that then. I guess I thought I was going to save these kids from chaos!

In an Aware Family, Cecelia would have moved more slowly, staying on the outside of Richard's relationship with his son, allowing him to set the rules with him. She would have noticed differences and talked to Richard about them, but in a tone more like someone trying to describe a piece of landscape accurately. Instead, Cecelia moved more like a bulldozer making space for a new house! In an Aware Family, Cecelia might have asked for a few changes, but would have put them into action through Richard and would not have initiated much on which she didn't have his full agreement. Conversely, in an Action Family, Richard would have moved aside and let Cecelia take over. He would either have been unaware of what was being asked of his children, or unable to express it. However, Richard, like most biological parents in a Mobilized Family, was both aware and expressive. He understood what was being asked of his children:

> That was tough for me. My first wife and I were fairly permissive. When we split, she had a lot of trouble controlling the kids. I was the weekend parent, and they acted fine with me. My kids weren't used to having boundaries and Cecelia was used to having them.

Like many part-time biological fathers, he felt torn between Cecelia and the fear of losing his first real opportunity to live with his son since the divorce:

> There was my son maybe wanting to live with me, and there was Cecelia making all these rules that were making it hard. I kept thinking, "He really made a conscious move to live with me, and I don't want to do anything that will make him leave." Even when I really believed in what Cecelia was saying, it was hard for me because I felt, "If I do that, Jon may not love me."

Richard began to struggle vigorously with Cecelia, not just over the rules, but equally important, over Cecelia's unrealistic expectations of Jon:

> I think Cecelia needed Jon to love her. I kept saying it wasn't in the cards for him to love her. That it was a very unrealistic need to have from a teenager who's not your son. I kept saying he did have to respect her, but she couldn't expect him to love her.

In those first few years, Richard and Cecelia fought a lot. However, typical of successful Mobilized Families, one gets a sense of how equally matched they were, and of the goodwill and respect Richard and Cecelia had for each other as they engaged over a raft of issues. Richard, for instance, rarely disagreed with Cecelia in front of his children. He argued with her in private, out of the children's earshot. Couples in less sucessful Mobilized Families argue with much less mutual respect and caring. As we listen to Cecelia and Richard, we can also feel the commitment that underlies their efforts. Richard:

We fought well. In Florida the weather is warm a lot, and we sat out on the back patio, and we confronted each other a lot. It wasn't always pretty.

But even though it was hard, we knew it was important, and we had enough goodwill and caring for each other that we didn't tear the relationship apart while we were fighting.

Cecelia continues:

There were a lot of those porch evenings. What really helped was that we thought of it as in the interests of the kids, that the worst thing would be for us to split up. And you know, we are the only couple in my stepdaughter's life. Her mother is involved in her third divorce.

It is as if this commitment to working it out formed a kind of middle ground for Richard and Cecelia that held them together despite the large differences in the way they wanted to function with his children. The fact that Richard and Corin's relationship remained very strong, providing some area of easy functioning for the family, must have added to the sense of a shared middle ground despite their differences.

This sense of having a place where they felt joined may have helped keep Cecelia and Richard's anxiety level low enough so that their fights, although not always pretty, strengthened their marriage rather than eroding it. Like the Mobilized Harry and Andrea, the Johnstons have a specific, informative fighting style that gives each member of the couple a chance to learn something about the other each time they fight.

In a double stepfamily, the fact that each adult inhabits both the step and the biological parent role can be divisive or unifying. For the Johnstons, it was the latter. Another man in Richard's position might have used his easier relationship with Corin against Cecelia ("Why can't you be as easygoing with my kids as I am with yours?"). However, both Cecelia and Richard understood that Corin was much more accessible and available than Richard's children. Both knew he also had had much steadier parenting in his young life—Richard's ex-wife had lived with a series of abusive men who had left their mark on his children.

Cecelia's relationship with Corin also gave her a resting place where she could be an insider and feel empathy for the dilemma she was creating for Richard by pushing his son so hard:

Having my own son helped. I had a place where I *was* connected. And it helped me to understand the bind I was putting Richard in by pushing his kids so hard.

The easier relationship with Corin, then, continued to function as an area of easy middle ground in the family. For all these reasons, as they fought, Richard and Cecelia began to get through to each other. Cecelia also had some outside assistance from a therapist who helped her to soften her fantasies about Jon:

I had a great woman therapist who helped me to see that my fantasies about my stepson and me were way out of line, that my need for closeness with him was out of line. He needed to be out in the world, she told me, having girlfriends. She really helped me to let go.

Cecelia began to understand that she couldn't become the mom Jon hadn't had, and she began to back off. Like many stepparents who have painfully relinquished closely held fantasies, Cecelia's new awareness is tinged with regret for not having known:

I know now that you can't convince a teenager they have to love someone else. And it doesn't have to do with the *person* you are. But I wish I'd known to give Jon the distance. If you run after a squirrel, it will run faster than you do. All you can do is put out your hand with a nut. And if you're fortunate, the squirrel will come to you.

On the other side, Richard began to understand Cecelia's need for more order and system in her relationship with his kids and her need for some control over their behavior. With these hard-won pieces of information in place, Cecelia and Richard were able to carve out one area where Cecelia *could* have a role—she would hand out the allowances. However, the new system was not set up by Cecelia, but by the whole family:

I wanted some realistic way to stay involved, and this worked. We set up contracts for each kid: how much money, for how often they had to clean up their room, etc. We all agreed. Since I was home more, that eliminated my nagging them, too. If they didn't do a particular chore, they got a certain amount of money off.

It was all agreed beforehand. Because his children were accustomed to asking Richard for money, this system naturally had its problems. Cecelia:

The kids were used to going to their dad for money. Now things had changed, and they were supposed to come to me. But sometimes they would go to Richard, and he would say, "Fine," and give them money. And I would feel trapped and undercut.

But, just as when Richard disagreed with Cecelia's rules, "We almost never fought with each other in public." Cecelia confronted Richard on this issue out of the children's earshot. Richard:

We didn't always feel united, but we almost never crossed each other openly in front of the kids.

In the midst of all this hard work, Richard and Cecelia also found some easier paths to thickening the middle ground in their new family:

We invented a "family night." Each Sunday we ate together. One person got to decide a family activity, and everyone else had to do it. We took turns. The person whose family night it was also got to call a family meeting any time they wanted to that week.

As Cecelia moved out of her precipitously mobilized parenting role with her stepchildren, she began to develop more empathy for them. One night Cecelia heard Mary talking to her boyfriend and crying. When the phone call ended, Cecelia, who had not been close to Mary, went up to her and said, "You really miss your mom, don't you?" "She hugged me," said Cecelia. Cecelia's map of the family had now enlarged considerably, and that helped her to make a bridge to Mary.

As things quieted down, more Action pieces began to fall into place. And, as understanding deepened and her relationship with her husband solidified, Cecelia's step-re-moved position with Richard's children became more and more comfortable and workable. Now in the Resolution Stage, the Johnston family includes three very different step-parent-child relationships. Corin calls Richard "Dad." He has invented a convention that gives him space for both Richard and his biological father, whom he visits occasionally. "Whichever one I'm with," says Corin, "I call that one 'Dad' and the other one by his first name." After seven years, Cece-lia and Mary have developed a very special stepmother-step-daughter relationship. Mary calls Cecelia her "motherly friend," and Cecelia has a fully mature intimate-outsider role with her stepdaughter. Jon remains somewhat outside the family. He has always been his mother's support and so may be in more of a loyalty bind than either of the other children. As we saw in Chapter Five, he still asks immediately to speak to his dad when Cecelia answers the phone.

As with most stepfamilies, new issues arise in the Reso-lution Stage that take the family back to some earlier terri-tory. For the Johnstons, it was Mary's wedding. As they en-tered the eighth year of their marriage, well into the Resolution Stage, Cecelia discovered that her stepdaughter, Mary, had listed only her biological parents on her wedding invitation. Cecelia found herself in the throes of some very old feelings:

I've been so close to Mary, and now I'm pushed out again. It hurts. It really hurts.

In the early years of her Mobilized Family, Cecelia might have taken a very strong stand with Mary or with her hus-band. Now in the Resolution Stage, Cecelia and Richard functioned much more like an Aware Family. Cecelia talked to Richard and cried in his arms. She called her friends who were stepmothers, "who understood perfectly how I felt. That helped more than anything!" With some effort Cecelia began to understand that Mary was reworking her feelings about having so many extra people in her life. However, the wedding loomed as a potentially very painful event for Cecelia, who knew she would feel very much the outsider in the presence of Mary's mother.

To admit there's another woman who is more entitled than I am is so painful for me all over again. I'm so envious of her. I'm not proud of feeling that way. But I know I do.

A stepmother in Cecelia's position in the early years of an Immersed Family would have chastised herself for her difficulty. Cecelia knew her worries were real. With her now expanded empathic map, Cecelia also knew that Richard, even as supportive as he wanted to be, would be full of his own feelings in the presence of his ex-wife at their daughter's wedding. Cecelia set about taking care of herself. She invited a close friend, another stepmother, to the wedding. The friend had never met Mary. "I told her not to bring a gift," said Cecelia. "I told her she should just bring herself, and that what I needed from her was to just sit next to me and be my buddy and gossip with me, so that I'd have a place where I could be real comfortable. That was her gift to Mary." And indeed, Cecelia supported herself well enough so that she could be the gracious outsider that Mary needed her to be.

We leave the Johnstons fully into the Resolution Stage. While progress for them has not been as smooth as for the Aware Family in Case One, their lively, highly engaged style has served them well in forging a satisfying, nourishing life together.

Case Four: The Wentworths, An Action Family

Arlene Goldfarb, 33, and her second husband, Michael Wentworth, 34, were clients of a supervisee who worked in a local clinic. Arlene's first husband had died suddenly in a helicopter crash when her son, Jonah, was 2, and her daughter, Leah, was 6. Five years later, after dating very little,

Arlene ran into Michael at a high-school reunion. When they married a year later, Arlene changed her name to Wentworth, and Michael adopted Arlene's children, "so the children wouldn't have a different last name, and we would really be a family."

When Arlene and Michael came for help toward the end of their first year of marriage, Jonah was 9 and Leah had just turned 13 years old. Like many Action Families, the Wentworths came in around a child-centered problem. Leah's grades were falling, and her teachers were noting that her behavior in class was increasingly aggressive, and her mother added, she had become "downright insolent" with Michael.

The Wentworths are an example of an Action Family with few complicating psychodynamic issues, who were able to respond to education, grief work focused on relinquishing fantasies, and some active coaching by the supervisee. They also illustrate some of the particular pitfalls that await a stepfamily formed by death. These dynamics were further complicated by the fact that when Arlene remarried, Michael became stepfather to a 12-year-old girl. Research tells us the stepfather-stepdaughter combination is likely to be especially harrowing at this age.

Most disturbing to me, this is a case in which stepfamily dynamics were crucial, but were almost missed. Leah's teachers, her school guidance counselor, the school social worker, and my supervisee all referred to Michael as Leah's father. The supervisee had attributed Leah's difficulties to the fact that the family had recently moved into the school system, requiring that Leah shift from an open classroom in a small rural school to a much more structured one in a very large urban school. She had concentrated on helping Arlene and Michael to help Leah's teachers and guidance counselor understand this change. The fact that this was a stepfamily did not emerge until the second time my supervisee presented the case, and then only because she mentioned that Leah, in response to a directive from Michael to clean up her room, had said, "I don't have to, and besides you're not my father."

Only then did I find out that Arlene and Michael had just been married a year and that he was, in fact, the children's stepfather. "I just didn't think it was important," said the embarrassed supervisee to the chagrined stepfamily expert! In fact, my supervisee, a very empathic young woman, had in many ways been in tune with Arlene and Michael's heartfelt desire to present themselves as an "ordinary" family. The guidance counselor, who did know that the couple was recently married, said, "I just didn't think it was important. They seemed so happy together, and he's so involved, and I thought, 'Isn't this nice—they're making this new family together!' "

The fact that this was a stepfamily put Leah's dilemma in a very different context. Arlene and her children had been a single-parent family for five years before she met Michael. Like many single-parent mothers and their daughters, Arlene and Leah had been very close. Their closeness had been intensified by the fact that Arlene had dated very little. Then suddenly Arlene had fallen "head over heels in love" with Michael.

An interview with Leah revealed that she, in fact, had felt quite abandoned when her mother became involved with Michael. With her deepened awareness of what might be happening, the supervisee was now able to provide Leah with a much more empathic ear, and the story came tumbling out. With the marriage had come not only a stranger in the house and a new last name, but a host of new, stricter rules. The move had come a few months after the remarriage. So within a few months, Leah had lost her name, her close relationship with her mother, her friends, her old neighborhood, a home she had lived in since birth, and her school. The move forced her to cope with a brand-new, much larger and much stricter school, without close friends, without her close relationship with her mother, in a strange urban environment, and with a new man she was calling "Dad" but who was a stranger to her. The family now had very little familiar middle ground for her to retreat to. This fact was made even more palpable by a marked difference in Leah's physical features. She is blond and large-boned like her father. Both Arlene and Michael are small and dark-haired. Most confusing, the pressure to treat Michael as a daddy left Leah feeling as though she were losing her real father. As if this weren't enough, Arlene and her children were Jewish. Michael was not. The first year they lived together, Michael insisted on having a Christmas tree. Jonah had loved it, but Leah had been furious. "How could you let him do that?" she had screamed at her mother. "It's no wonder you're having a hard time," the supervisee had been able to say. For Leah, just having all of this named and understood was a tremendous relief.

Typical of the differences researchers are finding between boys and girls in the shift from single-parent family to stepfamily, Jonah, now at the end of two years with Michael, had begun to settle down, and actually enjoyed having a man with whom to do "boy things." Although he didn't like the new rules either, he had not been as heartbroken. After an initial dip, his grades had actually gone up a bit. We surmised that his mother's remarriage was less of a loss and more of a gain for Jonah.

The next task was to help Arlene and Michael face the fact that they just couldn't go on as if they were a first-time family. The supervisee was instructed to proceed on the assumption that Arlene and Michael were missing some crucial information *and* that taking in this information would involve a loss they would find painful. She was instructed to say something like, "You two are really working hard, and it's obvious you're really trying to do the best possible by these kids." She was then to move gently to, "Did you know that you have some special challenges with this kind of family?" Predictably, Arlene responded with, "What kind of family?" "Well, for starters, you [looking at Arlene] have been with these children a lot longer than you [Michael] have. That makes your relationships with them very different." "Oh, Michael really loves the kids," said Arlene. "I can sure see that," said the supervisee, who had been instructed to empathically join with Arlene and Michael each time they pushed her away. "You've obviously really put your all into this new family. The problem isn't that you don't love the kids enough. It's that there are some special things about stepfamilies that, if you know them, make it much easier, and if you don't know them, make life much more difficult than it has to be." "But Michael adopted the children," said Arlene. The supervisee had by now grasped her task fully and came up with an appropriate metaphor. "Yes, and you really are working very hard to make this a good family for everyone. But it's sort of like you can swim upstream, or you can swim downstream. Downstream's a lot easier. So the news I've got for you is that Leah, in her own way, is telling you that you are trying to swim upstream, and she can't do it." Michael protested, "But Leah's behavior is absolutely inexcusable." And Arlene added, "She's been so ungrateful. He's tried so hard with her!" "Well, the good news I have," continued the supervisee, "is that there are some ways to swim downstream in this kind of family. I think there are some things we can do that will make life easier for both you and her."

The supervisee then began looking for a way to empathize with Arlene's loss of her fantasy about making her family whole again. She said, "I'm betting that you're telling me I'm saying something that hurts." She worked with Arlene and Michael to help them accept the realities of their stepfamily structure and to grieve the fact that Michael, for all his good intentions, was a step removed from the children. She drew pictures (see Chapter Two, Figure 2.5a to 2.5e, pp. 48–49), sent them to the local chapter of the Stepfamily Association of America, and gave them articles to read. She helped Michael to articulate, with some relief, the ways in which he did feel like an outsider and a stranger.

With the family's individual awareness work well under way, it was time to broaden the family map. The supervisee then brought Leah, Jonah, Michael, and Arlene together to do what I call a kind of "travelogue." Each family member was asked to tell the story of what the past three years had been like for him or her. Leah told her story of heartbreak and loss and confusion. Arlene wept. With some help from the supervisee, Arlene told her daughter how sad she was that she had understood so little. She then pulled the girl (who is much taller than her petite mother) on to her lap and held her, and they both cried.

Michael talked about how different *his* life had been, living alone in an apartment in the city. Jonah, apparently out of pure curiosity, asked Michael to describe his apartment. "What color were the rugs?" "That's irrelevant," Leah had said derisively. "White," Michael answered. Jonah began to laugh. "You really didn't know nothing about living with kids. Can you imagine a white rug in our house?" Michael talked about his excitement at "becoming a father," his pain at how hard it had actually been to live with so many people and so much mess, and to be treated like an ogre. Arlene talked about how lonely she had been as a single parent, how wonderful it had been to meet Michael again (they had been high-school sweethearts, which must have provided more fuel for the fantasy of living "happily ever after"). Jonah talked about his first meeting with Michael. "He *smelled* like a man!" said Jonah. He went on to say that he was scared and didn't like the new rules, especially cleaning up his room, but that he and Michael play baseball and, "He taught me to hit. Mom can't even *see* a baseball, much less hit one!"

The supervisee then coached the family to retrace their steps with each other and to begin acknowledging that they were a special kind of family. She helped Arlene and Michael to loosen the new rules a bit, so that the family could function for a while on some of the children's old familiar ground. She gave the adults "scripts" like, "Yeah, you're right, I'm not your father, even though I adopted you. You had a daddy who will always be your dad. You and I will get to know each other slowly, and I hope we'll have a special relationship some day. Meanwhile, these are your mom's rules, and I'm in charge right now, and, yes, you do have to wash the dishes tonight. No, you don't have to love me."

She suggested that both Leah and Jonah be allowed to invite some of their former friends for weekends. She encouraged Arlene to find some reliable one-to-one time with Leah. Since Jonah was more ready for a relationship with Michael, she suggested that the two do some "boy things" alone together (go to a baseball game, perhaps go on a camping trip overnight), leaving Leah some time with her mother. She helped Michael to design a slightly more distant stance with Leah, giving her positive verbal acknowledgment, but from a distance, and leaving the discipline to Arlene. Though Arlene was not pleased to become the disciplinarian again ("That's part of why I married him. I was *tired* of doing it all myself!"), she was coached to turn to Michael for advice and input ("What should I do about this?"). Michael was coached to provide Arlene support ("Terrific, keep it up. I think that's a good limit you set with her."), rather than to step in directly with Leah.

Like many remarried parents who lost a spouse when their children were young, Arlene, it developed, had some difficulty relinquishing her longing to be able to move on from the loss of her first husband and the many lonely years of single-parenting. "I don't want to remember him," she kept saying. She had felt "awful" for years after his death and was more than glad to be beyond that pain. The supervisee helped her to see that though she, as an adult partner, could move on from her first husband, he remained forever part of her children and that they needed her to remember him for them. She coached Arlene to tell the children stories about their father, to tell them how he felt and what he said when they were conceived, when they were born. Leah, who was beginning to struggle with identity issues, was particularly responsive to this move. "I think I was mad at Michael for not being my father," she said to her guidance counselor.

It is important to note that although Arlene and Michael came from different religious traditions, they actually shared much more middle ground than Arlene and her first husband. He had been a rather shy person, without many aesthetic interests. Michael, like Arlene, was enthusiastic and outgoing. They both loved music, loved to dance (they had won the dance contest at the high-school reunion), liked to cook together, and they both said they felt "spiritually connected" despite their religious differences. The supervisee was instructed to help Arlene and Michael to articulate their shared middle ground, and to find time alone in which they could cherish their new start as a couple without asking the children to abandon so much of their familiar ground. Couple time was also seen as providing support to both Michael, who was being asked to function on more foreign territory, and to Arlene, who was being asked to take back some of the childrearing burdens she had hoped to hand over to Michael.

The supervisee had now helped this family to move from pseudo-Action back to Awareness. She had helped each family member to describe the dilemmas he or she had experienced in the new family and then helped them to share this information with each other. She had gently helped the adults to mourn their fantasies of a first-time family and had shown them how to slow down enough so they weren't straining to be what they could not be. Leah's grades improved considerably, although she still "hated" the school. She and her stepfather remained somewhat distant, but were no longer at war when the supervisee's internship ended.

Not all Action Families (and not all supervisees!) are as responsive to intervention, but many are as earnest and well-meaning as Arlene and Michael were in their attempt to make a "real family" for themselves and the children. Some well-informed intervention and an infusion of sensitively and gently offered realistic information made a big difference in this family's life together.

Conclusion

A family's progress through the Stepfamily Cycle is influenced by many factors. These include the accuracy of the map members bring to their new lives together; their previous personal histories; the availability of supports (both educational and personal); the amount of already existing middle ground shared by members; the particular mix of personalities in various roles; the degree of family interest and skill in creative problem solving; the family's size and structure (higher numbers of children and more complex families are more challenging); the family's financial resources; and the gender of the children.

These factors seem to create four common stepfamily types. Names are derived from the stage of the Stepfamily Cycle where the family begins its life together, and describe the dominant style of dealing with differences.

The *Aware Family* (illustrated by the Davidson/Millers) begins its life together with realistic expectations. The varied needs of biological and step subsystems within their new family are met with interest and empathy rather than blame or denial. Members help each other to complete both individual and joint awareness tasks before moving into Action on most issues. These are the faster families that complete the entire Stepfamily Cycle in about four years.

The *Immersed Family* (illustrated by the Tolmans) centers around the dominant role of the biological parent-child subsystem. Differences between insiders and outsiders are met with confusion, denial, and/or blame. The special needs of outsiders are likely to be misunderstood or unvoiced. Successful Immersed Families eventually move on, often initially through the efforts of a mobilized stepparent. Movement may also be facilitated by a crisis or an infusion of outside support.

The *Mobilized Family* (the Johnstons) begins with two vocal adults (or two evenly matched adult-child subsystems) who immediately square off on a host of step issues. If the fighting style is constructive, enough information can be generated so that this high level of engagement can yield sufficient mutual understanding to complete awareness tasks and move the family forward. If the fighting style is destructive and does not generate useful information, Mobilized Families may remain in chronic conflict or may quickly blow apart.

The *Action Family* (the Wentworths) is characterized by an adult couple who deal with the uncertainties and conflicts of early stepfamily life by immediately forming a tight unit and instituting a host of new step rules and rituals. Often the needs of the stepcouple supersede the parent-child relationship. Children are particularly at risk in the Action Family and may often provide the point of entry into the mental health system. Successful Action Families eventually slow down and return to the Awareness Stage to complete unfinished tasks.

It is important to reiterate that although each of these family types will come to Resolution by a different path, all have the potential to complete the Stepfamily cycle and to create a satisfying, workable remarried family life.

Chapter 7

PROBLEMS IN STEPFAMILY DEVELOPMENT: INTERVENTION

U sing the Stepfamily Cycle
as a guide to intervention, psychotherapists, as well as guidance counselors, clergy, pastoral counselors, and medical
personnel with some knowledge of stepfamily dynamics and
developmental tasks can make the difference between hope-
less struggle and constructive movement in a floundering
stepfamily. It *is* possible to do almost irreparable damage by
treating stepfamilies as if they were first-time families. On
the other hand, it is usually not necessary for well-trained
helping professionals to develop an entirely new array of
skills in order to facilitate the process of becoming a stepfamily. Clinicians and other helping professionals can, like the

supervisee in Chapter Six, Case Four, draw on already existing skills in individual and systems therapy. The interventions to be described in this chapter range from primarily
educational, appropriate to a wide range of people who inter-
face with stepfamilies (clergy, teachers, medical personnel),
to primarily therapeutic, appropriate for those with in-depth
clinical training.

For additional information on psychotherapy with
stepfamilies, the reader may wish to consult the excellent
work of Sager and his colleagues (1983) or Visher and Visher
(1979, 1988). For other descriptions of Gestalt systems work
see Edwin Nevis's book on Gestalt organizational consulting
(1987) and any of the articles on the reference list by Sonia
Nevis and/or Joseph Zinker.

We begin with some general principles for working
with stepfamilies. We then proceed to more specific interventions relevant to facilitating movement at each stage of the
Stepfamily Cycle. The chapter ends with guidelines for attending to some of the special issues of stepfamily living (new
babies, families formed by death of a previous spouse, and
"older" children).

Basic Principles of Working with Stepfamilies

Principle One: Separate (and Weave Together) Psychodynamic and Step Issues

The stepfamily is a structure that creates powerful, uncomfortable feelings in the healthiest of us. One of the first tasks
in working with a stepfamily is to differentiate normal feelings created by this structure from feelings rooted in previous history. For example, to attribute a stepparent's jealousy
entirely to issues brought from his or her family of origin
only deepens the shame of already painful feelings and discounts the powerful impact of current realities. However,
when a stepparent's feelings are so intense that realistic information and reliable emotional support seem to have little

impact, it is important to look for underlying psychodynamics that may be intensifying an already difficult experience. Likewise, to attribute a biological parent's anxiety about "making it all work" entirely to the fact that he or she was the child who kept his or her alcoholic family of origin functioning would be a disservice. On the other hand, to work on stepfamily dynamics without attending to this parent's childhood experience would be unrealistic.

We will see below that previously incurred "bruises" may make the bumps of stepfamily living almost unbearably painful. The first task is always to name and fully validate the current sources of those feelings in stepfamily events. Only then does the task shift to exploring the earlier sore spots that make those events even more painful. The work often then proceeds with weaving back and forth between step issues and family-of-origin issues. (See, for example, the Tolmans, in Chapter Six.) In some cases, individual psychotherapy may be necessary in order for family work to move on:

Margaret Brewster, part of a stepcouple I had been seeing, called in a crisis. She reported that she had found herself "collapsed on the floor sobbing uncontrollably" after a fight with Ed, her husband, over his children. "I couldn't stop," she said, "I just couldn't stop crying."

This was the first time that Ed's children had ever spent their Christmas vacation in Ed and Margaret's home. Ed had become totally absorbed with his children, giving Margaret very little time or attention.

The breaking point came when Margaret discovered that her husband had changed his work schedule in order to take his son to the museum. Margaret had been asking Ed for months to do this for her, and he had protested that he couldn't leave work. Clearly, some normal stepfamily dynamics were at work here—*and* Margaret's response was particularly intense.

We looked first at the normal stepfamily dynamics and their impact on Margaret. She *was* left out. Ed had been paying very little attention to her. She had until now been the insider in the family (her two children had lived with the couple for most of their lives together), and this was her first experience as the outsider. It *was* painful that Ed could do for his children what he wouldn't do for her. And, most painful was that Ed was so absorbed with his children that he was unable to provide the empathy and attention that would have made it easier for Margaret to bear her feelings. My message to Margaret in this portion of the hour was, "You're not crazy, you're an outsider."

As Margaret began to relax, we started to explore some of the old bruises that made this a particularly difficult experience for her. "Anyone would find this hard," I said. "But your history might make this especially painful." "Yeah, I completely lost it." "Do you have any sense of what this evokes for you?" Margaret comes from a critical unresponsive family in which it was almost impossible to make her needs known. "Tell me some stories," I said. As we recaptured Margaret's early experience of a family life in which she could make no impact on her parents, the pain evoked by her inability to influence her husband's behavior became more understandable and more bearable.

Principle Two: Respect Multiple Realities— Keep a Systemic Viewpoint

As we have seen, for every event in a stepfamily, particularly in the Early Stages, there are as many different stories as there are people involved. This fact has a powerful impact on a person sitting with a stepfamily, or with any one of its members. Feelings on all sides are intense, and the behavior of the people in the family who reside "across the gap" is often so out of place that it seems purposefully destructive. Listening to any one stepfamily member tell his or her story, the pull to take sides is strong. "How could that child be so rude to you!" we feel when listening to a beleaguered stepmother, forgetting that she is probably describing a child in a loyalty bind. "How could she be so demanding," we wonder sitting with a child as he tells us about his "bossy" stepmother. We have forgotten that he is talking about a woman with no map for her task, no empathic support in her family, and who expects (and is expected by her husband) to step in and take over. "How could he be so insensitive and self-centered," we feel moved to object, listening to a mother tell us about her second husband's outburst when she canceled a date with him to care for a sick child. We have forgotten that this man has very likely already felt displaced and pushed out in countless subtle ways by her connection to her children.

Taking sides is rarely helpful in any couple or family system, but it is particularly dangerous in a stepfamily because the structure is so vulnerable to fracture. Each stepfamily member is often struggling and needs validation and empathy (sometimes desperately) for his or her experience of the family. It is especially important that clinicians involved with any part of a stepfamily system intervene with empathy for, and some awareness of, the unique feelings generated by each place in the stepfamily structure. Whether doing individual, couple, or family therapy, the clinician must hold a picture of the entire stepfamily map, particularly when individual members or subsystems each hold only a picture of their own piece of the territory. A school psychologist, for instance, must first empathize with a child's difficulties concerning an intrusive or rejecting stepparent. He or she may then also need to raise the family's awareness of the stepparent's struggles to begin a new relationship in the presence of what is probably an intense biological parent-child bond and in the face of consistent indifference or rejection. Therapists looking for victims and villains will slow or stall developmental progress.

Principle Three: Educate

Clinicians who are rigidly committed to remaining a "blank screen" will not be helpful enough to most stepfamily members. People in stepfamilies very often need new information in order to be successful. "If only we'd known!" couples so often say after I've spoken. "Where were you when we needed you 10 years ago? You would have saved us so much wasted effort trying to be what we couldn't be!" And even more encouraging, "I heard you speak last year, and it saved our marriage. We were killing each other over things we didn't know were normal!" Though statements such as these are affirming to me, they also provide heartbreaking evidence that stepfamilies all too often spend considerable energy straining to do the impossible, or wander hopelessly lost for lack of an accurate map of the territory they are trying to traverse together. Case Four in Chapter Six illustrates the impact that basic information and some sensitive coaching had on a stepfamily that had set out in a potentially disastrous direction and likely would have remained lost in troublesome terrain.

The willingness to coach actively and share information with stepfamilies includes encouraging them to make use of the Stepfamily Association of America (SAA). I tell my patients that SAA membership is much less expensive than therapy and that it provides resources therapy cannot offer: access to other people in the same boat, a wealth of good information about the varieties of ways in which other stepfamilies are making it, and, perhaps most important, people with whom to laugh about the foibles of this kind of family life. Membership in the national association buys membership in a local SAA chapter. SAA chapters provide education and support, usually within a monthly meeting format. The fee also includes easy access to a full line of hard-to-find books on stepfamilies, often available at a discount, as well as a subscription to the *Stepfamily Bulletin*, a quarterly newsletter full of useful articles about stepfamily living. Therapists, clergy, guidance counselors, medical personnel, and others involved with stepfamilies should be able to offer either the telephone number of the local SAA chapter or the address and telephone number of the headquarters (see Appendix B).

Furthermore, we perform a simple, but all too often neglected, preventive intervention when we place articles in our waiting rooms, pamphlets and local SAA chapter meeting announcements on our bulletin boards, and books on stepfamilies (for both adults and children) in our schools, churches, doctors' offices, hospitals, and child-care centers. Investing in the SAA's *Stepfamily Bulletin* and a few copies of *Stepfamilies Stepping Ahead* manual (1989) (a short, readable, educational guide and workbook published by SAA), and placing them in waiting rooms fills a critical information gap. When they disappear from my office (which they do with great regularity), I figure I have just done an important and inexpensive piece of *pro bono* work. Often the effect is multiplied when a friend (or aunt or neighbor) passes on a pamphlet or a phone number.

Principle Four: Attend Empathically to Resistance

> What usually passes for resisistance is not a dumb barrier to be removed but a creative force for managing a difficult world. (Polster & Polster, 1974)

The active coaching and educational role that is so often necessary to help stepfamilies move forward requires extra sensitivity to "resistance." By awareness of resistance, I mean attention to the places where the system, or the person, cannot or will not move. Resistance is an unfortunate word, as it implies stubbornness or laziness and evokes the urge to remove the offending obstacle. The Polsters remind us to be respectful, empathic, and curious when we sense that something is "stuck." Completing awareness tasks in a stepfamily requires bearing some very uncomfortable feelings (jealousy, resentment, loneliness, losses, etc.) and facing some profound disappointments: "My partner and I will never feel the same about my child," "My partner's child may never really love me or even like me," "My mommy and daddy will never again live together with me in the same family." And these distressing truths will be that much more painful if they reopen even older wounds.

Resistance in stepfamilies, as in most clinical work, is often not expressed directly or verbally. Rather, the therapist will sense a kind of invisible barrier. Failing to stop or continuing to push a stepfamily member to take in a piece of information or to try a new task will produce an anxious stalemate or uncommitted compliance followed by broken appointments. Stopping to pay attention—"This seems hard for you." "Something about this must be painful for you." "Am I telling you something that's really hard to hear?" "You're saying 'yes', but your whole body looks like 'no.' "—if it is done with enough empathy, will often uncover a deeply held, but unexpressed, fantasy or a painful piece of unresolved history. Attending to resistance may vary from presenting difficult-to-bear information with empathy and gentleness (as we saw with the Wentworths), to halting forward motion in order to explore an unexpressed fantasy (recall the Tolman family's exploration of lost wishes in Chapter Six, Case Two), to outright grief work. It may be useful to assume that anytime a stepfamily member seems to be resisting, there is some underlying loss that makes the change difficult to bear.

Early Stages: Helping Stepfamilies to Get Started

We have two primary therapeutic tasks in the Early Stages: to help stepfamily members attend to fantasies and to facilitate the completion of individual and shared Awareness Stage tasks.

Fantasy: Lifting the Invisible Burden

Although Fantasy is the first stage of the Stepfamily Cycle, unresolved wishes for what cannot be can continue to form significant impediments to stepfamily travel throughout the Early and Middle Stages, and even occasionally into the Resolution Stage.

These wishes often lie beneath the surface of what is being said, forming the unarticulated subtext. For this reason they are easy to miss, leaving the clinician (and the family) toiling to move forward against an invisible but powerful undertow. The first task of the helping professional, then, is to sense the presence of an unvoiced longing for something that cannot be. The next task is to resist the urge to attack directly. Like the parents and stepparents we met in the Fantasy Stage in Chapter Three, most people feel a mixture of regret, shame, chagrin, and embarrassment for having been "so wrong." And, as if the shame were not enough, relinquishing fantasies may require painful grief work. The challenge is to bring attention to these fantasies, but with great respect and caring. Depending upon how deeply entangled the fantasies are with their owner's sense of self, lifting the "invisible burden" can range from a purely educational task to a primarily clinical one.

When there are no other complicated issues, an infusion of good information can be enough to help stepfamily members put down, with great relief, the burden of straining to create what cannot be. A tuned-in minister, teacher, nurse practitioner, or family physician can provide the kind of educational intervention that will make the difference. Raising awareness that the stepfamily is a different kind of family might sound like: "Most of us go into the important things we do in life (parenting, teaching, starting a second-time family) with very little information. It turns out that there are some things to know about second-time families, and it also turns out that the people who know the most do the best. Are you interested?" This might be followed with a couple of articles and a referral to the local (or national) SAA chapter. A slightly more ambitious intervention might go on with something like: "It turns out there are a whole lot of fantasies that people normally have going into a second marriage . . . (such as). . . . Recognize any of them?"

In the work with Arlene Wentworth (Case Four in Chapter Six), providing missing information was crucial, but it was not in itself sufficient. Helping Arlene to take in this information required helping her to bear a number of losses—the reality that she could not entirely remove her first husband from her new family, that her new husband could not immediately lift her parenting burden, and, most important, that he could not replace her children's father. This kind of work, though it goes another step toward clinical, rather than educational, work, could be carried off by a sensitive day-care teacher, nurse, minister, or pediatrician.

In the following case, we return to Joanne Gray whom we met in Chapter Three (see pp. 77–78). In contrast to Arlene Wentworth, Joanne's resistance to the reality of her new family is more deeply rooted and entangled. It is embedded in a particularly strong fantasy of "family" that is unfortunately supported by Joanne's parents, with whom she has an enmeshed relationship. In addition, some of Joanne's characterological dynamics impede the necessary grief work:

Joanne, a new mother, was enraged by the inclusion of her husband's son from a previous marriage in their new daughter's christening. I tried in vain to explain her husband's attachment to his little boy. Having spent considerable effort explaining and cajoling, I finally stopped and acknowledged to myself that I was missing something. The word "picture" in Joanne's conversation intrigued me. I said, "I'll bet you had a very different picture of what it would be like to have your first child." Joanne became silent. "You know, I think you're right. . . . I just wanted at least the christening pictures to be just us."

As we explored what she had thought might happen to her husband's little boy when they married, Joanne realized that when they were courting, her husband saw very little of his son. "I guess I thought he would just stay out of the picture!"
I probed further: "So this is not the picture you had imagined as a little girl?" [Beginning to underline the loss]

Starting to soften very slightly, Joanne responded, "No. I thought it would be just my husband and me, and then the two of us together would be in awe of this tiny baby. Instead, when we look at her together, *I'm* crying, because I'm just so moved that we've made this child together. But it reminds him of his son and how much he misses him. He starts talking about how much he misses his son, and it's like he's not there with me. It's not at *all* what I imagined!"

As we went on, Joanne began to cry. We explored how alone she felt, how very different her original picture had been. Her grief work had begun.

Because I knew Joanne was close to her parents and that they were very conservative, I wondered about their role in this new stepfamily's difficulties. Stories of their disparaging remarks about Joanne's stepson emerged: "What's that boy doing there?" "The nerve of him expecting you to include that child." "See, this is what happens when you marry a divorced man." Clearly, the grandparents had their own work to do in relinquishing a particular picture of "family," a task that, we agreed, might merit an extended family therapy session.

We then turned to looking at how Joanne handles her disappointment, the ways in which she hardens when she is disappointed rather than softening and reaching out.

"Do you usually get angry when you're sad? Because you know you started out so angry, but it sure looks like you're real sad. It's almost like you have some mourning to do—grieving that picture on your mother's dresser. But something in you won't let you do it."

As is often the case, our work then focused on the juncture between Joanne's step and family-of-origin issues. In Joanne's family, the rules were clear and rigid. Joanne was the center of attention and yet her parents had very little empathic connection with her. Therefore, although "everything was fine and I had a great childhood," Joanne has little tolerance for "negative" or "weak" feelings in herself, a hard time empathizing with others, and great difficulty in stretching any of her pictures of how things "should" be. For Joanne, successful completion of Awareness Stage tasks depended on addressing some of these issues.

Awareness: Helping Stepfamilies Map the Territory

The most critical work with stepfamilies centers on facilitating completion of the individual and joint mapping tasks of the Awareness Stage. Awareness work can be appropriately done with an individual, couple, stepfamily, binuclear family, or the entire extended suprasystem (including grandparents), depending, as we have said, on the locus of the problem, the strengths of the particular family members, and the skills of their therapist.

The first task is to ascertain how fully the *individual* awareness tasks have been completed. Does each family member have words for his or her place in the structure? Can all family members connect negative, potentially shameful feelings to real events? Can they separate "shoulds" from realities? Finally, can each person name a few realistic needs from other family members? Gently (over and over) the therapist must attend to fantasies that block awareness.

Facilitating movement from Immersion to Awareness can quite appropriately be done in individual therapy with any stepfamily member, as long as the therapist does not give in to the pull to see absent family members as villains. In fact, sometimes individual awareness work is impeded by the pressure of dealing with other family members' needs and feelings.

When these individual maps are more firmly in place, we can to move to completing the *joint* task: we want to assess how much each member knows about the other members' experience. Does the stepparent have some inkling of what the biological parent feels as the insider? Do biological parents have some understanding of the strains of being an outsider? Are adults aware of children's needs? Are family members giving each other information and asking each other questions that expand each person's picture of the other parts of the family territory? In some cases, the therapist can begin providing missing map pieces in the context of individual therapy. However, "geography lessons" are best done in a couple, family, or extended suprasystem.

We begin with a discussion of individual awareness work with stepparents, biological parents, and children. We then move on to facilitating enhanced mutual understanding in couple, stepfamily, and binuclear work.

From Immersion to Awareness: Individual Work with Stepparents. In the Early Stages, the adult stepfamily member who is most likely to feel distressed enough to ask for help is the stepparent. He or she is likely to be floundering in the Immersion Stage: "Something's wrong here and it must be me." "I thought I was good with kids. Now I'm not so sure." "I don't know why I'm so depressed." "I'm so ashamed of how I feel." "I can't believe I'm jealous of a 6-year-old" (or a 15-year-old or a 30-year-old).

The task is to move the stepparent from "What's wrong with me?" (Immersion), to "I can name my feelings and they make sense" (Awareness), and finally to "These are a few things I need that will help me feel better in my outside position." Educational work with stepparents begins with "Did you know your feelings are normal?" and "You *are* an outsider. Your position is really different from a biological parent's position. Do you want to hear how?"

Stepparents in Immersion come in feeling vaguely terrible about themselves. They need help accurately naming their feelings and tying them to specific actual events. They may need assistance acknowledging their jealousy and tying it to being outside special relationships that precede them, and help connecting their feelings of loneliness and inadequacy to being constantly left out of intimate relationships. Normalizing the surprise is also helpful: "It's stunning, isn't it?" "Isn't it surprising how hard it is?"—to get a stepchild to respond or a spouse to hear his or her very different experience. Throughout, therapists must attend empathically to the shame these experiences generate for many stepparents.

Some stepparents will need help relinquishing fantasies of biological-like parenting. Stepparents also need a sympathetic (but not one-sided) ear for the strain of operating in a foreign culture and for the discomfort and inconvenience of sharing control with an absent but all too present ex-spouse. Simply naming some of the cultural differences can help to make their effects understandable: "You're a person who likes a great deal of order, and you've married a very hang-loose family! That must be hard for all of you!" (Note that the empathy in the last statement is not one-sided.)

"It's no wonder you feel that way" is the message we are communicating. "Anyone would." Because stepfamily structure offers so little empathic mirroring, stepparents in the Immersion Stage especially need the experience of being heard and understood. Drawing pictures (see Chapter Two, Figure 2.5) that graphically describe the stepparent's outsider position, offering articles (Papernow, 1984a, 1987) and books (see the starred books in the bibliography), and making a referral to the local Stepfamily Association supports the movement from Immersion to Awareness. The following is an example of this kind of work with Marsha Salzman, who had become a full-time stepmother to two school-age children.

M.: I've been feeling left out. I know it's my issue. [Note the self-blame of the Immersion Stage.]
P.: Well, maybe it would help if we could look at exactly what happened that made you feel that way.
M.: OK. Well, we were decorating the Christmas tree. They were real welcoming and warm to me. So welcoming.

And I *still* felt left out. [She answers but remains quite general, staying focused on her "inadequacy," not on the real events that generated her feelings.]

P.: Tell me some stories. Some little stories of things that happened that made you feel left out.

M.: Well, they'd pick up an ornament, and one would say, "Oh, remember when we got that one?" or "We always put this one on top!" It's so petty that I felt left out! Then they took out one of those little balls with a picture of their mom on it. And I just felt *awful*. I don't know why. I'm really embarrassed. And my husband is really upset with me. [She still blames herself, but the events that generated her feelings are now clear to me.]

P.: Well, you know what?

M.: What?

P.: You *are* left out! They have a history that they share, that you weren't part of. When they say, "Oh, remember . . . " you weren't there! That's what's making you feel so outside! You are outside of that history. You weren't there during all those years of putting those ornaments on the tree. Each one is new and strange and different to you.

M.: (Big sigh). Yeah . . . Yeah, you're right. It's true. . . . But it's so embarrassing!

P.: I can see. . . . Can you say some more about what feels so embarrassing?

M.: They're so welcoming. What's wrong with me that I still feel this way?

P.: Would you like an answer? [I want to teach her something, but I want to know first if she wants to be a student. She nods.] Well, it *is* truly wonderful that they're so welcoming. It would be much worse for you if they weren't. That's the good news. The bad news is that it doesn't change the fact that all those ornaments hold layers of memories that they share and you don't!

M.: Yeah. [Another sigh and a little smile.] I get it.

P.: And am I forgetting something or are you Jewish?

M.: I'm Jewish.

P.: That would make the tree even more foreign for you, right?

M.: That does seem rather obvious. (We both laugh.)

P.:   Well, I wonder if part of what's so embarrassing that
      you forget these "obvious" things is that your husband
      really doesn't get it.
M.:   He's so upset with me.
P.:   He really wishes being welcoming would be enough to
      make you feel part of the family. And his disappoint-
      ment is hard for you to bear. [I am beginning a geogra-
      phy lesson. "And it's no wonder he feels the way he
      does" is the message that is being communicated here.]
      The conflict is because of the structure of your family,
      not because someone's wrong or crazy. [I am beginning
      to try to capture both sides of the dilemma, so that Mar-
      sha can accept her own feelings *and* deepen her empathy
      for her husband's loss.]

Over the next few sessions, we went on to the final piece of
the individual awareness task, naming some of the things
Marsha might need to make herself more comfortable as an
outsider—some time for herself, time alone with her husband, a few changes in the rules. We talked about how it
would be Marsha's role to bring the bad news that she was
still an outsider and that she needed to do it tenderly.

Weaving current and past realities, we also began to explore
the fact that for Marsha, this was a repeat of her family-of-
origin role as the one person who openly stated that her
father was abusive. We talked about finding her some other
stepparents who could provide the empathy and responsive
understanding that would continue to be missing in her new
stepfamily for a while and that had always been missing in
her family of origin. Sometimes the step issues were central,
at other times they moved to the background as we explored
different areas of concern.

      Attending to shoulds provides another area of work
that helps stepparents move from Immersion to Awareness.
Shoulds carry fantasies of how the family "ought" to be. Although they are usually treated by their owners as realistic
expectations, they in fact impede awareness of how things
really are. Simply listing all of the shoulds on a piece of paper

begins the process of literally placing them on the table, outside the client, for more distant and sober consideration.

Josie Bridges was an art student in her mid-20s raised in a fundamentalist
family. She came in complaining of depression. Further exploration revealed that Manny, the man with whom she lived, had a 5-year-old son,
Carlos, who visited on weekends. The apartment was small and Carlos
stayed in Josie's studio, making the expectable amount of mess and chaos
that a 5-year-old would create in an art studio. Josie and Manny "mysteriously" had a terrible fight every Sunday night after Carlos left, followed
by an especially serious bout of depression for Josie.

Josie was relieved and interested to trace the roots of her depression and
the mysterious fights to the difficulties of feeling displaced by Carlos, both
with Manny and in her studio space. However, her language remained full
of shoulds that clearly impeded her ability to move fully into Awareness. So
we listed them on newsprint: "I should love this child." "I shouldn't be
jealous." "I shouldn't be resentful." "This should be easier."

We then went back to each item, slowly, one at a time. "So now let's take
each of these and really look at them. It's not that we shouldn't have
shoulds. It's that so many of them establish themselves without much
relationship to reality. So let's check each of these with reality. Let's look
at what's true and what's not true about each of these statements for you
right now. Take a deep breath, sit back, and go way inside. Let's figure
out how to make a true statement, rather than a wishful thinking statement, out of each of these, starting with the first one."

Despite her fundamentalist upbringing, Josie was very responsive to this
exercise. "Well, I *don't* love Carlos. That's true. I wish I did. But I don't.
Which actually makes sense if I think about it. Like you said, we're strangers! And he drives me nuts sometimes." To the next one she said, "Well,
I am jealous. But now it makes more sense. It does make sense. I guess
it's OK with me to feel jealous if I don't do something mean about it."

As with Josie, it sometimes helps to replace the harsher
"I should" with a softer "I sure wish" as in "I sure wish this
child could be more cooperative." "I sure wish this could be
easier." As shoulds loosen, stepparents can go on to name a
few more realistic needs they can mobilize around:

By the next session, Josie's depression had lifted considerably. She was
now fully in Awareness and had begun to feel clearer about the sources
of her irritation, many of which centered on being a rather neat and
orderly woman trying to share space with two messy males. We worked to
find one or two things she could ask for from Manny that might make a

difference to her. Josie decided that she wanted Manny and Carlos to put the toilet seat down so that she had fewer rude surprises when going to the bathroom in the night, and to replace the toothpaste cap! We called these "the two T's."

Manny was not interested in coming in. Instead, I coached Josie to raise the issues with him in an unthreatening, informative way, rather than in her usual sulking Sunday night attack style. She did beautifully. "I know I've been really irritable and it's been hard when Carlos is here," she was coached to say. "I think I've figured out a couple of things that would make a difference."

In fact, Manny was thrilled to know how to make Josie more comfortable. She had been instructed to ask Manny to request the changes from Carlos, with the understanding that when they forgot (as they surely would at times), she would remind them.

For people whose shoulds are more deeply embedded, making expectations realistic is a more challenging task:

Fran Werner, part-time stepmother to two children, relentlessly accused herself of not being a good enough stepmother. Unlike Marsha, realistic information had little impact. Despite my valiant efforts, she seemed to be unable to give herself even a few inches of leeway in making her shoulds more realistic. A canceled session signaled me that I needed to take a more empathic, accepting stance toward her expectations of herself. In the next session, I mended my ways.

"You really feel this is how you should be, huh?" "Yes," she said, and went on to describe a few more of her "failings." "How long have you been expecting superhuman feats of yourself?" I asked. "Well, my mother was a saint," she said without skipping a beat.

She went on to graphically describe a highly stressed family. Fran is the oldest of six children. Her mother, we ascertained, was, in fact, a member of that 1 percent of the population that qualifies for sainthood (with the major exception, Fran was able to note later in her work, that her mother did not teach any of her children how to say no). Fran's father was abusive and demanding. Her mother never complained, never raised her voice, and yet managed to keep the household fully organized. Each child had his or her own set of household tasks that almost always got accomplished. The standard of excellence was unremitting high. For Fran 98 percent was almost "successful." Ninety-five percent was barely passing. Eighty-nine percent was close to failing. For the moment fully respecting this skewed scale, we laid out in great detail what stepmother behaviors would be 98 percent and which ones would be 95 or 89 percent. This exercise in itself seemed to give Fran a clearer picture of what she was expecting of herself. She also began to be able to joke, just the tiniest bit, about her impossibly high standards.

As with firmly held fantasies, attacking deeply entrenched shoulds directly only strengthens resistance and embarrasses the client. Attending empathically to the roots of her expectations, describing them in greater detail, and weaving between step and earlier issues allowed Fran to begin to loosen their hold on her.

Again, it is destructive to begin an exploration of the feelings generated by stepfamily living by blaming them on the client's internal neurotic dilemmas. To do so implies that the jealousy, inadequacy, and resentment stepparents feel are entirely self-generated. This deepens the humiliation of already shameful feelings and impedes awareness work. On the other hand, when these feelings will not lift, or are especially intense, it is then often helpful to ask about family history. Stepparents who felt unimportant as children, who were not heard, who were rarely "put first," or who had a more favored sibling will find the stepparent role more painful, as will stepparents who learned to feel ashamed of negative feelings. Often just naming where the old bruises are and measuring their depth and width moves stepparents from Immersion ("What's wrong with me?") to Awareness ("Now I see why this hurts").

Individual Awareness Work with Biological Parents. Except when they are already in treatment for other issues, the insider biological parent rarely appears in a counselor's office in the Early Stages. He or she is more likely to show up after the outsider stepparent has mobilized and is pressuring for changes. At this point, the biological parent often needs help catching up, returning to the Awareness Stage to gain a firmer hold on his or her experience of the new family.

Like the outsider stepparent, the biological parent needs help putting words on the feelings the insider role creates. These feelings are fully described in Part II (Chapters Three, Four and Five). Biological parents in stepfamilies can almost always respond to empathic statements about feeling torn, as needs of new partners conflict with needs of children, and the need to keep the peace with an ex-spouse conflicts with the current spouse's needs for change. As with stepparents, the pictures in Chapter Two, Figure 2.5, can help to clarify the structural causes of the insider's experience.

Other evocative words for biological parents may include: "frustrated" by their inability to make it all work, "heartbroken" that this isn't the family they wished it was, "lonely" because they can't share their feelings and dilemmas about their parenting as fully as they would like with their new partners, "frightened" about the pressure to loosen a close and nourishing relationship with a child, and "guilty" about their children's pain. Biological parents may also be helped by gentle acknowledgment of the shame and fear of another failure evoked by these feelings. Noncustodial fathers and mothers also need a place to share their guilt about being asked to parent their new partner's children when "I can't parent my own kids."

The shoulds that biological parents may need help acknowledging include: "I should be able to make everyone happy." "My child shouldn't be upset when I talk to my partner." "My adult partner shouldn't be upset when I am intimate with my child." "This should be easier." "I shouldn't have to compartmentalize myself."

Biological parents form the center of their new families. Developing some understanding of the experience of other family members will make the linking job more doable. However, the amount of awareness insiders carry can be overwhelming. For insiders, the final individual awareness task of naming needs may include identifying the need to step out of the middle. Other needs therapists might be aware of for biological parents may include the need for empathy for feeling constantly torn; the need to slow down the pace of change; the need for one-to-one relationships; and the need for some time alone.

It can be especially helpful to say to a biological parent, "You *do* have to compartmentalize. It will go easier that way—try making some separate time for each of these relationships so you're not in the middle all the time."

Again, it is crucial to empathize with the resistance: "I know it doesn't feel 'family-like.' I can see how much you really wish it would work for you all to be a whole and happy family. I think you will at some point. But that's going to take time. And even then, even in first-time families, family life goes better when everyone has some one-to-one time with each other."

When resistance is more deeply rooted, we need to look for previous history that makes the insider role more painful and that impedes the work of relinquishing fantasies and shoulds. A mother who as a child was the "hero" or "rescuer" in a dysfunctional family (Black, 1981) will find her inability to smooth over the chaos of early stepfamily life particularly anxiety-provoking. A father who is vulnerable to narcissistic injury will experience his partner's discomfort and his children's pain as shameful and injurious. He will respond with despair or criticism rather than empathy and comfort. Biological parents who have not completed their own grieving process may sacrifice adult couple time to avoid bearing their children's sadness and anger at being left out.

Remarried biological fathers who have lost access to their own children often need help with this kind of grief work as they begin a new family. Despite changes in divorce law which have increased joint custody and visitation rights for men, mothers still retain custody in a majority of cases. As a result, awareness work with noncustodial fathers who have been deprived of contact with their own children is all too often a critical and painful piece of facilitating development in a new stepfamily. We return to Alan Simmons whom we met in Chapter Three ("Noncustodial Fathers: Old Loyalties, New Ties," p. 107).

Alan is a computer engineer who is in a new relationship with Diana, a healthy satisfying relationship except for the fact that Diana wants children and Alan feels "blocked for some reason." He was referred to me by a colleague for a consultation on stepfamily and divorce issues.

Alan and his first wife separated when their son Brad was 2. After an extremely hostile divorce, Alan's ex-wife interfered so substantially in his relationship with his son that visitation, when it happened, was a miserable experience for both father and son. Alan came in "haunted" by the fact that he had only seen his son intermittently since the child was three.

Attempts to get his ex-wife in for a joint session failed. In a telephone conversation she seemed to be not only extremely bitter about her divorce from Alan but had remarried and was firmly attached to the fantasy of a biological-like new family with her new husband and Brad. My best attempts to interest her on Brad's behalf proved fruitless.

Alan did not have the funds to mount a custody battle. We began by talking about the reality of this loss for both Alan and his son. We explored Alan's troubling feeling that, "I ought to be able to do something about this," and the shame he experienced at his inability to father his own son. Alan's shame and grief, it emerged, were made doubly painful by the fact that he had lost his own father in a hostile divorce. Like many men in Alan's situation, he had carried these feeling "inside without hardly even knowing about them" and with little awareness of the size of his pain or its impact on his willingness to incur yet another potential loss by fathering another child.

Our work focused on validating for Alan the reality of his losses, both as a child and now, giving weight and language to his pain. We talked about his sense of powerlessness and the shame that evoked for him as a man. We began sorting out the loss of his own father from the loss of his son, and articulating the sense of betrayal of what should have been for Alan, both as a father and as a son, and for Brad. I encouraged Alan to begin talking to Diana about all of this and to bring the grief and shame of both losses back to his original therapist.

We also looked together at where Alan did have power. I encouraged him join a political group of non-custodial fathers. I supported his decision to continue his once-a-month visits with his son, partly as a strategy for staying "at the doorway" and available for a time when his son was free to make his own choice. I suggested that he keep a "Father Journal" of his thoughts and experiences for Brad to see when he started to ask questions about, "Why weren't you more involved?" We also talked about some ways that Alan could respond constructively and empathetically to his son's pained accusations. We developed a series of little scripts based on statements from Brad that Alan reported feeling "stopped" by. They are repeated here because they are asked for so frequently:

Brad: Why did you leave us?
Alan: I didn't want to leave *you*. I never wanted to leave you. I love you very much.
B.: Then why did you leave?

A.: Your mother and I couldn't get along. Just like sometimes you and your friends don't get along. We tried hard to work it out. But we couldn't. So one of us had to leave.

B.: Mom says if you really loved me you wouldn't have left me.

A.: I know that's what Mom says. It must be very confusing to you. Sometimes when people are really hurt they say funny things. I'm sorry Mommy said that. Sometime I hope she won't say that any more. She's hurting now. Sometime I hope she won't hurt so much and then maybe she won't have to say those things to you. You know that I love you. Mommy forgets sometimes.

B.: Why did you hurt Mommy?

A.: I didn't want to hurt Mommy. Remember when you and Billy weren't getting along? You didn't want to play but he still wanted to come over? That was hard, remember? It's sort of like that. I didn't want to hurt Mommy. But I did. And I'm sorry she hurts.

B.: Mommy says Joe's my Daddy now.

A.: What do you think about that?

B.: (Alan feels he would get no response from Brad.)

A.: Sometimes when people remarry like Mom and Joe, they say that. That must be confusing for you. You and Joe will have lots of time to get to know each other. And I hope you'll have a special relationship with him. But I will always be your Daddy and I'll always love you. And sometime maybe you'll love Joe, too, but in a different way. I'll always be your Daddy.

B.: Mommy says I have to call Joe "Daddy."

A.: What would you like to call Joe?

B.: (Alan feels Brad would have no answer. We talked about Brad's loyalty bind: if he crossed his mother he risked punishment. If not he betrayed his father.)

A.: (We tried to think up something Alan could say that would relieve Brad's loyalty bind without incurring his mother's wrath.) Whatever you call Joe is fine with me. People's hearts are very big. I know your heart has lots of room in it. There's room in there for Joe, and I know there will always be a special place for me, just like there is a big special place for you in my heart, and it will always be there. You'll always be my son and I'll always be your Daddy. No matter what.

Armed with these suggestions, and with his underlying feelings more fully identified, Alan returned to his own therapist to continue this work.

Like Alan, noncustodial fathers often bring unresolved grief that makes engaging fully in their new families mysteriously difficult. For Alan ongoing movement into the Awareness Stage from the Immersion Stage will require weaving between validating the feelings generated by his particular stepfamily circumstances, and working through the previous losses which further deepen his pain and sense of betrayal.

Helping Children Complete Awareness Tasks. In Case One (Chapter Six), Jan and Chuck anticipated and helped to articulate many of the issues for their children, greatly easing Gabby and Kevin's transition into their new family. When adults in stepfamilies are too absorbed or too uninformed to do this for their children, a counselor sensitive to step issues can help children to put words on their own story, and then can provide assistance in voicing it to the family. The work with Leah Goldfarb Wentworth in Chapter Six (Case Four) illustrates this. Note that work with Leah's mother and her new husband was important in preparing the adults to hear the child's story. Children in Action Families and in highly conflicted binuclear systems may particularly appreciate having a neutral outsider to whom they can talk.

Children in the Early Stages have a special need for the adults in their lives to help them acknowledge and loosen their loyalty binds, and to understand and comfort them about their losses. Coaching parents is often the best way to be helpful to children, especially young children, in the Early Stages. Both Lena Taylor and John Smith, the adults in the following family, bring considerable "baggage" from their families of origin into their new couple relationship, and both have a tendency toward depression. However, their psychological difficulties did not impinge on their ability to face the realities of their stepfamily. This case is drawn from my clinical practice. However, an astute and sensitive teacher or minister might have been able to provide similar, equally effective coaching.

Lena was a 27-year-old, newly divorced mother of two young children. She and her children had just moved in with John, a man she experienced as much more loving and reliable than her husband. Together they were involved in creating a new family. However, Lena's 5-year-old daughter Jenny was not as pleased. Jenny continually ignored John, criticized the way he ate, dressed, walked, and talked and got her 3-year-old brother to join her in choruses of "We don't like you, we don't like you." Jenny's teacher had already complained about her aggressiveness.

Lena's response had been to discipline the children for acting badly and to enumerate John's good qualities, telling the children how much he loved them. John had alternated between saintly lovingness, self-deprecating irritation, and sullen withdrawal.

John and Lena sought help quite early in their relationship and were eager to learn about normal stepfamily development. They quickly recognized their own in my list of fantasies people often have in these kinds of families. Together they were able to acknowledge that their fantasy of an instant "better" family for themselves and Lena's kids was creating a great deal of pressure for both the adults and the children. They were willing to try anything to make their stepfamily work.

We began with a basic lesson in how stepfamilies are different. I drew the diagrams in Figure 2.5 (Chapter Two), which enabled us to talk about the ways in which Lena's experience as an insider in the family differed from John's experience as an outsider. We then talked about the losses and loyalty binds children in stepfamilies face.

With this greater understanding in place, the adults were interested in what they could do to acknowledge the children's losses and help them loosen their loyalty binds. I asked the adults to see if we could list all the changes in these children's lives. It emerged that, in addition to losing daily contact with their father, these children had been moved to a new state, had lost all of their old friends, and were beginning a new school. When added to the changes wrought by their new step situation (losing time with mommy, changed rules, a stranger in their house), the list was quite overwhelming.

With some coaching, Lena was able to sit down with her children and somewhat awkwardly tell them that she was counting up the number of changes in their lives and that it was a really big number. With them she began to construct a list. The children were in different stages of mastering counting, which made this an exciting task for them. Most stunning to Lena and John were the details they as adults just hadn't imagined: "We don't eat sugar cereal anymore." "We don't have Piggy (a guinea pig) anymore." "We don't have wobbly pancakes anymore" (their dad had made odd-shaped pancakes for them every weekend). John had been instructed to be present as an outsider, at a distance but nonetheless there so the children knew that he could bear hearing this information, and so that he could gain some understanding of their behavior. "Gosh, that's a lot of changes," he had said spontaneously. "No wonder it's been hard for you to be nice to me!"

Jenny characteristically rejected this bit of empathy with, "I'm not talking to *you!*" "Ooops, guess I interrupted," John replied, in his saintly mode. This time, however, Lena saw that he had been hurt. She reached over and touched his shoulder. "Boy, did that make a difference," John later reported. "I felt like I did the right thing. I felt like Lena saw it and appreciated it. So I didn't feel so empty and resentful."

Later, when Jenny blurted out her inevitiable, "You're not my daddy," John was able to say directly and firmly (as he had been coached), "You're right. It must be kind of confusing for you sometimes. I'm not your daddy. But I'm the grown-up here right now, and these are the rules of the house." Lena had also been coached to expect this. Rather than chastising her daughter, she sat down with her later and said something like, "You're absolutely right. John's not your daddy. You have a daddy, and he's in Minnesota. Do you miss him?" Over time Lena had a series of conversations with her children about how much they missed their father, how frightened they were that caring for John would mean losing their father. She reassured her children that their father would always be their daddy, and that the children and John would get to know each other slowly like strangers do, and it would take time. She said that they did not have to love him, or even like him, but that saying mean things was not OK.

Like Lena and John, adults in stepfamilies need to know that children may need help naming their fears and putting them to rest. Parents need to know that children's feelings are likely to come in "drifts," rising in intensity, abating, and then returning again. Children may have to hear *over and over again* that their hearts have lots of room, and that they will always have a very special place for their biological parents, and that when they are ready, and if they want to, they will have enough room to make a different kind of place for stepparents.

Whether facilitated by parents or by a therapist, in a family or individual session, the issues that children may require help articulating include: losses (of friends, of the original family, of time with custodial parent, of access to noncustodial parent, of familiar routines); loyalty conflicts (mom complains about dad to the child, child feels worried about caring for a new stepfather for fear of losing her dad); for insider children, feeling invaded and displaced; for outsider children, not having a place, functioning under unfamiliar rules and foreign rituals (see Chapter Three, Stages Two and Three for more detail).

Like their parents, children may also need help naming needs from their new family. These might include: time alone with a biological parent, some input into rule changes, no more bad-mouthing of one parent by the other, a say in family rituals, a slower pace of change, some space that is "mine" (i.e., a dresser for a visiting child, a blank wall for the outsider child to decorate, etc.).

Books can be especially helpful to children in completing awareness tasks and opening conversation in touchy areas. Larry Ganong and Marilyn Coleman's *Bibliotherapy with Stepchildren* (1988a) thoroughly reviews both the fictional and self-help children's literature on stepfamilies. Their favorites, which I have included in the reference list, include: for adolescents, Linda Craven's book *Stepfamilies: New Patterns of Harmony*; for school-age children, Bradley's *Where Do I Belong? A Kid's Guide to Stepfamilies*; for somewhat younger children, Helen Coale Lewis's *All About Families the Second Time Around*. I tell parents to expose their children to a number of different books—children will usually gravitate toward those that meet their needs best. (All books appropriate for children are starred on the reference list at the back of this book.)

Puppets (operated by the therapist or by a coached parent) can help very young children digest their stepfamily experience: "Mr. Raccoon's parents are divorced, too. And do you know what? Mr. Raccoon thought that if he loved his mom's new friend John, then he couldn't love his Daddy anymore." As Mr. Raccoon begins to talk ("I get really worried about this. Do you ever worry about this?" or, "I miss my dad when I'm with my mommy, and I miss my mommy when I'm with my daddy. Does that ever happen to you?"), young children can often engage surprisingly freely in a conversation that provides considerable relief.

Stepfamily Geography Lessons. As each stepfamily member begins to find words for his or her experience, it is time to begin voicing them to one another so that each family member develops some understanding of the others' territory. In my own practice I am most frequently referred with a couple or with a stepparent. In the latter case, I work individually until the stepparent's awareness solidifies. I then ask the couple to come in, perhaps balancing the alliance during a few sessions alone with the new partner. When the couple feels more solid, I like to bring the whole family in for several sessions. The focus of these family sessions is initially almost always on completing Awareness Stage tasks—putting words to each member's experience, helping them tell each other, helping them to hear each other, and identifying blocks to their contact with themselves and each other.

As we saw in Case One, Aware Families begin accomplishing the joint awareness task in a low-key, empathic style. They try to imagine each other's feelings when they aren't voiced. They are more likely to tell each other what they're thinking, and to listen to each other. They more often help one another figure out what they need. Immersed Families and Mobilized Families are more likely to begin this task in the highly charged atmosphere of the Mobilization Stage—"beating some understanding into each other," as one woman said. Whether we are moving a family forward from the Immersion Stage, or backward from Mobilization or premature Action, helping stepfamilies to develop a family-wide map is essential to developmental progress.

An effective and quite simple way to help adults and children accomplish this task together is to ask each person to give a kind of travelogue. "You know everyone in your family has traveled a long way even to get where you are now. Maybe it seems as if everyone's been going through the same thing because you're all in the same family. But, in fact, it's likely that in this kind of family you have each had to travel a very different path to get here. Maybe we could start by just having each of you describe, chronologically, what it has been like for you in this family, perhaps starting from just before you first met one another. I want the others to listen just the way you'd listen to someone who has been on a trip to a land you've never seen. Ask questions, and try to imagine what it must have been like."

This was the technique used by the supervisee in the Chapter Six Wentworth case (Case Four p. 294). In that example it was preceded by an individual session with the child, Leah, and a separate session with the adult couple, during which family members had an opportunity to find their individual voices without worrying about how they would be heard. This simple exercise can have powerful results.

When there is resistance, it may be rooted in unacknowledged fantasies or losses that will need attention before work can proceed. Or it may lie closer to the surface, in the irritation, frustration, and difficulty of naming assumptions and putting words to things that family members have never had to say out loud before. Sharing very different perceptions is a task that requires acknowledging how alone we each really are in the world—that others just don't "get it" as we'd like. Providing metaphors for the task can make it more palatable: "How to make this family work is sort of like a mystery story. Only you each have different clues, and everyone needs all of the clues together to solve the mystery." "You're like the three blind men feeling an elephant, only you each have your hands in a different spot. That's the way stepfamily structure is, each spot feels really different from the other spots. So one of you has your hand on the tail, and one of you has a hand under the foot, and another of you is feeling the tusk."

Whether using the travelogue exercise or in ordinary conversation, there are a number of things therapists can do to raise the quality of a family's geography lessons:

1. **Help family members to complete their connections with each other**. When one person finishes talking, turn to others and ask: "What did you hear that you didn't know? What do you understand differently?" followed by, "Can you tell him/her?" and then, "How did it feel to hear that John understood you?"

2. **Help family members to improve the quality of the information they give each other.** Encourage them to give *specific examples* of behavior rather than exchanging vague accusations or generalized compliments: "Yesterday when I walked into the room I asked you a question and you didn't look up," is more recognizable and useful than, "You never acknowledge my existence." "This morning you smiled directly at me, and it made such a difference to me," communicates more than, "You were nice to me today."

It is important to support good information-sharing behavior with positive feedback: "You not only keep talking to each other about hard things, you're very specific so that each person knows exactly what the other one is talking about." Families that do not give each other recognizable information need feedback: "You are all trying very hard to tell each other what this family is like. But nobody quite gets it. What would help is to be more specific. Try giving each other examples and try asking each other for concrete details."

When the family does not yet have the hope or the energy to do this themselves, the therapist can do it for them. For instance, when a child in this kind of family says, "It was hard in the beginning, but then it got easier," the therapist can say to the child, "Tell us one thing that was especially hard. Tell us one story of when it got easier." Whenever possible, we need to teach families to do this for themselves. "You look confused, John. Are you? I wonder what stopped you from asking your daughter for an example?"

3. **Encourage families (and couples) to be curious about each other.** Do family members say, "Go on some more about that," or "Tell me what that was like." If so, support the behavior with specific feedback: "You are generous in encouraging each other to talk. You ask one another a lot of questions. You're willing to let each other know when you don't understand. That really helps you deepen your understanding of one another." For families that do not do this task well, "You each do a good job of saying where you are. But I notice almost no one asks anyone else to say more. It's as if you're not curious about each other! Do you recognize what I'm describing?"

4. **Help family members take turns**. This is central in every family, but it is especially important in a stepfamily—where the unheard voice speaks for a very different experience—to ensure that each person's experience will be acknowledged. The therapist can structure the conversation (as in the travelogue) or teach the couple or family to do this themselves: "I notice that you seem really good at having John talk and Ellen listen. John says where he is and how he is feeling, and Ellen asks lots of questions and listens quietly." If John is the biological parent and Ellen is the stepparent in this couple, the family is in danger of remaining in the Immersion Stage: the biological subsystem's point of view will be expressed whereas the step experience will remain unarticulated. If the reverse is true, then the family is in danger of shooting into Action prematurely: the step-member's needs for rapid change will be voiced and acted upon, but children's needs for stability and comfort will remain unheard. The flow of information must go both ways for the family to progress: "I wonder if you can each try the other end. John, can you ask the questions and listen quietly? Ellen, can you talk about where you are and how you are feeling?" Often attempts to reverse the flow reveal that John is better at talking and lousy at listening, and Ellen is good at listening but has a very hard time voicing her own thoughts and feelings. Members of couples like these need help teaching each other their very different skills.

Attending to Needs: Making Life in the Early Stages Less Bumpy. Sitting on a firm cushion and wearing a seatbelt do not take the bumps out of the road, but they do make the ride more comfortable and safer. The divided structure of early stepfamily life can be extremely anxiety-provoking. Anxiety does not foster the kind of atmosphere in which the curiosity and empathy necessary to complete awareness tasks thrives.

When stepfamilies are coached to meet a few of the basic needs created by their unique structure, and if they are helped to avoid the large potholes, the ride through the Early Stages and into the Middle Stages can be much more comfortable, and the journey will be a safer and more fruitful one.

In a structure made up of insiders and outsiders, we can tell families that stepparents will be less anxious if they have access to the things that make it easier for anyone in an outsider position: acknowledgment that they are operating on foreign territory, reliable intimate time with their partners, a few familiar routines and belongings, sources of mastery and nourishment outside the stepfamily (job and friends), and a few people who fully understand and can validate their feelings of jealousy, resentment, and inadequacy. It is important that they know they will often be bringing bad news. They must understand that they are more likely to be change agents in their families, and like all good political activists, they have to decide on a couple of agenda items that really matter and let go of the rest.

Biological parents will be more comfortable in the insider role that early stepfamily structure assigns to them if they compartmentalize, that is, arrange to spend some separate time and space with each child and with their new partner. They must have acknowledgment that they are managing a lot of people and feelings, and some relief from that task occasionally. They must realize that they will often be speaking for their children's needs and that they will frequently be the advocates for maintaining the status quo in their new family. They may need to be coached to provide the empathy and intimacy that outsider stepparents require.

Parents can be coached to tell their children what will stay the same and what will be different. Most children need clear, reliable time with their biologial parents. Like Lena Taylor, parents can be coached to provide empathy and support for their children's losses rather than just propaganda about how wonderful everything will be. As we have repeatedly stressed, research to date consistently indicates that children do much better in divorce and remarriage when their parents are not in conflict. Parents and stepparents may need help to curb their impulses to compete for children's loyalties. Children must have active ongoing support from all sides for their relationships with all of the members of their binuclear family. Outsider children should have a space of their own and some input into household rules and rituals. Insider children need to know what territory they can keep as their own and what they must share.

The new stepfamily as a whole also has some needs that, if met, will ease travel through the Early and into the Middle Stages. New stepfamilies should be encouraged to spend most of their time in minifamilies. Paradoxically, not attempting to blend all activities immediately will make life more nourishing for everyone in a new stepfamily. Time in minifamilies provides the older biological subsystems (parent-child, sibling) some time when they don't have to adjust their familiar routines to include a stranger. It gives the new subsystems (stepcouple, stepparent-child, or stepsiblings) time when they can identify their existing middle ground without competing with the thicker, more established ground of biological subsystems. In addition, new stepfamilies must identify a few areas where they can function together easily. They need encouragement to look actively for existing middle ground, whether it is a shared penchant for Chinese food or a particular dessert.

Rituals such as a "family night" offer an option for creating new middle ground without the heavy negotiating that is best saved for the Action Stage. One night a week is designated during which everyone will be home by a certain time. Each family member gets a turn organizing family night (within a particular budget, if necessary). The rule is that everyone will join in. If the activity is foreign or distasteful, family members are encouraged to remember that they will want the others to participate when it is their turn. Family night might include determining the menu. Therefore, on the 3-year-old's night the dinner may be hot dogs, and the activity may be watching "Mr. Rogers." On the stepfather's night the dinner may be a formal meal with candlelight and china, and the activity may be chess lessons. On Mom's night the program may be lasagna and a movie. On her teenager's night the menu may be peanut butter sandwiches and "make-your-own ice cream sundaes," and the activity may be trying on clothes.

Finding holidays not yet defined in either family provides another source of easy middle ground in early stepfamily life. Negotiating about holidays where rituals are already defined means that any change will wrest away something precious from someone. In the Early Stages, we can help stepfamilies find "virgin territory" where neither family has staked out a claim for how things should go, and where all family members participate in creating a new family ritual. The ritual might include a meal that has some favorite foods for each person in the family. In the Middle Stages the family is ready to turn to creating holiday rituals that must be forged out of mismatched pieces of already tightly woven cloth. In the Early Stages, "virgin" holidays give the vulnerable new stepfamily space where spontaneous moves are less likely to get snuffed out by already existing ideas on how things ought to be done. In this way the new stepfamily creates a few places in which the fabric of their lives together can be woven easily, thread by thread, more like a first-time family.

Families that map their territory accurately will figure out some of these things for themselves. However, actively coaching stepfamilies to meet some of these needs may increase everyone's comfort, making the remaining disappointments and difficulties less disturbing and leaving attention available for more difficult developmental challenges.

Middle Stages: Facilitating the Restructuring Process

Mobilization: Putting the Conflict into Context

For each of the past five years I have been asked as a step expert to speak at our local SAA chapter about stages of development in stepfamilies. Last year, as I looked around the room, I spied several couples who were repeat customers. One couple had heard me speak for at least the last four years in a row. Though it was flattering, I wondered what they could possibly get out of hearing me tell some of the same stories over again. Nonetheless, I launched into my talk.

When I finished speaking, the woman of the couple, a part-time stepmother to three children, raised her hand. "I just want to say that this is the fifth time we've heard you give this presentation, and we almost didn't come tonight. And I'm so glad we did. We had an absolutely *awful* summer. Really truly horrendous. And now listening to you, I realize that we have just been through the Mobilization Stage! And I'm *so* relieved! I had been thinking of this summer as a real slide backward, a real failure. You've just put it in a totally different context. And I can see we really have accomplished something. Our differences are really out in the open now, and we have gone back and learned some more about each other, and now I can see we're really ready to move on to Action." This woman gave me yet another lesson in the power of placing stressful events within a normal developmental framework.

In the Mobilization Stage, it is often couples who appear for help. The conflict is now clearly located between family members who are arguing wildly over a whole raft of what may seem to be petty issues and feeling extraordinarily anxious and disturbed. Much of the work of this stage involves lowering the anxiety and panic enough so that the couple or family can return to complete missing Awareness Stage tasks. Like the repeat customers above, placing the conflict within a developmental context can be very comforting. "Congratulations, you're in the Mobilization Stage, which is already the fourth stage of stepfamily development. Some people never get here! You're airing your differences openly. It may be more frightening this way, but you can't begin to function as a team until you do this."

In an Immersed Family the rabble rouser will be an outsider stepparent. In an Action Family it will be a child, or a previously silent insider biological parent who finally finds his or her voice in the Mobilization Stage. For these families, the Mobilization Stage can mean a very upsetting turn of events in stepfamily life. In an Immersed Family, for instance, the biological parent has been married until now to an apparently cooperative (though perhaps sullen and withdrawn) outsider. As outsiders find their voices they often feel quite relieved. Their spouses, however, often feel suddenly and surprisingly beleaguered by the unexpected assault. Both may be frightened and disturbed by the change. Mobilized Familes like the Johnstons (Case Three in Chapter Six) begin their lives together in the Mobilization Stage with all of their differences out in the open. But, biological parents in Immersed Families (and both adults in an Action Family) may have been completely unaware of trouble brewing beneath the surface, or they may simply be surprised at the force with which it seems to suddenly erupt.

It is useful in assessing couples and families who come in during the Mobilization Stage to know whether they are an Immersed Family (in which case their fighting is a hard-won accomplishment) or a Mobilized Family (in which case their fighting is a life-style). We also need to assess the level of completion of Awareness Stage tasks. Do they know enough about themselves to communicate specific, useful information about their feelings and needs? If so, with a few listening skills they may be able to move on quickly. On the other hand, if they are hurling vague accusations at each other, more work in the Awareness Stage will be needed before their fighting will be fruitful.

Because the primary task is often to return to the Awareness Stage, all of the questions and interventions listed earlier in this chapter (see "Stepfamily Geography Lessons," pp. 330-333) are relevant in work with Mobilized couples or families. Often, however, the therapist's most challenging task is to lower the anxiety enough so that family members can get interested in each other. In addition to placing the conflict within a developmental context, the following strategies may be useful here.

Give Positive Feedback. Positive feedback is crucial for all couples and families, but it is particularly important for stepfamilies. Everyday life in a stepfamily, especially in the Mobilization Stage, presents many seemingly unsolvable problems and proceeds with little direction. Positive feedback not only provides some relief, but it also says, "There are some things you are doing right, and if you keep doing them, you'll get somewhere." My own rule is that *every* intervention in a stepfamily begins with positive feedback for what that family is doing well. Sonia Nevis and Joseph Zinker, of the Gestalt Institute of Cleveland, begin their family therapy practicum with the instruction to provide *only* positive feedback. A violently fighting couple can be told, "Well, I hear two strong voices here. It's not like one person has a voice and the other is silent." Or "It's clear you really care about what goes on here. Nobody's sitting in the background letting things slide by." "It's clear you're not indifferent to each other!" I said (rather in desperation) to a couple who had quarreled for an entire session. To my surprise, both of them softened, and they exchanged the most loving looks I had seen in three sessions of sitting with them! The previous cases all underscore this point— each intervention is preceded by a piece of positive feedback.

"Increase the Grease." Increasing the amount of empathy and responsive mirroring family members give each other lowers anxiety and facilitates the flow of information. Families in which people say, "Oooh, that must have hurt!" and, "No wonder you've been so upset," make each other feel heard and cared about despite differences. If tension is very high, the therapist must provide this function. Eventually we need to teach family members to do this for one another: "I notice each person in this family has his or her say. And each of you is fairly articulate. But do you know what is missing? It's the 'That sounds hard!' and 'That must have been scary.' These little responsive moves don't mean that you necessarily agree. But they make the other person feel less alone, and they make it much easier to talk about frightening things. I wonder if you'd be willing to experiment with adding some of this 'grease' and see what happens."

Therapists working with stepfamilies need to help family members cherish the tender moments that result. "Oh, did you see how her face changed when you said that? You didn't? Well look now. See how she softened toward you when you simply stopped long enough to let her know you heard her."

Slow Down. Another tool for helping a Mobilized couple slow down enough to hear each other is a simple but surprisingly challenging exercise devised by staff at the Gestalt Institute of Cleveland. Each person is asked to speak only a sentence or two at a time. The other member of the couple is asked to repeat the essence of what he or she has heard before stating a new sentence. The exercise continues as the first person repeats back the essence of what she or he has heard and then adds only a new sentence or two. What appears to be a ridiculously simple exercise often proves to be both very difficult and very effective. The therapist frequently must intervene to remind one or both partners to repeat what she or he heard before jumping in with a new thought. One or both partners may need encouragement to "check to see whether you got it," because, in fact, the listener left out a central piece. The impact can be powerful. Just hearing one's words accurately repeated in itself stops spiraling anxiety by providing some of the feeling of being seen and heard and understood that is usually missing in the Mobilization Stage. I joke with my clients sometimes, calling this the "rote empathy" exercise. "If you can't do the real thing, then do it by rote. Even doing it by rote slows things down enough so you can begin to hear each other."

The following illustrates the effect this exercise can have on a warring couple. A stepfather (let's assume he is a noncustodial father) and his wife are engaged in a heated argument. Let's imagine that this is an Immersed couple that has just catapulted into the Mobilization Stage as the stepfather has begun to take a firmer stand on securing reliable intimate couple time with his wife. Like most newly Mobilized stepparents, he is not very graceful. As is true with most biological parents in an Immersed couple, his wife does not welcome his newly found voice. Although all the dialogue here is invented, it is constructed from many other very similiar real ones:

Stepfather: You never have any time for me!

Biological Mother: I have two children who need me. What do you think I am, superwoman?

Stepfather: I don't treat you that way when my kids are around. I don't see why you can't return the courtesy!

Biological Mother: What do you mean? When your kids are around I *never* see you! Why can't you be the grownup and wait your turn!

Compare the above with the following:

Stepfather: You never have any time for me!

Biological Mother: You feel I never have time for you. [His mouth softens ever so slightly and he nods.] Well, sometimes I think you have no idea how hard it is for me to try to take care of two kids and pay attention to you at the same time. [She is angry, but already her language is less accusing and more informative.]

Stepfather: You feel I don't know how hard it is for you. [She nods and breathes what looks like a sigh of relief.] Well, sometimes I think you don't know I exist!

Biological Mother: You feel I forget that you exist. [He nods and sighs]. Well, maybe sometimes I'm just so absorbed with my daughters that I can't pay attention to you. And I'm exhausted by trying to do it all.

Stepfather: You get tired trying to pay attention to so many people. [He has shifted from rote replay of her words to putting her feelings into his words. I imagine he has taken her in just a little more deeply. She tears up as he acknowledges the effort required in her role. He breaks the silence.] But I'm lonely.

Biological Mother: [Hardening again slightly.] You're the adult. [His mouth tightens and he sits back.]

P: Ooops. You forgot to repeat first.

Biological Mother: You're lonely. [His eyes tear ever so slightly, and he nods. They look directly at each other, and there is another small moment of connection.]

P: Do you feel the difference when you stop and repeat back?

Stepfather: Yeah. It's like we're together, just a little bit, even though we're apart in what we each feel.

This exercise constructs moments of empathic connection that serve like little drops of glue to hold the couple together as they traverse potentially polarizing territory. Because they are forced to hear each other, the couple can also begin to broaden its area of shared awareness. In this case, the couple might go on to help the mother to compartmentalize her time with her children and her husband more clearly, freeing her from being constantly pulled in many directions, and giving her husband reliable intimate time with her. However, even when differences cannot be resolved, more fully shared understanding of each person's dilemma can provide a sense of togetherness. Over time this excercise can become a model for conversing about differences in a way that builds up the relationship rather than tearing it apart.

Underline Moments of Contact. Another way therapists can lower anxiety for couples and families in the Mobilization

Stage is to ensure that when contact is made, it is acknowledged. In the press of the struggle, precious moments of tenderness often get lost. "Did you see the effect," I ask the speaker as the shoulders of a partner who has just been heard visibly drop and relax, and her face softens into a tiny smile. "Look what happens when you just let her know you heard her, even though you don't agree!"

Look for Losses. As always, work in the Mobilization Stage may be impeded by unvoiced fantasies. Therapists need always to stay in tune with losses that must be borne in order to hear. The anger of the Mobilization Stage may be rooted in unvoiced grief.

Explore Family-of-Origin Issues. Sometimes the roots of a highly mobilized conflict lie not in step issues but in bruises from the family of origin. Sager et al. (1983) offer many examples of resolving stepfamily conflict by exploring its roots in family-of-origin relationships.

The following describes a session that demonstrates several of these strategies at work with a couple in the Mobilization Stage. Vicky Corino and Bruce King have been living together for three years. Both are recovering alcoholics who have been involved in the 12-step program, and both have been in individual therapy, which made it possible to accomplish in one session what might have taken much longer with a less responsive couple.

It is our first session. Vicky has come in raging. They had had a fight on the subway en route to my office. She is furious at Bruce's children. "I'm sick and tired of the way they treat me." He is defensive. They start to fight about whether his children should greet her or not. Vicky has clearly moved fully into the Mobilization Stage and is trying to bring Bruce with her. She seems more aware of her feelings than he is of his but neither seems to have a clue about what the other is feeling. The atmosphere is so charged that I decide to begin by talking to them individually.

P.: It may be no comfort at all, but do you have any idea how normal your feelings are?

V. and B.: [Shake their heads "No."]

P.: I'm going to guess. You tell me if I'm right. You [looking at Vicky] joined this man who had kids. You're a nice person. You reach out.

You try to be friendly. They ignore you. They call their dad on the phone and don't even speak to you if you answer the phone. [I am trying to normalize the experience for Vicky by predicting her feelings. I'm also providing an empathic ear for her for the first time. She relaxes a bit.]

V.: Yeah, yeah! How'd you know!?

P.: Well, it's not magic. It's because this kind of structure sets up the kids to treat you that way. Want to know why they do it? [I give her a very brief description of the children's loyalty bind in the context of saying, "It's no wonder you feel this way."]

V.: But my feelings are so big!

P.: It's stunning, isn't it! [Empathizing with the surprise.]

V.: I get so embarrassed. I don't know what the people on the train thought of me.

P.: They're nobody's favorite feelings, the feelings your position in these kinds of families creates. It's hard to feel so pushed away and left out! Lots of people feel embarrassed about this. [Empathizing with the embarrassment and teaching a bit about where the feelings come from.]

P.: [Turning to Bruce] Hard to bear all her feelings, huh?

B.: Yeah, especially when they're directed at *me*!

P.: Well, now let me guess about you. You ready? You tell me what's right and what's wrong about my guesses, OK? I'll bet you're feeling really torn. You love her. You love your kids. She's upset. You can't fix her upset. And the more you tell her to calm down, the more upset she gets.

B.: Right! Right! [He brightens up and begins talking. He talks at length about his recovery and about how hard it is to be learning now to be a father and a lover at the same time.]

P.: It must break your heart at times [underlining the loss].

B.: *All* the time! So I've been seeing less of my kids.

P.: [Turning to Vicky—I want to begin to make some connections between them now that they've calmed down a bit.] What's it like listening to him?

V.: I didn't know how hard it was for him!

P.: Tell him. [Now they are ready to talk to each other. They do well for a while and then begin quarreling again. She begins accusing, and he gets defensive. I'm guessing there's a fantasy, some longing underneath, that hasn't found a voice yet. Bruce has given me a clue in his heartbreak.]

P.: [To Bruce] You look really frustrated and angry. Right? [He nods.] But I wonder if under your frustration and anger you might be really sad. I bet you really wish this were easier. I bet you wish she could love your kids like you do. [In fact, I've guessed wrong, but my guessing and the language of "wishing" have opened the door.]

B.: [In a low, almost inaudible voice] No, it's that I wish I didn't have children. I had them before I knew who I was.

P.: You wish you could start over fresh, huh? With this woman you love, without all these pushes and pulls. [I'm telling her indirectly that he loves her, and she is listening intently to his painful dilemma. He begins to weep, and Vicky's face warms visibly, but Bruce is looking at the floor.] Bruce? Can you see Vicky? [He is sobbing uncontrollably now.] Can you tell Vicky how *much* you wish you could just be lovers with her, and start fresh? [He looks at her and tells her. She begins crying.] "God, me too," she says.

B.: I've been so afraid to talk about these things.

V.: I had no idea it was so hard for you! I feel that loss, too. I wish I'd met you before you had kids!

P.: [Both are crying.] You know, maybe you can hold each other and cry together. [Silence as they cry together.] I tell them that it doesn't change the reality, but it helps to hold hands and grieve together instead of each being so isolated and alone. We've found a place where they can join together. They are in hard territory, but at least they are stumbling around together for the moment.

Later, with them sitting on the couch holding hands, I can insert a little piece of the children's experience—they *did* lose their father when he got involved with Vicky, and no wonder they're upset!

This moving session was not the end of Bruce and Vicky's struggles. They had a honeymoon for several weeks and then got entangled again. We then began exploring Bruce and Vicky's previous family history, identifying the old bruises and their habitual responses to them. Vicky's parents were alcoholics. In that context where there was no comfort available, she learned to withdraw or attack when she got hurt. Bruce is also from an alcoholic family in which he was often shamed and diminished. As Vicky moved from Immersion, where she was in her withdrawal mode, to Awareness and Mobilization, she voiced her concerns about step issues in the only way she knew—with stinging criticism. Bruce would shrink almost visibly under Vicky's attacks, responding defensively and unempathically. Bruce's apparent lack of empathy and supportiveness increased Vicky's anxiety, intensifying her attack. As a result, this couple's fights in the Mobilization Stage were not the least bit informative or useful. Rather, they inevitably deepened Bruce's shame and Vicky's despair.

Over time we explored Vicky's panic, raising her hope that in *this* relationship she could afford to identify her needs and to ask for them to be met rather than retreating or attacking. We explored Bruce's shame, helping him to learn how in this relationship he could keep his size and comfort Vicky's scared inner child rather than defending himself. As with many couples who get stuck in the Mobilization Stage, the work with Vicky and Bruce continues to weave between step issues and the couple and individual dynamics that exacerbate them.

Action: Helping Stepfamilies Go into Business Together

As the individual and mutual awareness tasks on a particular issue are completed, the family is ready to move into the Action Stage. We have talked about supporting the development of step middle ground in Early Stages by spending time in minifamilies and finding some "virgin territory" for easy middle ground. In the Action Stage, the family has sufficient information and strong enough relationships to turn its attention to heavy negotiating about already defined territory. The task now is to forge new fully shared agreements about how they will function as a stepfamily.

Action Stage Aesthetics. Stepfamilies and their therapists need to have a good aesthetic sense about when to move into the Action Stage on an issue. When the family never begins joint decision making, the outsider stepparent or subsystem languishes (see Chapter Two, Figures 2.3 and 2.4), creating a stuck Immersed Family that functions by the dominant biological subsystem's rules. When joint decision making moves too quickly to establish new step rules and rituals, children languish, creating a stuck Action Family. Where there is active disagreement, but no resolution of the conflict, a stuck Mobilized Family is created. Generally, successful Action Stage moves leave some of the biological subsystem's old middle ground in place. Some areas of already existing shared middle ground are identified and incorporated, and some brand-new areas are constructed and added.

A useful metaphor for this process is that stepfamilies and their therapists need to function on any one issue like respectful real estate developers. They must assess what pieces of the landscape are especially precious or vital to their inhabitants and what changes would make the area more livable for newcomers. The task is to alter the terrain enough to create a joint homestead, leaving some of the cherished areas of the old landscape intact and changing others. Moving in with a bulldozer may seem expedient but will render the land unrecognizable, stripping it of its most special qualities. On the other hand, changing nothing will leave some of the members of the new stepfamily homeless.

The Action Stage stories in Chapter Four provide models of successful inventions. Local Stepfamily Associations (see Appendix B) offer another source of helpful ideas for forging workable rituals out of two (or more) traditions. *Each successful attempt in itself adds to the family's feeling of well-being and mastery* and thickens the new step middle ground.

Attending to All Levels. Drawing from Wolin and Bennett (1984), Mary Whiteside (1988a, 1989) writes about the importance of three levels of ritual that need to be negotiated in a new stepfamily: ordinary *daily routines* such as meals and household rules; regularly occurring *traditions* such as holiday celebrations that symbolically represent the family; and *life cycle events* such as weddings and graduations that are likely to include the entire extended stepfamily suprasystem. In a stepfamily, rituals on any of these levels are embedded in previous legacies, many of them supported by an entire team. "What was once invisible and automatic," says Whiteside, "becomes explicit and endlessly negotiated" (1988a, p. 280). Work with stepfamilies in the Action Stage must over time bring attention to all three of these levels.

Assessing Awareness Stage Task Completion. In working with stepfamilies in the Action Stage, the first step is to assess the level of Awareness Stage task completion for a given issue. As we have seen, therapists often need to push a couple or family back into the Awareness Stage before they can move effectively into the Action Stage. A family that is fighting wildly (in the Mobilization Stage) cannot move into Action until each of its members is able to articulate his or her feelings and needs. Each member (particularly those on the adult team) also needs to find some interest in and knowledge of the others' needs.

As in earlier stages, when work in the Action Stage seems to get stuck, it is important to stop and attend to unspoken fantasies that the new action might threaten, losses this action might create, or previous painful family history the dilemma may be activating. Continuing to engage in Action tasks when the work of earlier stages is incomplete can be disastrous. A failed case illustrates the pitfalls. We return to Angela Ricci who spoke in Chapter Three of her determination to have her stepdaughter Molly "follow my rules" and "learn some manners" (see p. 130).

Angela had become the full-time stepmother of Molly, age 10, a year ago. She and her husband Frank came for help in "making some decisions together." The Riccis were an Action Family. Frank had immediately supported Angela's rules for his daughter. Molly had become increasingly resistant, openly ignoring Angela's requests of her. Much to Angela's distress, Frank was beginning to disagree with her more often.

I mistakenly treated this as an Action Stage dilemma, helping Angela and Frank to choose one issue at a time and to figure out what a reasonable, workable compromise might be. They were rarely able to complete this task, and could not keep agreements.

It became clear that both Angela and Frank were laboring under the fantasy that with Angela's corrective parenting Molly would straighten out, and their new family would provide the secure home Frank and Molly (and Angela, it later emerged) had missed. Neither Angela nor Frank was responsive to information about normal stepfamily functioning. Attempting to get them to understand how impossible was the task they had set for Angela and Molly produced a series of canceled appointments and a premature termination.

Looking back over this case, it was clear that I not only began work in the wrong stage but had failed to deal empathetically with family-of-origin issues. I had responded to Angela and Frank's request for Action Stage help in "making decisions." However their awareness work remained substantially incomplete. Although Angela was very clear about her own needs, she had no understanding of Molly's difficulty in accommodating such a long list of changes. Frank was just beginning to find his voice, and his daughter Molly seemed only able to express herself by acting out.

Furthermore, Angela and Frank's resistance to new information should have sparked my curiosity. Attention to Angela's history would have provided some clues to the function of her fantasies, and her powerful but unrealistic need for control and order. She was the oldest child in an abusive alcoholic family. From the age of 10 (Molly's age), she had kept her younger brothers fed and clothed, and had done most of the housework while getting straight A's in school.

In asking Angela to relinquish the notion that she could do the same with her stepdaughter, I was stripping her of a precious survival skill. Angela's brothers were both alcoholics. She was the only one in her family to have finished college. Angela's need for control was problematic and unrealistic in her new stepfamily. However, it had kept her sane in a chaotic and terrifying family.

In this case, the principle of respecting resistance meant understanding that giving up control over her stepdaughter required helping Angela to face a level of despair that had drowned her brothers, a therapeutic task not conducive to mere provision of information!

On her partner's side, Frank's mother had been manic-depressive. His first wife had been an alcoholic. His marriage to a woman as steady and well-organized as Angela must have seemed like his chance to fix it all and to have the family of which he had been twice deprived. I delivered my news without empathy or respect for this, and in so doing left them with no choice but to protect themselves.

Teaching Good Problem-Solving Skills. As we saw in Chapter Two, Gestalt therapy works from a model of healthy functioning. In addition to therapeutic work that completes "unfinished business" and heals old wounds, we are interested in teaching our clients skills that will make their lives more satisfying. The Gestalt Interactive Cycle provides an especially cogent description of the skills stepfamilies need for the kind of problem solving necessary to complete the Middle Stages.

In facilitating progress through the Early Stages, we have focused on teaching awareness skills: putting names on feelings, attaching them to real events, voicing them so they can be heard, asking questions of and empathizing with the intimate others in one's life. These remain crucial. However, the problem solving and negotiating tasks of the Action Stage now require stepfamilies to complete entire interactive cycles together.

Let us review the skills involved in each stage of the Gestalt Interactive Cycle, applying them now to work in the Action Stage of the Stepfamily Cycle. In the Action Stage of the Stepamily Cycle, the Interactive Cycle helps the therapist to identify what skills this couple or family brings to Action Stage tasks (What does this system do well that we can support and underline?) and to choose a specific point of intervention (What is the next thing they could learn that would help them to be better problem-solvers?).

Awareness. As always, the therapist needs to first assess the level of each individual's awareness. Do insider and outsider, adult and child perspectives each have a voice on this issue? Are the adults and the older children gaining some understanding of the whole picture? Are family members being specific with each other, asking for examples when they are not, saying "tell me more" when there is a misunderstanding? Do they linger long enough in this stage to gather sufficient information to make an accurate map? Those who catapult into Mobilization or slip back into uneasy silence will not generate enough information to invent workable plans on Action Stage issues. The interventions described in previous sections of this chapter apply in teaching these skills. This is the first area of work. It must be in place before the family can proceed on any one issue.

Energy/Action Skills. Once the family has generated enough information on an issue, does someone move to try to influence others ("Let's try this . . . " "I'd really like to . . . "), or does everyone wait for someone else to make a move ("After you, Alphonse")? As the couple or family members become energized, are they able to focus on one or two items, or do they flood themselves with a whole raft of issues at once? Positive feedback to stepcouples and stepfamilies that do this well supports these important skills: "Faced with a full plate of compelling issues, this family knows how to take one thing and really stay with it. And you can see the results." As always, teaching interventions will be more effective if they begin with positive feedback:

This is a family that gets very excited about a whole lot of things at once. You really know how to get engaged and involved. The problem is that I'm not sure anyone's watching to see if the plate is too full! I wonder if you could try working together to take one thing at a time. What do you think about that?

When families and couples cannot focus on one issue, the problem may be lack of skill, or it may lie in losses that must be faced, a fantasy that would be painful to relinquish, or family-of-origin issues that prevent movement. As the case of Angela and Frank Ricci illustrated, attempting to help the family complete Action Stage tasks will be premature and frustrating for all.

Other energy/action skills include: checking for what was left out ("Oops, we forgot that Danny hates peanut butter."); checking for agreement ("OK, here's what we've agreed. Is that it?") rather than leaving it vague and then getting disappointed because each person had a different picture of what would happen; and checking for who's going to do what ("OK, I'm gonna . . . and you're gonna . . . and Johnny's gonna . . . Is that right?"). All of these skills require that family members step outside their own particular pieces of territory and take a look at how the whole operation is proceeding.

Contact Skills. Do the members of this family stop and congratulate each other or push right on to the next problem? Stepfamilies are often so overwhelmed by multiple pressing dilemmas that they rush on to the next problem without stopping to savor work they have accomplished and without taking time to feel the new ground they have forged together. As discussed in the section on Mobilization earlier in this chapter, underlining moments of contact in Mobilization serves to emphasize and heighten these connections (p. 341).

Resolution Skills. Good resolution skills provide time for digestion before proceeding. They ensure that the couple or family or group learns from its often heroic efforts in the Action Stage. "So what did we learn about what works and what doesn't work on the weekends your kids come?" "Well *that* was a fiasco! What do you suppose we missed in planning for it?"

First-time families, because they can develop most of their rules and rituals and celebrations over time, little by little, can get by with less careful resolution work. Stepfamilies must bring together many different needs and ideas and histories within a very short period of time. What appeared to be a terrific plan may go awry when unspoken, often previously unaware assumptions and divergent habits are suddenly exposed. Good resolution skills help family members to figure out what happened rather than blame each other for being uncooperative or uncaring.

Most couples and families need to be taught to do this. As helping professionals, we can model good resolution skills by stopping a few minutes early to give some time for digestion and asking members to lean back, take a breath, and say what stood out for them, what adjectives would describe the session for them, or what they liked and didn't like about a session. This simple exercise in itself can provide the most poignant, vivid moments of an entire session as family members distill into a few words what mattered to them and voice it to each other.

Withdrawal Skills. The Action Stage involves stepfamilies in much hard work. Families that solve a problem and then rush off to the next one without a break not only deprive themselves of appreciating what they have accomplished, but will exhaust themselves more quickly. Sitting back and making a clear ending is like clearing the table between courses. "OK, that's done." "Whew! We got through that. Let's rest a moment."

It is important to support this skill in stepfamilies and couples that do it well: "This family finishes things well. You really take time to stop and notice what you've done, and then you rest. You take a little break before you move on. That really helps you live well together." Those who do not do this well will need some help making little resting places, for without them the sheer amount of work involved in sorting out stepfamily rules and rituals can be overwhelming:

"Did you know that you have just completed a huge amount of work together and that you are rushing on to the next thing? That keeps life exciting, but you'll wear yourselves out! Can I interest you in sitting back and taking a breath before you tackle another issue? There. How do you like the way that feels?"

First-time families that have these skills in Interactive Cycle completion have much healthier and more satisfying lives together. However, they can get away with a lower level of communication. Developmental progress in becoming a stepfamily is much more dependent on these skills, particularly in the Action Stage.

Strategic Planning. Some events in stepfamily life create predictable hot spots that strain problem-solving skills to their limits. "Strategic planning," by which I mean predicting difficulties and planning for them ahead of time before goodwill is enveloped in anxiety, can greatly increase chances of success. Typical hot spots in stepfamilies include family celebrations where biological and step rituals are already fully (and differently) defined (Christmas, Passover, birthdays, etc.); events that bring together the binuclear family system (a school play); and life-cycle celebrations that bring the new family into contact with people tied to the previous family (an aunt's birthday party where the aunt was close to the ex-spouse, a grandparent's anniversary, weddings, and graduations). These kinds of family rituals can heighten differences in culture, underscore losses, intensify loyalty binds and expose insider/outsider dilemmas. However, they can also provide opportunities for thickening the new family's middle ground.

As in any Action task, strategic planning begins with awareness work. Families may need help asking each other and articulating exactly how each person in the family imagines Christmas Eve and Christmas Day. What will be done when and with whom? What will be eaten and when? To what pieces of the ritual are family members most attached? What differences evoke the most pain and anxiety? Anxiety will be lowered if we remind the family that the first step is to map out all the different territories in the family, which must precede any decision making. The family then has enough data to concoct workable new traditions that creatively meet a variety of needs.

Life-cycle events that include the binuclear or extended stepfamily require a special kind of strategic planning. The insider/outsider issues, losses and loyalty binds that resurface at suprasystem events often surprise stepcouples. Predicting some of them can be extraordinarily helpful: A biological father at his daughter's wedding may be flooded by memories of the bride as a baby and youngster, memories he shares with that child's mother, not with his second wife. His second wife may find herself feeling surprisingly awkward and left out as she experiences her husband's apparent withdrawal, or watches an aunt who was close to the ex-wife speak intimately with her. Strategic planning begins here with helping the couple or family to anticipate and talk about these feelings and events and to build in supports. An intimate date before potentially divisive family gatherings may provide extra glue for the stepcouple. The outsider, like the stepmother Cecelia in Case Three (Chapter Six), may want to bring along a close friend who can provide a protective insider relationship. The couples may want to arrange an intimate break—a walk during which they share what has come up for them and provide each other with an empathic ear.

The section on "Older Stepchildren" at the end of this chapter more fully explores some of the dilemmas that weddings, graduations, bar and bat mitzvahs pose for stepfamilies. Therapists, religious leaders, and school personnel involved in life-cycle events can play an important role in establishing norms of binuclear cooperation. When the event revolves around a child, a joint session may help the adults to cooperate in loosening children's loyalty binds.

Families must often be reminded to work resolution skills into the planning. I often say, "I assume that since this is the first time you've tried this, lots of things will go wrong. So let's think of this as a bold experiment rather than an ultimate solution. What you do with an experiment is try it and see how things go—then you talk about what you learned and put your experience to work the next time." This framework not only lays the foundation for some resolution, but it predicts and mitigates the effects of inevitable disappointments when carefully constructed plans do not succeed. In teaching resolution skills, we are teaching stepfamilies to use these inevitable disasters to build their understanding of each other rather than to further fracture their new family.

The kind of effort strategic planning requires often doesn't feel family-like. It may help to remind members of remarried families that they are a different kind of family whose members do not share a history. Attempting a merger without well-thought-out plans for integrating and respecting differences invites disaster. On the other hand, careful planning can ensure that celebrations will serve their function of adding glue to the new family rather than deepening cracks.

Later Stages: Helping Families to Hold on and to Let Go

Supporting Contact: Appreciating What Has Been Accomplished

The Contact Stage gives stepfamilies a well-deserved honeymoon. Helping professionals are rarely needed at this time. Teachers, psychotherapists (who may be involved around other issues), clergy, and medical and school personnel can best support stepfamilies in this stage by openly recognizing what has been accomplished. "I remember when you and your stepdaughter hardly talked to each other. Now you sit here talking at a school conference (making summer vacation plans, preparing for a bat mitzvah), discussing these things with such ease and openness. Congratulations. It must feel good." Statements such as these give stepfamily members an opportunity to sit back and appreciate how far they have come. "I hadn't thought about it. It's true, isn't it! Boy, does that feel good! We've worked our tails off, and we've really done it," is often the kind of response I hear.

Supporting Families in the Resolution Stage

By the Resolution Stage, much of what required effort in earlier stages has moved to the background. New issues arise within the context of solid reliable step relationships. Adults now function as a team. Stepparent and child(ren) have developed mutually suitable relationships. The family now has an identity. Nonetheless, new or recurring issues occasionally send Resolution Stage stepfamilies back to earlier stages. Insider/outsider issues that had long ago receded may reemerge as a custody shift introduces a new full-time stepchild. Impending college costs may revive old conflicts over the stepparent's financial role. A wedding may reawaken long dormant tension between ex-spouses.

Placing New Issues in Context. Resolution Stage stepfamilies who appear for help often need to be reminded of all that they have accomplished. Helping a family struggling over college finances to remember that they have already solved many problems together may in itself provide relief and hope. Stepfamilies that find themselves back in an earlier stage may need assurance that this slippage is not an indication of ultimate failure but is instead a common and normal developmental occurrence.

Assessing Stage. Work in the Resolution Stage then proceeds according to the stage in which the family is functioning on this issue. Sometimes a new life event revives an old fantasy. The impending birth of an "ours" child may stir up a remarried father's wish that he could be full-time parent to his child of the first marriage, provoking a sudden custody fight. Regrieving the loss of full-time parenting will be necessary before the custody discussion can be fruitful. If the family is stuck in Immersion (one or several voices silent), the first order of business is to create space for each family member to put words on feelings and find a voice for them. If the family has begun Awareness Stage work and all family members can voice their thoughts and feelings, they may simply need to use the therapist as a safe neutral space in which to continue exploring a charged subject. They may need help completing the joint awareness task: asking each other questions, checking for understanding, etc. If they have jumped to Mobilization, the strategies described earlier in this chapter may help them to slow down and lower anxiety (pp. 337–346).

Whom to see in the Resolution Stage depends upon both the Stepfamily Cycle Stage the family has slipped back into and the locus of the problem. A struggle over whether to have a new baby may be an individual problem (Immersed biological parent isn't sure he or she wants another child and needs some individual help to sort out feelings), or a couples problem (biological parent does not want another child, but previously single stepparent does). A child's failing school grades may begin as an individual problem (remarriage of a second parent has placed the child in an intense loyalty bind, and he or she needs someone safe to talk to), become a suprasystem problem (the extended family works together to understand and loosen the bind), and then move back to a couples issue (stepparent in one couple is feeling pressured for a custody shift).

Resolution Stage issues often involve the binuclear family. For therapists who are comfortable dealing with large family systems, weddings, college costs, and custody shifts provide an opportunity to bring the suprasystem together to provide much-needed system-wide geography lessons and to loosen long-standing loyalty binds.

Special Issues: New Babies, Stepfamilies Formed by Death, and "Older" Stepchildren

In addition to characteristic ongoing developmental issues, there is a wide range of specific issues that the stepfamily may find itself confronting.

New Babies

Stepcouples often ask their therapists, ministers, or pediatricians whether a new baby will glue their new family together. This wish for a child who will cement the stepfamily has led Ganong and Coleman (1988b) to call the new child of a stepfamily the "concrete baby." In fact, Ganong and Coleman found that a new baby made no difference in the quality of stepfamily relationships. My own interpretation of these results is that a new baby may increase or decrease the glue in a stepfamily depending upon the developmental stage of the family into which the child is born.

Although each family is different, therapists can use the following information to provide some guidance to clients in their decision making. Simple stepfamilies (only one adult brings children) in the Early Stages are vulnerable to splitting along biological lines with the previously single stepparent bonding to the new child, leaving the biological parent with his or her children from the previous marriage. Like the Tolmans (Case Two, Chapter Six) and Joanne Gray and Jeff Rudnick (in Chapters Three and Seven), further exploration often reveals that the adults carry two divergent fantasies: The stepparent had imagined "our new family" as "you, me, and our new baby." The biological parent had imagined "our new family" as "you, me, our new baby, and my children." Exploring these families in detail and grieving them can be useful. Helping professionals working with expectant couples in the Early Stages can head off these painful splits by aiding couples in articulating these fantasies before they find themselves in the midst of them. The question can be asked directly ("Often in these kinds of families, members have different pictures of what their family will look like after a new baby is born. What are yours?"). Asking each member of the couple or family to imagine who will be present and what will happen at a family celebration also provides access to these various individual pictures: "Perhaps you each could describe what you think Christmas/Passover will be like in your new family."

In normalizing the dilemmas created by the birth of an "ours" child, it may be helpful for both stepparents and biological parents to know that for stepparents who have never been parents, the birth of a biological child will clarify and intensify the differences between biological parenting and stepparenting. Robert Keefe, a previously childless stepparent, talks about his experience at the birth of his first biological child:

It was such a surprise, that passionate attachment. Right from the start, there is something that your own baby pulls out of you that I missed with my stepdaughter. It's just so close right away.

Barbara Abramson, a stepmother and mother to a new baby boy:

I love my stepdaughter. But I don't have that solid feeling that I have with David [her son], that I absolutely love this kid, I adore him.

For previously single stepparents who are on their way to working through Awareness Stage tasks, this experience of biological parenting provides confirmation and relief, and actually facilitates movement from the "What's wrong with me" of the Immersion Stage to "I'm not crazy, I'm just a stepparent" of the Awareness Stage:

Now I know what I've been missing. It's not that I was inadequate. It's that being a stepparent and being a biological parent are different, real different. And now I can feel the difference. Now I know for sure I'm not nuts.

However, if the fantasy that "I should love my stepchildren as my own" remains, these intense feelings of attachment provide devastating evidence of the stepparent's inability to parent a stepchild like a biological child. This statement from Robert Keefe illustrates the way in which biological parenthood can intensify the shame of the Immersion Stage:

I could see the difference. I could see what people expected of me with Becky (his stepdaughter). I could feel it. And I began to take it on for myself. I was always making comparisons for myself, feeling how the quality of my love for Becky was lacking.

When remarried parents still hold the hope for biological-like attachments between stepparents and stepchildren, they will agree with stepparents such as Robert. For these families the birth of a new biological child will actually deepen the mire of the Immersion Stage, raising the anxiety level of the family. Work in these families begins in the Early Stages and may go back to family-of-origin issues that hold fantasies in place.

In contrast, for stepparents who have moved far enough developmentally through the Stepfamily Cycle, the birth of a biological child may provide the last bit of clarity needed to more effectively confront their still-fantasizing biological parent spouses about step and biological differences. In these families, the birth of a new baby precipitates movement into the Mobilization Stage. Often the couple appears for help in these cases, fighting and frightened. For these families, the section on work in the Mobilization Stage is applicable.

When new babies are born in the Middle Stages, the family may also initially divide along biological lines. Stepfamilies that are closer to the Action Stage are likely to have enough teamwork in place to find their way back together again. If this has begun to happen, positive feedback from the therapist can facilitate the process: "In stepfamilies it's very common that the birth of a new baby creates this kind of split. It looks like that happened in this family and that you two are working your way back toward each other. Congratulations. Here are some things I see you doing to mend the split. First and most important, I see you talking to each other about how differently you each view this situation, and I see you really listening. It's as if you are able to hold each other's hands through a painful passage. Not many couples can do this, and it makes all the difference."

If the couple is stuck in Mobilization, then the interventions from that section apply here: giving whatever positive feedback is possible, providing some of the missing empathy for each side, helping the couple to slow down and hear each other, normalizing the struggle for this kind of family, and looking for fantasies and family-of-origin issues that impede awareness.

In my experience, new babies born into families in the Later Stages do seem to provide the glue for which stepfamilies hope. Families that can wait until the tasks of early stepfamily development have been accomplished are less vulnerable to being polarized by a new child. Step relationships are reliable and firm and it is safe to talk about the differences in step and biological attachments that emerge with the birth of an "ours" child.

Whatever the developmental stage of the family, therapists, ministers, day-care teachers, guidance counselors, pediatricians, nurses, teachers, and others involved with stepfamilies can be very helpful in preparing children for the arrival of a half-sibling. Older children, particularly those in a highly conflicted family, may appreciate having some time apart from their family with an empathic, neutral ear. Others may absolutely refuse to see "a shrink," in which case the therapist can act as consultant to the child's parents. With younger children, I feel it is often more supportive of parental competence as well as of the child's self-esteem to coach parents to anticipate and deal with children's feelings rather than to involve children in a therapeutic setting.

Stepchildren vary tremendously in their feelings about the birth of a new child. Some are very excited about having an "ours" child. Others may experience a particular twist on the natural fear of losing one's place to a new baby (Papernow, 1984b). For stepchildren, as for adults, the birth of a new child may highlight a variety of painful differences between step and biological relationships. Stepparents will now have a "more real" child. Their stepchildren may fear being displaced. Others may fear losing their own parents to this "more mutual" child of the new family. Both adults and children may need help to articulate and acknowledge these feelings. Younger children can be told stories:

Once upon a time, there was a little girl who had a daddy and a mommy. Her daddy and mommy got divorced. Then her daddy remarried a woman named Jane. At first the little girl thought that if she loved Jane she would lose her mommy. Pretty soon she found out that she could have both a mommy and a stepmom. Then Jane got pregnant. The little girl was really worried. She was afraid Jane would love the new baby more than her, because the new baby would really be Jane's baby. Did you ever feel that way?

Well, then the baby was born and Jane did have a sort of different relationship with the baby than with the little girl. But Jane and the little girl had always had very special feelings about each other, and when the baby arrived they still did—they had their very own different kind of very special relationship, just as the little girl had a different relationship with *her* mommy and another kind of special relationship with Jane.

Older children can be dealt with more directly. Often simply expressing the feelings and having them heard helps children to feel freer to welcome a new sibling. Parents may need to be coached to respond to feelings: "Tell me some more about what worries you the most," rather than, "You have nothing to worry about."

Stepfamilies Formed by Death

Stepfamilies formed by the death of a parent present somewhat different dilemmas than those formed by divorce, as do stepfamilies where a parent has disappeared. Because there is no competing ex-spouse, these families are particularly vulnerable to becoming stuck Immersed Families (dominated by the biological parent-child subsystem) or Action Families (dominated by the adult couple subsystem) in which there is no acknowledgment of step issues. Often in these cases, the stepparent adopts his or her stepchildren, further sealing the fantasy, for the adults at least, that this family can operate as if it were a first-time family. Robert Keefe, the stepfather whose feelings for his own new baby caused such agony, was from such a family, a stuck Immersed Family in which the first husband, a drug addict, had completely disappeared. The Wentworths in Chapter Six illustrate an Action Family formed by death.

Members of these kinds of stepfamilies may come to therapy in a variety of ways. The stepparent may appear for help, perhaps complaining of depression, but usually around other issues. He or she will often refer to the stepchild as "my daughter" or "my son." A therapist experienced in step issues will find, upon further probing, that though the step relationship has never been acknowledged, it is a daily source of discomfort. Cathy Olson, a midwestern Protestant stepmother, talks about Betty, her Italian stepdaughter, whom she adopted when the child was 3. The child's mother had died of cancer.

We don't look alike. There's no *mirror* there. It's not like my son [mutual child] who is blonde like me. I look at Betty and she's dark. *In 14 years of parenting this child, I have never even said this out loud before, and it's such a relief.*

Cathy had come for help "feeling low and inadequate all the time." Although there were other sources of her depression, she was also clearly a stepparent in Immersion. Helping her to name and voice her feelings gave her considerable relief:

I never felt my husband let me in with his daughter. Never. There was always this expectation that I'm the mom now. And yet I always felt he and Betty had a special relationship that I was left out of, that his opinion would always be the one that won. That was not true with our [mutual] son. But I could never say it until now. What a relief. It doesn't change the reality, but I feel so much better just saying out loud what it is.

Because Cathy's individual therapy with me was important, this couple was referred to another therapist as Cathy entered the Mobilization Stage. For couples like Cathy and her husband Nick, awareness work will often include the biological parent's unfinished grief work.

These families also come to the attention of helping professionals through children, as in the Wentworth case (Case Four, Chapter Six). Children may have questions about their biological parents that they have been unable to ask ("What did he look like? What did he say when I was born? What did we do together?"). Sometimes their parents will say, "But we've talked to the children about their father." I tell widowed parents that talking to children about a parent who has died is a lot like sex education. You do it over and over again, at different ages, listening for children's questions, anticipating them sometimes, giving them the amount of information they can process at each particular age. The Action Stage task of these stepfamilies, establishing and maintaining a "boundary with a hole in it," extends to helping children maintain access to their absent biological parent even when that parent has died or disappeared. Although adults can move on from bereavement into a new family, children's identity remains inextricably tied to that parent. Helping professionals need to keep in mind that re-including a dead spouse may be a painful task for a surviving parent. As Ben Wilson, a widower about to be remarried, said to me:

> My first wife's cancer was one of the most painful times in my life, and I am just glad to be through with it. I don't want to go back to it. I hate even thinking about it.

Widowed parents like Ben need empathy for their dilemma: they can, and would very much like to, replace their previous spouse, but she remains part of their children, both psychologically and physically.

Teenage children like Betty, above, who were adopted as young children, provide another entry point for these families. As identity issues become more pressing, these children sometimes find themselves mysteriously troubled. Jeannie Caponi, whose father had died when she was 4, was in this situation. She had, in fact, attempted suicide when she was 15, and was now at 18 looking back. She had been hospitalized, and, fortunately, had worked with someone sensitive to her step issues:

> My father died when I was 4 and my mom married my dad, well, really my stepdad, but I always called him my dad. I don't remember my real father.

> But my stepfather is big and dark. My mom and I are little and we have freckles. I never thought about it consciously, but something must have been going on because when I got to be a teenager I started treating my dad, really my stepdad, real badly.

> I think now that it was that I wanted my real dad. And I was mad
> about it. Because, you see, we never talked about it. But I needed
> to know about my real dad: what he looked like, what he felt like
> when I was a baby, if he held me, what he said about me.

For this child and many adolescents who have lost a parent
through abandonment or death, her own Action Stage involved re-including her father in her family.

Older Stepchildren

Our parents remain part of our identities for life. Nowhere
is this more obvious than in the response of grown children
when their parents divorce or remarry. To "wait until the
kids are grown" does not, in fact, protect children as much
as we would wish (Crosbie-Burnett, 1987; Kaufman, 1987).
Because the parents of these young adults may feel freer
to confide in them as equals, loyalty binds can be intense.
Graduations, weddings, and other life-cycle events that
should be sources of pride become painful reminders of a
divided household, or worse, battlegrounds for warring ex-
spouses. When their parents divorce or remarry at this time,
it is as if these children lose a foundation from which to push
off. The resulting sense of uneasiness can be profound for
young adults, whose developmental task is to launch themselves into the world.

The following work with Sally Kelly, a graduate student
in music, focuses on awareness work: naming her feelings,
tying them to real events, placing them within a normal context, and, finally, naming her needs. We then brought those
needs into the room and into her present life. As is often
true of young adults in remarried families, Sally came into
therapy around other issues. The therapy had first focused
on her internal harsh "critical parent" and the unrealistic
expectations she placed on herself. By the time of the following exchange we had worked on her need to exhaust herself
taking care of others, and its roots in her familial role as
a "parentified" child. She had begun to set more realistic
expectations, to ask her friends for help more often, and to

tell her mother and her brothers a bit more about her real feelings. Then she got stuck writing what her advisors felt was a great thesis. At the time of this session, she had also just finished a well-received piano performance, and yet she didn't seem proud or excited.

Sally's father had just remarried. Her mother, who had remained alone and very needy since the divorce, had "lost it" at the news of her ex-husband's remarriage. This information made me wonder what Sally thought her parents' response to her work might be:

S.: I *have* accomplished a lot. But it's like there's no place to take it to! My dad's acting like a teenager in love and my mom is going nuts. They're both too self-absorbed to notice. It's like there's no place to take it to!

P.: Nobody to celebrate you as a young adult?

S.: Yeah. [Silence.] And so I find myself saying it's not important what I've done. It's like I make it not matter.

P.: But it does matter?

S.: I don't want it to.

P.: Because then it would hurt?

S.: But why should it matter? It's so embarrassing that I should need this. I'm not a little kid.

P.: Is that a real question? [Sally doesn't seem ready to feel sad for the loss of parents to be proud of her. I want to feed her some information that might lift some of her shame and make internal space for her feelings. But I don't want to force-feed her.]

S.: Yes. [Said firmly, and with some energy.]

P.: Well, then, I'll answer it! What you're saying is that there's nobody to celebrate you as a young adult! Not as a little child. You know, you're at the age when you don't need your parents for advice or to tell you what to do, or even for financial support.

S.: Right. That's right.

P.: But you do need them to be *interested* in what you're doing in the world. And to be proud of what you're mastering in the world, and to ask you about your thesis, and be thrilled with your piano performance. And they don't have that for you.

S.: Yeah. It's almost like they're in the same stage I am! My dad wants me to like his new wife and tells me all about his new house, and dotes on his new stepson and ignores my brothers. It's like he's so busy getting *my* approval. [Now she is beginning to find a voice for her experience.]

P.: He's not being a dad? [Her cheeks are pink and her eyes are tearing.] You do need someone to be proud of you, huh? [Now she's more ready to face the loss.]

S.: [Nods. She's very teary.]

P.: [Silence for a while.] No wonder it's been hard to be excited about your thesis! [We talked for a while about this, Sally facing her sadness over the loss of parents to be proud of her.]

S.: It makes sense now. I do feel better that this makes sense. [She looks relieved, and her eyes are brighter. A piece of work remains — to bring her reawakened awareness of her needs to bear on her current relationships.]

P.: So, are you bragging enough with me?

The session ended with a very lively exchange in which Sally and I confronted the ways in which she might ask more of me and others in her life. "I didn't think you'd be there," she said, close to tears. Sally's despair and shame over her unmet needs from her parents had dulled her appetite in the present. Naming her loss and grieving for it freed her to want more for herself.

Once their grief work is well underway I like to interest adult children in the dilemmas of their remarried parents and their new spouses. Behavior that had seemed cruel and insensitive can become understandable as adult children form a clearer picture of a stepparent's outsider experience and a parent's feeling of being torn. It is important to remember, too, that a parent's new spouse may, in fact, be a new resource for the young adult. If this seems possible, I often encourage older children to make some direct contact with this person. Sally's father's wife, Dora, seemed very promising. When Sally's father insisted that Dora attend Sally's graduation with him, I helped Sally write her an empathic but direct letter saying what she understood about

Dora's feelings about being excluded from Sally's graduation. She went on to tell Dora some of her struggle in taking in a new person and her loyalty bind with her own mother, and she asked for Dora's help in solving the problem. Dora responded graciously, laying the groundwork for Sally to form an intimate outsider relationship with a steadier, more sensible adult.

Not only do young adults feel the loss of foundation when their parents remarry. The following is an example of how a nurse practitioner attuned to step issues was able to help an "older child" (of 50!) move from Immersion ("I have all these feelings, what's wrong with me?") to the beginning of Awareness ("I have a lot of feelings, and I have some ideas about where they're coming from.").

Jerry Burke, a 50-year-old man, appeared for an annual checkup complaining of feeling lethargic and having no energy. When his nurse practitioner asked about recent changes in his life, Jerry replied, "Not much," though he casually mentioned his father's remarriage.

The nurse practitioner said, "It is surprising how powerful your feelings can be about these things, isn't it?" Jerry looked stunned and then relieved, and said that he hadn't thought about it. But, yes, in fact, it was very upsetting, surprisingly so.

Further questioning revealed that the remarriage had resulted in a number of unsettling changes including the sale of the house in which Jerry had grown up, and a radical shift in the yearly family Christmas (Jerry was upset that the newlyweds had gone to Europe instead of hosting the family celebration). In addition, sibling relationships had become strained as brothers and sisters lined up "for" and "against" the new marriage.

With these multiple losses identified, the nurse practitioner referred Jerry for some short-term counseling.

Keeping the wider picture in mind, we can imagine that Jerry's father was both hurt and stunned by his grown son's difficulty in accepting what must have felt like very positive changes in the father's life.

Likewise, stepcouples (and their therapists) often assume that children who have moved out of the house will not be affected by the birth of a new baby in a remarried household. In fact for older children the birth of an "ours" child may be a complex event that puts them in the painful position of watching their parents (particularly their remarried fathers) providing a quality of nurturing that they had never received. Similar feelings may be evoked when a father becomes involved with a woman who has younger children. These events can provide a rich opportunity for older children in individual therapy to reexperience and rework their relationships with parents. We can also encourage remarried parents of "ours" babies to explore what they did and didn't give the children of their first marriage. We can encourage them to talk to their adult children or to invite them into a joint session.

The work with Sally Kelly also illustrates the impact of remarriage on life-cycle events for young adults. Religious leaders, school personnel, and therapists can encourage exspouses to bury the hatchet for their children's important moments. Where conflict remains high, creative solutions can be urged.

Peter Norstadt was planning his wedding. His parents had divorced when he was 16 years old. His father had remarried a much younger woman and planned to attend the wedding with his new wife. Peter's mother had remained single and bitter since the divorce. The spectre loomed of a wedding spoiled by Peter's mother's histrionics. The minister involved was told that Peter's parents were "impossible" to work with. However, Peter's fiancée's parents were quite willing to help out. The minister helped Peter and his fiancée, Wendy, to devise the following plan to diffuse the tension: Peter's father and his wife were seated as far as possible from Peter's mother. Wendy's parents were willing to split up, each accompanying one of Peter's parents. Friends of Peter's who had remained close to his mother were dispatched to sit with his mother and engage her as actively as possible. A friend of Wendy's was seated near Peter's father's new wife, with directions to be friendly and welcoming. Peter and Wendy were told to assume that their friends and Wendy's parents would take care of his parents, leaving the young couple free to enjoy their wedding.

The detailed strategic planning required to extricate Peter from his loyalty bind may feel distinctly uncelebratory. However, without this careful planning, Peter's marriage would have started as yet another chapter in his parents' divorce. The planning paid off in a ritual that, despite some tension, truly celebrated Peter and Wendy and left the entire extended family feeling more whole than it had in years.

The remarriage of a parent affects children of all ages. Just as for younger children, awareness of the feelings evoked and the needs involved of older children can make the difference between mysterious depression and active coping.

Conclusion

In this chapter we have used the Stepfamily Cycle to provide the helping professional, whether in a clinical or an educational role, with a framework for effective intervention. Appendix C summarizes these intervention strategies. Here let us review the principles that guide all work with stepfamilies.

Keeping in mind that awareness is the primary building block and the foundation on which development rests, the first task is always to name and validate the experience of current and real dilemmas of stepfamily living. As we have seen, conveying accurate information about normal stepfamilies is often enough to ease the strain and redirect attention from achieving the impossible to tackling real challenges. Toward this end all helping professionals involved with stepfamilies ought to have access to their local (or the national) Stepfamily Association of America group (see Appendix B for SAA address and telephone number), as well as appropriate articles and books, many of which are available from SAA. (See also the starred references in the bibliography.)

When education is not sufficient therapists can look for "old bruises" that may be making the inherently bumpy experience of stepfamily life much more painful. The therapeutic task then moves to separating and weaving together the past and the present.

Work with stepfamilies requires remaining impeccably systemic. When doing individual work, we do first empathize with the dilemma of the person in front of us. But we must offer our empathy without blaming the absent players, always holding in our own awareness the fact that the apparent bad guy who is not in the room has an equally compelling story to tell. When our clients are ready, we then interest them in that story as well. In work with remarried couples or families, the fragility of members' connections with each other makes the pull to take sides especially destructive. Developmental progress with stepfamilies requires that the helping professional provide appreciation (often missing in the family) for the dilemma of each person in the room.

Finally, as in all therapeutic work, apparent resistance must be treated with respect and tenderness. Stepfamilies are born of loss. What looks like stubbornness or rigidity is often the only protection available against the painful awareness of a wish that cannot be.

It seems appropriate to have ended this chapter with the story of Peter's wedding which I believe captures the creativity and vitality that stepfamily life calls forth from its members and the helping professionals involved with them. Peter's story reminds us as well of the possibilities for healing inherent in beginning a new life with awareness of the old.

PART IV

EPILOGUE:

What Stepfamilies Can Teach Us

We have come a long way since meeting the Tolmans in Chapter One just after their disastrous New Hampshire weekend. We have established the need for a developmental model that would have helped them make sense of their experience much earlier and with less anxiety and blaming. We have described several powerful conceptual tools drawn from Gestalt psychology, and we have used them to highlight the developmental challenges for stepfamilies.

We have listened to the voices of stepparents, biological parents, and children in stepfamilies describing their progress through the Stepfamily Cycle. We have followed them through the Early Stages, hearing their wishes and fantasies. We have traveled with them through their initial experience of the realities of stepfamily living and their gathering clarity (and sometimes empathy) about the diverse needs and feelings in their new family. We have moved with many of them into the Middle Stages as old biologically based structures began to loosen and new step relationships strengthened. And we have savored with them the fruits of the Later Stages, when step relationships became more intimate and authentic and their stepfamilies gained solidity and reliability.

We have seen how four families, including the Tolmans, have found their way by very different paths, sometimes with help, through the Stepfamily Cycle to nourishing and workable lives together. Finally, we have explored ways in which stepfamilies can be assisted in their development.

Both helping professionals and members of stepfamilies will find relief and direction in a conceptual framework that points the way through the sometimes baffling process of becoming a stepfamily. It is hoped that the vivid stories of stepfamily members in the Later Stages, describing their achievements with pride and deep personal satisfaction, will encourage others who are still toiling through the uphill stages of the Stepfamily Cycle.

The complexity of the issues to be faced and the effort involved may leave the reader feeling educated and enlightened but at the same time overwhelmed and even terrified at the prospect of building a new marriage and forging a workable stepfamily. Nevertheless, the widespread, deeply-held conviction that marriage and family life, even with their shortcomings, provide something precious permeates these chapters. Census data on remarriage rates suggest that, recalling Samuel Johnson's famous line, hope continues to triumph over experience. Hesitant prospective stepcouples may wish to know that despite his remarks, made in reference to an individual who had endured a particularly long and dismal marital experience, Johnson himself extolled the advantages of companionable coupled life and was overheard to remark that "even ill-assorted marriages were preferable to cheerless celibacy" (Boswell, 1979).

I would like to end this book by expanding upon what we can be hopeful about. I invite you to turn your attention to what stepfamilies can teach us, and how this family form creates opportunities for personal growth and satisfaction often not achieved in first-time families—in short, why it *is* worth making the effort.

First, it may be comforting to note that the challenges facing stepfamilies are not different in *kind* from the challenges of living well in any human group. It is true that first-time families, particularly those who begin their lives together with substantial shared middle ground, can sometimes get by with less conscious attention to these things. However, stepfamily living simply requires doing with more awareness things which are essential to any satisfying relationship:

—Relinquishing fantasies of what could or should be and attending to what is.

—Being able to say, "Tell me more," rather than "What's wrong with you?" or "What's wrong with me?" when confronted with a misunderstanding.

—Being willing to ask questions and remain curious in the face of apparently inexplicable differences.

—Making the effort to treat one's own and others' feelings with respect and empathy.

—Developing the capacity to be interested in, to find words for, and to bear a wide range of feelings both negative and positive.

—Attending to the needs of those who are strangers as well as those who are very familiar, and finding ways to live respectfully with diverse traditions. Thinking inventively about meeting diverse needs.

—Searching hard for shared ground when none seems available (Roger Fisher's book *Getting to Yes* provides additional practical guidance for this complex art).

—Forming a developmentally realistic picture of what must be lived with for now and what will change over time, as well as a realistic sense of what is unlikely to change or do so only with considerable effort.

—And, finally, staying open to learning from experience—viewing minor and major disasters as the consequence of gaps in understanding rather than evidence of betrayal.

These, then, are the tasks of living well in any group. Again, a first-time family, with its shared history and more equal parental ties, is more likely to be able to gradually build shared norms and rituals with less awareness of these things. Stepfamily living, to repeat this essential point, requires doing with greater awareness things that a first-time family may get away with taking for granted.

On the other hand, the very fact that stepfamily living requires reconsidering habitual ways of doing things opens the door to a world of experience that first-time families may miss. A first-time family may well suffer for years with entire arenas of family norms and rituals remaining unarticulated and unquestioned despite the fact that nobody chose them and/or they no longer satisfy anyone. In stepfamily living this kind of unexamined dissatisfaction is often impossible. And, paradoxically, herein lies the promise. It is in the very necessity of finding language for things that had been done unconsciously, of voicing, doing and re-doing, that much of the richness of stepfamily living lies. If we listen between the lines, the stories in the Action Stage tell us of the liveliness and sense of mastery that are engendered as families look at their habitual ways of functioning, find out what matters, and create rituals and rules made out of pieces that satisfy each family member. We can hear the excitement of inventive solutions like "Santa sees double" and a Thanksgiving where a gooey chocolate cake replaces cranberry sauce and sweet potatoes.

It is true that dealing with differences in family cultures, in attachments, in aesthetics and rhythms and rituals, is challenging. What I find hopeful is that this challenge, while sometimes irritating, often inconvenient, and sometimes painful, is also potentially exciting and enhancing. I am fond of saying to my patients that stepfamilies provide opportunities for foreign travel on an intimate level. Even at times when no resolution of the differences is possible, the necessity of fully encountering and considering another's experience holds the possibility of enriching each stepfamily member's awareness of how many ways there are to see the world.

A friend who read parts of this manuscript said, "But this looks so hard. I'd rather keep my life simple." Putting aside the fact that life with intimate others is rarely simple, the truth is that this old and seductive vision, of a simple life of shared history and automatic understanding, does not fit the reality of today's world. On both a national and a global scale we do not live only among peoples who look like us and think like we do. Seismic international political shifts face us with the fact that we must all learn to live well with peoples who share neither our history nor our culture nor our assumptions about reality.

As in an Early Stage stepfamily, dangers abound. Like an Immersed family, an old set of norms may be allowed to dominate while new members lose their voices. Like a stuck

Action Family new ways of functioning may be pasted together too quickly with results that satisfy too few people or no one. Like a stuck Mobilized Family, we may remain mired in conflict. The stakes are enormous, for failure to meet the challenge of living peacefully and creatively in the world community means facing the real possibility of not living at all. Living well in a stepfamily teaches us at an intimate level the skills and lessons we must master on a larger level if we are to travel safely into the next century.

Shifting the focus now to helping professionals, just as the tasks involved in living well in a stepfamily are like those of any group—except that they require that closer attention be paid to them—the skills required to do good work with stepfamilies are not isolated and specialized. It is true that helping stepfamilies requires knowing something about the special dynamics and developmental tasks of this particular family form. However, most of the principles in the beginning of Chapter Seven are basic to any good therapy. What is different is that therapists working with stepfamilies must heed these principles much more impeccably, lest disaster ensue. In this way, working with stepfamilies demands the best of us. It requires, for example, that we remain rigorously systemic, keeping in mind the very different stories of family members who are not present in the room lest we contribute to fracturing an already divided family. It requires balancing a willingness to step in and teach while maintaining tremendous respect for resistance.

Likewise, the interplay of current and past dynamics is a part of every therapy. Working with stepfamilies underlines for us the necessity of weaving between these domains. It requires that we attend, with full respect, to the normal feelings and dilemmas stepfamily structure generates while staying tuned to past hurts which might make these dilemmas more painful or impossible to resolve by present focus alone. Stepfamilies acutely remind us of the importance of attending to both the power of the present and the lingering impact of the past.

In these ways, stepfamilies can provide their therapists with a kind of professional aerobic training. Like any exercise, if done at the right level, concentrated effort can be invigorating and strengthening, even inspiring, to us. And like any exercise, we need to take on a level of work that matches our skills.

Finally, stepfamilies have a lesson to teach us about the fact that living and loving over time requires accumulating losses. It is one of the ubiquitous challenges in life to grieve these "necessary losses" (Viorst, 1986), let them go and reinvest, rather than to narrow our lives through resignation or hypervigilant efforts to control the uncontrollable.

One of the most challenging aspects of living in and working with stepfamilies, and potentially one of the most fruitful, is that the work requires directly encountering this fact. I am so often impressed with what can be gained as stepfamily members are gently helped to grieve what cannot be rather than denying reality. I have watched my clients face and resolve family-of-origin losses that they had been able to get by without attending to until now, moving beyond the narrow territory they had come to inhabit in their attempts to avoid further loss. In this way, what begins as one of the most painful aspects of stepfamily living can ultimately provide some of the richest opportunities for releasing new energy for living and loving.

Several years ago as I neared the end of an airplane trip my seatmate turned and asked me where I was going. "To a national conference on stepfamilies," I replied. "That sounds boring," he said. "Not a chance," I replied. What is lost in predictability and security is more than gained in an exciting and invigorating family life. It is the very fact that healthy stepfamily living requires full engagement in living well that I find most hopeful, and that makes this work worth it to me.

APPENDIX A:
STEPFAMILY CYCLE SUMMARY

The Early Stages: Getting Started Versus Getting Stuck
(Stages 1, 2, 3: Fantasy, Immersion, Awareness)

Family Structure remains biologically organized throughout the Early Stages. Most common ground remains within biological parent-child units. Differences between fast, average, slow and stuck movement through the Stepfamily Cycle lie primarily in the amount of time spent accomplishing Awareness Stage tasks.

STAGE 1. FANTASY: THE INVISIBLE BURDEN.

Family members bring fantasies and wishes to their new relationships that result from (1) previous losses and the legacy of hope inherent in becoming a stepfamily, (2) individual members' family-of-origin histories, and (3) lack of accurate information about stepfamily dynamics. These fantasies and wishes, while they may be unrealistic, are often deeply held and must be treated with respect and care. For many, relinquishing them will involve significant grief work.

Developmental Tasks. To bring to awareness and to articulate the fantasies, wishes and shoulds each member has for the new family. To let go of (and grieve for) unrealistic hopes.

Dangers/Dilemmas. When fantasies and wishes harden into coercive requirements, these become an invisible burden blocking the work of building individual and shared information about the family.

381

STAGE 2. IMMERSION: SINKING VERSUS SWIMMING.

Pressure, confusion, and distress may mount throughout this
stage as differences in insider/outsider, step/biological and
adult/child perspectives become increasingly obvious. There
is little clarity yet concerning the sources inherent in stepfamily structure which create predictable, but sometimes intensely painful, emotions (jealousy, feeling torn, lost or invaded, isolation, missing an absent parent, loyalty binds, etc.).
Children and outsider adults may be more uncomfortable
than insider adults in this stage.
Developmental Tasks. To "keep swimming" through this period, bearing the discomfort long enough to accurately name
feelings and to hear other family members' experiences.
Dangers/Dilemmas. Unrealistic expectations, especially a conviction that stepfamilies should function like first-time families despite mounting evidence to the contrary, make early
glitches feel like "failures." The danger is that family members will sink into shame ("Something's wrong here and it
must be me") or blame ("Something's wrong here and it must
be you"). When shaming and blaming block effective communication, families may become mired in Immersion, unable to move on to Awareness. Immersed Families begin at
this point in the Stepfamily Cycle and remain here longer.

STAGE 3. AWARENESS: MAPPING THE TERRITORY.

This is the single most critical stage for the successful completion of the Stepfamily Cycle. It is characterized by curious,
empathic exploration of one's own and others' perceptions
and needs. Clarity and self-acceptance begin to replace confusion and self-doubt. Members begin to create a more accurate map of the territory they inhabit individually and together. The resulting enhanced mutual understanding
provides the foundation for joint decision making in the Middle Stages. Aware Families start their journey through the
Stepfamily Cycle here, spending relatively little time in Immersion.

Developmental Tasks. Each person must begin to accurately name his or her own feelings and needs in the new family structure. More challenging, each member must also develop an accurate picture of the territory other family members inhabit. The task is to maintain enough curiosity ("Tell me more") and empathy ("That must be tough") in the face of differences and disappointments, so that each member's joys, pains, suggestions, and requests can be voiced and heard.

Dangers/Dilemmas. Because the feelings evoked by insider/outsider issues may be experienced as shameful and dangerous, the task of bringing them to awareness and exposing them can be difficult. Tightly held fantasies of an easily blended family, shame and blame may mire families in Immersion or propel them precipitously into Mobilization or Action.

The Middle Stages: Restructuring the Family
(Stages 4, 5: Mobilization, Action)

During this period the family embarks on a period of major reconstruction, shifting its structure from a collection of biologically organized minifamilies to a working stepfamily. Conflict is aired in Mobilization and resolved during Action. Movement is not linear. Sometimes a trip back to the Awareness Stage is necessary to complete unfinished tasks. Furthermore, families may have moved to Action on one issue and remain further back (or have proceeded further ahead) on other issues. By the beginning of the Action Stage the family needs sufficient information and strong enough relationships to begin heavy negotiations about already defined territory and to forge fully shared agreements about how the stepfamily will function. Prior to completion of the Action Stage a major event such as the birth of a new baby is more likely to increase the split between insiders and outsiders.

STAGE 4. MOBILIZATION: EXPOSING THE GAPS.

An atmosphere of highly charged emotional conflict results as the stepfamily moves into more openly airing differences and more actively influencing each other over step issues. In many families this stage is ushered in by the outsider stepparent taking a firm stand in some area. This stage is less pronounced and less highly polarized in Aware Families.

Developmental Tasks. To actively confront differences between family cultures, between insider and outsider needs, and between adults' and children's experiences of the family without shaming or blaming; to begin constructively influencing each other for changes without breaking the family apart.

Dangers/Dilemmas. As the outsider/stepparent finds his or her voice, some families lurch from Immersion into Mobilization. If the resulting collisions over step issues are constructive enough, they may forge enough fresh understanding to help the family complete Awareness tasks. However, accompanying anguish, shame, and recrimination may propel the family back to the silent, pained Awareness Stage; even further back to the confusion of the Immersion Stage; or prematurely forward into action. Particularly for the insider biological parent, the intense conflict after what may have seemed a peaceful Early Stage may feel like failure.

Mobilized Stepfamilies begin here and remain here longer. In these families, all voices are heard early on, but members' expectations may be unrealistic and awareness work may be missing. Mobilized Families must complete Awareness Stage tasks before further development is possible.

STAGE 5. ACTION: GOING INTO BUSINESS TOGETHER.

This is a hard-work period in which the family has sufficient information to institute new rules, create new family traditions, and identify new areas of family activities. Biological ties loosen and clearer boundaries are established around step relationships.

Developmental Tasks. To use the understanding developed during Awareness and Mobilization to generate new stepfamily rituals, customs, and codes of conduct in which all members of the family can invest. New "middle ground" must be constructed leaving some old ground from original subsystems in place.

Dangers/Dilemmas. Couples who have trouble bearing the anxiety of the Early Stages may move too quickly into the Action Stage without doing the work of getting to know one another and finding a voice for the needs of each family member. In these Action Families, adults quickly become a tight unit, setting a raft of new rules and regulations. For children, the consequent resentment, depression, and/or sense of being overwhelmed by unmanageable new requirements may lead to behavior problems and/or depression. Action Families must return to complete Awareness Stage tasks before development can proceed.

The Later Stages: Solidifying the Stepfamily
(Stages 6, 7: Contact, Resolution)

By the time the family enters the Later Stages, the old biological ties have substantially loosened and firm new boundaries define emerging step relationships. By the end of this period, solid middle ground unites most members and a mature "intimate outsider" role has taken shape in at least some of the family's stepparent-stepchild relationships. The couple is now an intimate sanctuary even on step issues. The family feels "whole" and is well-equipped to provide for its members.

STAGE 6. CONTACT: INTIMACY AND AUTHENTICITY IN STEP RELATIONSHIPS.

The stepfamily at last has its hard-earned honeymoon. Satisfying communications now characterize step relationships. An "intimate outsider" stepparent role sanctioned by all family members has jelled.

Developmental Tasks. To enjoy the honeymoon; to continue the awareness process as new issues arise; and to further solidify the stepparent role.

Dangers/Dilemmas. Adults from dysfunctional families-of-origin, who may find it especially hard to trust increasing intimacy in new relationships, may create crises that return the family to earlier stages.

STAGE 7. RESOLUTION: HOLDING ON AND LETTING GO.

The new system of relationships has become a fully-functioning stepfamily. Insider and outsider roles now shift easily within the group. Stepfamily boundaries are more flexible than in first-time families and biological relationships remain special and different. Middle ground has become firm in most step relationships, and there is a strong sense of "family." Issues that were nagging sources of discomfort in the Early Stages and subjects of intense discussion in the Middle Stages now require little attention. Children are secure members of two households and feel nourished by the multiple relationships and cultures available to them.

Developmental Task. To "hold on" to the depth and nourishment of mature stepfamily relationships while revisiting unresolved grief about "once removed" step status and the necessity of sharing children with ex-spouses. For both children and adults, life cycle events such as weddings, college graduations may offer (sometimes unexpected) opportunities to rework divorce, death, and loyalty conflicts.

Dangers/Dilemmas. New step issues (childbearing, custody shifts, weddings and graduations) may revive old insider/outsider disputes and return the family to earlier stages. Divorced adults who are unable to cooperate around life cycle events may reactivate intense loyalty binds for children. The pain of relinquishing what cannot be in step relationships may be intensified by issues such as family-of-origin losses and infertility.

Length of Time Usually Required for Families to Complete the Stepfamily Cycle

	Fast-paced* *Families*	Average** *Families*	Slow/Stuck** *Families*
Early Stages	1-2 years	2-3 years	4+ years
Middle Stages***	1-2 years	2-3 years	2-3+ years
Later Stages	1-2 years	1-2 years	1-2 years
Total	c. 4 years	c. 7 years	c. 9+ years

*Fast-paced families are primarily Aware Families. They spend little time in Fantasy or Immersion and tend to begin their lives together in the Awareness Stage, moving into Action with comparatively little conflict (i.e., with a shorter, less polarized Mobilization Stage).

**Average and slow/stuck families may be Immersed, Mobilized, or Action Families. Some may not reach the Later Stages.

***Mobilized and Action Families begin their lives together in the Middle Stages. However, developmental progress is usually not possible until they return to the Early Stages to complete Awareness tasks.

APPENDIX B:
SELF-HELP GUIDE FOR
STEPFAMILIES

The Early Stages: Getting Started Versus Getting Stuck
(Stages 1, 2, 3: Fantasy, Immersion, Awareness)

Suggestions
1. **Educate yourself.** Build an accurate picture of the challenges and dilemmas stepfamilies face. Read (see starred items in the bibliography and the S.A.A. booklist, below). Talk to other people in stepfamilies.
2. **Join the Stepfamily Association of America:**
   212 Lincoln Center
   215 So. Centennial Mall
   Lincoln, NE 68508
   Telephone: (402) 477-7837

   Order a copy of *Stepfamilies Stepping Ahead,* a basic compendium of information about stepfamilies. S.A.A. membership will also get you: a quarterly newsletter full of articles and book reviews about stepfamilies; a very complete list of books which can be easily ordered on stepfamilies for both children and adults: information about S.A.A.'s yearly national conference; a list of local chapters.
3. **Join your local S.A.A. chapter.** Monthly meetings provide members with a wealth of practical tips for everyday coping and a reference group that helps put things in perspective. Also (very important) a place to laugh at

the foibles of stepfamily living. S.A.A. will help you start a chapter if none exists in your area.

4. **Find one or two people who understand** (they may not be in your family) and talk to them regularly. If you decide to seek help from a mental health professional, make sure he or she either knows enough about step-families or is willing to read a few things before working with you.

5. **Spend reliable one-to-one time** with each member of your family. Children need reliable time alone with their biological parents without having to adjust to a competing new adult. The new couple needs time alone without children. Set a regular couple *business time* to discuss stepfamily issues. Make regular *intimate time* where business is put aside. Give stepparent and each stepchild time alone together to be strangers and get to know each other without the intrusion of a more expert biological parent. Remember when stepfamilies blend too fast, someone usually gets creamed.

6. **The stepparent role** works best in the Early Stages as a support to the biological parent rather than as primary disciplinarian ("sounding board not savior"). Steppar-ents can function more like a babysitter or an aunt or uncle than as a parent: enforce the rules of the house rather than create a host of new rules, get to know children, show interest in their activities, assist in areas where children are interested in the stepparent's special strengths (helping with homework, teaching a child to throw a baseball, teach a child to swim, etc.).

7. **Attend to needs of both insiders and outsiders. Outsider stepparents:** Get acknowledgement of the dif-ficulties of operating on foreign territory. Ask for reli-able intimate time with your spouse without children present. Ask for a *few* rule changes in the new family (choose one or two that really matter to you and let the rest go for now). Maintain or establish additional support outside the new family—keep old friendships, stay in a satisfying job, talk to other stepparents. Older

stepdaughters (pre-teen and up) may need more distance from stepfathers (give verbal, not physical affection and let Mom do the disciplining) and clear reliable time with their biological parent.

Insider/biological parent: Ask for acknowledgement
for feeling invaded and for feeling overwhelmed by
competing needs (of new partner, children, and often,
ex-spouse). "Compartmentalize": Make reliable one-to-
one time with your children when you can engage with
them without worrying about your new partner. Make
reliable intimate time with your partner without children present. Give yourself permission to take time
alone. Try to actively anticipate and empathize with
your partner's feelings. Remember that in the Early
Stages you are both the voice for children's needs for
stability *and* the only source of comfort and empathy
for your outsider/stepparent spouse.

Children do best in the Early Stages (and throughout)
if their parents are not in conflict over them. They need
reliable one-to-one time with each of their biological
parents and freedom to get to know their stepparents
slowly. Adults can actively help to reduce children's loyalty binds by not bad-mouthing an ex-spouse to a child,
and encouraging children's relationships with their absent parents. Children need clear information about
what will change and what will not. They need empathy
for the multiple losses and disorienting changes en-
tailed for them in becoming a stepfamily. They need to
know they have time to get to know the strangers in
their new family. They do not have to love their new
stepparents and stepsiblings; they do have to be civil.

8. **When an ex-spouse is doing the badmouthing,** here
are some things to say: "I know Mommy says that. That
must be confusing for you. Sometimes when people are
hurting they say things like that. Here's what I think is
true . . . *I'm sorry you're in the middle.* It's not fair to you
that your Mommy and Daddy are fighting. It's not your
fault. We are blowing it. That's why we're divorced. I

love you. Mommy loves you." (See the vignette of Alan Simmons in Chapter Seven for more detail.)

Fantasy Stage Exercises (adapted from Stepfamily Workshops)

Fantasies evolve gradually from accumulated experience throughout our lives. Unless a crisis challenges them, we simply take these pictures for granted, assuming our expectations are realistic and normal. If you have been living longer than a few months in a stepfamily, some of your fantasies have already been challenged. Remember that outsiders will often have to face their fantasies more quickly than insiders.

1. Which of the fantasies and wishes listed in Chapter Three do I recognize as mine? Are there others not listed there that I am becoming aware of?
2. Can you remember the first time (or a time) you "knew" that reality and your wishes were not the same? What happened?
3. Which of your wishes or fantasies feel easy to let go of? Which feel harder to relinquish?
4. What do you feel like inside as you contemplate giving up the latter?
5. Share first with someone else in your role or a close friend who understands. Then with your partner. Job of the listener is just that. Listen. Absorb. Ask questions. Do not attempt to convince, fix, or change the person. Be more like a sponge than a faucet.

Immersion Stage Exercises (adapted from Stepfamily Workshops)

1. What feelings have been most painful and confusing for you in your new stepfamily?
2. A theme of this stage is "something's wrong here and it must be me." How do you blame yourself for what goes "wrong" in your new family?
3. Look at your answer to #2. Sit back. Take a deep breath. Get in touch with the part of you that is very wise and knows what is true and what's not true. What, realistically is your part in what's not going well? What is someone else's part?

4. List some of the "shoulds" you have for yourself in your role in your stepfamily. With another person (probably not your partner yet) use the strategy in #3.
   Sit back. Breathe. Write down what is realistic about each should and what is not.

Awareness Exercises (adapted from Stepfamily Workshops)
   1. Name one or two things that are going well in your stepfamily and one or two things that are hard, disorienting, or upsetting.
   2. Take one of the "negative" things above and list your feelings. (What *you* are feeling inside, not what you think about what other family members feel or think.) List the actual things that happened that made you feel that way (stick to "data": What an anthropologist would *see or hear*).
   3. For each other family member: what do you think is going well for him/her? What do you imagine, *from his or her point of view* is hardest or most disorienting?
   4. Take your lists of #2 and #3. Sit down with each family member and share lists. Where were you/they accurate? On #3 where inaccurate? Be sure to ask for a reality check on your #3 items.
   5. For each member of your family, write down two or three questions beginning with "Would you tell me more about . . ." or "What's it like for you when . . ." For yourself write down two or three requests, beginning with, "I would like you to ask me more about . . ." Ask one of these questions of each family member each week.

The Middle Stages: Restructuring the Family
(Stages 4, 5: Mobilization, Action)

Suggestions
   1. **Learn to fight fairly and constructively.** Concentrate on sending "I messages" ("I feel left out when you don't

look up and say hello to me") versus "You messages" ("You never include me and you obviously don't care").

2. **When your partner raises an issue** begin with, "Tell me more." Sit back, breathe, ask questions and listen to the answers for at least ten minutes before you respond. When you are raising an issue, ask your partner to just listen, and try to understand what it's like for you *without trying to fix it* for at least ten minutes.

3. **As you begin to make new rules and new traditions,** take time to find out what each person involved needs (insiders and outsider, adults and children, step and biological family members). Use your local S.A.A. chapter as a resource for generating pragmatic ideas. The stories in Chapter Four may also help you stay with it until you have identified and creatively combined different needs and expectations into something everyone can buy into.

4. **Plan ahead for family events** that are likely to expose step versus biological and insider versus outsider differences, i.e., holidays, birthdays, extended family events such as weddings and graduations. (Peter Norstadt's wedding at the end of Chapter Seven provides an example of the latter.)

5. **Stepparents** can begin to take a more active role with some (but perhaps not all) stepchildren.

6. **If you need extra help,** couple or family therapy is usually most appropriate in the Middle Stages. *Be sure to choose someone who knows about stepfamily dynamics,* or who is willing to read and learn.

Mobilization and Action Stage Exercises (adapted from Stepfamily Workshops)

1. List two or three things which the members of each step pair in your family have in common (i.e., stepcouple, stepparent—child, stepsiblings). What one or two activities would each pair like to do more of that would deepen existing common ground?

2. Name one or two things you like about *how* your stepfamily handles its differences. Name one or two things

you don't like about *how* your family handles its differences.
3. Name one difference you've resolved in your new family. How did you resolve it? What do you like about how
   it was resolved? What would it take to resolve one more
   unresolved issue in this way?
4. List one family tradition or rule where different people
   want different things. Get *each* person to write down:
   what one or two things would you like to see us *keep on
   doing* regarding this rule or tradition? What one or two
   things would you like to see us *do more of* to make this
   rule or tradition better? What one or two things would
   you like to see us *do less of*? Say them all out loud. No
   judgements, only clarifying questions allowed.

   Now, take a breath. Take a sheet of paper for
   each *other* person in the family. *Guess* about what he or
   she would like the family to *keep on doing, do less of,* and
   do more of on this tradition. Share your lists. Where
   were you right? Where were you wrong? Identify all the
   areas where you agree. Underline them. Take *one* area
   of disagreement and see if you can invent something
   that satisfies both/all sides.

   What did we *like* so far about *how* we handled this
   disagreement? What could we do more of/less of? Take
   the next issue and work on it together applying what
   we've just said. How did we do?

The Later Stages: Solidifying the Stepfamily
(Stages 6, 7: Content and Resolution)

1. **Identify the "intimate outsider" role** that is likely
   emerging between stepparent and at least one stepchild.
   This mentor-like relationship when it happens is one of
   the real gifts of stepfamily life. Of the following qualities of a mature stepparent role, which have begun to
   happen in your family?

- Stepparent role does not usurp or compete with the parental role of the absent same-sex parent.
- It often capitalizes on differences the stepparent brings to the new family in style, strengths, particular rules. (Allow yourselves to appreciate that some of these same qualities were sources of trouble in the Early or Middle Stages.)
- It observes an intergenerational boundary.
- The stepparent role is "mutually suitable" for stepparent *and* stepchild.
- It is actively supported by the child's parent.

2. **Take time to appreciate the little "honeymoons"** of the Contact Stage—moments where stepparent and biological parent remain an intimate team on a step issue that had previously divided you, moments where stepparent is functioning in a clear, fully supported role, moments when the family feels "whole" and there is a distinct sense of "us."

3. **Continue to actively reduce loyalty binds** for children as life cycle events bring ex-spouses together for graduations, weddings, etc. Get skilled outside help if necessary.

4. **Frame apparent regressions** as new issues arise within the context of the fact that the solidity of your family is no longer threatened.

5. **Expect a new round of awareness of losses** (of uninterrupted parenting, of infant and first-family memories at a child's wedding, of a biological-like relationship with stepchildren).

Contact and Resolution Exercises (adapted from Stepfamily Workshops)

1. Name two or three areas in your family life that used to be anxious or difficult and now flow more easily.

2. Describe two or three step issues that are now resolved in your family. How did you do that? Write down two or three things each person did to help resolve those issues. Sometime this week tell those family members

what they did over the years that made a difference to you.

3. Name a loss, something you're aware of being sad about, or something you wish could be but can't in your stepfamily. Think of one person you can share that with who will "get it." He or she may not (still!) be in your family.

4. Describe one or two times in the last year where your stepfamily felt really whole and good.

5. Name two or three things you like or love that you have in your life now that you wouldn't have had if you had remained in your original family.

APPENDIX C:
SUMMARY OF
CLINICAL INTERVENTION
STRATEGIES

The Early Stages: Getting Started Versus Getting Stuck
(Stages 1, 2, 3: Fantasy, Immersion, Awareness)

1. Draw attention to unvoiced longings for something that cannot be.
2. Provide information to place fantasies in perspective and normalize feelings.
3. Help connect feelings (of jealousy, resentment, inadequacy, loyalty binds) to real events. Separate "shoulds" from realities.
4. Train members to "mirror" one another.
5. Facilitate "mapping" at individual, couple, stepfamily, binuclear or entire extended family levels, including grandparents.
6. Explore losses involved in relinquishing fantasies and provide empathic support for necessary grief work.
7. Look for influences external to the immediate stepfamily that may be contributing to counterproductive fantasies or developmental delay (an over-involved grandparent allied to the previous family). In some families it may be appropriate to refer individuals who need psychodynamic assistance. Death of a previous spouse leaves families particularly vulnerable to stuck fantasies of becoming a biological-like family, and additional grief work may be needed.

The Middle Stages: Restructuring the Family
(Stages 4, 5: Mobilization, Action)

Mobilized couples often appear in the Middle Stages needing help lowering anxiety and accomplishing awareness tasks. Child referrals may be the result of premature movement to Action changes.

1. Provide the missing "grease" for Mobilized systems, giving substantial positive feedback on what the family is doing well.
2. In conflicted relationships, provide empathy and "mirroring" for *both* insider and outsider, child and adult dilemmas. Do not further fracture an already divided system by taking sides.
3. Help mobilized couples and families to slow down and listen to each other (see "rote empathy" exercises in Chapter Seven)[1].
4. Draw attention to moments of genuine contact.
5. Look for unexpressed losses, family-of-origin issues that may drive adults into premature Action or stuck Mobilization.
6. Help family members to hear adults' and children's, stepparents' and biological parents' very different experiences of the same events (see "Travelogue"[2] and "rote empathy"[1] exercises).
7. Explore family-of-origin issues that make the "outsider" or "insider" roles especially painful.
8. Teach problem-solving and communication skills.
9. Assist with strategic planning on potentially problematic family events.

The Later Stages: Solidifying the Stepfamily
(Stages 6, 7: Contact, Resolution)

1. Stepfamilies rarely need help in the Contact Stage. Individual family members who grew up in dysfunctional

---

[1] "Rote Empathy" exercise can be found on page 340 in Chapter Seven.
[2] Travelogue exercise can be found on page 298 in Chapter Six and page 330 in Chapter Seven.

families may need assistance if they find themselves sabotaging good feelings.

2. Resolution Stage issues may require work at the individual (family-of-origin loss blocks final resolution of what cannot be), couple (conflict over a custody shift or childbearing), family (a college-age stepchild moves in for the semester), or binuclear level across households (college costs, how to minimize loyalty conflicts and provide sufficient support for all extended family members in a wedding or graduation).

3. Families often need help normalizing apparent "regression" and placing new challenges in the context of firmly established stepfamily ties.

4. As always assess level of completion of Awareness tasks, if necessary complete earlier stage tasks for this issue.

APPENDIX D:
FAMILY PROFILES

NOTES

Where there are two last names in the family, full information is listed under the first one that appears alphabetically. Stepchildren's names are indented under their parent's name. Children of the new marriage are listed unindented under both parents' names. In the case of adult children, custody information refers to arrangements before they left home. Where no custody information is given, the children were grown at the time of stepfamily formation. All ages and numbers of years married are at the time of the last interview.

ABRAMSON/DAYTON (m. 1 yr; lived together 3 yrs)
    Barbara Abramson (34) D
    Jim Dayton (38) D
        Emmie (8) FT
        David (9 months)
    Katerina Dayton (37) (Emmie's mother, Jim's first wife.)
ALLEN/BETTS (m. 2 yrs.)
    Barry Allen (38) S
    Doreen Betts (35) D
        Sophie (12) FT
        Sammy (5) FT
ANDREWS/SHAPIRO (m. 3 yrs)
    Cheryl Andrews (40) D
        Jill Andrews (18) FT
        Son (16) FT
        Son (14) FT
    Mark Shapiro (52) D
        Daughter (31) V
        Son (24) V
BECKER
    Zoe Becker (18) PT w. father
BERRY (m. 1 yr.)
    Dennis Berry (55) D
        Son (33)
        Son (31)
    Doris Berry (50) D

Daughter (28)
BLACK/JONES (m. 2 yrs)
LuAnne Black (43) D
Jennifer (13) FT
Mara (11) FT
Don Jones (38) D
Trisha (10) FT
Bobby (8) FT
BREWSTER/SCHMIDT (m. 8 yrs)
Ed Brewster (60) D
Son (30) NC
Daughter (25) NC
Son (23) V
Margaret Brewster (45) D
Larry Schmidt (25) FT
Kim Schmidt (21) FT
BRIDGES/DOMINGUEZ (dating 1 yr.)
Josie Bridges (24) S
Manuel Dominguez (26) D
Carlos (5) PT
BROWN/GREENFIELD (m. 3 yrs)
Walter Brown (43) D
Julie (10) PT
Trisha Greenfield (40) S
BURKE (m. 1 1/2 yrs.)
John Burke (77) W
Jerry Burke (50)
Daughter (52)
Daughter (45)
Daughter (42)
Rita Burke (John's new wife) (68) W
BURNS/LIPPMAN (m. 1 1/2 yrs. lived together 5 yrs.)
Gregory Burns (33) S
Lynn Lippmann (38) D
Jason (18) HT
Judy (15) HT
CAMPBELL/MORRISON (m. 4 yrs)
Chris Campbell (36) D

   Son (20) V
   Son (12) V
  Karen Morrison (32) S
   Carl (3)
   Caitlin (2)
CAPONI (m. 10 yrs.)
  Tina Caponi (39) W
   Jeannie Caponi (18) FT
  Ralph Caponi (42) S
COHEN/LIEBERMAN (m. 6 yrs)
  Mickey Cohen (40) D
   Josh (13) HT
   Aaron (10) HT
  Ann Lieberman (38) S
   Melissa (3)
CORINO/KING (living together 3 yrs.)
  Vicky Corino (39) D
  Bruce King (45) D
   Daughter (19) NC
   Daughter (17) NC
   Daughter (14) NC
   Son (12) NC
COX/MCNALLY (m. 4 yrs.)
  Reginald Cox (46) D
   Son (18) V
   Son (17) FT
   Daughter (16) FT
  Gina McNally (36) S
CUMMINGS (m. 3 yrs)
  Eric Cummings (38) D
   Ingrid (17) FT (PT w. mother on weekends)
   Ellen (15) FT (PT w. mother on weekends)
  Nancy Cummings (stepmother) (39) D
   Teddy (13) FT
   Jerry (11) FT
  Cheryl Cummings (mother, Eric's ex-wife) (40)
DANIELSON/ROBERTS (m. 4 yrs.)
  George Danielson (37) D

Pamela (15) PT
Cindy (12) PT
Beth Roberts (34) D
Melissa (8) FT
DAVIDSON/MILLER (m. 1 yr.)
Jan Davidson (38) S
Gabby Davidson (11) FT
Chuck Miller (42) D
Kevin Miller (12) HT
DAVIS (m. 4 1/2 yrs.)
Gene Davis (32) S
Joan Goodman Davis (33) D
Wendy Goodman (10) FT
DAYTON (See **ABRAMSON/DAYTON)**
ERICKSON (m. 7 yrs.)
Christine Erickson (28) S
Roger Erickson (34) D
Kate (15) PT
Pam (11) PT
EVANS (m. 1 yr.)
Abigail Evans (32) D
Jeremy (13) FT
Bob Singer (41) D
Dylan (12) PT
FISHMAN/LEVINSON (m. 5 yrs.)
Ron Levinson (42) D
Marty Levinson (17) HT
Mara Fishman (40) D
Sarah Fishman (16) FT
Son (14) FT
FRANKLIN (living together 2 yrs.)
Hope Franklin (42) D
Nicole (4) FT
Julian Paglia (38) S
GENTILE/OLSON (m. 14 yrs.)
Nick Gentile (42) W
Betty (17) FT
Cathy Olson (40) S

Nicky (12)
GOLDFARB/WENTWORTH (m. 1 yr.)
    Arlene Goldfarb Wentworth (33) W
        Leah (13) FT
        Jonah (9) FT
    Michael Wentworth (34) S
GREENFIELD (See **BROWN/GREENFIELD)**
GRAY/RUDNICK (m. 3 yrs.)
    Joanne Gray (32) S
    Jeff Rudnick (33) D
        Son (8) V
        Hilary (2)
GRINNELLI/JAMES (m. 3 yrs.)
    Anton Grinnelli (36) D
        Son (16) PT
        Son (12) PT
    Jane James (30) D
        Ellen (9) FT
GUNNARS/NISSENBAUM (m. 5 yrs.)
    Michelle Gunnars (34) S
    Dan Nissenbaum (36) D
        Meggan (13) HT
HALEY (m. 14 yrs.)
    Hank Haley (43) S
    Helen Haley (42) W
        Daryl (20) FT
        Don (18) FT
        Winnie (17) FT
        Billie (13)
HOBBES (m. 4 1/2 yrs.)
    Bill Hobbes (32) S
    Paula Hobbes (36) D
        Patsy Handlon (10) FT (visits father)
        Sylvia (3)
JAMES (See **GRINNELLI/JAMES**)
JOHNSTON (m. 8 yrs)
    Cecelia Johnston (38) D
        Corin Wells (11) FT (visits father)

Richard Johnston (45) D
    Jon (22) V (FT and PT over the years)
    Mary (24) V (PT at times)
JONES (See **BLACK/JONES**)
KEEFE (m. 7 yrs.)
    Robert Keefe (40) S
    Elizabeth Keefe (33) D
        Becky (11) FT
        Sarah (3 1/2)
        Jamie (1 1/12)
KELLY (m. 1 yr.)
    Al Kelly (49) D
        Sally Kelly (25)
        Son (24)
        Son (22)
    Dora Kearns (43) D
        Son (12) FT
        Daughter (8) FT
    Martha Kelly (48) D (Sally's mother, Al's first wife)
KING (See **CORINO/KING**)
KOHL
    Leslie Kohl (26)
LEVI (m. 2 yrs.)
    Arnold Levi (43) D
        Timothy Levi (22) V
    Alla Levi (37) D
        Son (6) FT
        Son (4) FT
LEVINSON (See **FISHMAN/LEVINSON**)
LIEBERMAN (See **COHEN/LIEBERMAN**)
LIPPMAN (See **BURNS/LIPPMAN**)
MCNALLY (See **COX/MCNALLY**)
MORRISON (See **CAMPBELL/MORRISON**)
NELSON (m. 5 yrs.)
    Peg Nelson Peters (47) W
        Jessie Nelson (20) FT
    Dennis Peters (60) D
NISSENBAUM (See **GUNNARS/NISSENBAUM**)

NORSTADT (m. 4 yrs.)
    Nelson Norstadt (53) D
        Peter Norstadt (26)
    Glenna Norstadt (38) S (Nelson's second wife)
    Gillie Norstadt (53) (Peter's mother)
O'BRIEN (m. 2 yrs.)
    Fred O'Brien (47) D
        Daughter (25) NC
        Daughter (23) NC
    Delia O'Brien (38) D
        Daughter (9) FT
        Son (6) FT
OLSON (See **GENTILE/OLSON**)
PEABODY
    Rusty Peabody (30) (FT w. mother, visited father)
PETERSON (3 yrs.)
    Terry Peterson (42) D
        Son (12) FT
        Daughter (10) FT
    Bill Waters (40) S
PIERCE/RASKIN (m. 6 yrs.)
    Liz Pierce (40) D
        Kate (14) FT
    Andrew Raskin (41)
        Joe (18) FT
        Alex (16) FT
RASKIN (See **PIERCE/RASKIN**)
RICCI (m. 1 yr.)
    Angela Ricci (32) S
    Frank Ricci (36) D
        Molly (10) FT
ROBERTS (See **DANIELSON/ROBERTS**)
ROSEMAN (m. 2 yrs.)
    Harvey Roseman (36) S
    Jannine Roseman (40) D
        Cory Stevens (13) HT
RUDNICK (See **GRAY/RUDNICK**)
SALVI (m. 1 yr.)

Maria Salvi (32) D
    Anna (6) FT
    Nicki (4) FT
Joe Salvi (33) D
    Daughter (16) NC
    Daughter (14) NC
SALZMAN (m. 2 yrs.)
  Marsha Salzman (34) S
  Bruce Salzman (39) D
    Daughter (11) FT
    Son (8) FT
SAX (m. 5 yrs.)
  Rachel Sax (30) S
  Ira Sax (42) D
    Ben (19) V
    Adam (15) PT
SCHMIDT (See **BREWSTER/SCHMIDT**)
SHAPIRO (See **ANDREWS/SHAPIRO**)
SIMMONS (living together 2 yrs.)
  Alan Simmons (35) D
    Brad (6) NC
  Diana Salter (28) D
    Anna (8) FT
SMITH/TAYLOR (living together 6 mos.)
  John Smith (28) S
  Lena Taylor (24) D
    Jenny (5) FT
    Billy (3) FT
TOLMAN (m. 6 yrs.)
  Tom Tolman (37) D
    Ricky (14) PT
  Jenny Tolman (44) S
    Bobby (3)
TAYLOR (See **SMITH/TAYLOR**)
TURNER (m. 8 yrs.)
  Charlie Turner (45) D
    Wes (23) V
  Jessica Turner (52) D

   Daughter (20) FT
   Daughter (18) FT
WENTWORTH (See **GOLDFARB/WENTWORTH**)
WERNER (m. 1 1/2 yrs.)
  Fran Werner (38) S
  Nate Werner (45) D
   Daughter (11) PT
   Daughter (8) PT
WILSON (m. 3 yrs.)
  Ben Wilson (41) W
   Danny (12) FT
  Donna Drubec Wilson (35) W
WINSTON (m. 2 yrs.)
  Alicia Winston (42) S
  David Winston (41) D
   Mary (10) HT
   Mark (8) HT

BIBLIOGRAPHY

*Asterisk indicates popular literature that may be helpful to adults in stepfamilies.
**Indicates books appropriate for children in stepfamilies.

Ahrons, C.R. (1979). The binuclear family: Two households, one family. *Alternative Lifestyles, 2* (4), 499–515.

Ahrons, C.R. (1980a). Divorce: A crisis of family transition and change. *Family Relations, 29,* 533–540.

Ahrons, C.R. (1980b). Joint custody arrangements in the postdivorce family. *Journal of Divorce, 3,* 189–205.

Ahrons, C.R., & Wallisch, L. (1987). Parenting in the binuclear family: Relationships between biological and stepparents. In K. Pasley & M. Ihinger-Tallman (Eds.), *Remarriage and stepparenting: Current research and theory* (pp. 225–256). New York: Guilford.

Beer, W.R. (Ed.). (1988). *Relative strangers: Studies of stepfamily processes.* Totowa, N.J.: Rowman & Littlefield.

Beer, W.R. (1989). *Strangers in the house: The world of stepsiblings and half-siblings.* New Brunswick: Transaction.

Bernstein, A. (1988). Unraveling the tangles: Children's understanding of stepfamily kinship. In W.R. Beer (Ed.), *Relative strangers: Studies of stepfamily processes (pp.83–11).* Totowa, N.J.: Rowman & Littlefield.

*Bernstein, A. (1989). *Yours, mine, and ours: How families change when remarried parents have a child together.* New York: Charles Scribner's Sons.

Black, C. (1981). *It will never happen to me.* Denver: M.A.C. Printing and Publications Division.

Bohannan, P. (1971). *Divorce and after.* New York: Doubleday.

Boss, P. (1977). A clarification of the concept of psychological father presence in families experiencing ambiguity of boundary. *Journal of Marriage and the Family, 39,* 141–151.

Boss, P. (1980). The relationship of wife's sex role perceptions, psychological father presence and functioning in the ambiguous father-absent MIA family. *Journal of Marriage and the Family, 42,* 541–549.

Boss, P., & Greenberg, J. (1984). Family boundary ambiguity: A new variable in family stress theory. *Family Process, 23,* 535–546.

411

Boswell, J. (1979). *The life of Johnson.* Edited by C. Hibbert. New York: Penguin Books. [Boswell's biography of Samuel Johnson was originally published in 1791.]

**Bradley, B. (1982). Where do I belong? A kid's guide to stepfamilies. Reading, Mass.: Addison-Wesley.

Brand, E., & Clingempeel, W.G. (1987). Interdependencies of marital and stepparent-stepchild relationships and children's psychological adjustment: Research findings and clinical implications. *Family Relations, 36,* 140–145.

Bray, J.H. (1988a). The effects of early remarriage on children's development: Preliminary analyses of the developmental issues in stepfamilies research project. In E.M. Hetherington & J. Arasteh (Eds.), *The impact of divorce, single-parenting, and step-parenting on children* (pp. 279–298). New York: Erlbaum.

Bray, J.H. (1988b, August). Children's development in stepfather families. Paper presented at the Annual Meeting of the American Psychological Association, Atlanta.

Bray, J.H., Gershenhorn, S., & Bennett, A. (1987, August). The role of the stepfather. In *Becoming a stepfamily.* Symposium conducted at the Annual Meeting of the American Psychological Society, New York.

Burt, M., & Burt, R. (1983). *What's special about our stepfamily?* New York: Doubleday.

Carter, E.A., & McGoldrick, M. (Eds.). (1980). *The family life cycle: A framework for family therapy.* New York: Gardner Press.

Cherlin, A. (1981). *Marriage, divorce, and remarriage.* Cambridge, Mass.: Harvard University Press.

Cherlin, A., & McCarthy J. (1985). Remarried couple households: Data from the June 1980 current population survey. *Journal of Marriage and the Family, 47,* 23–30.

Chollak, H. (1989). Stepfamily adaptability and cohesion: A normative study. (Doctoral dissertation, University of Pennsylvania).

Clingempeel, W.G., & Brand, E. (1985). Structural complexity, quasi-kin relationships, and marital quality in stepfamilies: A replication, extension, and clinical implications. *Family Relations, 34,* 401–409.

Clingempeel, W.G., Brand, E., & Ievoli, R. (1984). Stepparent-stepchild relationships in stepmother and stepfather families: A multimethod study. *Family Relations, 33*(3), 465–473.

Clingempeel, W.G., Ievoli, R., & Brand, E. (1984). Structural complexity and the quality of stepfather-stepchild relationships. *Family Process, 23,* 547-560.

Coleman, M., Ganong, L., & Gingrich, R. (1985). Stepfamily strengths: A review of the popular literature. *Family Relations, 34,* 583–589.

**Craven, L. (1982). *Stepfamilies: New patterns of harmony.* New York: Messner.

Crosbie-Burnett, M. (1984). The centrality of the step relationship: A challenge to family theory and practice. *Family Relations, 33*(3), 459–464.

Crosbie-Burnett, M. (1987). *College-aged stepchildren: Their unique stress.* Paper presented at the Big 10 Counseling Center Conference, Madison, Wisconsin.

Dahl, A.S., Cowgill, K.M., & Asmundsson, D. (1987). Life in remarried families. *Social Work, 32*(1), 40-44.

Day, R.D., & Bahr, S.J. (1986). Income changes following divorce and remarriage. *Journal of Divorce, 9*(3), 75–89.

Dean, G., & Gurak, D.T. (1978). Marital homogamy the second time around. *Journal of Marriage and the Family, 42,* 559–570.

Draughn, M. (1975). Stepmother's model of identification in relation to mourning in the child. *Psychological Reports, 36*(1), 183–189.

**Evans, M.D. (1986). *This is me and my two families.* New York: Brunner/Mazel.

**Fassler, D., Lash, M. & Ives, S.B. (1988). *Changing families: A guide for kids and grown-ups.* Burlington Vt.: Waterford.

Fast, I., & Cain, A.C. (1966). The stepparent role: Potential for disturbances in family functioning. *American Journal of Orthopsychiatry, 36*(3), 435–491.

*Fisher, R. & Ury, W. (1981). *Getting to yes.* Boston: Houghton Mifflin.

Furstenberg, F.F., & Spanier, G.B. (1984). *Recyling the family.* Beverly Hills, Calif.: Sage.

Ganong, L., & Coleman, M. (1984). The effects of remarriage on children: A review of the empirical literature. *Family Relations, 33*(3), 389–406.

Ganong, L. & Coleman, M. (1986). A comparison of clinical and empirical literature on children in stepfamilies. *Journal of Marriage and the Family, 48,* 309–318.

Ganong, L., & Coleman, M. (1987). Effects of parental remarriage on children: An updated comparison of theories, methods, and findings from clinical and empirical research.

Ganong, L., & Coleman, M. (1988a). *Bibliotherapy with stepchildren.* Springfield, Ill.:Charles C. Thomas.

Ganong, L., & Coleman, M. (1988b). Do mutual children cement bonds in stepfamilies? *Journal of Marriage and the Family 50,* 687–698.

Gestalt Institute of Cleveland (1988). Intensive postgraduate training program. Cleveland, Ohio.

**Getzoff, A. & McClenahan, C. (1984). *Stepkids: A survival guide for teenagers in stepfamilies and for stepparents doubtful of their own survival.* New York: Walker.

Gilligan, C. (1982). *In a different voice.* Cambridge, Mass.: Harvard University Press.

Glenn, N., & Weaver, C. (1977). The marital happiness of remarried divorced persons. *Journal of Marriage and the Family, 39,* 331–337.

Glenwick, D.S., & Mowrey, J.D. (1986). When parent becomes peer: Loss of intergenerational boundaries in single-parent families. *Family Relations, 35,* 57–62.

Glick, P.C. (1979). Children of divorced parents in demographic perspective. *Journal of Social Issues, 4,* 170–182.

Glick, P.C. (1980). Remarriage: Some recent changes and variations. *Journal of Family Issues, 1,* 455–478.

Glick, P.C. (1984). Marriage, divorce, and living arrangements: Prospective changes. *Journal of Family Issues, 5,* 7-26.

Glick, P.C. & Lin, S.G. (1986). Recent changes in divorce and remarriage. *Journal of Marriage and the Family, 48,* 737-747.

Goetting, A. (1982). The six stations of remarriage: Developmental tasks of remarriage after divorce. *Family Relations, 31,* 213–222.

Goldner, V. (1982). Remarried family: Structure, system, future. In L. Messinger (Ed.), *Therapy with remarried families* (pp. 189-206). Rockville, Md.: Aspen Systems Corp.

Hetherington, E.M. (1987). Family relations six years after divorce. In K. Pasley & M. Ihinger-Tallman (Eds.), *Remarriage and stepparenting: Current research and theory* (pp. 185–205). New York: Guilford.

Hetherington, E.M., Arnett, J.A., & Hollier, E.A. (1986). Adjustment of parents and children to remarriage. In S. Wolchik & P. Karoly (Eds.), *Children of divorce: Perspectives on adjustment.* New York: Gardner Press.

Hetherington, E.M., Cox, M., & Cox, R. (1985). Long-term effects of divorce and remarriage on the adjustment of children. *Journal of the American Academy of Psychology, 24*(5), 518–530.

Hobart, C. (1987). Parent-child relations in remarried families. *Journal of Family Issues, 8,* 259–277.

**Hyde, M. (1981). *My friend has four parents.* New York: McGraw-Hill.

Isaacs, M.B., Leon, G.H., & Kline, M. (1987). When is a parent out of the picture? Different custody, different perceptions. *Family Process, 26,* 101–110.

Jacobs, J.A., & Furstenberg, F.F., Jr. (1986). Changing places: Conjugal careers and women's marital mobility. *Social Forces, 64,* 714–732.

Jacobson, D.S. (1979). Stepfamilies: Myths and realities. *Social Work, 24,* 202–207.

Jacobson, D.S. (1987). Family type, visiting, and children's behavior in the stepfamily: A linked family system. In K. Pasley & M. Ihinger-Tallman (Eds.), *Remarriage and stepparenting: Current research and theory* (pp. 257–272). Beverly Hills, Calif.: Sage.

Jacobson, David. (1988, November). *Stress and support in stepfamily transition.* Paper presented to the Second Annual Wingspread Conference on the Remarried Family, Philadelphia.

Johnston, J.R., & Campbell, L.E.G. (1987). Instability in family networks of divorced and disputing parents. *Advances in Group Processes, 4,* 243–269.

Johnston, J., Coysh, W., Kline, M., & Nelson, R. (1988, August). *What visitation arrangements work best for whom?* Paper presented at the Annual Meeting of the American Psychological Association, Atlanta.

Johnston, J.R., Gonzales, R., & Campbell, L.E.G. (1987). Ongoing post-divorce conflict and child disturbance. *Journal of Abnormal Child Psychology, 15,* 493–509.

Kaufman, K.S. (1987). Parental separation and divorce during the college years: Gender differences in the response of young adults.

Unpublished doctoral dissertation, Harvard University Graduate School of Education.

Keshet, J.K. (1980). From separation to stepfamily: A subsystem analysis. *Journal of Family Issues, 1* (4), 517–532.

Kleinman, J., Rosenberg, E., & Whiteside, M. (1979). Common developmental tasks in forming reconstituted families. *Journal of Marital and Family Therapy, 5,* 79–86.

Kline, M., Tschann, J.M., Johnston, J.R., & Wallerstein, J.S. (1989). *Children's adjustment in joint and sole physical custody families. Developmental Psychology 25,* 430–438.

Kline, M., Johnston, J.R., & Tschann, J.M. (1991). The long shadow of marital conflict: A model of children's postdivorce adjustment, *J. of Marriage and the Family, 53,* 297–309.

Kohut, H. (1977). *The restoration of the self.* New York: International University Press.

Kolata, G. (1988, November). After divorce: Child splitting. *Psychology Today.*

**Lewis, H.C. (1980). All about families the second time around. Atlanta: Peachtree.

Lutz, P. (1983). The stepfamily: An adolescent perspective. *Family Relations, 32,* 367–376.

McGoldrick, M., & Carter, E.A. (1980). Forming a remarried family. In E.A. Carter and M. McGoldrick (Eds.), *The family life cycle: A framework for family therapy.* New York: Gardner Press.

Messinger, L. (1976). Remarriage between divorced people with children from previous marriages: A proposal for preparation for remarriage. *Journal of Marriage and Family Counseling, 2,* 193–200.

Messinger, L. (Ed.) (1982). *Therapy with remarried families.* Rockville, Md.: Aspen Systems Corp.

Miller, A. (1981) *Drama of the gifted child.* New York: Basic Books.

Mills, D.M., (1984). A model for stepfamily development. *Family Relations, 33,* 365–372.

Minuchin, S. (1974). *Families and family therapy.* Cambridge, Mass.: Harvard University Press.

Morrison, A.P. (1983). Working with shame in analytic treatment. *Journal of the American Psychoanalytic Association, 32* (3), 479–505.

Morrison, A.P. (1986). Shame, ideal self and narcissism. In A.P. Morrison (Ed.), *Essential papers on narcissism* (pp. 348–371). New York: New York University.

Morrison, A.P. (1989). *Shame: The underside of narcissism.* Hillsdale, N.J.: Analytic Press.

Mott, F.L., & Moore, S.F. (1982). Marital transitions and employment. In F.L. Mott (Ed.), *The employment revolution.* Boston: MIT Press.

Moynihan-Bradt, C. (1983). *The subtle revolution.* Paper presented to the Institute on Stepfamilies at the Annual Meeting of the American Orthopsychiatric Association, Boston.

Neubauer, P.D. (1960). The one-parent child and his oedipal development. *PsychoAnalytic Study of the Child, 15,* 286–309.

Nevis, E.C. (1987). *A gestalt approach to organizational consulting.* New York: Gestalt Institute of Cleveland/Gardner Press.

Nevis, S.M. (1980). *Psychological "gluon."* Unpublished presentation for Conference on Intimate Systems, Gestalt Institute of Cleveland.

Nevis, S.M. (1988). *Is awareness bearable?* Unpublished presentation of the Gestalt Institute of Cleveland Thirty-Fifth Anniversary Conference.

Nevis, S.M., & Warner, E.S. (1983). Conversing about gestalt couple and family therapy. *The Gestalt Journal, 6* (2), 40–50.

Nevis, S.M., & Zinker, J.C. (1982). *How gestalt therapy views couples, families, and the process of their psychotherapy.* Cleveland: Gestalt Institute of Cleveland.

Papernow, P.L. (1980). A phenomenological study of the developmental stages of becoming a stepparent: A gestalt and family systems approach (Doctoral dissertation, Boston University, 1980). *Dissertation Abstracts International, 41,* 8B, 3192–3193.

Papernow, P.L. (1984a). The stepfamily cycle: An experiential model of stepfamily development. *Family Relations, 33* (3), 355–363.

Papernow, P.L. (1984b, Winter). A baby in the house. *Stepfamily Bulletin,* pp. 1,4,5,8.

Papernow, P.L. (1987). Thickening the "middle ground": Dilemmas and vulnerabilities for remarried couples. *Psychotherapy, 24* (3S), 630–639.

Papernow, P.L. (1988). Stepparent role development: From outsider to intimate. In W. R. Beer (Ed.), *Relative strangers: Studies of stepfamily processes* (pp. 54–82). Totowa, N.J.: Rowman & Littlefield.

Papernow, P.L. (1989, Spring). Children in stepfamilies: What do we know? *Stepfamily Bulletin,* 16–18.

Parkes, C.M., & Weiss, R.L. (1983). *Recovery from Bereavement.* New York: Basic Books.

Pasley, K. (1987). Family boundary ambiguity: Perceptions of adult stepfamily members. In K. Pasley & M. Ihinger-Tallman (Eds.), *Remarriage and stepparenting: Current research and theory* (pp. 206–224). New York: Guilford.

Pasley, K. (1991). Recent research on stepfamilies and remarriage. Paper presented at the Wingspread Conference on Remarriage and Stepfamilies. Denver, Colo.

Pasley, K. & Ihinger-Tallman, M. (Eds.) (1987). *Remarriage and stepparenting: Current research and theory.* New York: Guilford.

*Paul, J., & Paul, M. (1983). *Do I have to give up me to be loved by you?* Minneapolis: CompCare.

*Paul, J., & Paul, M. (1987). *If you really loved me.* Minneapolis: CompCare.

Pill, C. (1988). Stepfamily cohesion, adaptability, and coping styles. (Doctoral Dissertation, Simmons College School of Social Work.)

Pill, C. (1990). Stepfamilies: Redefining the family. *Family Relations, 39,* 186–193.

Polster, E., & Polster, M. (1974). Gestalt therapy integrated. New York: Vintage.

Ransom, J.W., Schlesinger, S., & Derdeyn, A.P. (1979). A stepfamily in formation. *American Journal of Orthopsychiatry, 49* (1), 36–43.

Sager, C.J., Brown, H.S., Crohn, H., Engel, T., Rodstein, E., & Walker, L. (1983). *Treating the remarried family.* New York: Brunner/Mazel.

Santrock, J.W., & Sitterle, K.A. (1987). Parent-child relationship in step-mother families. In K. Pasley & M. Ihinger-Tallman (Eds.), *Remarriage and stepparenting: Current research and theory* (pp. 273–279). New York: Guilford.

Santrock, J.W., Warshak, R.A. Lindberg, C., & Meadows, L. (1982). Children's and parents' observed social behavior in stepfather families. *Child Development, 53,* 472–480.

Schulman, G. (1972). Myths that intrude on the adaptation of the step-family. *Social Casework, 53,* 131–139.

Shaw, D.S., & Emery, R.E. (1987). Parental conflict and other correlates of the adjustment of school-age children whose parents have separated. *Journal of Abnormal Child Pyschology, 15,* 269–281.

*Stepfamily Association of America (1989). *Stepfamilies stepping ahead.* Lincoln, Nebr.: Stepfamilies Press.

Stepfamily Association of America & the National Council on Family Relations (1988). Bibliography of academic and professional literature on remarriage and stepfamilies. Lincoln, Nebr.: Stepfamily Association of America.

Tschann, J.M., Johnston, J.R., Kline, M., & Wallerstein, J.S. (1989). Family process and children's functioning during divorce. *Journal of Marriage and the Family, 51,* 431–444.

**Vigna, J. (1984). *Grandmother without me.* Miles, Ill.: Albert Whitman.

*Viorst, J. (1986). *Necessary losses.* New York: Ballantine Books.

Visher, E.B., & Visher, J.S. (1978). Common problems of stepparents and their spouses. *American Journal of Orthopsychiatry, 48* (2), 252–262.

Visher, E.B., & Visher, J.S. (1979). *Stepfamilies: A guide to working with stepparents and stepchildren.* New York: Brunner/Mazel.

*Visher, E.B., & Visher, J.S. (1988). *Old loyalties, new ties.* New York: Brunner/Mazel.

Vital Health Statistics. (1980). *Remarriage of women 15-44 years of age whose first marriage ended in divorce: United States, 1976.* (No. 58, February 14.) Hyattsville, Md.: National Center of Health Statistics.

Waldron, J.A., & Whittington, R. (1979). The stepparent/stepfamily. *Journal of Operational Psychology, 10* (1), 47–50.

Wallerstein, J.S. (1984). Children of divorce: Preliminary report of a 10-year follow-up of young children. *American Journal of Orthopsychiatry, 56*(1), 444–458.

Wallerstein, J.S. (1986). Women after divorce: Preliminary report of a 10-year follow-up. *American Journal of Orthopsychiatry, 56* (1), 65–77.

*Wallerstein, J.S., & Kelly, J.B. (1980). *Surviving the breakup: How children and parents cope with divorce.* New York: Basic Books.

Weiss, R. (1975). *Marital separation.* New York: Basic Books.

Weiss, R. (1979). *Going it alone.* New York: Basic Books.

Weiss, R. (1985). Men and the family. *Family Process, 24,* 49–58.

Weltner, J.S. (1982). A structural approach to the single-parent family. *Family Process, 21,* 203–210.

White, L.K. (1979). Sex differentials in the effect of remarriage on global happiness. *Journal of Marriage and the Family, 41,* 869–876.

White, L.K., & Booth, A. (1985). The quality and stability of remarriages: The role of stepchildren. *American Sociological Review, 50,* 689–698.

Whiteside, M.F. (1988a). Creation of family identity through ritual performance in early remarriage. In E. Imber-Black, J. Roberts, & R. Whiting (Eds.), *Rituals in families and family therapy* (pp. 276–304). New York: Norton.

Whiteside, M.F. (1988b). Remarried systems. In L. Combrinck-Graham (Ed.), *Children in family contexts: Perspectives on Treatment* (pp. 135–160). New York: Guilford.

Whiteside, M.F. (1989). Family rituals as a key to kinship connections in remarried families. *Family Relations, 38,* 34–39.

Winnicott, D.W. (1958). *Through paediatrics to psychoanalysis.* New York: Basic Books.

Wolin, S.J. (1989). Family rituals. *Family Process, 38,* 401-420.

Zinker, J.C. (1977). Creative process in gestalt therapy. New York: Brunner/Mazel.

Zinker, J.C. (1983). Complementarity and the middle ground: Two forces for couples binding. *The Gestalt Journal, 6* (2).

Zinker, J.C., & Nevis, S.M. (1981). *The gestalt theory of couple and family interaction.* Cleveland: Gestalt Institute of Cleveland.

Index

A

Abandonment, in Immersion Stage, 105
Abramson, Barbara, 77, 79, 88, 91, 93, 94, 157, 160–161, 184–185, 201–202, 359
Action in Gestalt Experience Cycle, 24–25. *See also* Energy-action
Action Family: analysis of pattern for, 263-266; case study of, 293–300; described, 237–238, 302; insiders and outsiders in, 57–59; and Middle Stages, 156
Action Stage: analysis of, 171–196; boundaries in, 171–177; children in, 175–177, 191–193; couple boundaries in, 177–183; described, 16; intervention at, 346–355; stepfamily boundary at, 186–193; stepparent-stepchild boundary at, 183–186; summary on, 194–195
Ahrons, C. R., 4, 47, 131, 191, 227
Allen, Barry, 58, 264
Amy, 251–254, 255, 257, 258, 260–261, 263–264
Andrea, 251–254, 255, 257, 258, 260–261, 263–264
Andrews, Jill, 145, 146
Arnett, J. A., 185
Asmundsson, D., 19
Attachment, and stepfamily structure, 59–61
Aware Family: analysis of pattern for, 249–254; case history of, 266–278; described, 236, 301; and Middle Stages, 154; mirroring in, 240; sanctuaries in, 64
Awareness: in first-time family, 41; in Gestalt Experience Cycle, 22, 24; in Gestalt Interactive Cycle, 26, 28, 32, 33, 34, 35, 36, 37, 38, 53–54, 58, 62; skills of, 245, 350
Awareness Stage: analysis of, 118–150; background on, 118–120; for children, 140–149; described, 14; and gains and losses, 115; for insider parents, 131–140; intervention at, 313–336; and loyalty, 110, 143–144; for outsider stepparents, 120–131; patterns in, 236; and structure, 56, 62; summary on, 149–150

B

Baby, new. *See* Childbearing
Bahr, S. J., 137
Becker, Zoe, 112–113, 114–115, 116–117, 141, 144, 149
Bennett, A., 126
Bennett, 186, 347
Bernstein, A., 246
Berry, Dennis, 79, 96
Betts, Doreen, 58, 264
Betts, Sammy, 58, 265
Betts, Sophie, 58, 265

Biological forces: in Awareness
    Stage, 122, 134–135; in
    Resolution Stage, 218–219
Black, C., 240, 322
Black, Jennifer, 37, 38
Black, Lu Anne, 35–37, 51, 55, 59,
    74, 267
Black, Mara, 37
Bohannan, P., 4
Booth, A., 248, 266
Boss, P., 60
Boswell, J., 82, 376
Boundaries: in Action Stage,
    171–177, of couples, 177–183;
    and ex-spouses, 191–193; in
    Resolution Stage, 221–223,
    225–227; ruptured, 225–227;
    and stepfamily structure, 45,
    186–193; stepparent-stepchild,
    183–186
Bradley, B., 110, 328
Brand, E., 106, 116, 247, 248
Bray, J. H., 126–127
Brewster, Ed, 112, 305–306
Brewster, Margaret, 305–306
Bridges, Josie, 318–319
Brown, Julie, 88
Brown, Walter, 136–137, 173
Burden: easing, in Fantasy Stage,
    75–76; lifting invisible, 310–313;
    sharing, in Immersion Stage,
    103–104
Burke, Jerry, 149, 368
Burns, Gregory, 5, 89–90, 94, 99,
    156, 178–179, 184, 200–201,
    202–205, 219, 220, 230–231
Burt, M., 110, 130
Burt, R., 110, 130

C

Cain, A. C., 9, 45
Campbell, Chris, 190, 222
Campbell, L.E.G., 47, 246
Caponi, Jeannie, 365
Carter, E. A., 10
Change agents, stepparents as,
    158–160
Cherlin, A., 5, 175, 211

Childbearing: for first-time
    families, 42–43, 46; and
    interventions, 358–362; in
    Resolution Stage, 219–221
Children: in Action Families,
    264–265; in Action Stage,
    175–177, 191–193; and
    attachment, 60–61; in
    Awareness Stage, 140–149;
    developmental stages of,
    185–186; emotional shifts of,
    109–110, 116–117; in Fantasy
    Stage, 80–83; and full-time
    stepmothers, 94; gender
    differences of, 247–248,
    295–296; grief of, 223–224;
    grown, 96, 365–370; in
    Immersion Stage, 108–117;
    impact of, 246–248; insider-
    outsider split for, 56–57,
    145–146; interventions with,
    325–329; loyalty of, 110–111,
    143–144, 169, 193, 246–247,
    292, 324–329; in Mobilization
    Stage, 169–170; needs of,
    147–148, 334–335; and new
    babies, 361–362, 369; in
    Stepfamily Cycle, 70; and tasks,
    148–149; two households for,
    47, 144–145, 191–193
Chollak, H., 19
Clingempeel, W. G., 106, 116, 247,
    248
Cohen, Aaron, 109, 122
Cohen, Josh, 122
Cohen, Mickey, 163
Coleman, M., 5, 73, 110, 176, 242,
    266, 328, 358
Complex stepfamilies: as Aware,
    266–278; Gestalt Interactive
    Cycle for, 35–37; in Immersion
    Stage, 85–86; insider-outsider
    split for, 145–146; as Mobilized,
    262, 286–293; structure of,
    54–55
Conflicts: context for, 336–338;
    levels of, and impact, 246
Contact: in Gestalt Experience
    Cycle, 25; in Gestalt Interactive

Cycle, 29–30, 34, 37, 58; in Mobilization Stage, 342; skills for, 351–352

Contact Stage: analysis of, 198–213; background on, 198–199; described 16; family process in, 209–211; interventions at, 355–356; intimacy in, 200–209; stepcouple sanctuary in, 199–200; summary on, 212

Corino, Vicky, 343–346

Couple relations: in Action Stage, 177–183; in Fantasy Stage, 76–79; in Mobilization Stage, 162; for parenting, 180–183; as sanctuary, 199–200; of team solidity in Resolution Stage, 217–221

Cowgirl, K. M., 19

Coysh, W., 47, 246

Cox, M., 247

Cox, R., 247

Cox, Reginald, 133, 135–136, 164, 165

Craven, L., 110, 328

Crosbie-Burnett, M., 141, 208, 211, 286, 365

Culture: in Action Stage, 186–190; in Awareness Stage, 144–145; clashes of, 84; in Immersion Stage, 95, 112–113; and stepfamily structure, 50, 61–63

Cummings, Ingrid, 143, 227

Cycle. *See* Stepfamily Cycle

D

Dahl, A. S., 19

Daily routines, at Action Stage, 186–188

Danielson, Cindy, 141–142, 199

Danielson, George, 6, 136, 184, 199

Danielson, Pamela, 169

Davidson, Gabby, 82, 112, 113, 114, 115, 141, 147, 246, 266–278, 325

Davidson, Jan, 108, 114, 146, 242, 244, 250, 266–278, 325

Davis, Gene, 200, 214–215, 224

Davis, Joan, 166

Day, R. D., 137

Dayton, David, 359

Dayton, Emmie, 77, 88, 91, 93, 94, 144, 160–161, 184–185, 201–202

Dayton, Jim, 91, 94, 157, 161, 184–185, 202

Dayton, Katerina, 93, 161

Dean, G., 243

Death, stepfamilies formed by, 362–365

Denial, in Immersion Stage, 107–108

Derdeyn, A. P., 10

Developmental map, need for, 7–9

Developmental stages: of children, 185–186; described, 12–17; patterns of, 235–302; in Stepfamily Cycle, 12–17, 65–231

Developmental tasks, in Stepfamily Cycle, 15, 16. *See also* Tasks

Distance, in Awareness Stage, 127–128

Dominguez, Carlos, 318–319

Dominguez, Manny, 318–319

Double stepfamily. *See* Complex stepfamily

Draughn, M., 208

E

Early Stages: analysis of, 70–151; attending to needs in, 333–336; of Awareness, 118–150; childbearing at, 358–360; conclusion on, 150–151; described, 13–15; of Fantasy, 71–84; and Gestalt Interactive Cycle, 29–30; of Immersion, 84–118; intervention at, 310–336; structure in, 85–86, 150; time spent in, 18–19

Emery, R. E., 246

Emotions, in Immersion Stage, 109–110, 116–117

Empathy, rote exercise for, 340–342. *See also* Mirroring

Energy-action: in Gestalt Interactive Cycle, 28–29, 34, 35,

37, 38, 53, 58; skills for, 350–351
Erickson, Christine, 87, 97, 98, 185,
    218, 223
Erickson, Kate, 87
Erickson, Pam, 87, 97
Erickson, Roger, 87, 185, 218
Evans, Abigail, 75–76, 79
Evans, Bob, 75–76
Evans, Jeremy, 75–76
Evans, M. D., 110
Ex-spouses: at Action Stage,
    191–193; in Awareness Stage,
    131; in Immersion Stage, 93; in
    Mobilization Stage, 161; in
    Resolution Stage, 221–223
Expectations: in Action Stage,
    174–175; in Resolution Stage,
    218–219; as "shoulds," 317–320
Expressiveness, in Mobilization
    Stage, 160–163
Extended family: in Immersion
    Stage, 91–93; and middle
    ground, 52; strategic planning
    for, 354–355, 369–370

F

Failures: at Action Stage, 193–194;
    impact of, 241–242
Family: extended, 91–93, 354–355,
    369–370; first-time, 41–43, 46,
    47; as sanctuary, 52, 57, 64;
    single-parent, 43–45, 46; whole,
    in Fantasy Stage, 81. *See also*
    Action Family; Aware Family;
    Immersed Family; Mobilized
    Family; Stepfamilies
Family of origin: and fantasies, 74,
    239, 284; and Immersed
    Families, 257, 280; issues of, and
    step issues, 304–306, 343–346;
    and "shoulds," 241
Fantasy Stage: for adults, 72–79;
    analysis of, 71–84; background
    on, 71–72; for children, 80–83;
    described, 13; intervention at,
    310–313; summary on, 83–84
Fassler, D., 110
Fast, I., 9, 45

Fathers, noncustodial, loyalties of,
    in Immersion Stage, 105–107
Feedback, at Mobilization Stage,
    339
First-time family, structure of,
    41–43, 46, 47
Fisher, R., 377
Fishman, Sarah, 176–177
Fixing: in Awareness Stage,
    133–134; in Fantasy Stage,
    73–74, 80–81
Focus, in Awareness Stage,
    123–124
Franklin, Hope, 6, 111, 137, 138
Franklin, Nicole, 111
Furstenberg, F. F., 4, 10, 105, 106

G

Gains: in Awareness Stage,
    137–138, 146–147; in
    Immersion Stage, 115
Ganong, L., 5, 73, 110, 176, 242,
    266, 328, 358
Gary, 42
Gay parent, and parent-child time,
    108
Gentile, Betty, 163, 363–364
Gentile, Nick, 163
Gershenhorn, S., 126
Gestalt Experience Cycle: for
    individuals, 22–25; and
    Stepfamily Cycle, 67–68
Gestalt Institute of Cleveland, 23n,
    339, 340
Gestalt Interactive Cycle: in Contact
    Stage, 210–212; and skill
    development, 349–353; for
    stepfamilies, 25–33
Getzoff, A., 110
Gilligan, C., 99
Gingrich, R., 73
Glenn, N., 118
Glenwick, D. S., 44
Glick, P. C., 5, 105
Goetting, A., 10
Goldner, V., 62
Gonzales, R., 47, 246
Goodman, Wendy, 200, 214–215,

224
Grandparents, in Awareness Stage, 143
Gray, Joanne, 6, 77–79, 312–313
Greenfield, Trisha, 6, 88, 173
Grieving: in Awareness Stage, 136–137; in Immersion Stage, 101; for losses, 380; by older stepchildren, 367; in Resolution Stage, 223–225
Grinnelli, Anton, 92, 102–103, 104–105, 136
Gunnars, Michelle, 93, 166–167
Gurak, D. T., 243

H

Haley, Billie, 121, 178
Haley, Daryl, 97
Haley, Hank, 97–98, 121–122, 177–178
Haley, Helen, 177
Handlon, Patsy, 167, 214, 224
Harry, 251–254, 255, 257, 258, 260–261, 263–264
Hetherington, E. M., 116, 126, 185, 247, 248
Hobart, C., 47, 246
Hobbes, Bill, 167, 213, 214, 221–222, 224, 226–227
Hobbes, Paula, 167, 222
Hollier, E. A., 185
Hope, in Fantasy Stage, 82–83
Hyde, M., 110

I

Ideal family: in Fantasy Stage, 77–78, 81; in Immersion Stage, 104–105
Ievoli, R., 116, 247
Immersed Family: analysis of pattern for, 255–259; case history of, 278–286; described, 237, 301; pace of, 259
Immersion Stage: analysis of, 84–118; background on, 84–86; for children, 108–117; described, 13–14; to insider

parents, 100–108; intervention at, 314–320; for outsider stepparent, 86–100; summary on, 117–118
Information: for Action Family, 296–297; for Immersed Family, 256; impact of, 238–239; in interventions, 307–309, 311, 315–317, 331–332, 370–371
Insider-outsider split: in Aware Family, 266–278; for children, 56–57, 145–146; in stepfamily structure, 54–59
Insiders. *See* Parents
Interventions: at Action Stage, 346–355; attributes of, 303–371; at Awareness Stage, 313–336; background on, 303–304; and childbearing, 358–362; conclusion on, 370–371; at Contact Stage, 355–356; at Early Stages, 310–336; at Fantasy Stage, 310–313; at Immersion Stage, 314–320; at Later Stages, 355–358; at Middle Stages, 336–355; at Mobilization Stage, 336–346; with older stepchildren, 365–370; principles of, 304–310, 370–371; at Resolution Stage, 356–358; skills for, 379–380; and special issues, 358–370; for stepfamilies formed by death, 362–365
Intimacy, in Contact Stage, 200–209
Intimate outsider, stepparent as, 201–202, 208–209, 214–216, 276, 292, 368
Isaacs, M. B., 47, 246
Ives, S. B., 110

J

Jacobson, David, 113, 248
Jacobson, Doris S., 47, 71, 128
James, Ellen, 101, 111, 134, 143, 146
James, Jane, 74, 91–92, 101, 102–103, 104–105, 133, 134,

137, 143
Johnson, S., 82, 376
Johnston, Cecilia, 215, 216–217,
    221, 243, 246, 262, 263, 286–293
Johnston, J. R., 47, 246
Johnston, Jon, 216, 286–293
Johnston, Mary, 215, 216, 286–293
Johnston, Richard, 216, 221, 243,
    246, 262, 263, 286–293
Jones, Bobby, 36, 37
Jones, Don, 35–37, 51, 55, 59, 267
Jones, Trisha, 36–38

K

Kaufman, K. S., 141, 365
Kearns, Dora, 142, 368
Keefe, Becky, 90, 95, 360
Keefe, Elizabeth, 75, 90, 95
Keefe, Robert, 75, 79, 90, 95, 359,
    360, 363
Kelly, J. B., 4, 47, 80
Kelly, Sally, 111, 142, 143, 147, 148,
    366–368
Keshet, J. K., 10, 33
King, Bruce, 343–346
Kleinman, J., 11
Kline, M., 47, 246
Knowledge of others, in Awareness
    Stage, 124–125
Kohl, Leslie, 146–147, 169
Kohut, H., 240

L

Lash, M., 110
Later Stages: analysis of, 197–231;
    background on, 197–198;
    childbearing at, 361: conclusion
    on, 230–231; of Contact,
    198–213; described, 16–17;
    interventions at, 355–358; of
    Resolution, 213–230
Leon, G. H., 47, 246
Letting go, in Resolution Stage,
    221–227
Levi, Timothy, 6–7, 145–146,
    169–170, 185
Levinson, Marty, 215–216

Lewis, H. C., 110, 328
Lieberman, Ann, 122, 125, 131,
    163
Lin, S. G., 5
Lippman, Jack, 203–204
Lippman, Jason, 156, 202–204
Lippman, Judy, 156, 200–201,
    202–204
Lippman, Lynn, 89–90, 99, 108,
    178–179, 184, 202–205, 219,
    220
Loneliness, in Awareness Stage,
    122–123
Losses: in Awareness Stage,
    141–143, 146–147; in Fantasy
    Stage, 81–82; grieving for, 380;
    in Immersion Stage, 113–115;
    impact of, 239–242, 323; in
    Mobilization Stage, 343
Love: in Fantasy Stage, 72–73; in
    Immersion Stage, 89
Loyalty: in Action Stage, 193; in
    Awareness Stage, 143–144,
    246–247, 324–329; in
    Immersion Stage, 110–111; in
    Mobilization Stage, 169, 292; of
    noncustodial fathers, 105–107
Lutz, P., 116

M

McCarthy, J., 5
McClenahan, C., 110
McGoldrick, M., 10
McNally, Gina, 164, 165
Messinger, L., 45
Middle ground: in Action Family,
    299–300; in Action Stage,
    172–174; in Aware Families,
    250; competition for, 51–54;
    family rituals for, 335–336,
    346–347; in first-time family,
    42–43; in Immersion Stage, 108;
    importance of, 39–41, 63–64,
    243–244; in Later Stages, 198,
    205; in Middle Stages, 153; in
    Mobilization Stage, 158–159; in
    single-parent family, 44; for
    stepparent and stepchild, 125

Middle Stages: of Action, 171–196;
analysis of, 152–196;
background on, 152–156;
childbearing at, 360–361;
conclusion on, 195–196;
described, 15–16; interventions
at, 336–355; of Mobilization,
156–171; and structure, 62–63;
time spent in, 154–155
Miller, A., 240
Miller, Chuck, 108, 114, 242, 244,
250, 266–278, 325
Miller, Kevin, 82, 109, 110, 113,
114, 115, 143, 146, 147, 169,
246, 266–278, 325
Mills, D. M., 10, 124–125, 126
Minuchin, S., 45, 52, 57, 217
Mirroring: impact of, 240–241,
242; in interventions, 315–316,
339–340
Mobilization, in Gestalt Experience
Cycle, 24
Mobilization Stage: analysis of,
156–171; background on,
156–158; described, 15; insider
parent in, 164–169;
interventions at, 336–346; needs
stated in, 104; speed in,
167–168, 340–342; stepparents
in, 158–164; summary on,
170–171
Mobilized Family: analysis of
pattern for, 260–263; case
history of, 286–293; described,
237, 301; and Middle Stages,
155; pace of, 263
Moore, S. F., 137
Morrison, A. P., 240
Morrison, Karen, 190, 222–223
Mott, F. L., 137
Mowrey, J. D., 44
Moynihan-Bradt, C., 128
Mutual suitability: in Mobilized
Family, 286; of stepparent role,
208, 211, 216–217

N

National Council on Family
Relations, 5
Needs: in Awareness Stage, 127,
138, 147–148; in Early Stages,
333–336; in Mobilization Stage,
104
Nelson, Jessie, 116
Nelson, R., 47, 246
Neubauer, P. D., 45
Nevis, E. C., 22, 24, 26, 27n, 32–33,
304
Nevis, S. M., 22, 26, 39, 243, 262,
304, 339
Nissenbaum, Dan, 93, 167
Nissenbaum, Meggan, 93, 167
Nissenbaum, Susan, 93
Norstadt, Peter, 369–370
Norstadt, Wendy, 369–370

O

O'Brien, Fred, 6, 106–107
Olson, Cathy, 163, 363–364
Outsiders. *See* Insider-outsider
split; Stepparents

P

Paglia, Julian, 111, 137
Papernow, P. L., 19, 68n, 85, 88,
200, 207, 242, 256, 316, 362
Parenting: better, in Fantasy Stage,
74–75; couple team for,
180–183; expert, in Immersion
Stage, 89–91
Parents: and abandonment, 105: in
Awareness Stage, 131–140; and
biological forces, 134–135; and
burden sharing, 75–76,
103–104, 310–313; in Fantasy
Stage, 72–79; grief of, 224–225;
in Immersion Stage, 100–108;
interventions with, 320–325; in
middle role, 166–167; in
Mobilization Stage, 164–169;
multiple pulls on, 132–133;
needs of, 138, 334; and step
intimacy, 202–205; tasks for,
132, 138–140; widowed,
362–365

Parkes, C. M., 101
Pasley, K., 5, 10
Patterns of development: for
    Action Family, 263–266,
    293–300; analysis of, 235–302;
    for Aware Family, 249–254,
    266–278; background on,
    235–238; case histories of,
    266–300; conclusion on,
    300–302; differences in,
    238–248; for Immersed Family,
    254–259, 278–286; for
    Mobilized Family, 259–263,
    286–293; types of, 248–266
Paul, J., 267
Paul, M., 267
Peabody, Rusty, 80
Personality styles, impact of,
    244–245
Peterson, Terry, 108, 132
Pierce, Kate, 144, 181–182,
    188–189, 194, 206
Pierce, Liz, 181–182, 188–189, 194,
    206
Pill, C., 19, 79, 227–228, 229
Polster, E., 309
Polster, M., 309
Process, family: in Contact Stage,
    209–211; in Resolution Stage,
    227–228; in stepfamilies, 31–39

R

Ransom, J. W., 10
Raskin, Alex, 189, 194
Raskin, Andrew, 181–182,
    188–189, 194, 206
Raskin, Joe, 182, 189, 194, 206
Relationships, shifting, in
    Awareness Stage, 144. *See also*
    Couple relations; Stepparent-
    stepchild relationships
Resentment, in Awareness Stage,
    135–136
Resistance, attention to, 309–310,
    312–313, 320, 322, 330–331,
    349, 371
Resolution: in Gestalt Experience
    Cycle, 25; in Gestalt Interactive

Cycle, 30–31, 33, 34, 35, 37, 38,
    58; skills for, 352, 355
Resolution Stage: analysis of,
    213–230; assessing, 356–358;
    background on, 213–214;
    couple team in, 217–221;
    described, 16–17; family process
    in, 227–228; interventions at,
    356–358; letting go in, 221–227;
    pleasures of, 227, 229;
    stepparenting in, 214–217;
    summary on, 228–230
Ricci, Angela, 130–131, 134,
    348–349
Ricci, Frank, 348–349
Ricci, Molly, 6, 348–349
Roberts, Beth, 6, 108, 130, 137,
    159–160, 184, 199, 226
Roberts, Melissa, 159–160, 184, 226
Role of stepparent: emergence of,
    205–207; qualities of, 207–209;
    reasons for, 211–212
Roseman, Harvey, 162–163
Roseman, Jannine, 162
Rosenberg, E., 11
Rudnick, Jeff, 6, 77–79

S

Sager, C. J., 10, 43, 45, 47, 52, 304,
    343
Salter, Diana, 72, 323
Salvi, Anna, 34
Salvi, Joe, 33–35, 53–54, 55–56,
    59–60, 105
Salvi, Maria, 33–35, 53–54, 55–56,
    59–60, 105
Salvi, Nicky, 34
Salzman, Marsha, 99, 316–317
Sanctuary: in Action Stage,
    177–180; for couple in Contact
    Stage, 199–200; family as, 52,
    57, 64; in Resolution Stage, 217
Santrock, J. W., 78, 248
Sax, Adam, 123, 181
Sax, Ben, 123, 163–164
Sax, Ira, 72, 123, 164, 179, 181,
    220–221
Sax, Rachel, 72, 97, 98, 123,

163–164, 179, 181, 220–221, 223, 225
Schlesinger, S., 10
Schmidt, Kim, 112
Schmidt, Larry, 142, 177
Schulman, G., 71
Sensation: in Gestalt Experience Cycle, 22; in Immersion Stage, 85, 117
Shame: in Immersion Stage, 96–99, 107; impact of, 239–242, 323
Sharon, 42
Shaw, D. S., 246
Simmons, Alan, 72, 106, 107, 322–325
Simmons, Brad, 106, 323–324
Simple stepfamilies: childbearing issues in, 358–360; Gestalt Interactive Cycle for, 33–35; structure of, 46–47
Single-parent family, structure of, 43–45, 46
Sitterle, K. A., 78, 248
Skills: impact of, 245, 249–250; teaching, 349–353
Smith, John, 76, 325–327
Spanier, G. B., 4, 10, 105, 106
Stepchildren, grown: in Immersion Stage, 96; interventions with, 365–370
Stepfamilies: attention to, 3–20; boundaries of, at Action Stage, 186–193; challenges of, 376–377; conceptual tools for, 21–41; conclusion on, 63–64; developmental challenges for, 50–63; developmental map needed for, 7–9; extent of, 5; formed by death, 163, 362–365; Gestalt Interactive Cycle for, 26–33; interventions with, 303–371; issues for, 1–64; lessons from, 373–380; middle ground for, 39–41; needs of, 335; overview on becoming, 19–20; process in, 31–39, 209–211, 227–228; richness of, 378–379; sessions with, 329–333; structure of, 21–64;

suprasystem for, 52, 91–93, 354–355, 369–370; systemic view of, 306–307, 371; types of, 248–266. *See also* Complex stepfamilies; Families; Simple stepfamilies
Stepfamily Association of America (SAA), 5, 110; address of, 388; and interventions, 308–309, 311, 316, 336, 347, 371; resources from, 308–309; support from, 98, 188, 190, 239, 242, 243, 257, 297
Stepfamily Cycle: attributes of, 9–19; background on, 9–12; developmental stages in, 12–17, 65–231; differing completion rates for, 18–19; Early Stages of, 70–151; interventions with problems in, 303–371; Later Stages of, 197–231; Middle Stages of, 152–196; overview of, 67–69; and patterns of development, 235–302; theoretical basis of, 9–10
Stepmothers, full-time: in Awareness Stage, 128; in Immersion Stage, 94–95
Stepparent-stepchild relationship: boundary for, 183–186; intimacy in, 200–209; middle ground for, 125
Stepparents: at Awareness Stage, 120–131; and biological forces, 122; as change agents, 158–160; distance for, 127–128; at Fantasy Stage, 72–79; firmness by, 163–164; grief of, 224; at Immersion Stage, 86–100; interventions with, 314–320; as intimate outsiders, 201–202, 208–209, 214–216, 276, 292, 368; loneliness of, 122–123; in Mobilization Stage, 158–164; needs of, 127, 333–334; at Resolution Stage, 214–217; role of, 205–209, 211–212; as sounding board, 125–127; tasks of, 129–131

Stevens, Cory, 162–163
Straining: in Awareness Stage, 133–134; in Immersion Stage, 99–100, 107–108
Strategic planning, for traditions, 353–355, 369–370
Structure: and attachment, 59–61; and cultures, 50, 61–63; in Early Stages, 85–86, 150; of first-time family, 41–43, 46, 47; insiders and outsiders in, 54–59; for stepfamilies, 45–49
Support: amount and timing of, 18–19; for Immersed Family, 256–257; impact of, 242–243

T

Tasks: in Awareness Stage, 119–120, 129–131, 132, 138–140, 148–149, 313–314, 321–322, 347–349; in Middle Stages, 153–154, 156, 171, 184
Taylor, Jenny, 115, 326–327
Taylor, Lena, 76, 115, 325–327
Tolman, Bobby, 278, 284–285
Tolman, Jenny, 3–4, 5, 8–9, 54, 60, 73, 75, 103, 104, 108, 127, 243, 278–286
Tolman, Ricky, 3–4, 8–9, 73, 75, 103, 104, 278–286
Tolman, Tom, 3–4, 5, 8–9, 54, 60, 73, 75, 103, 104, 107–108, 127, 243, 278–286
Traditions: at Action Stage, 188–190; strategic planning for, 353–355, 369–370
Tschann, J. M., 246
Turner, Charlie, 217–218
Turner, Jessica, 217–218
Turner, Wes, 217–218

V

Vigna, J., 110

Viorst, J., 240, 380
Visher, E. B., 10, 11, 45, 71, 304
Visher, J. S., 10, 11, 45, 71, 304
Vital Health Statistics, 101

W

Waldron, J. A., 10, 11, 208
Wallerstein, J. S., 4, 47, 80, 191, 246, 248
Warner, E. S., 39, 243, 262
Wallisch, L., 131
Weaver, C., 118
Weiss, R., 4, 44, 101, 128
Wells, Corin, 216, 286–293
Weltner, J. S., 44
Wentworth, Arlene Goldfarb, 115, 243, 293–300, 311
Wentworth, Jonah, 294–300
Wentworth, Leah, 115, 294–300, 325, 330
Wentworth, Michael, 243, 293–300
Werner, Fran, 319–320
White, L. K., 118, 248, 266
Whiteside, M. F., 11, 126, 185, 186, 191, 246, 347
Whittington, R., 10, 11, 208
Wilson, Ben, 165, 364
Wilson, Danny, 113, 148, 165
Wilson, Donna Drubec, 113, 165
Winnicott, D. W., 119, 240
Winston, Alicia, 121, 123–124
Winston, David, 121
Winston, Mark, 121
Withdrawal: in Gestalt Experience Cycle, 25–26; in Gestalt Interactive Cycle, 30, 34, 37; in Immersion Stage, 99–100; skills for, 352–353
Wolin, S. J., 186, 347

Z

Zinker, J. C., 22, 26, 40, 63, 304, 339